AI, Learning Analytics, and Educational Design

Gürhan Durak
https://orcid.org/0000-0003-2944-3713
The Open University, UK

Serkan Çankaya
https://orcid.org/0000-0002-3951-9809
İzmir Democracy University, Turkey

IGI Global
Scientific Publishing
Publishing Tomorrow's Research Today

Vice President of Editorial	Melissa Wagner
Director of Acquisitions	Mikaela Felty
Director of Book Development	Jocelynn Hessler
Production Manager	Mike Brehm
Cover Design	Jose Rosado

Published in the United States of America by
IGI Global Scientific Publishing
701 East Chocolate Avenue
Hershey, PA, 17033, USA
Tel: 717-533-8845 | Fax: 717-533-7115
Website: https://www.igi-global.com E-mail: cust@igi-global.com

Library of Congress Cataloging-in-Publication Data

No LCCN (CIP Data Pending)
ISBN13: 9798337388052
Isbn13Softcover: 9798337388069
EISBN13: 9798337388076
British Cataloguing in Publication Data
A Cataloguing in Publication record for this book is available from the British Library.

Table of Contents

Preface x

Chapter 1
Inclusive Curriculum Design Innovations Facilitated by AI 1
S. Ida Evangeline, Government College of Engineering, Tirunelveli, India

Chapter 2
Mapping the Future: Spatial Data Science in Education Policy Development.... 27
Valisher Sapayev, Mamun University, Uzbekistan
Rejon Kumar Ray, Gannon University, USA
Sulurkhan Rakhimova, Urgench State Pedagogical Institute, Uzbekistan
Rayhon Sapaeva, Urgench State University, Uzbekistan
Munir Ahmad, Survey of Pakistan, Pakistan

Chapter 3
Prompt Engineering in Higher Education: Perceptions, Practices, and Pedagogical Potentials 55
Seçil Tümen Akyıldız, Fırat Üniversitesi, Turkey

Chapter 4
Enhanced Framework for Automated University Questionnaire Creation 83
Satwik Jambula, Lamar University, USA

Chapter 5
AI-Based Adaptive Learning Systems for Developing Writing Skills in Primary Education: A Model Proposal.. 119
Güliz Şahin, Balikesir University, Turkey

Chapter 6
Artificial Intelligence Project-Based Learning English for Specific Purposes Nexus: Advancing Language Learning and Communication 149
Jean Mathieu Tsoumou, Universidad Europea de Madrid, Spain

Chapter 7
Young Adults' Attitudes Toward Generative Artificial Intelligence and Its Role in STEM Education 183
Merve Çolakoğlu, Independent Researcher, Turkey
Semiral Öncü, Balikesir University, Turkey
Hüseyin Colak, Northeastern Illinois University, USA

Chapter 8
Predicting Student Success in Distance Learning Using Machine Learning and Explainable AI for LMS Data 207
Çağatay Bal, Muğla Sitki Koçman University, Turkey
Eralp Doğu, Muğla Sitki Koçman University, Turkey
Müge Adnan, Muğla Sitki Koçman University, Turkey

Chapter 9
An Analysis of AI Trends in Instructional Technology From a Bibliometric Perspective 237
Hamid Derviş, Kastamonu University, Turkey

Compilation of References 269

About the Contributors 307

Index 311

Detailed Table of Contents

Preface x

Chapter 1
Inclusive Curriculum Design Innovations Facilitated by AI 1
S. Ida Evangeline, Government College of Engineering, Tirunelveli, India

The emergence of generative artificial intelligence (AI) offers an unprecedented possibility to make the curriculum a more inclusive, responsive and culturally sensitive process. This chapter discusses how AI-based technologies can overcome the shortcomings of traditional curriculum models (e.g. limited representation, rigid pacing and inconsistent access) by allowing the dynamic generation of curriculum content that represents diversity in identity, language and ability. Using the concepts of educational theory, Universal Design for Learning (UDL), culturally responsive pedagogy, and differentiated instruction, the text points out the most practical ways to incorporate inclusivity into AI-enhanced study plans. Case studies based on different educational settings exemplify how AI can be used to achieve the creation of multilingual resources, customized instruction based on the profiles of learners, and provide culturally applicable examples at scale.

Chapter 2
Mapping the Future: Spatial Data Science in Education Policy Development.... 27
Valisher Sapayev, Mamun University, Uzbekistan
Rejon Kumar Ray, Gannon University, USA
Sulurkhan Rakhimova, Urgench State Pedagogical Institute, Uzbekistan
Rayhon Sapaeva, Urgench State University, Uzbekistan
Munir Ahmad, Survey of Pakistan, Pakistan

This chapter emphasizes the strategic importance of Spatial Data Science (SDS) in transforming education policy and planning. SDS enables the identification of geographic disparities, supports data-driven decision-making, and fosters equity, transparency, and sustainability. To realize its full potential, the chapter recommends strengthening spatially enriched EMIS, ensuring open and interoperable data systems, and investing in technical capacity. Ethical data governance and community engagement are essential. Integrating SDS into the education policy cycle is a vital step toward building equitable and future-ready education systems.

Chapter 3
Prompt Engineering in Higher Education: Perceptions, Practices, and Pedagogical Potentials 55
Seçil Tümen Akyıldız, Fırat Üniversitesi, Turkey

This study examines how university instructors in Eastern Türkiye perceive and use prompt engineering in higher education. Using an interpretivist/constructivist stance, a generic qualitative design and reflexive thematic analysis were employed. Fifteen instructors from five state universities were interviewed until saturation. Four perception areas emerged: a practical, instruction-focused view; recognition of student-centered potential; challenges from lack of training; and varying motivation. In practice, prompts supported material design, assessment, and critical thinking, while research use was limited to idea generation, summaries, and tool drafting. Ethical concerns were stronger among senior staff, while early-career academics were more confident. The study suggests tailored professional development, collaboration with computing units, and clear AI policies. Though region- and interview-based, findings indicate prompt engineering can become a key pedagogical and methodological skill in universities.

Chapter 4
Enhanced Framework for Automated University Questionnaire Creation 83
Satwik Jambula, Lamar University, USA

This chapter presents an enhanced framework for automated university questionnaire creation using generative artificial intelligence technologies. The authors propose a comprehensive system integrating AI capabilities with inclusive educational practices, universal design principles, and rigorous survey methodology. The framework addresses growing demand for scalable, personalized, and ethically sound assessment solutions in higher education through four core components: intelligent question generation systems, adaptive response mechanisms, inclusive design protocols, and comprehensive evaluation metrics. Implementation strategies and illustrative case studies demonstrate practical applications across diverse academic contexts. This resource guides educators, administrators, and technology professionals in implementing automated questionnaire systems that enhance educational equity while maintaining academic rigor and institutional integrity.

Chapter 5
AI-Based Adaptive Learning Systems for Developing Writing Skills in Primary Education: A Model Proposal........ 119
Güliz Şahin, Balikesir University, Turkey

This chapter explores the potential of artificial intelligence (AI)-based adaptive learning systems in supporting the development of writing skills among primary school students. Building on theoretical foundations such as Vygotsky's Zone of Proximal Development, Bruner's stages of cognitive growth, and process-based writing instruction, the chapter introduces the AI-Assisted Adaptive Writing Instruction with Teacher Scaffolding (AAWIT) Model. The model integrates real-time AI feedback with teacher guidance, aiming to enhance cognitive, affective, and social learning outcomes while ensuring inclusivity and educational equity. The chapter discusses the stages of the model, highlights the dual roles of teachers and digital systems, and outlines potential benefits such as improved metacognitive awareness, personalized learning, and systematic monitoring of student progress. Limitations related to developmental appropriateness, teacher competence, digital inequality, and ethical data use are critically examined, followed by recommendations for future research and implementation.

Chapter 6
Artificial Intelligence Project-Based Learning English for Specific Purposes Nexus: Advancing Language Learning and Communication 149
Jean Mathieu Tsoumou, Universidad Europea de Madrid, Spain

The aim of this paper is to demonstrate how PBL and AI can be implemented in English for Specific Purposes (ESP) classrooms. The primary goal is to encourage students to develop critical thinking, problem-solving, collaboration, and communication skills while applying knowledge and concepts from various disciplines. If there is a need to ensure that students use AI responsibly, PBL stands out as an effective alternative approach in ESP classrooms. PBL enables students to (re)negotiate their learning. In a PBL context, the final product no longer has to be a traditional written essay or paper but rather a solution to a real-life problem. For instance, students might develop an app or a computer program that is beneficial not only for the fields of physics and aerospace engineering but also for society at large.

Chapter 7
Young Adults' Attitudes Toward Generative Artificial Intelligence and Its Role in STEM Education 183
Merve Çolakoğlu, Independent Researcher, Turkey
Semiral Öncü, Balikesir University, Turkey
Hüseyin Colak, Northeastern Illinois University, USA

Using artificial intelligence (AI) tools in education is a contemporary method that enhances the evaluation, transformation, and promotion of learning and teaching processes. Integrating AI tools into the learning process in STEM fields contributes to the development of students' metacognitive abilities. This study aims to learn and evaluate adolescents' opinions and insights regarding the use of AI tools in STEM fields. Our research examines students' attitudes, confidence, and perceptions towards using AI tools and their perspectives on current global issues. Their views on the use of digital AI tools to solve these problems are also explored. Face-to-face interviews were conducted with eight participants for the study. The collected data were analyzed using content analysis methods. A review of the relevant literature revealed no studies similar to the methodology of this study. In this regard, we believe that the results of our study will benefit researchers conducting studies on the use of AI tools in education especially towards STEM education.

Chapter 8
Predicting Student Success in Distance Learning Using Machine Learning and Explainable AI for LMS Data 207
Çağatay Bal, Muğla Sitki Koçman University, Turkey
Eralp Doğu, Muğla Sitki Koçman University, Turkey
Müge Adnan, Muğla Sitki Koçman University, Turkey

In the era of distance education, understanding student behaviours through learning analytics has become crucial for improving educational outcomes. This study analyses log data obtained from a Learning Management System (LMS) to explore the relationship between student engagement patterns and academic performance. Student's interaction with various activity contexts were extracted as features and evaluated through machine learning methods. A Random Forest model, supported with Local Interpretable Model-Agnostic Explanations (LIME) interpretability, was applied to classify outcomes. The model achieved an accuracy of 81.67%, revealing that attendance patterns and exam duration are critical factors influencing success. Findings offer practical implications for instructors and supporting the design of targeted interventions, early warning systems, and personalised feedback mechanisms. Ultimately, the research demonstrates the potential of log-based analytics and Explainable Artificial Intelligence to deliver evidence-driven improvements in distance education and student support.

Chapter 9
An Analysis of AI Trends in Instructional Technology From a Bibliometric Perspective 237
Hamid Derviş, Kastamonu University, Turkey

Artificial intelligence (AI) has significantly impacted both conventional and online education, particularly the latter. Digital learning ecosystems now encompass a broad spectrum, from intelligent tutoring systems such as Cognitive Tutor developed at Carnegie Mellon University and AutoTutor at the University of Memphis, to contemporary AI-based tools like chatbots and adaptive learning platforms. On the other hand, bibliometric analysis offers a systematic and transparent approach to reviewing scholarly communication, identifying thematic clusters, and tracing the evolution of AI applications within instructional technology. This chapter analyzes AI and instructional technology trends using bibliometric methods, focusing on publication patterns, research hotspots, collaboration networks, and evolving methodologies. Beyond mapping scientific trends, the study also highlights the ethical implications of AI integration in education, emphasizing fairness, transparency, inclusivity, and acccuntability.

Compilation of References 269

About the Contributors 307

Index 311

Preface

INTRODUCTION

The rapid evolution of artificial intelligence (AI) has reshaped nearly every facet of education—from personalizing learning experiences to transforming assessment, instructional design, and policy development. As institutions adapt to a new era of technology-enhanced learning, researchers and educators increasingly seek integrative frameworks that blend pedagogy, analytics, and computational innovation. This book was developed in response to that global momentum, aiming to provide a comprehensive, research-driven examination of how AI and learning analytics can effectively support modern educational design.

At the same time, the expansion of AI tools has generated renewed interest in inclusivity, ethics, and equity within digital learning environments. Whether constructing accessible curricula, designing adaptive systems, or applying machine learning for student success prediction, educational ecosystems now face both unprecedented opportunities and complex challenges. These dual forces make it essential to engage thoughtfully with AI's pedagogical, methodological, and societal implications.

The chapters in this volume collectively contribute to a deeper understanding of how AI-supported educational practices can empower learners, inform teaching strategies, and guide institutional decision-making. By bringing together international perspectives and multidisciplinary approaches, this book highlights emerging trends, showcases practical implementations, and underscores the significance of ethical, culturally sensitive design. Our aim is to support educators, administrators, researchers, and policymakers in making informed, future-oriented decisions about AI in education.

CHAPTER OVERVIEW

Chapter 1 explores how generative AI can facilitate inclusive curriculum design. Drawing on Universal Design for Learning, culturally responsive pedagogy, and differentiated instruction, the author demonstrates how AI can help build multilingual, culturally relevant, and learner-centered study plans at scale.

Chapter 2 examines the role of Spatial Data Science (SDS) in shaping equitable education policy. The chapter highlights how spatially enriched data systems can reveal geographic disparities, inform strategic planning, and strengthen transparency, while stressing the importance of ethical governance and community involvement.

Chapter 3 investigates higher-education instructors' perceptions and practices related to prompt engineering. Through qualitative analysis, the chapter uncovers the pedagogical uses of prompts, barriers to adoption, ethical concerns, and the need for targeted professional development and institutional AI policies.

Chapter 4 proposes an enhanced framework for automated questionnaire generation in universities using generative AI. Integrating inclusive design, adaptive response features, and methodological rigor, this chapter provides practical strategies and case applications for data-driven assessment.

Chapter 5 presents the AAWIT Model—an AI-assisted adaptive writing instruction system designed for primary education. By blending real-time AI feedback with teacher scaffolding, the chapter illustrates how writing instruction can become more personalized, equitable, and developmentally aligned, while addressing key limitations and ethical considerations.

Chapter 6 demonstrates how project-based learning (PBL) and AI can jointly enhance English for Specific Purposes (ESP) education. The author highlights AI's potential to support creativity, collaboration, and problem-solving while ensuring responsible use and authentic, interdisciplinary learning outcomes.

Chapter 7 analyzes young adults' attitudes toward generative AI in STEM education. Through qualitative inquiry, the chapter reveals students' perceptions, confidence levels, ethical concerns, and views on global issues, offering insights into how AI tools can strengthen metacognitive skills and STEM engagement.

Chapter 8 investigates student success prediction in distance learning using machine learning models enriched with explainable AI (LIME). The findings underscore the importance of engagement patterns and exam behavior while offering practical implications for early-warning systems, targeted interventions, and personalized feedback.

Chapter 9 provides a bibliometric analysis of AI trends within instructional technology. Mapping research patterns, thematic clusters, and collaboration networks, the chapter illustrates the evolution of AI-related scholarship while emphasizing the need for ethical, transparent, and inclusive adoption in digital learning ecosystems.

CONCLUSION

As AI becomes increasingly embedded within educational systems worldwide, it is crucial to balance innovation with responsible, learner-centered design. The chapters in this volume collectively show that AI can advance accessibility, improve instructional quality, and deepen analytics-driven insights—but only when integrated with thoughtful pedagogy, robust ethics, and a clear understanding of learner diversity. Across contexts, the contributors emphasize that technology must serve educational goals, not the reverse.

Another key theme emerging from this book is the importance of interdisciplinary collaboration. Effective AI-enhanced education draws on expertise from data science, cognitive psychology, instructional design, linguistics, policy studies, and beyond. Such cross-disciplinary engagement ensures that AI tools are grounded in real educational needs, culturally sensitive practices, and evidence-based frameworks that empower both teachers and learners.

We hope this book serves not only as a reference for current research but also as a catalyst for future inquiry and innovation. By highlighting practical models, international case studies, and emerging methodologies, this volume aims to support those shaping the next generation of educational technologies. As AI continues to transform learning environments, we invite researchers and practitioners to build upon these insights, ensuring that advances in learning analytics and educational design contribute meaningfully to more inclusive, equitable, and future-ready education systems.

Chapter 1
Inclusive Curriculum Design Innovations Facilitated by AI

S. Ida Evangeline
https://orcid.org/0000-0003-2997-7897
Government College of Engineering, Tirunelveli, India

ABSTRACT

The emergence of generative artificial intelligence (AI) offers an unprecedented possibility to make the curriculum a more inclusive, responsive and culturally sensitive process. This chapter discusses how AI-based technologies can overcome the shortcomings of traditional curriculum models (e.g. limited representation, rigid pacing and inconsistent access) by allowing the dynamic generation of curriculum content that represents diversity in identity, language and ability. Using the concepts of educational theory, Universal Design for Learning (UDL), culturally responsive pedagogy, and differentiated instruction, the text points out the most practical ways to incorporate inclusivity into AI-enhanced study plans. Case studies based on different educational settings exemplify how AI can be used to achieve the creation of multilingual resources, customized instruction based on the profiles of learners, and provide culturally applicable examples at scale.

1. INTRODUCTION

The rapidly rising incorporation of generative artificial intelligence (AI) into educational settings is a fundamental transition in the generation and delivery of knowledge as experienced by end-users. Over decades, curriculum design has been heavily influenced, and enacted by, a combination of human actors, curriculum

DOI: 10.4018/979-8-3373-8805-2.ch001

committees, subject experts, and textbook publishers who act within institutional, cultural, and policy limits. Although these processes have delivered positive frameworks of teaching and learning, they have largely failed to proactively represent the diversity, accessibility requirements as well as cultural affiliation of the modern-day learners. Even the standard curriculum has, in most instances, been based on an ideal of the so-called average student, and has served to side-line those whose linguistic, cultural, cognitive or socio-economic situation does not conform to the perceived norm (Mao et al. 2024).

Generative AI offers a new, one-of-a-kind chance to resolve these constraints. Through its ability to create on-the-fly text, images, simulations and adaptive learning pathways, educators are now able to do away with one-size-fits-all, static curriculum development, in favor of learner-centered, up-to-date curriculum design. The natural language processing powers of AI can enable the near-instantaneous generation of material that can be immediately scaled to reading level, language, and cultural references, and adaptive algorithms may enable material to be structured in terms of sequence and difficulty with respect to how individual learners progress and learn. It cannot be a question of efficiency only but rather equity, of curriculum being able to cater to different learner profiles in a scale that was not logistically possible before (Cooper, 2023).

Demographic and technological trends are putting more pressure on the pressing need of such an innovation. Classrooms (both physical and virtual) are becoming more heterogeneous in nature taking into account students with different linguistic backgrounds, abilities as well as different cultural traditions. Change to online and hybrid learning environment has also expanded the range of learner needs, where educators may be challenged to provide inclusive resources that are entertaining and applicable in any context. Simultaneously, generalized availability of AI tools that facilitate generative technology (conversational agents, intelligent tutoring system, and so on) has not only introduced the technological possibility of altering the traditional approach to curriculum development, but also the institutional necessity of doing so (Bahroun et al. 2023).

The chapter has placed generative AI not as a content-creation automation machine, but as a potentially landmark partner in the co-building of diverse curricula. It will critically discuss opportunities on how AI can be used to incorporate a multiplicity of outlooks, cultural responsiveness, and differentiated instructions in the design of curriculum systems. In that respect, it will also provide the ethical considerations, risks, and governance system required to safeguard that the AI-enhanced curriculum design also follows the ethical principles of equity, diversity, and universal design of learning (UDL).

Finally, it is necessary to reiterate the goal of this chapter, which is to reconcile the discussion behind educational theory, AI ethics and curriculum innovation in practice. In synthesizing case studies, theory and critical reflection, it will offer a conceptual and practical guide that may be used both by educators, policymakers, and ultimately developers to help capture the promise of generative AI that goes beyond the success of efficiency and personalization, to promote justice and inclusion in education. This introduction sets the stage to examine, in the chapters that will follow, ways in which inclusive curriculum design may change in the age of generative AI: ways both that, should this often-discussed paradigm shift be led by human-centered values, could help make education a more accessible and empowering experience to all learners.

2. LIMITATIONS OF CONVENTIONAL CURRICULUM MODELS

Even the best pedagogical innovation of the previous decades has not been able to address the needs of these students using conventional curriculum models. These models are based on standardized models and are frequently limited by national or institutional requirements, so have been aimed rather at uniformity than at flexibility. Although it can be a convenient way to implement consistency and ease of evaluation, this strategy has a side effect of reproducing inequality because it favors some narratives, thinking styles and language conventions over others (Walder, 2014).

A major constraint is the question of representation. Conventional curricula are likely to capture the views and experiences, histories and knowledge systems of the dominant cultural groups with the experience and contributions of the marginalized communities poorly or distortedly represented. As an illustration, the literature curriculum may incorporate literary classics that represent a much smaller group of cultural backgrounds, whereas history curricula can skip latent or downplay incidents in non-Western history. These gaps not only minimize the depth of the learning process, they also have the risk of pushing students out of the various situations in which their identities and their experiences have either been left out of what they are studying or reduced to what they are studying (Walder, 2017).

The second challenge is connected with the notion of accessibility. There is problem in traditional curriculum formulation in that not all students have been factored in diverse abilities, learning methods and needs of the students. Accessible education is required by law and guidelines; in the United States, this includes the Americans with Disabilities Act (ADA), which governs it, or, in other countries, comparable policies; however, the actual inclusion of accessible design in curriculum development has been mixed. As an example, the learning materials might not provide alternative text to images, be overwhelming towards the visual or audio representation without alternatives, or contain information frequently encountered in forms hard to interpret by the assistive technology. This has the effect of creating a wall that does not allow the full participation of learners in curriculum (Law, 2014).

In addition, traditional curriculums have the paradigm of one-size- fits- all, where learning processes may be constrained on a personalization process of learning routes. The pacing, assessment procedures, and sequencing in most cases presuppose that all students will begin at the same point without taking into consideration that students will have different background knowledge, language abilities, as well as the speed of processing thoughts. Such inflexibility will harm those students who need additional time to learn a concept and those who are prepared to move faster giving rise to apathy on both ends of the scales (Carvalho et al. 2021).

The fact that the curricular materials are not dynamic aggravates the problem. Textbooks and other foundational materials are generally predetermined to be modified on multi-year cycles hence their information can be outdated fast in high-rate fields or can not react to newly arising societal and cultural concerns. This stagnation can reinforce the old-fashioned assumptions, exclude the examples of such contemporary world and ignore the possibility of using current events or local contexts in accessing this learning process.

Lastly, these challenges are worsened by the difference in resources that the institutions have. With adequately funded schools there are schools that can afford to add other resources to the official curricula whereas the under-resourced schools are limited with little room to adapt to the centrally mandated materials. The effect is an increased disparity in the openness and meaningfulness of curricula, most likely impacting those students who are members of marginalized or underserved communities (Silver et al. 2019).

While the benefits of inclusive curriculum are widely acknowledged, scholarly views differ on how it should be conceptualized and implemented. Florian and Black-Hawkins (2011) emphasize that inclusion should involve designing learning for all, rather than creating separate tracks or compensatory programs for marginalized students. In contrast, Slee (2013) critiques the notion that inclusion can be meaningfully achieved within existing systems that prioritize standardization and performance metrics, arguing instead for a more radical restructuring of education. This divergence points to a persistent research gap: the lack of consensus on practical models that reconcile inclusive ideals with systemic constraints — especially as digital and AI-based tools begin to reshape curriculum delivery (Akyildiz, 2025).

Briefly, the traditional curriculum models have ensured stability and order in the educational system, but because of their unavoidable restrictions, such as (but not limited to) cultural absence, variable accessibility, linear movement, the obsoleteness of its material and lack of resources equity, they form controlled structures of exclusivity. It is against this backdrop, however, that generative AI is an emerging potential game-changer. Section two will discuss the capabilities of AI in breaking out of these limitations, and in being able to develop curricula that not only become increasingly responsive to a wider range of learner's needs, but that will also be more adaptable to a changing, globalized information world at large.

3. GENERATIVE AI AS A CATALYST FOR INCLUSIVE CURRICULUM INNOVATION

The shortcomings of traditional curriculum designs provide an avenue to innovative ways and generative artificial intelligence (AI) is thus at the center of this revolution. Generative AI differs with prior educational technology waves in two fundamental ways. First, most early technology development was aimed at putting existing content through a digitization form, or automating administrative tasks in the K-12 or higher ed space. Generative AI adds the new capability of producing content on the fly that is, in real time, malleable to the contextual needs of a given situation. The depth of this capacity has far-reaching implication to matters of inclusivity since it enables that the curricula are designed not only to focus on the standard learning results but also on individual identities, backgrounds, and learning preferences of separate students (Kayabas, 2024).

The essence of generative AI can be summed up as machines that can generate new text, images, audio and other media based on user prompts with the use of machine learning, especially large language models, and multimodal architectures. The systems have been able to synthesize large volumes of data, learn and identify patterns in language on imagery and generate coherent and context relevant, outputs that seem to replicate the creative power of a human. Applied to education, this translates to the ability of AI not only to suggest resources, but to in fact develop lesson plans, interactive simulations, differentiated assessments, and even culturally responsive educational material that is specific to a given cohort or even to an individual learner (Tariq, 2024).

Dynamic content adaptation is probably one of the most promising uses. Generative AI can take concepts that are too intricate and rewrite them in user-friendly terms to provide more scaffolding to those students not ready to dive deep into the subject, or go deeper into the concepts and give a more in-depth treatment to those capable of a more rigorous pursuit. As regards multilingual classrooms, the AI-powered translation tool will instantly translate the content into various languages and preserve contextual accuracy, giving the students the possibility to read the materials in the preferred linguistic medium. This is especially relevant in globalised world of learning where linguistic diversity is a common form of inaccessibility to fair participation (Singha & Singha, 2024).

However, not all researchers agree on the readiness or reliability of generative AI for high-stakes inclusion work. Luckin et al., (2022) warns that generative systems, while promising, still lack nuanced understanding of learner context — a gap that can hinder genuine personalization. In contrast, authors like Holmes et al. (2022) argue that even limited adaptive capacity can outperform rigid, traditional methods in supporting diverse learners. This divergence highlights an emerging research gap: the need for empirical studies comparing human-led and AI-assisted inclusivity interventions across contexts (Temel & Yılmaz, 2025).

Right along with AI is its capability of being culturally responsive. Generic curricula have the problem of lacking local or culturally-specific examples, but GAI has the capability of utilizing a wide data set to localize curriculum to be meaningful to students. An example is how to frame a computational problem with locally relevant problems, or having a literature assignment with the narratives of non popular communities. This scalable option of personalizing contents fills a long-standing void in the educational world: the students need to ensure that learning is personally significant to them (Dai et al. 2023).

Generative AI can also provide customised learning routes, which change the content, as well as its order and pace. AI-fueled adaptive learning platforms have the power continuously evaluate the performance of the students and modify the learning process. This guarantees that those students who need more time on the basic concepts are provided with time, and the students that are ready to do advanced material are not in danger of being left behind in a fixed agenda. This flexibility encourages a learning culture where any learner is enabled to advance upon the capacities, requirements and aspirations- the characteristics of an inclusive education method.

Recent empirical insights support this vision. A global survey found that 64% of educators and 77% of parents of students with intellectual and developmental disabilities (IDD) believe AI holds significant potential for advancing inclusive education. Their views emphasize AI's role in offering differentiated instruction, adaptive interfaces, and multilingual access — aligning directly with the inclusive mechanisms described above[REMOVED HYPERLINK FIELD]. This evidence reinforces the argument that generative AI is not merely theoretically inclusive, but already recognized by stakeholders as a tool for reducing real-world learning barriers (Xiao et al., 2024).

Evidence from large-scale adaptive learning deployments supports this claim. In the Indian state of Andhra Pradesh, a personalized adaptive learning program leveraging AI tools led to learning gains equivalent to 1.9 years of additional progress over 17 months, compared to peers in non-PAL schools. Such measurable outcomes illustrate the scalable impact of AI in closing learning gaps, particularly for students historically marginalized by one-size-fits-all curricula (Rizvi et al., 2025).

Disability-wise, AI has been better able to incorporate universal design of learning (UDL) principles in the curricular materials than traditional delivery modalities have. Students with disabilities will have fewer barriers created due to the possibility to generate text-to-speech, speech-to-text, alternative image descriptions as well as multimodal information representation on demand. Moreover, AI has the ability to generate several different versions of the same idea e.g. a textual explanation, an interactive visual model, and an audio narrative to provide learners with the option of how they may prefer to interact with content (Tanweer & Ismail, 2024).

A systematic review of AI in education for students with learning disabilities found that out of 16 studies analyzed, the majority focused on adaptive learning platforms—particularly for students with dyslexia and dyscalculia. These AI-driven tools showed promising results in improving learner engagement, task comprehension, and confidence, while enabling personalization that traditional formats lacked (Panjwani-Charania & Zhai, 2024). This evidence reinforces the role of generative AI in delivering not only accessible content but also pedagogically effective support tailored to neurodiverse learners.

Nevertheless, generative AI is not limited in its ability to promote inclusivity only through producing content. It also helps to design collaborative curriculum enabling teachers, course designers and even students to co-develop learning content using AI as a co-creator. The participatory approach does not only democratize curriculum design, but also assures diversity of the voices that shape the narratives, examples, and learning modalities the curriculum contains.

Recent scholarship proposes structured frameworks for designing inclusive AI-based learning environments. These models emphasize principles such as adaptability, accessibility, learner agency, and cultural responsiveness in the development process itself — not just in the AI output. For example, Song et al., (2024) outline a four-stage inclusive AI learning design process that integrates stakeholder co-design, algorithmic transparency, and multimodal feedback to ensure equity is embedded throughout the learning experience (Song et al., 2024)[REMOVED HYPERLINK FIELD]. Such frameworks are essential for translating the promise of generative AI into truly inclusive educational practice.

This observation implies that in this respect, generative AI may create a balance between social justice and effectiveness as a scalability powerhouse and personalizator. Its ability to generate responsive, accessible, and culturally-aware text at scale is able to combat the very issues posed by traditional curricula that have never been defeated. However, achieving this potential is deeper than technology capability but must instead be a strong pledge to ethical protection, pedagogical mindfulness, and mutual control so that AI does not merely reproduce the disparities that exist but quicker and more full-scale. However, empirical work remains scarcer than conceptual work: a pilot study of two students in a resource room setting used an AI-analytics environment to explore inclusive learning, but the sample size was very small and the authors stressed the need for larger scale studies (Toyokawa et al., 2023).

4. FROM VISION TO PRACTICE: IMPLEMENTATION FRAMEWORKS FOR INCLUSIVE AI IN EDUCATION

While the promise of generative AI for inclusive curriculum is compelling, realizing its full potential requires deliberate and context-sensitive implementation. Educators, policymakers, and technologists must collaboratively translate theoretical insights into actionable strategies that ensure accessibility, equity, and pedagogical integrity. This section outlines a practical framework across three domains: implementation strategies, educator training, and policy implications.

4.1 Implementation Strategies in the Classroom

To avoid techno-solutionism and ensure that AI genuinely supports inclusivity, schools should prioritize low-barrier, high-impact applications of AI tools. For instance, integrating AI into formative assessments—where students receive adaptive feedback or real-time language scaffolds—can enhance engagement without overhauling the core curriculum. Similarly, AI-powered translation and summarization tools can break language barriers in multilingual classrooms by providing materials in students' preferred languages.

Another key strategy is participatory design. Teachers, students (especially those with disabilities or from marginalized groups), and curriculum developers should co-develop and test AI-integrated learning modules. This collaborative process ensures that outputs are responsive to local needs and cultural contexts. Schools can also adopt modular AI-enhanced components—such as personalized reading aides, adaptive quizzes, or content simplifiers—that seamlessly integrate into existing syllabi without disrupting established pedagogies (Melo-López et al., 2025).

4.2 Educator Training and Professional Development

The shift toward AI-enhanced inclusivity demands a new layer of teacher capacity: AI literacy. Professional development programs must equip educators not only with technical know-how (e.g., how to prompt AI systems or assess generated content) but also with critical frameworks for evaluating bias, fairness, and alignment with inclusive pedagogies such as Universal Design for Learning (UDL) and Culturally Responsive Pedagogy (CRP).

Training modules should adopt practice-based learning environments where teachers can simulate the integration of generative AI into lesson planning and classroom delivery. These sandbox settings allow educators to build confidence, troubleshoot challenges, and see the inclusive potential of AI in action. Embedding interdisciplinary knowledge—from ethics to accessibility standards—into such training is essential to prevent misuse and ensure human-centered deployment (Marras et al., 2025).

4.3 Policy Implications for Equitable AI Integration

At the policy level, frameworks must move beyond access and address inclusive design mandates. Procurement policies should require AI educational tools to undergo inclusivity audits—assessing for accessibility, cultural representation, and potential bias. Moreover, clear data governance standards must be enacted to safeguard learner data, especially among vulnerable populations.

Governments and education ministries should also consider incentivizing inclusive AI innovation through targeted funding schemes, grants, and public-private partnerships. Pilot programs, for example, can support schools in rural or under-resourced areas to experiment with AI-enhanced curriculum under guided protocols. Finally, establishing multi-stakeholder advisory boards—including teachers, technologists, disability advocates, and students—can ensure that AI adoption in education remains equitable, ethical, and evidence-based (Murari & Parmar, 2025).

5. DESIGNING FOR INCLUSIVITY WITH AI

The generative AI in education is not only a transformative force, but only when used with a purpose to purposefully incorporate inclusivity throughout all the tiers of curriculum planning. Although it is well known that AI can be used in automation and personalization, when these features are incorporated with the use of pedagogical concepts like culturally responsive teaching, differentiated instruction, and universal design for learning (UDL), AI reaches its full potential. Collectively, these models provide a guide to the successful application of AI not only to provide content, but also to establish fair learning experiences with due regard to and celebration of diversity (Holmes & Tuomi, 2022).

This work is based on culturally responsive curriculum design. Development of culturally relevant learning materials has traditionally been a costly endeavor, one that usually required the background knowledge, as well as lived experiences, of individual educators. Generative AI of course may be able to scale this and can use large and diverse datasets to incorporate multiple cultural narratives, perspectives and examples in to curricular materials. As an example, a service on migration history can be changed challenging with a lively attitude it can be diversified with the regional migration narratives with the input of local history of the students attending a specific classroom. In the same effect, the concerns of science can be put in quandaries that can be easily relatable in scenarios such as in local settings or even community concerns so that the students can relate abstract ideas to what they face daily. This way, AI would contribute to bridging the distance between the culture of students and the content of what they have to study in school (Zhai et al. 2021).

DI, or distincted instruction, the strategy of adjusting the approaches to teaching to fit the different needs of learners, also makes use of AI significantly. Conventional means of differentiation can be quite time-consuming in that the educator has to plan duplicate copies of the same lesson or homework assignment in varying calibrations of learning levels, learning paces, or modalities. Generative AI is able to automate much of this with tiered assignments being generated at will or reading levels of the same text being generated in different tones or multiple problem sets addressing the same concept but in different forms. Take the case of a mathematical concept which can be elaborated to one group, in terms of a narrative-story, to another group, by means of visual simulation and to another group in terms of symbolic notation to access advanced application. Differentiating in an education setting would more closely be possible by using AI, thus enabling a teacher to dedicate their time towards building relationships and offering individualized assistance as opposed to preparing the repetitive content (Schiff, 2022).

Universal design for learning (UDL) framework additionally consolidates the connection among AI and inclusiveness. UDL focuses on the use of multiple representations (presentation of the material available), engagements (the presentation of motivational strategies to learn) and expressions (presentation of the ways students show their knowledge). Generative AI has the potential to make these principles operational in the sense of producing different versions of instruction materials on demand. To take just one example, an AI engine might produce a lesson in the form of a podcast, visual infographic, interactive simulation, and a classic text-based lesson, each one set to the same target learning objectives but aimed at the various sensory and cognitive processing styles. In the same way, AI can assist the students in deciding how to reflect their mastery, where they could have a choice of doing a written reflection, a recorded oral presentation, or multimedia work, all properly scaffolded to their level of ability (Selwyn, 2022).

Notably, inclusivity in designing with AI is not only about the content which is created, but also about the process of management. To achieve relevance and authenticity, collaborative design processes whereby the educators and students and even community stakeholder define the parameters of the AI and assess the output are significant. This collaborative method reduces the chance of cultural misrepresentation or overgeneralization that may happen in case of a training a certain AI model which utilizes the data that has its own prejudices. This may be achieved practically through co-designing prompts with students, editing AI-generated materials regarding cultural insensitivities, and subsequently iterating on the writing per feedback in the classroom based.

However, despite its potent functionality, AI still is unable to replicate the subtle judgment, empathy, and situational consciousness that human educators can contribute to the design process. Instead, it is worth viewing AI as a multiplier of human creativity and inclusivity, an enabler that stretches possibilities but still one which human beings must oversee consciously as we ensure that the outputs of AI reflect in balance with the value of education. Texanized generative AI can transform how educators behave by moving them away in the role of content deliverers into those of learning architects designing a hyperlocal learning experience that meets learners where they are (Srinivasa et al. 2022).

When strengths of culturally responsive pedagogy, differentiated instruction and UDL are combined with the adaptive capability of AI, inclusive curriculum design stops being a hopeful ideal and becomes a realisable scale. In the following section, we will see that these principles are already being applied in practice by giving practical case studies, to provide the examples of how inclusion of AI is actually occurring in curriculum building.

6. CASE STUDIES AND PRACTICAL APPLICATIONS

Although the generative AI is temptingly persuasive in the theoretical context of inclusive curriculum design, its transformation potential is the most apparent in practice. As examples of schools, university research efforts, and grass roots education around the world are starting to incorporate AI tools in their curriculum development, more and more concrete outcomes in terms of inclusivity, accessibility and learner participation are starting to be achieved. Despite the dissimilarities in terms of scope and context, these examples present the overview of the ways in which the principles explained above cultural responsiveness, differentiated instruction, and universal design for learning may be implemented with the help of AI technologies (Su & Zhong, 2022).

A good example is the case of a multilingual secondary school in Canada where teachers colluded with a team of researchers in one of the universities to pilot the application of AI-aided translation and adaptation of science curricula. In this project generative AI was utilised to generate lesson content in the first languages of students- which could include mandarin to arabic- as well as adding in or simplifying explanations, based on the specific reading level of the student (Çoban & Yıldız, 2025). Teachers described more active participation of students in discussion and their better conceptualization of content in science, as students who previously could not well engage with science materials because of language barriers. The proved capacity of the AI system to adjust the complexity to individualize learning combined with the preservation of the subject-specific accuracy of translation highlights directly how linguistic disparities can be overcome in the classroom setting with the help of technological adaptation (Somasundaram et al. 2020).

The public school system in Brazil has emerged as an example of an edtech startup serving as a partner to the local Ministry of Education, in order to utilize AI, to create mathematically relevant issues based on the local experiences of the students of the regions as well as their cultural backgrounds. As an example, word problems involving agricultural themes were used in rural areas whereas issues related to fishing and shipping were used in coastal areas. This process did not only reduce faceless abstractions in understanding them, but also justified local culture identities as worth being included in academic studies. The teachers observed increased student engagement and their desire to tackle problems and problem-solving tasks, which implies that cultural contextualization plays a significant role in motivation when conducted with the help of AI in the context of content generation (Torrisi-Steele, 2026).

In higher education an inclusive design project within a European university involved the use of generative AI to develop a series of adaptive learning pathways to allow students to work through an introductory course on programming. The AI system used real-time analysis of coding submissions to suggest customized problem sets, alternative explanations and scaffolded tutorials, all specific to the strengths and weaknesses of each learner (Aslan & Sever, 2025). Notably, all of the generated resources were equipped with accessibility options, including screen-reader-friendly code formatting and a narrated explanation, to make sure that any student with impaired vision will be involved in the expanses. The initiative showed that placing a focus on accessibility in the design of the AI in the initial phases of this process, inclusion can be achieved on a large scale, without the need to develop a set of special materials dedicated to specific groups of learners, which normalizes the existence of diverse learners (Chu & Ashraf, 2025).

Grassroot initiatives have also developed, including one community-centered AI curriculum project in Kenya where local educators partnered with technologists to co-design open educational resources in the Kiswahili language and indigenous languages. Generative AI was employed to create drafts of learning modules which were further fine-tuned after teacher workshops in order to make them accurate culturally and contextually relevant. The given participatory model stresses the responsibility of human control and community-based knowledge to make sure that the content generated by AI can be introduced to communities in an authentic manner, not to impose some homogenized or alien worldview.

These case examples are connected by the following aspects: the capacity of AI to process the materials in a short time to personalize them to the learners at scale, the capacity of AI to introduce the cultural and linguistic relevancy at scale, and the need to ensure that human agencies are present and helps with preserving the contextual integrity. They also show that the uses of AI in aiding inclusivity that can have the most significant impact are not those that are aiming to boot out human educators, but they are those that will help them shed mundane content creation and concentrate on facilitating learning, mentoring, and bonding with learners (Chiu et al. 2021).

Even the firstseveral deployments offer valuable lessons: generative AI can democratize, scale, and bring inclusivity to new life like never before, yet only when it is deployed consciously, ethically, and comes hand in hand with careful attention of educators, as well as learners. In the following part, I am going to focus on the hazardous byproduct of such innovations, including risks and ethical concerns that should not be overlooked, lest the push toward inclusion ends up fruitlessly reinstating the same inequality it was aimed to eliminate.

7. RISKS AND ETHICAL CONSIDERATIONS

The variety of opportunities of increased inclusivity beyond generative AI integration in the curriculum is therefore indisputable, but all of it is accompanied by the risk of failure to meet the goals due to unaddressed risks that generative AI integration into curriculums may unintentionally result in. Technology is not neutral, in that it reflects the assumptions, values and limitations of those who build it and those in whose interests its interests are built. With regards to inclusive education, this implies that unless AI is governed carefully, it may unwillingly perpetuate inequality, cause reinforced prejudice, and the decline of trust toward the educational systems. It is necessary to understand these risks to create the safeguards that would ensure AI becomes a tool of inclusion as opposed to looking over its shoulder (Borenstein & Howard, 2021).

A concern of the greatest concerns is algorithmic bias. Generative AI models are trained by a large data that tends to impose societal biases and inequity over previous generations. When such biases remain unrecognized and unaddressed, such AI can create curriculum materials that tacitly favor some cultural norms, linguistic form, or worldview at the expense of others. In another, ethical involvement example, an AI producing historical content may give undue attention to Eurocentric historical accounts should it be trained more on Western historical records, or in other cases may reproduce gender stereotypes through examples and imagery. The results of such outputs can lead to the institutionalization exclusion within a curriculum upholding inclusivity as an objective.

Along with this there is the peril of homogenization of content. Although AI has the capacity to produce more material in a short time, this might be generic, safe and locally unspecific as it is limited to using pattern recognition. This may compromise the cultural specificity which gives learning resources cultural sensitivity to different communities. In their search of a universal applicability of the curricula generated through AI, there is a risk of obliterating local identity so as to offer a globalized yet shallow culturally aware version of the knowledge that tends to remain outside the interests of the learners (Holmes et al. 2022).

The nature of ethical issues concerning data privacy and consent needs to be considered well. A vast number of AI systems depend on learner data aggregations and analyses, which allow personalizing the content as much as possible. This can be revealing of sensitive information of the learning needs, disabilities, or socio-economic backgrounds of the students without good privacy safeguards. Under the circumstances of communities with already existing surveillance concerns, including the mistrust towards the educational process, applied AI may overemphasize the suspicion, particularly, in cases unless learners and their families are provided with clear communications regarding the way their data is used, kept, and shared.

Giving excessive decision-making to the educational process is the other challenge. Although AI may assist the educators by recommending them or by creating content, the danger is that when such systems are made to appear objective authorities, the amount of human supervision is decreased. An AI can suggest learning pathways or evaluations using partial or ill informed information and cause mismatched training. When they do, instructors might feel they are under pressure to abide by the AI because doing otherwise in an under-resourced environment with limited time and resources will go against best professional practice (Biagini, 2025).

Moreover, the ethics of AI-generated content would be complicated in the cases when it harms someone or replicates exclusion. It can be quite difficult to assign any responsibility in multi-stakeholder settings be it the AI developer, the school institution itself or individual teachers. In the absence of well-defined accountability structures, there is a threat of unaddressed harms, where victims of the harms cannot do anything about them, further reinforcing injustices in the systems or organization.

Acts and the inclusivity of curriculum design enabled by AI are also influenced by the digital divide. As much as AI stands to democratize access, the benefits could be enjoyed overwhelmingly by better-resourced schools and institutions that could afford a strong digital infrastructure, training and technical assistance. This may have the unforeseen effect of magnifying the educational disparities that already exist between city and country schools, or between the high-income and lower-income population, or defeat the democratic ideal of education that strives to bend-down education to all.

Last but not least, the teacher independence is an issue. There is a danger that with no obvious boundaries between generative AI and themselves, teachers risk being converted into mere facilitators of generated AI productions as opposed to designers of the learning process. This would de-professionalise teaching and minimise the scope of innovation and destabilise the human relationships at the heart of any effective education (Raji et al. 2021).

Overall, although there are terrifically non-trivial potentials of generative AI in the field of inclusivity development in curriculum plans, there are also tremendous dangers that cannot be overlooked. These are the challenges that can only be addressed through the active design decisions, ethical principles, clarity of governmental management, and constant communication between teachers, technologists, politicians and students. The following section will concern itself with frameworks to make AI-driven curriculum innovation human centered, equity informed and embrincipied by the values of universal design for learning.

8. FRAMEWORKS FOR HUMAN-CENTERED, INCLUSIVE AI CURRICULUM DESIGN

It is not merely technical expertise that is needed to ensure the enhancement of inclusivity with help of generative AI or prevent harm caused by it; it is rather principled and conscious design, deployment, and evaluation. That includes positioning AI as an assistant and not a self-governing agent in the educational sphere, and envisioning it as a resource and as a part of much more human and humanistic systems within which the teachings and instructions are held positively by equity, cultural responsiveness, and universal access. These frameworks serve as guide-rails, and can be used to make innovations by steering the outcomes in ethically sound, pedagogically robust, and socially considerate ways (Zhao et al. 2024).

One of the places to begin is the Collaborative Design Model where educators, students, AI developers, and policymakers would serve as collaborators in the design of the educational curricula. The model acknowledges that inclusivity cannot be `` programmed `` on the outside; it is a result of the lived experiences, values, and priorities of people that the curriculum is aimed to serve. In practice this would entail teachers and learners being involved in defining the parameters of AI-generated content, reviewing and correcting demonstrations of accuracy and cultural accuracy, and creating the feedback loops wherein the technology could be continually refined in response to reality as encountered in the classroom. This form of participatory engagement can make sure that AI will not become a dictator in the industry of curriculum design (Chu & Ashraf, 2025).

A second framework is focused on Ethical AI Governance namely a set of policies and checks, balances, aimed at ensuring transparency, fairness and accountability in using AI. This includes:

- Transparency: Openness to educators and learners to how the AI functions, what information is used and what weaknesses its systems have.
- Fairness: AI outputs to be systematically audited on bias with corrective action taken where inequities can be identified.
- Accountability: Clear lines of accountability, so that curriculum content had the last decision resting with education professionals.

The willingness to enshrine such governance principles in institutional policy serves to work to engender trust, and presents a protective mechanism against the risks of non-transparent/unchecked applications of AI.

The third pillar is the Alignment with Universal Design Learning (UDL). When taking UDL as a non-negotiable basis, AI-generated curriculum could systematically offer a variety of means of representation, engagement and expression. To illustrate, when a unit is created, the AI can automatically generate accessible adaptations, e.g. audio interpretations, visual interpretations, text and interactive, means that the educators do not need to make orders regarding separate adaptations at all. Design-stage embedding of UDL should make inclusivity proactive as opposed to reactive (Mosly, 2024).

Another quality assurance is provided by the Cultural Responsiveness Protocol. This entails the AI outputs evaluated in a perspective of cultural integrity and relevancy, with both checks of automation and human check. Teachers, community members, and cultural specialists can be employed in an effort to make sure that examples, stories, and situations are suitable within the social and cultural life of the learners. In multilingual environments, it was also verified that this protocol is applied but rather than being linguistically correct, the AI translations have to be idiomatically true and sensitive.

Lastly, AI adoption has to be integrated with Capacity-Building and Professional Development. Teachers must be able to work with AI tools technically; conversely, they will need critical literacy to question and work with the content such tools generate. The professional development programs must cover the how and why of AI in teaching and learning- allow educators to make use of the benefits but avoid complacency and the over-dependence trap, while remaining creative and pedagogically authorial (Long et al. 2025).

Collectively, the frameworks can develop a multi-tiered strategy toward AI enabled curriculum design a strategy that is not only technologically thoughtful, but ethically and socially concerned. By doing so, AI has the potential to act as an enabler of the transformation in education by extending the importance of equity, diversity, and inclusion that identify the values inherent to the mission of modern education.

The next section will be a prospective reflection on transforming developments and the directions, where the future development of generative AI may create additional change in the field of inclusive curriculum design and what research and policy should be done to make such a change follow human-centered values.

9. FUTURE DIRECTIONS

With generative AI technologies developing at a blistering rate, the implications of their use will only continue to grow and diversify in regards to all-inclusive curriculum design. The next ten years will bring changes that not only increase the customizability and autonomy of learning content, but also hold the faculty, policy makers and developers as more equipped to draw a new paradigm in the role of technology and pedagogy in address the challenges of equity. These developments are all likely to have profound impacts on just how much AI is built into the context of educational justice and whether it serves to widen existing gaps or curb it (Ullah et al. 2025).

Another growth area will be multimodal generative AI which will enable a coherent generative production and synthesis of text, images, audio, video, simulations, and even haptic feedback all operating seamlessly within a learning experience. In the inclusive curriculum design, it implies that one concept, e.g. the structure of DNA could be presented in parallel form by audio descriptions of animations, computer models that students could interact with using 3D modeling software, physical models accessible to students with visual impairments, and culturally appropriate analogies. Whether this multimodal combination promises to be a dramatic enlargement and improvement in accessibility and engagement may mean offering high level learning to students irrespective of sensory, cognitive, and linguistics variations (Abbasi et al. 2025).

The other disruptive innovation includes real-time adaptive learning environments. It is also possible that future artificial intelligence systems will enable the evaluation of learners on their engagement, comprehension and emotions according to their consumption of content and modify material in real time. This has the potential to take curriculum design in an altogether different direction by pushing it towards a respondent, adaptive learning experience in which the curriculum changes in each learner at every moment, dynamically. This presents unparalleled possibilities of individualization however it also poses challenging issues based on privacy of data, consent and extent of technology imposing itself on learning process in human beings.

New policy frameworks will also be catalyzed by the spread of AI across the globe in education. Guidance on how to ethically use AI in the educational field is already starting to take shape in international bodies like UNESCO, the OECD, and education and educational research ministries of regions. New policies would most certainly look at measures regarding the standard of inclusivity measures, bias auditing, accessiblity concerns and cross-border data protection. In terms of curriculum design, this may refer to developing internationally agreed benchmarks of what may be considered as an inclusive AI generated learning resource, which will facilitate the assessment and dissemination of best practices in a cross-contextual manner (Karataş et al. 2025).

The other frontier is localization of the AI technology with village-level datasets. Future systems will be characterized less by all-purpose globally trained models that can impart cultural biases into the systems--and more by locally-focused community-curated knowledge bases. This would permit AI to create documents that are heavily aware of local history, language, and experience lived reinforcement of culture that would not sacrifice educational excellence. These directions may also provide communities with the strength to become co-owners of AI systems, changing the power hold on to central tech providers and making them more democratic and participatory in curriculum innovation (Tatar et al. 2025).

Research priorities, simultaneously, will have to change in order to keep up with these new technological potentials. It will be necessary to have longitudinal research questions on the effectiveness of AI-based inclusive curricula, comparative studies across various socio-economic and cultural settings, and substantive research on learning outcomes. Investigations of the psychological and social processes of AI-enhanced learning, i.e., the impact on student motivation, teacher agency, and the perception of educational justice, will also be of great importance.

Technology however will not be the only factor that shaping the future. The values and governance structures under which AI is used, will be the strongest influence towards or against inclusion. Unless there is a long-term commitment to equity, diversity and universal access, even AI tools that are most sophisticated will simply recreate the exclusions of the past, but do so even more efficiently. Otherwise, with its human-centered principles elucidated by inclusive policies, generative AI can make personalized, culturally relevant, and accessible learning the norm rather than an exception (Vettriselvan & Ramya, 2025).

Moreover, as educators, policymakers and developers look forward, their challenge is not merely to embrace the AI, but to build it-- to make the future of curriculum design in which technology and the person become technologically sophisticated and humanly civilized. The final part of this chapter will summarize the main findings of the discussion and reiterate the main argument which is that generative AI, when ideally applied to inclusive educational values, is going to assist in establishing an educational learning environment where students can grow and flourish (Alfayez & Rasool, 2025).

10. CONCLUSION

Generative AI is about as big of a paradigm shift to how a curriculum is handled since mass-scale public education. The scale of its ability to produce, adaptive, culturally responsive and accessible learning material questions the long held drawbacks of traditional curriculum models. Throughout the above discussion, this chapter has addressed the (seemingly) futuristic potential of this transformation, as well as the dangers of it becoming reality--suggesting that being inclusive is not an incidental and imminent outcome of adopting AI, but a dynamic part of the enshrinement of a set of beliefs.

There is a powerful case to be made on the side of AI-enabled inclusivity. The use of dynamic language adaptation, incorporation of multiple cultural narrative, individualized learning routes, universal access, etc., can redesign the structure of curricula thinking, development, and implementation in fundamental ways, with a combination of AI capabilities. These advantages do not occur automatically, however. They demand good governance, design with others, critical auditing of bias, and alignment with pedagogy like culturally responsive teaching, differentiated instructions, universal design of learning (UDL).

The dangers are also blatant. Unless addressed, algorithmic bias, content homogenization, privacy issues and the digital divide will negate the inclusive possibility of AI. Resistance to AI is not an issue, as much as this chapter has stressed, but shaping it to reflect and enforce principles of equity, diversity, and human dignity in its application in designing curriculums.

It is on the path forward to think of AI not as a substitute, but as a creative companion, to human educators: one that enhances teacher authority, empowers learner agency, and helps to overcome missing access and representation gaps. With the help of the generative AI and within the frameworks of inclusivity, it will be possible not only to have responsive curriculum that individual needs, but also a curriculum that is cognizant to the cultural and cognitive richness of our learning populations.

Ultimately, the potential of AI in inclusive curriculum design is not technical, it lies in the decision-making we place on implementing it. With the choices being informed by a dedication to justice, representation, and accessibility, AI will be able to help make education all the more aligned with its most idealistic vision: the chance to succeed as an education system accessible and available to all learners regardless of their background or ability.

REFERENCES

Abbasi, B. N., Wu, Y., & Luo, Z. (2025). Exploring the impact of artificial intelligence on curriculum development in global higher education institutions. *Education and Information Technologies*, *30*(1), 547–581.

Akyildiz, Y. (2025). The impact of virtual reality on vocabulary learning and cognitive efficiency. *Journal of Educational Technology and Online Learning*, *8*(2), 152–163.

Alfayez, A. A., & Rasool, A. (2025). Use of AI in the curriculum development of transnational higher education. In *Bridging Global Divides for Transnational Higher Education in the AI Era* (pp. 401–422). IGI Global Scientific Publishing.

Aslan, I. A., & Sever, G. (2025). Fine arts high school students' experiences on the use of Tonic, an interactive instrument practice application. *Journal of Educational Technology and Online Learning*, *8*(3), 330–350.

Bahroun, Z., Anane, C., Ahmed, V., & Zacca, A. (2023). Transforming education: A comprehensive review of generative artificial intelligence in educational settings through bibliometric and content analysis. *Sustainability*, *15*(17), 12983.

Biagini, G. (2025). Towards an AI-Literate Future: A systematic literature review exploring education, ethics, and applications. *International Journal of Artificial Intelligence in Education*, **•••**, 1–51.

Borenstein, J., & Howard, A. (2021). Emerging challenges in AI and the need for AI ethics education. *AI and Ethics*, *1*(1), 61–65. PMID: 38624388

Carvalho, A., Teixeira, S. J., Olim, L., Campanella, S. D., & Costa, T. (2021). Pedagogical innovation in higher education and active learning methodologies–a case study. *Education + Training*, *63*(2), 195–213.

Chiu, T. K., Meng, H., Chai, C. S., King, I., Wong, S., & Yam, Y. (2021). Creation and evaluation of a pretertiary artificial intelligence (AI) curriculum. *IEEE Transactions on Education*, *65*(1), 30–39.

Chu, T. S., & Ashraf, M. (2025). Artificial Intelligence in Curriculum Design: A Data-Driven Approach to Higher Education Innovation. *Knowledge (Beverly Hills, Calif.)*, *5*(3), 14.

Çoban, D., & Yıldız, D. G. (2025). An evaluation of the 10th grade robotic coding curriculum (2020) within a participant oriented curriculum evaluation approach. *Journal of Educational Technology and Online Learning*, *8*(2), 226–250.

Cooper, G. (2023). Examining science education in ChatGPT: An exploratory study of generative artificial intelligence. *Journal of Science Education and Technology*, *32*(3), 444–452.

Dai, Y., Liu, A., & Lim, C. P. (2023). Reconceptualizing ChatGPT and generative AI as a student-driven innovation in higher education. *Procedia CIRP*, *119*, 84–90.

Florian, L., & Black-Hawkins, K. (2011). Exploring inclusive pedagogy. *British Educational Research Journal*, *37*(5), 813–828.

Holmes, W., Porayska-Pomsta, K., Holstein, K., Sutherland, E., Baker, T., Shum, S. B., & Koedinger, K. R. (2022). Ethics of AI in education: Towards a community-wide framework. *International Journal of Artificial Intelligence in Education*, *32*(3), 504–526.

Holmes, W., & Tuomi, I. (2022). State of the art and practice in AI in education. *European Journal of Education*, *57*(4), 542–570.

Karataş, F., Eriçok, B., & Tanrikulu, L. (2025). Reshaping curriculum adaptation in the age of artificial intelligence: Mapping teachers' AI-driven curriculum adaptation patterns. *British Educational Research Journal*, *51*(1), 154–180.

Kayabas, İ. (2024). Innovative curriculum development and content creation with generative AI. In *Transforming Education With Generative AI: Prompt Engineering and Synthetic Content Creation* (pp. 462-473). IGI Global Scientific Publishing.

Law, N. (2014). Comparing pedagogical innovations. In *Comparative education research: Approaches and methods* (pp. 333–364). Springer International Publishing.

Long, T. T., Lam, N. T., & Cuong, T. Q. (2025, January). AI Integration into Curriculum Design and Development: Theoretical Framework and Application. In *International Conference on Mathematical Modeling and Computational Science* (pp. 352-361). Cham: Springer Nature Switzerland.

Luckin, R., Cukurova, M., Kent, C., & Du Boulay, B. (2022). Empowering educators to be AI-ready. *Computers and Education: Artificial Intelligence*, *3*, 100076.

Mao, J., Chen, B., & Liu, J. C. (2024). Generative artificial intelligence in education and its implications for assessment. *TechTrends*, *68*(1), 58–66.

Marras, A., Fornara, F., & Pasqualotto, A. (2025). Harnessing AI for Inclusive Teaching: Professional Development Strategies for Early Educators. *AI in Early Education: Integrating Artificial Intelligence for Inclusive and Effective Learning*, 267-290.

Melo-López, V. A., Basantes-Andrade, A., Gudiño-Mejía, C. B., & Hernández-Martínez, E. (2025). The Impact of Artificial Intelligence on Inclusive Education: A Systematic Review. *Education Sciences*, *15*(5), 539.

Mosly, I. (2024). Artificial intelligence's opportunities and challenges in engineering curricular design: A combined review and focus group study. *Societies (Basel, Switzerland)*, *14*(6), 89.

Murari, U. K., & Parmar, H. (2025). Ethical Integration of Artificial Intelligence in Inclusive Education: Addressing Challenges and Advancing Opportunities for Equitable Learning. In *Ethics and AI Integration Into Modern Classrooms* (pp. 439-470). IGI Global Scientific Publishing.

Panjwani-Charania, S., & Zhai, X. (2024). AI for Students with Learning Disabilities: A Systematic Review. *Uses of Artificial Intelligence in STEM Education*, 469.

Raji, I. D., Scheuerman, M. K., & Amironesei, R. (2021, March). You can't sit with us: Exclusionary pedagogy in ai ethics education. In *Proceedings of the 2021 ACM conference on fairness, accountability, and transparency* (pp. 515-525).

Rizvi, I., Bose, C., & Tripathi, N. (2025). Transforming Education: Adaptive Learning, AI, and Online Platforms for Personalization. In *Technology for Societal Transformation: Exploring the Intersection of Information Technology and Societal Development* (pp. 45–62). Springer Nature Singapore.

Schiff, D. (2022). Education for AI, not AI for education: The role of education and ethics in national AI policy strategies. *International Journal of Artificial Intelligence in Education*, *32*(3), 527–563.

Selwyn, N. (2022). The future of AI and education: Some cautionary notes. *European Journal of Education*, *57*(4), 620–631.

Silver, R. E., Kogut, G., & Huynh, T. C. D. (2019). Learning "new" instructional strategies: Pedagogical innovation, teacher professional development, understanding and concerns. *Journal of Teacher Education*, *70*(5), 552–566.

Singha, S., & Singha, R. (2024). Revolutionizing content creation and curriculum development through generative AI. In *Transforming Education With Generative AI: Prompt Engineering and Synthetic Content Creation* (pp. 261-280). IGI Global Scientific Publishing.

Slee, R. (2013). How do we make inclusive education happen when exclusion is a political predisposition? *International Journal of Inclusive Education*, *17*(8), 895–907.

Somasundaram, M., Latha, P., & Pandian, S. S. (2020). Curriculum design using artificial intelligence (AI) back propagation method. *Procedia Computer Science, 172*, 134–138.

Song, Y., Weisberg, L. R., Zhang, S., Tian, X., Boyer, K. E., & Israel, M. (2024). A framework for inclusive AI learning design for diverse learners. *Computers and Education: Artificial Intelligence, 6*, 100212.

Srinivasa, K. G., Kurni, M., & Saritha, K. (2022). Harnessing the Power of AI to Education. In *Learning, teaching, and assessment methods for contemporary learners: pedagogy for the digital generation* (pp. 311–342). Springer Nature Singapore.

Su, J., & Zhong, Y. (2022). Artificial Intelligence (AI) in early childhood education: Curriculum design and future directions. *Computers and Education: Artificial Intelligence, 3*, 100072.

Tanweer, M., & Ismail, A. (2024). Generative AI in curriculum development: A framework for adaptive, customized, and personalized learning. In *Impacts of generative AI on creativity in higher education* (pp. 193–226). IGI Global.

Tariq, M. U. (2024). Generative AI in curriculum development in higher education. In *Impacts of generative AI on creativity in higher education* (pp. 227–258). IGI Global.

Tatar, C., Jiang, S., Rosé, C. P., & Chao, J. (2025). Exploring teachers' views and confidence in the integration of an artificial intelligence curriculum into their classrooms: A case study of curricular co-design program. *International Journal of Artificial Intelligence in Education, 35*(2), 702–735.

Temel, T., & Yılmaz, C. (2025). Investigating the impact of digital storytelling on EFL learners' language motivation levels. *Journal of Educational Technology and Online Learning, 8*(2), 164–189.

Torrisi-Steele, G. (2026). AI and Curriculum: Designing for the Future. In *Foundations and Frameworks for AI in Education* (pp. 147-170). IGI Global Scientific Publishing.

Toyokawa, Y., Horikoshi, I., Majumdar, R., & Ogata, H. (2023). Challenges and opportunities of AI in inclusive education: A case study of data-enhanced active reading in Japan. *Smart Learning Environments, 10*(1), 67.

Ullah, R. S., Hashim, F., Bandeali, M. M., & Akbar, A. (2025). Artificial Intelligence in Curriculum Design a Roadmap for Adaptive and Personalized Learning in Higher Education. *The Critical Review of Social Sciences Studies, 3*(3), 304–322.

Vettriselvan, R., & Ramya, R. (2025). Sustainable Curriculum Design and Development: A Comprehensive Approach. In *Smart Education and Sustainable Learning Environments in Smart Cities* (pp. 471-486). IGI Global Scientific Publishing.

Walder, A. M. (2014). The concept of pedagogical innovation in higher education. *Education Journal*, *3*(3), 195–202.

Walder, A. M. (2017). Pedagogical Innovation in Canadian higher education: Professors' perspectives on its effects on teaching and learning. *Studies in Educational Evaluation*, *54*, 71–82.

Xiao, R., Xu, P., Liang, X. L., Zou, Z., Zhong, J. G., Xiang, M. Q., & Hou, X. H. (2024). Effects of the special olympics unified sports soccer training program on executive function in adolescents with intellectual disabilities. *Journal of Exercise Science and Fitness*, *22*(2), 103–110. PMID: 38268818

Zhai, X., Chu, X., Chai, C. S., Jong, M. S. Y., Istenic, A., Spector, M., & Li, Y. (2021). A Review of Artificial Intelligence (AI) in Education from 2010 to 2020. *Complexity*, *2021*(1), 8812542.

Zhao, H. G., Li, X. Z., & Kang, X. (2024). Development of an artificial intelligence curriculum design for children in Taiwan and its impact on learning outcomes. *Humanities & Social Sciences Communications*, *11*(1), 1–17.

KEY TERMS AND DEFINITIONS

Accessibility: The development of learning materials and learning environments that are easily applicable by all learners including learners with disabilities and the need to have specialized adaptation is not required.

Adaptive Learning: An instruction method, whereby technology varies the rate, sequence and delivery of information according to learner activity and performance monitored in real-time.

Algorithmic Bias: Reproducible and systematic flaws in the output given by the AI causing unfair results that are commonly caused by the biases in the data in which the AI model was trained.

Culturally Minded Pedagogy: A pedagogical model that integrates the cultural sources of students, their experiences and identities into learning to make content more relevantly and more engaging as well as affirming.

Differentiated Instruction: A teaching plan, which adjusts the topic of the learning, process or product to fit the varied levels of readiness, interests and students and their learning styles.

Educational Equity: The idea and act of equitably providing resources, opportunities, and assistance to every learner should be given equal access to regardless of their identity, background, and ability.

Generative Artificial Intelligence (Generative AI): A branch of artificial intelligence that is optimized by machine learning models to create new material--text, pictures, audio, or simulations--using patterns found in large data sets. Generative AI has the potential to produce new adaptive and individually personalized instructional content in real time in education.

Human-Centered Design: An approach in design that considers needs, experiences and opinions of people, in this case, educators and learners, in both the development and implementation of curriculum tools based on AI.

Inclusive Curriculum Design; A curriculum development approach in which the various cultural: linguistic, cognitive, and accessibility requirements of all pupils are actively considered and incorporated, and thus given equal chances to access and receive the value of education material.

Universal design for learning (UDL): A learning environment in which there is an educational setup, encouraging the flexibility of learning in which the various forms of representation, engagement, and expression through means of providing the various ways where a learner could be accommodated.

Chapter 2
Mapping the Future:
Spatial Data Science in Education Policy Development

Valisher Sapayev
https://orcid.org/0000-0002-6751-5864
Mamun University, Uzbekistan

Rejon Kumar Ray
https://orcid.org/0009-0009-1549-844X
Gannon University, USA

Sulurkhan Rakhimova
Urgench State Pedagogical Institute, Uzbekistan

Rayhon Sapaeva
Urgench State University, Uzbekistan

Munir Ahmad
https://orcid.org/0000-0003-4836-6151
Survey of Pakistan, Pakistan

ABSTRACT

This chapter emphasizes the strategic importance of Spatial Data Science (SDS) in transforming education policy and planning. SDS enables the identification of geographic disparities, supports data-driven decision-making, and fosters equity, transparency, and sustainability. To realize its full potential, the chapter recommends strengthening spatially enriched EMIS, ensuring open and interoperable data systems, and investing in technical capacity. Ethical data governance and community engagement are essential. Integrating SDS into the education policy cycle is a vital step toward building equitable and future-ready education systems.

DOI: 10.4018/979-8-3373-8805-2.ch002

INTRODUCTION

Within such a time when data-driven decision-making is transforming the governance of the public sector, Spatial Data Science (SDS) becomes an emergent and promising interdisciplinary study that links the domains of geography, data analytics, and computational modeling to reveal the spatial patterns and relations in the given data. SDS is a union of geographic information systems (GIS) and spatial statistics, remote sensing, and machine learning methodologies that are used to analyze and draw meaning out of spatial data. Also, in contrast to traditional data science, where geographic locations of data points might not be important, SDS places particular focus on where phenomena are happening and how location determination results in trends, behaviors, and results. This space dimension is vital in the interpretation of social systems, and the case of education is no exception since it forms part of the geographical and demographic settings. (Anselin, 2024; Anselin & Rey, 2022; Janowicz, 2023; Pebesma & Bivand, 2023).

Spatial thinking is important, especially in education policy, since access, quality, and equity of education heavily depend on the geography. Distribution of schools, commuting distance of students, socio-economic differences of neighborhood, as well as the quality of infrastructure at the local level, all differ depending on the location. With the absence of a spatial lens, there is a danger of policymakers relying on aggregate data to hide the disparities and contextual nuance of the data. Through the SDS analysis, the stakeholders can have a clearer picture of the geographic disparities, such as underserved rural areas or overcrowded urban schools, and create specific interventions to cope with the problems at a local level. Spatial analysis can also facilitate a prediction of future requirements, school infrastructure planning, and the influence of socio-environmental processes (such as natural hazards or pollution) on the learning outcomes. (Helfenbein, 2021; Martin et al., 2022; Wong, 2022).

The involvement of spatial data science in the development of education policy may result in a greater degree of informed and fair education policy decisions. The chapter starts with the technical and conceptual underpinnings of SDS and proceeds to provide examples of applying spatial approaches to the perception of educational differences and planning policies to address those. The chapter shows the practical role of SDS in resource distribution, planning of access, and information-based governance within the education sector through case studies and real-life examples. Lastly, it takes into account ethical and operational issues, and strategic directions on how to enroot SDS in long-term policy formulations.

FOUNDATIONS OF SPATIAL DATA SCIENCE

In order to realize the potential of SDS in the field of education policy, one needs to learn the background and main practices, as well as the technological base of SDS. SDS reflects an intersection of various fields: geography, computer science, statistics, and public policymaking in generating meaningful insights from spatially referenced data. This section presents the dominant spatial concepts, describes the categories of spatial data applicable to educational policy, and provides a brief overview of the tools interpreted by spatial data scientists and policy practitioners.

Key Concepts in Spatial Data Science

Rooted in the core idea of the concept of a location being non-neutral is SDS. Unlike the typical data analysis procedure based on a disregard of spatial context, SDS also focuses on highlighting the roles spatial relationships play in defining policy-relevant phenomena. Spatial relationships Space is the relationship and position indicator of objects in a geographic space: whether schools are located in neighborhoods or industrial parks, are isolated along routes, or are surrounded by cities with a huge population. This kind of positioning affects access, exposure, opportunity, and outcome (Carniel & Schneider, 2021; Moraga, 2023; Sarker, 2021; Shi, 2022). As another example, two schools with equally disadvantaged populations can exhibit highly divergent patterns of performance over time, not due to differences in funding or teaching practice, but because one school is in a high-walkable area with no history of floods, and one school is in a low-walkable area that is prone to flooding or lacked ready access to services. Such spatial dynamics are at the essence of the policy utility of SDS through recognition and quantification.

One of the most useful analytical notions in SDS, spatial autocorrelation, measures the degree of similarity between a phenomenon in one geographic region and in regions that are near to it. (Gedamu et al., 2024). When a spatial autocorrelation is positive within an educational indicator like literacy rates or student attendance, then it means that there is more than likely to be a geographic cluster within the indicator with similar values falling in a particular area, like having a group of districts with low school enrollment. On the other hand, negative spatial autocorrelation means that highs and lows can alternate with each other, or in other words, that there is more diversification towards the location. The most popular methods to quantify the concept of spatial autocorrelation and identify areas to be concerned about are Moran's I and Getis-Ord Gi*. With these statistical tools, the education planners can find out: hotspots that are emerging, such as a high rate of dropouts in a region or the presence of ongoing teacher allocation disparities that cannot be seen using a non-spatial average or tabulation.

SDS, besides spatial correlation and spatial proximity, is based on several fundamental technologies and methodological platforms. Probably the most obvious of these is GIS, which provides the power to make maps, analyze, and interactively query spatial data in multiple layers and multiple scales. (Li & Ning, 2023). With GIS, an analyst is able to plot student enrolment information with infrastructure networks, areas of hazard or poverty index, and create a composite picture, which otherwise would not be possible using only spreadsheets. Remote sensing is also another pillar of SDS and is the process of retrieving spatial data from a satellite or an aerial image. In education, remote sensing is employed in monitoring the conditions of school presentation, the identification of new environmental hazards around schools, and the quantification of the growth of cities or rural isolation, which impacts school access. Lastly, spatial statistics adds a quantitative rigor to SDS, enabling the analyst to create tests on clustering, spatial outliers, diffusion patterns, and geographic dependencies. The whole body of approaches converts raw geographic data to meaningful evidence, meaning specific and situation-responsive policy actions.

Overview of Relevant Spatial Data Sources

The use of SDS in the education policy closely depends on the access and consolidation of various spatial data. The source of these datasets is different, as well as their temporal frequency, spatial resolution, and thematic focus. Combined, they offer a multidimensional perspective of the terrain of the educational world, with the capture of who is served, when, where, and how. The census data becomes the basis of most education spatial analysis because it provides detailed, nationally equivalent demographic, socioeconomic, and housing characteristics (Walker, 2023). This type of data is normally disaggregated at a national level or a provincial level, district level, or even a block level, giving a chance to the person analyzing the data to look at regional variations in literacy levels, education levels, household earnings, population density, etc. Coupled with other indicators of education, the census thus becomes an effective means of detecting the presence in society of systemic imbalances in the form of automatic associations between poverty and school attendance or gender differences in secondary schooling.

Coupled with the census data, satellite imagery offers a crucial spatial component that is especially useful where ground data collection is either limited or not consistent enough (Burke et al., 2021; Zhao et al., 2022). Satellite anomalous data available in high resolution can allow an analyst to map school catchment areas, screen the feasibility of accessing the schools based on road conditions and terrain, and track environmental hazards (flooding, landslide, or air pollution) around school locations. Satellite-based mapping has also been implemented to estimate satellite-based mapping estimates of informal settlement and underserved areas in most developing regions where there are little or no accurate official estimates. Remote sensing uses dynamic and frequently real-time information sections, which are of the essence to planning in unstable situations or in emergencies like a war or drought-related displacement.

Also of importance is the school administrative data, which is usually kept in the Ministries of Education, by means of their Education Management Information Systems (EMIS). Such datasets may contain highly granular school-level data, including GPS-marked locations, class and gender breakdown of population, teaching staff qualifications, availability of infrastructure (water, toilets, electricity), and student evaluation. After georeferencing and being combined with demographic or environmental data, this information allows one to conduct very fine-grained geospatial analyses to understand the characteristic patterns of resources, unmet service access needs, and equitable outcomes. As an example, analysts can find the merged systems of such schools to have poor structures in the regions with densely populated areas or locate the locality where the schools underperform in socioeconomically vulnerable neighborhoods.

In addition to these key datasets, other more supportive sources of spatial data enhance learning on education policies. The data in transportation networks (frequently provided by national road authorities or on open platforms) allows for analyzing movements and the accessibility of students using the networks. Spatial relationships. Public health indicators may be associated with school attendance to determine the influence of disease burden or sanitation on school attendance. Decisions on construction site areas of new schools are made based on the land use and land cover data, much of which depends on the urban growth, fields, or nature reserves. There is also the availability of open data sources such as OpenStreetMap and Google Earth Engine, which offer global shared geospatial imagery as well as API enabling fast, flexible spatial analysis. The platforms are most suitable for education systems that want low-cost and highly scalable geospatial intelligence solutions. Table 1 shows the integration of data types (e.g., census, satellite, EMIS, open data) with their sources, spatial scale, typical use cases, and applications in education planning.

Table 1. Types and Sources of Spatial Data for Education Policy

Data Source	Origin	Spatial Scale	Sample Attributes	Policy Application
Census	Statistical Bureaus	National to Local	Population, Literacy Rate, Age	School Siting, Resource Allocation
Satellite Imagery	Remote Sensing Agencies (NASA, ESA)	Global to Local	Land Use, Urban Expansion, Vegetation	Urban Planning, Risk Mapping
School Administrative	Ministry of Education / Local Authorities	School-level	Enrollment, Dropout, Facilities	Monitoring, Budgeting, Planning
Transportation	Transport Departments / GIS Surveys	Urban/Rural Routes & Networks	Road Access, Travel Time	Access to Schools, Travel Barriers
Health Data	Health Ministries / WHO	Health Facility Catchment Areas	Child Mortality, Nutrition	Health-Education Nexus Planning
Open Mapping Platforms	Crowdsourced (e.g., OpenStreetMap)	Street to Community Level	School Locations, Roads, Boundaries	Gap Analysis, Community Engagement

Analytical Tools for Spatial Data Science

The transfer of the spatial data into meaningful information entails a strong arsenal of analysis tools, which aid in the collection, processing, visualizing, and modeling of geographic information. At the heart of this toolkit lie GIS modules, where one can overlay and play with layers of spatial and non-spatial information. Some of the most popular GIS platforms, both academically and in policymaking circles, are ArcGIS and QGIS. Being a free and open-source software project, QGIS gained popularity because of its easy accessibility, extensibility with the help of extensions, and the availability of a global user base. It can support many operations, including spatial querying and digitization, map styling, and geostatistical modeling, which makes it appropriate for education planners with limited budgets (Pereira et al., 2022; Titti et al., 2022).

Esri develops ArcGIS, a commercial alternative distributed in governmental institutions and non-governmental development organizations. Its desktop, web, cloud component, and integrated tool suite permit sophisticated spatial analysis, real-time data dashboards, and professional cartography. The special services of ArcGIS, including network analysis, 3D visualization, and StoryMaps, are of special value to the users of the public sector who need both high-functional and administrative support. They allow GIS manipulations of both non-programmers (as the interface of these GIS platforms is usable and intuitive) and scripting to streamline certain applications and handle personalization needs (Caquard & Dimitrovas, 2017; Vojteková et al., 2022).

Higher-level or larger-scale geospatial workflows may be achieved using Python and R and can be much more flexible, and can integrate into other geospatial modules and other data science processes. Python has many libraries to assist in geospatial data wrangling, geometry transformation, raster analysis, and interactive web mapping, including GeoPandas, Shapely, Fiona, Rasterio, and Folium. Python is especially beneficial for creating reproducible pipelines, machine learning models, and spatial-based dashboards. Equally, the R programming language has extensively developed geospatial packages such as sf, spdep, ggmap, and tmap, so popular in academic studies on analyzing spatial data, exploring spatial capabilities, spatial economics, and cartographic representations (Chen et al., 2024; Rawat et al., 2025; Vaz, 2024).

Such tools of analysis are critical in the conversion of raw geographical data to an informative policy in education. These tools allow evidence-based planning and interventions by making evidence-based customized planning and interventions through the facilitation of functions, such as accessibility mapping, school location optimization, resource distribution modeling, and hotspot identification. In addition, spatial analytics can enable education officials and stakeholders with real-time situational awareness and decision support links when implemented into web-based dashboards or mobile applications.

Competence in these analytical settings is the basis of contemporary spatial data science applications in teaching. They fill the divide that exists between esoteric information and practical courses of action, making policy models that are capable of being designed, tested, and revised with a precision never before seen, accessible to the decision-maker. Figure 1 shows a conceptual workflow diagram depicting key tools across GIS platforms, programming environments, and output applications.

Figure 1. Spatial Data Science Toolchain for Education Analytics

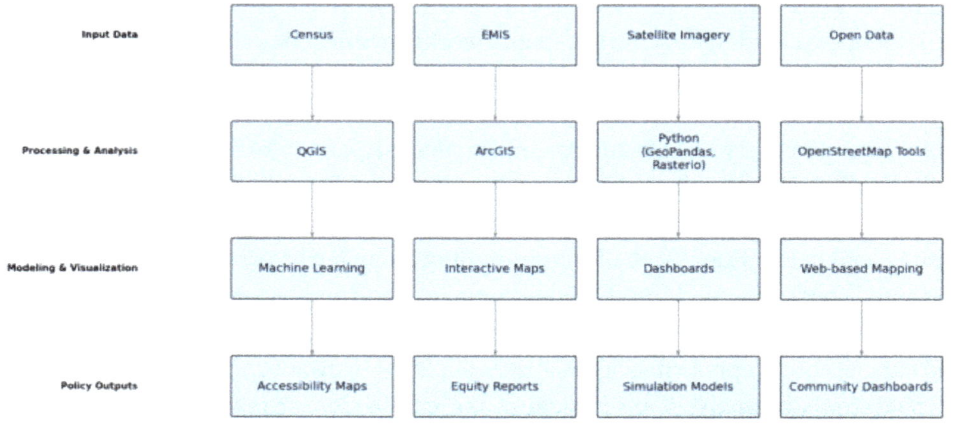

MAPPING EDUCATION

The ability of SDS to shed some light on the geographic aspect of inequality is one of the strongest contributions that the system can make to education policy. The spatial analysis can enable policymakers to visualize the access, quality, and outcome of education at the regional level and show a hidden mapping of issues that are usually lost when examining aggregate statistics. SDS provides empirical support to more spatially focused and equal education interventions by mapping disparities and identifying spatial clusters of relative disadvantage or opportunity (Adeleke & Alabede, 2022; Akudo et al., 2021; Kolhe et al., 2023; Venkatesan & Mappillairaju, 2023).

Mapping School Access, Teacher Distribution, and Dropout Hotspots

Mapping school accessibility is one of the brightest and most immediate applications of spatial data science in education. Combining the georeferenced locations of schools in the map with the population density layers, networks of roads, and topography features, the spatial analyst evaluates whether communities can be within the reach of education establishments in reality. The physical catchment area may be drawn by drawing circular areas around existing schools, indicating the physical area within which a school can admit students. This is achieved through buffer analysis, where school boundary areas are created and the radius around these schools is used to show the extent to which this school may accommodate pupils (usually 1-3 km in the case of primary schools). In contrast, a more realistic model of the commutes of students is based on network analysis, taking into consideration the real-world travel paths, distances, and road conditions. Such analyses are particularly important in locations that are geographically disadvantaged or high-risk areas, as terrain and infrastructure shortages create significant difficulties when it comes to accessing education. Evidence-based planning on locations of new schools, mobile classrooms, or the improvement of transport services can be made using insights from such spatial models.

Physical access aside, spatial mapping also throws some light on the unfair distribution of teachers. Placing the locations of schools over other administrative datasets containing figures of staff, level of qualification, and student-to-teacher ratios using spatial analysis, disparities within the system at the district or sub-regional level may be identified. An example of such information can be that the schools in the peri-urban slums or remote villages have a consistent rate of teacher shortage or can be understaffed with untrained members, as opposed to the schools in the central district that can be well-equipped. Taken together in scale, these differences can enable the education authorities to intervene directly by rotating teachers in and out of planning teacher schedules, hardship allowances, or locally based training regimes to ensure that staffing is maintained reasonably, even at operational levels across the underserved regions.

Spatial analysis of school dropout patterns is also equally significant, as this trend is usually associated with complicated socio-economic and environmental factors (Venkatesan & Mappillairaju, 2023). Combining the dropout statistics with some indicator such as the household income, flood risk, or gender disparity index, and access to sanitation or potentially electricity, one can demonstrate using a heatmap or kernel density estimation (KDE) that there are areas where the dropout can be primarily concentrated. These geographical loci of student dropout provide a spatial dimension to the complex of vulnerabilities in student retention. Regardless of the reason, poverty, chronic under-resourcing, or exposure to environmental hazards, such spatial intelligence allows more targeted use of social protection programs, community-based retention initiatives, or conditional cash transfers. A combination of these spatial studies makes a complete vision of access, equity, and vulnerability within the education landscape. Not only can they assist in determining who and where the left-behind individuals and groups are, but also inform the careful design and surveillance of policy response, therefore making education planning more dynamic, specific, and fair.

Uncovering Spatial Disparities Across Social and Geographic Dimensions

Although increasing the physical infrastructures keep them as the main issue, the real equity in education is moving past the mere access to the physical building and exploring the socio-cultural and economic factors that construct the educational prospects. A greater appreciation of these inequalities is possible through Spatial Data Science (SDS), which combines layers of geospatial with demographic, gender, and socio-economic data to uncover unsuspected structures of marginalization. As an illustration, by overlapping the rate of attendance with data by gender disaggregation of the censuses, analysts can be able to detect geographic aggregations where the representation of girls at school is relatively low. Such differences can be rooted in cultural impediments, early marriage, or risks of commuting over great distances home to stay safe; all factors that largely cannot be seen in nationally related statistics, yet become explicitly noticeable when drawn onto the maps (Ahmed, 2024; Couillard et al., 2021; Madanipour et al., 2022).

Spatial analysis makes visible divides, such as urban-rural divides, that are common in most developing education systems but are not measurable. Cities and towns tend to have more schools, such that they have higher concentrations (they are found more closely together and are also better equipped and more capacitated with skilled teachers). On the contrary, rural regions are often characterized by dense settlements, rugged landscapes, and logistical challenges to the delivery of education regularly. Spatial depictions render such disparities perceptible, demonstrating, e.g., how long villages are outside the radius of a school or how rural schools almost always perform below national averages in terms of learning achievement. Measuring such differences, SDS also enables policymakers to create targeted responses, such as mobile learning units, distance education technology, or local teacher training programmes adapted to the realities prevailing in rural settings.

SDS goes beyond the binary of urban or rural to unravel intersectional inequalities, the compound disadvantage experienced by learners caused by the intersection of various factors like poverty, language exclusion, disability, or being an ethnic minority. Vulnerability profiles of various regions can be created, giving multi-layered supremacy, by integrating information conveyed by household survey enumerations, language dissemination maps, and income quintile pointers as applied by the spatial analysts. Such profiles not only show where educational access is restricted, they also explain why some populations are left behind, it is because of the combination of barriers that cannot be addressed in a single step, but in a cross-sectoral manner. This kind of granular, place-based knowledge is then used in making inclusive policies, e.g., multilingual learning materials, targeted subsidies, or culturally relevant pedagogy, in a manner that national strategies can be too blanket or nonspecific.

Applying Spatial Clustering and Interpolation in Educational Planning

With the increase in inequality and the desire to allocate resources as efficiently as possible, highly developed SDS methods, including spatial clustering and interpolation, can become very effective to embed in strategic planning. The methods can move beyond simple maps to determine statistically meaningful trends and fill unrecorded missing values, and thus make more predictive and information-based policymaking.

The spatial clustering techniques to identify "hotspots" (i.e., non-random groupings of high or low performance, attendance, quality of infrastructure, or availability of resources) include Getis-Ord Gi*, DBSCAN, and Local Moran I. As an illustration, a Local Moran I test would show that the home of bad performance among schools is in concentrated spaces in vanguards of rural zones or incommunicado areas. The results assist policymakers in targeting specific interventions, special training programs, or even the need to investigate the factors of the issue, like health or socio-economic situations.

Simultaneously, spatial interpolation methods make up for missing information in regions where there are no direct education indicators present. Such methods are Inverse Distance Weighting (IDW) and Kriging, in which a known data point can be used to extrapolate values in unknown areas to create smooth surfaces of estimates of student teacher ratios, likelihoods of dropout, or sufficiency of infrastructure. It is especially helpful in situations displaying an unequal reporting structure, like the remote provinces or war-ridden areas. Interpolation helps policymakers to have a scenario of expected conditions in the whole geography, and this leads to more fair and informed decisions. Clustering and interpolation combined help commercialize the raw data of the spatial data into intelligence that can be acted on. They not only provide some knowledge about the present situation but also the possibility to forecast needs, the optimal use of resources, and the spatial effects of transformations in the course of time. In the process, SDS raises mapping above the status of a descriptive activity to a fundamental element of evidence-based educational justice and inclusion.

SPATIAL DATA SCIENCE IN ACTION

To translate spatial knowledge into useful policy, more is needed than a map and model; development of a systematic methodology that enables the connection between the collection of data, rigorous analysis of rigor, and action of practical decision-making.

Data to Decisions Workflow

Education policymaking is an ideal example of SDS implementation as it needs a systematic framework for transferring raw geospatial information about a region into policy recommendations. It usually follows three main steps that include data acquisition, spatial analysis, and generation of policy insights, all of which are key in making evidence-based decisions.

Data acquisition would be the initial stage and can entail the gathering of geographically referenced data to describe the education system as well as its wider surroundings. Primary sources of information cover school places data, student demographics, transportation services, socio-economic factors, environmental risk areas, and high-definition satellite photos. They can be found especially in government Education Management Information Systems (EMIS), national census bureaus, or on open platforms such as OpenStreetMap or Google Earth Engine. At this point, it is essential to ensure the interoperability, precision, and temporal consistency of data, as such aspects directly influence the validity of downstream analyses.

During the next stage, which is the spatial analysis, the GIS, like QGIS or ArcGIS, and map libraries in Python or R are deployed to process and analyze the data (Karelkhan et al., 2023; Lee et al., 2022). Spatial joins, network and buffer analysis, hotspots, clustering, and the use of interpolation come in handy to enable people to reveal patterns not noticeable in raw data. In particular, analysts can be able to discover gaps in the coverage of schools, evaluate the ratio of teacher-to-student in space, or areas with high levels of dropout rates, producing spatial intelligence by reflecting the inequality in real life. The last step is the generation of policy insights, whereby the results of the analysis are converted into definite decisions. This can provide a way to the setting of priority areas, in which the school should be constructed, the most efficient transportation lines, the redistribution of teaching resources, or the creation of regional interventions, connected with particular vulnerabilities. Most importantly, such insights are shared with the stakeholders in the form of interactive dashboards, thematic maps, and story maps that improve clarity, transparency, and strategy addition to education planning.

Following this three-step approach to SDS workflow, policymakers can be able to ensure that the interventions made rely on strong spatial evidence. The method not only reinforces the technical merits of education strategies but also increases their intelligibility, repeatability, and adaptability to the varied demands of the different learners in different geographical and social settings. Figure 2 outlines the three-phase workflow of spatial data science in education policy, from acquiring and processing geographic data to generating actionable insights and communicating them effectively to planners and decision-makers.

Figure 2. SDS Workflow for Education Policy

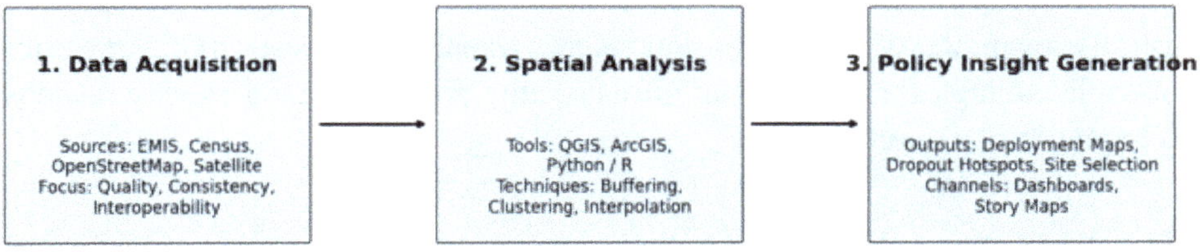

From Mapping to Meaningful Action

With the maturity of spatial data science (SDS), more and more education systems are turning to its abilities to inform successful, place-based decisions. These are not just mapping apps; there is a great deal more- SDS allows education departments to prioritize interventions, resources, and responses to risk with agility.

As an example, we can consider a case of national school location optimization. Spatial analysts can create models of ideal areas to construct new schools by combining the layers of data, e.g., population density, schools currently in place, road systems, and the age structure of students. The result is a priority heat map that identifies where schools are being built that would make the greatest reduction in commuter distances, in particular to underserved school-age children in rural settings, informal settlements, or urbanizing fringe areas. These models prevent blanket policies and rather foster a specific infrastructure planning.

The other important use is for preparedness and mitigation of emergencies. In disaster-prone situations, e.g., in areas where the natural hazard (floodplains, landslide zones, or seismic belts) can be mapped, education planners can overlay the school infrastructure map with the hazard map to determine where the vulnerability clusters can be found. Such understanding guides retrofitting of existing school buildings, moving of school buildings, and establishment of emergency response procedures, including evacuation pathways and short-term learning centers. SDS has taken place in Bangladesh to find out which schools are affected by seasonal floods, and both the infrastructure and academic calendar are being changed.

In war or refugee areas, SDS promotes the organization of mobile and transitory learning services. Humanitarian support zones, their theoretical layering with the spatial representation of displaced populations, and learning centers allow education planners and NGO organizations to prevent duplication, bridge the gaps in service provision, and guarantee continuous learning opportunities in the volatile environment. Collectively, these two case studies reveal that SDS does not exist as merely a diagnostic tool but as a catalyst for scalable, evidence-based action. Equity, resilience, and inclusion in the planning of education are all promoted through the application of spatial intelligence when done in the right way. Figure 3 presents three illustrative examples of how spatial data science transforms education challenges into actionable strategies, ranging from infrastructure planning to emergency response and humanitarian coordination.

Figure 3. Use Cases of SDS in Education

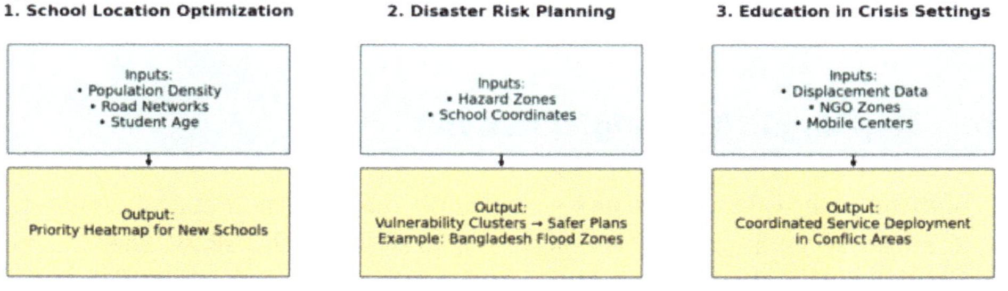

Integrating SDS into National Education Information Systems

A lasting impact of SDS would require the data science to be integrated within the digital infrastructure and institutional systems of national education systems. The increasing trend is being adopted in more countries where they are integrating geospatial intelligence in traditional Education Management Information Systems (EMIS). These new generation EMIS systems enable ministries to view real-time dashboards, carry out spatial equity studies, and associate performance outcomes (such as enrollments, test scores, or the availability of infrastructure) with geographic locations. Table 2 contrasts traditional EMIS platforms with next-generation, SDS-integrated systems, showing how spatial intelligence transforms education data into a powerful tool for planning and governance.

Table 2. Evolution of EMIS Platforms with Integrated SDS Capabilities

Feature	Traditional EMIS	SDS-Enabled EMIS
Data Type	Tabular	Spatial + Tabular
Visualization	Static charts/tables	Interactive geospatial dashboards
Analysis	Descriptive statistics	Spatial gap analysis, clustering, prediction
Decision Support	Limited to reporting	Real-time, location-specific policy actions
Accessibility	Internal use	Public portals for transparency

continued on following page

Table 2. Continued

Feature	Traditional EMIS	SDS-Enabled EMIS
Data Integration	Isolated datasets	Linked with census, health, and hazard maps
Skills Required	Basic ICT	GIS, remote sensing, spatial analytics

In a few countries, national spatial education portals have been issued, on which school location and student enrollment, teacher distribution, and infrastructure status are mapped and freely available. Such platforms can enhance transparency and decision-making capacity on specific areas of interest, and can provide stakeholders, such as the civil society and local education planners, the tools to track developments in achieving certain ideals like universal access, gender parity, and spatial equity.

More importantly, the institutionalization of SDS requires human and technical capacity investment. Ministries of Education and subnational offices should develop GIS and data literacy and good data governance processes and practices, and lead cross-sectoral data links (e.g., with the health, transport, and disaster management sectors). Such activities can make spatial insights a normal part of the education policy cycle; that is, planning, budgeting, implementation, and monitoring. Mainstreaming SDS in the national education systems spells the difference between reactive policy making to proactive, place-sensitive and predictive governance in ensuring inclusive, resilient, and equitable education to all. Figure 4 illustrates the core technical and institutional components required for embedding SDS into national education information systems, supporting data-driven governance and inclusive planning.

Figure 4. Components of an SDS-Integrated National Education Information System

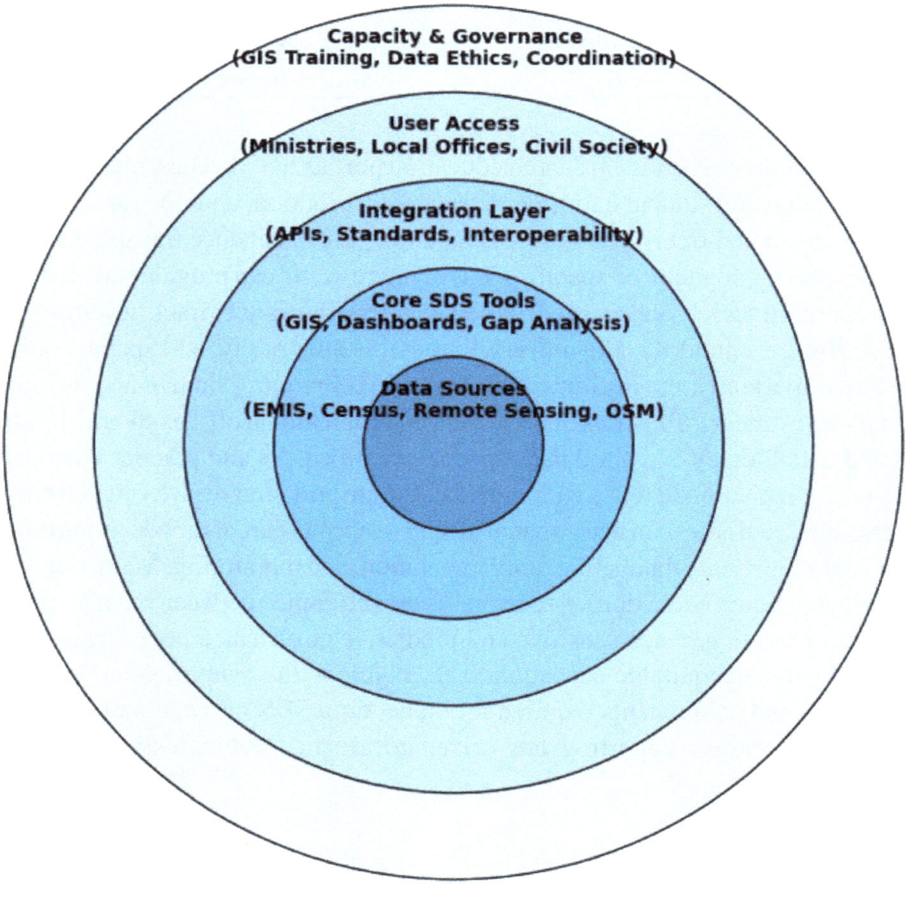

SMARTER EDUCATION POLICIES

Although the inclusion of SDS in the educational policy has enormous potential, extensive adoption is not without issues. Concerns toward data privacy, technical capacity, and ethical application of spatial intelligence also require significant attention in order to make sure that SDS promotes rather than undermines equity, inclusion, and trust in the field of education. Meanwhile, right now, there are new technological applications to be exploited, like artificial intelligence (AI), spatial machine learning, and real-time geospatial dashboards.

Data Privacy, Quality, and Governance

The most fundamental aspect of SDS is the data it contains; it is high-resolution, contains context (is contextual), and may be very sensitive. This data covers the geocoded location of schools, disaggregated enrolment data, student performance data, teacher data, and infrastructure data in the field of education. In spite of the incredible value of this granularity when it comes to locality and precision of the insights, it also manifests a set of ethical risks, especially when the data points can unintentionally end up identifying a marginalized community, or in the case of a vulnerable group in the student population. This exposure to conflict, displacement, and systematic inequality in impacted regions may lead to stigmatization and physical safety threats as well. Consequently, the concept of data privacy is not the only legal requirement, but it is one of the principles of ethical SDS practice.

Protecting privacy in spatial-enabled education systems can require intensive legal and technical protection by the countries implementing them. This involves the optimization of all data processes in relation to the laws of the country on data protection and such further international requirements as the General Data Protection Regulation (GDPR). Privacy-protection methods should be included in the SDS work processes as early as possible: anonymization of personally identifiable information (PII), aggregation (concealing individual data by clustering it spatially), and role-based access controls (limiting access to sensitive data to only authorized users). Besides, there would be a need to have secure platforms with encryption protocols and an audit to maintain access and accountability. Otherwise, the educational policy on his spatial intelligence may lose its validity in both integrity and credibility through mass disapproval or misconduct as a result of the lack of such protections. Table 3 outlines the most common risks and strategic responses across the three foundational dimensions of SDS integration: privacy, quality, and governance.

Table 3. Strategic Considerations for Ethical and Effective SDS Deployment

Dimension	Key Risks	Strategic Interventions
Data Privacy	Exposure of vulnerable populations	Anonymization, aggregation, access control, and legal compliance
Data Quality	Misleading insights due to data errors	Validation, standardization, regular updates, and field verification
Data Governance	Fragmentation, misuse, and lack of coordination	Defined ownership, ethical oversight, and inter-agency agreements

Other than privacy, information integrity and dependability are also important. Chronic problems of data quality, such as missing data or datasets, stale records, data inconsistency, incorrect spatial tagging, or invalid geocoding, are common in many education systems. Such drawbacks could distort spatial analysis, leading to incorrectly located investment in infrastructure, missed interventions, or spurious suggestions to policy. To illustrate, when the school sites are not correctly identified during mapping, resource allocation models may over- or under-report the requirement in specific places, and lead to more inequalities than reducing them. To mitigate these risks, education ministries and data providers must formalize data quality assurance procedures of providers. These are the implementation of similar data collection processes in all provinces, implementation of procedures to carry out routine updates, field validation practice, and incorporation of compatible data standards to make spatial data usable when combined with demographic, performance, or financial data.

It is also necessary to create an effective data governance environment. Data governance means the regulations, rules, procedures, and duties that put necessity to the way data is collected, stored, accessed as well and utilized. Within SDS, governance systems should provide a clear custodian of the datasets (be that at the central ministry level, subnational department level, or external data provider) and allow cross-sectoral collaborations between health, planning, or disaster risk management sectors. Powerful governance procedures can assist in alleviating the threat of data hubs, duplicity, or clashing realities. They also allow setting up the structure that can apply ethical monitoring, ensure adherence to the law, and the trust of the people in spatially aware decision making. In its absence, the SDS efforts might turn out to be too splintered, where the datasets can just be stored in isolation or might not be updated regularly, or might not be under the control of manipulation.

Privacy, quality, and governance, when combined, constitute three pillars of ethical and efficient integration of SDS into the education systems. The sustenance of these pillars is not a temporary process but an institutional commitment, which is ongoing through legislation, technology, human capacity, and cross-agency orientation. Figure 5 visualizes the foundational pillars that uphold trust and effectiveness in spatial data science for education policy. Each pillar is essential and mutually reinforcing.

Figure 5. The SDS Trust Framework: Privacy, Quality, and Governance as Pillars

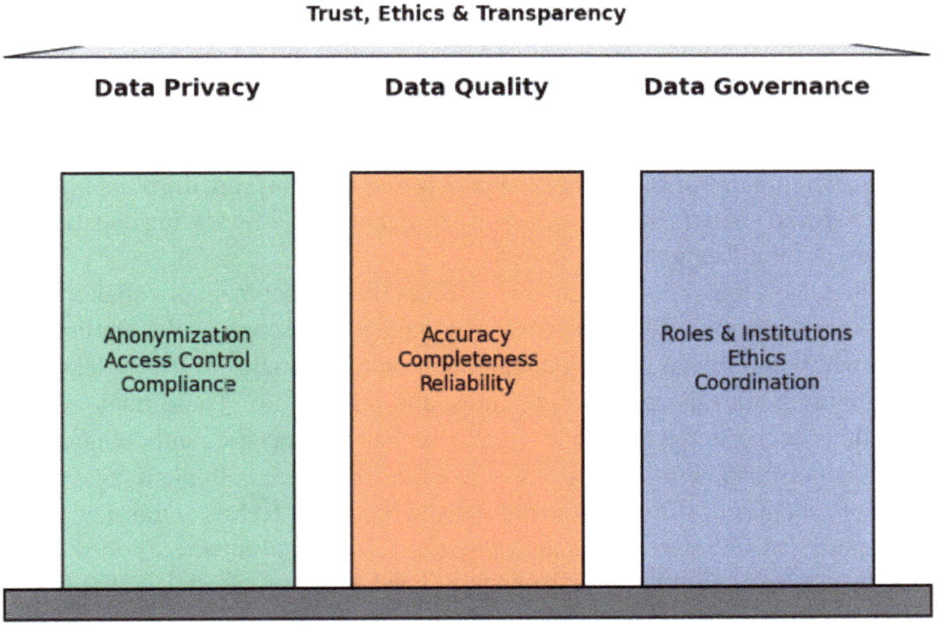

Building Capacity and Digital Literacy

The future of Spatial Data Science (SDS), going beyond the currently experimental pilot programs to become an institutional approach to education sector reform, rests on the ability to make long-term commitments to human capital development and institutional infrastructure. At present, numerous teachers, planners, administrators, and even policymakers in education systems and departments do not have the technical skills required to make sense of data derived in a geospatial manner or make use of spatial tools. This skill impediment usually restricts the adoption of spatial intelligence in policy-making procedures, supporting the adherence to non-spatial data sources that are traditional and intuitive planning. Education systems need to broadly take two paths to enable the revolutionary power of SDS: 1) the development of technical skills in the subject matter using GIS, spatial analysis, remote sensing, and visualization, and 2) the production of data-driven cultures that recognize the importance of spatial thinking and evidence-based decision-making throughout the administration.

The duration of capacity-building cannot be limited to single-time, training workshops or technical seminars. Rather, it should be addressed as a continuous, system order initiative that is built into policies of workforce development. Ministries of education ought to create special SDS units that can be equipped with spatial data analysts, planners, and IT experts able to assist in the near-term planning, emergency, and strategic reforms over the long term. These departments may become centers of excellence within the organization, wherein they can do spatial analysis as needed, direct map-based analysis, and administer geospatial databases. In locations where the formation of new units might not be practical in the short run, the other plan can be to slot spatial analysts into the structure of current problem-tackling departments (planning or monitoring and evaluation).

Capacity building of the institutions involves the development of collaborations outside the educational sector as well. The quality and scope of the applications of SDS can be improved through cooperation with national statistics bureaus, urban planning bodies, geographic institutes, and universities. These trans-sectoral connections promote the exchange of data, technical expertise, and collaborative development of spatial tools responsive to educational needs in planning. Virtual centers of excellence: Universities, in particular, can offer technical training, create locally pertinent GIS curriculum, and provide experienced tutelage, policy teams in spatial strategies. Similarly, liaisons with local planning officials at the city or district level may help school location planning processes and outcomes become parts of a larger city planning process in which educational facilities are aligned with population growth and change. Figure 6 presents a multi-layered capacity-building ecosystem needed to institutionalize spatial data science in education policymaking. Each layer represents reinforcing elements that move SDS from isolated use to systemic integration.

Figure 6. Enabling SDS Capacity in Education Policy

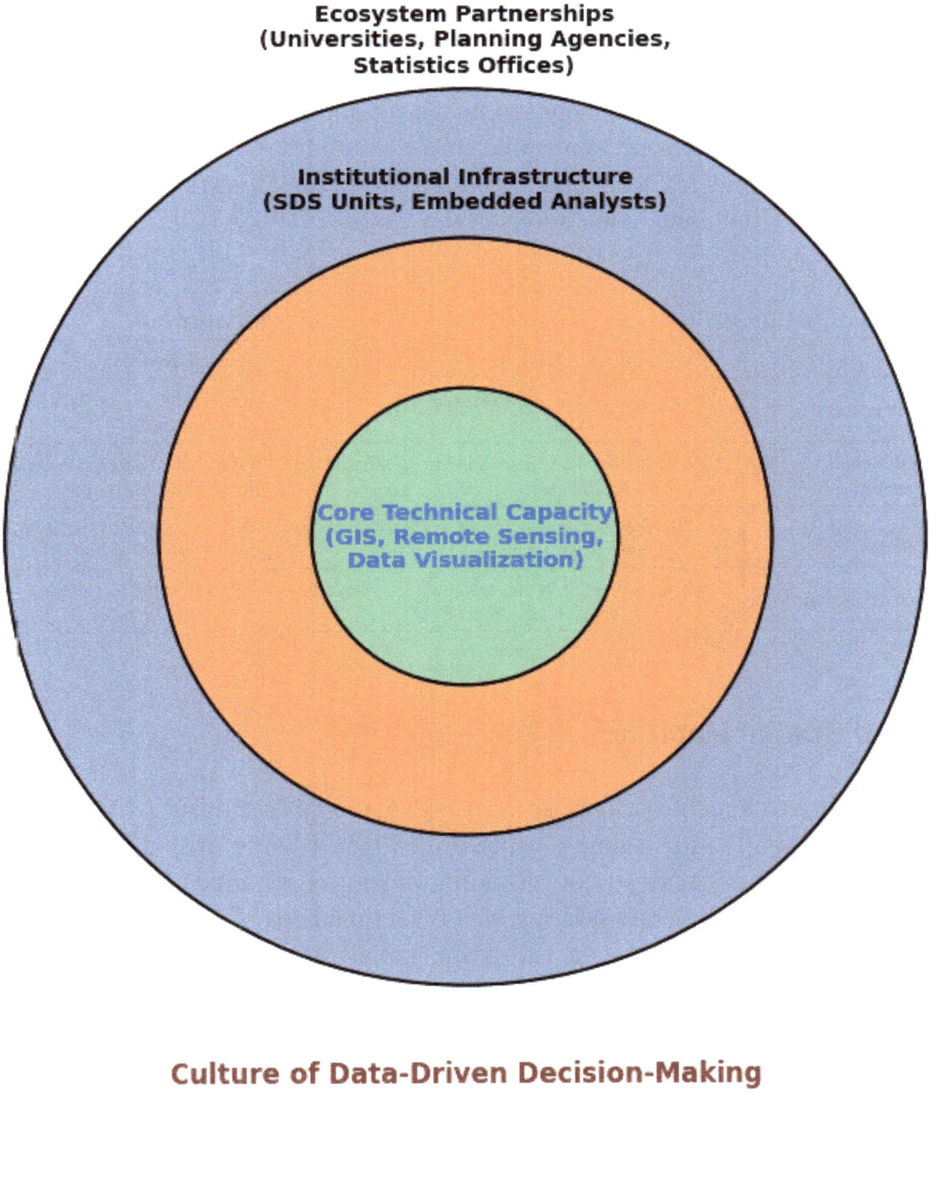

Similarly to the crucial role of technical training, the inclusive and accessible SDS tools are also required. Simplified dashboards, map-based short policy briefings, and interactive spatial storytelling websites can be helpful to many non-technical stakeholders, such as senior policymakers, local officials, or school administrators. These tools need to be made to be usable by concentrating on the clarity, relevancy, and visual appeal instead of technical sophistication. Without exception, when used properly, spatial interfaces enable decision-makers to see the gaps in the services, evaluate the equity issues, and simulate policy scenarios in an easy-to-use and understandable format. The concept of democratizing access to geospatial insights is the main idea of systemic integration of SDS into everyday policymaking governing the education domain, not only among the specialists but also in the context of the policymaking ecosystem as a whole. Table 4 outlines the main challenges and corresponding strategies in building individual, institutional, and systemic capacity for meaningful SDS integration into education policy.

Table 4. Key Capacity-Building Strategies for SDS Institutionalization

Focus Area	Capacity Challenge	Strategic Response
Individual Skills	Low proficiency in GIS or spatial tools	Structured training programs, certification, and mentoring
Institutional Capability	Lack of SDS-dedicated units in the education sector	Create SDS units or embed analysts within planning departments
Cross-Sector Collaboration	Siloed expertise and limited knowledge exchange	Build partnerships with academia, planning agencies, and NSOs
User Accessibility	Low engagement from non-technical stakeholders	Develop dashboards, spatial storytelling tools, and visual maps

AI and Spatial Machine Learning

Emerging technologies, more specifically, Artificial Intelligence (AI), spatial machine learning, and real-time geospatial intelligence, are swiftly displacing the future of the SDS in education policy. This innovation is re-energizing the possibilities of data-guided planning and offering new potent methods of modeling, tracking, and controlling education systems. The more granular the education data is and the more it is spatially connected, the more predictive and prescriptive insights that may be gleaned from such data are exponentially expanded.

Spatial machine learning models and AI already have great potential in predicting educational outcomes and guiding policy-making. For example, through monetarily adding a geospatial tag to school data, demography, access to transportation, and physical features of infrastructure, analysts might forecast future areas of school enrollment growth and identify vulnerable to dropping out of school, and locate future places to install educational services. The algorithms are also able to identify spatial inequalities, such as the occurrence of poor performance or resource deprivation that may not appear with conventional statistical methods. These capabilities are not only able to increase the diagnostic accuracy, but also enable policymakers to model different intervention scenarios and select the best policy levers using the evidence. Figure 7 illustrates how AI, spatial machine learning, and real-time dashboards converge within SDS platforms to inform adaptive, equity-oriented education policies.

Figure 7. Emerging Technological Applications in SDS for Education Policy

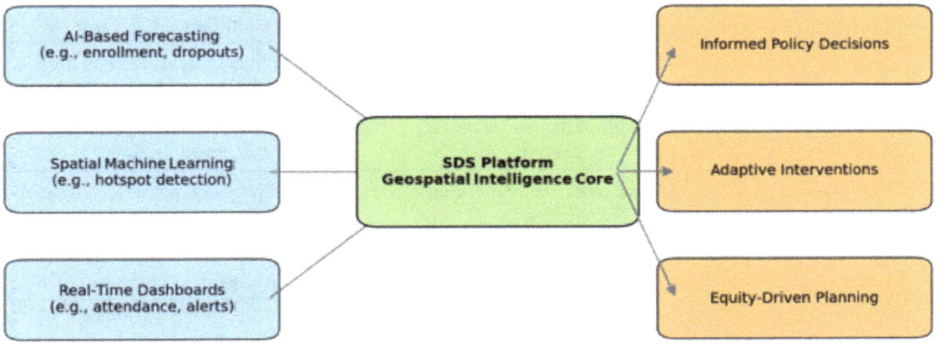

Real-time geospatial dashboards are equally disruptive because they allow policymakers to shift towards an anticipatory governance model. They may combine live feeds of mobile surveys, remote sensing systems, IoT, or crowdsourcing-based reporting systems, so as to offer dynamic perspectives of the education environment. As an example, a real-time spatial on-screen dashboard could indicate a school as temporarily out of operation because of flash flooding, roads being blocked, or damage to infrastructure, so that district officials could immediately begin response assisting on this or other tasks as a temporary reallocation of resources. Routine monitoring of student attendance patterns, maintenance of infrastructure, or even tracking the progress of an ongoing construction can also be carried out on a location-specific and dynamic basis by such systems.

In the future, SDS combined with frontier technologies can allow more responsive, specific, and situation-sensitive policymaking in the educational realm. It is here, however, that the path should be critically influenced by data justice, data ethics, and universal design principles of use. Advanced technologies have the potential to either open or eliminate equity disparities- this can depend on the manner in which they are devised, implemented, and controlled. Marginalized populations can be underrepresented in training sets, their spatial cues misinterpreted, or locked out of the system design, causing policy blind spots. To maximize the potential of SDS initiatives, transparency in the algorithms, equitable distribution of spatial decision tools, and participatory governance is therefore very crucial. The final objective is not technological progress alone, but rather a more attentive and all-inclusive system of education that can be able to adjust itself intelligently to the demands of all students. Table 5 presents selected technological innovations in SDS and their corresponding applications in education planning and governance, highlighting their transformative impact and policy relevance.

Table 5. Future-Forward SDS Capabilities and Policy Applications

Technology	Core Capability	Education Policy Use Case
AI-Based Prediction	Learning from complex historical patterns	Forecast enrollment surges; identify dropout risk zones
Spatial Machine Learning	Spatial clustering and anomaly detection	Detect underserved regions; optimize school catchment areas
Real-Time Geospatial Dashboards	Integration of live spatial data streams	Monitor disruptions; support rapid disaster response
Simulation Models	Scenario testing and spatial impact modeling	Evaluate the placement of new schools or transport schemes

CONCLUSION AND POLICY RECOMMENDATIONS

SDS provides a revolutionary perspective on learning about and responding to the complex place-based issues that govern the education systems. SDS can help policymakers to leave behind the overall thinking of one-size-fits-all solutions and engineer specific instruments of intervention based on local facts on the ground by revealing geographic inequalities, mapping access and equity gaps, and supporting data-driven planning. The fulfillment of the spatial analysis as a part of an educational policy makes not only the strategic decision process more effective but also transparent, inclusive, and long-term sustainable.

To make prudent use of the SDS potential, the policymakers and the education departments are advised to focus more on developing spatially rich education management information systems, data infrastructures that are open and interoperable, and provide the staff at all levels with the technical training that they will require. All spatial initiatives must be imbued with ethical data governance, privacy protection, and community involvement. In the future, a more proactive approach to planning education is also possible due to the integration of more innovative tools, including artificial intelligence, spatial modeling, and real-time dashboards. Making SDS mainstream in the policy cycle is not only a technical enhancement, but it is a strategic necessity to create equitable, resilient, and future-proof education systems.

REFERENCES

Adeleke, R., & Alabede, O. (2022). Geographical determinants and hotspots of out-of-school children in Nigeria. *Open Education Studies*, *4*(1), 345–355. DOI: 10.1515/EDU-2022-0176

Ahmed, D. F. (2024) Mapping Inequality: Spatial Dimensions of Social and Economic Disparities. *Liberal Journal of Language & Literature Review, 2*(01), 1–12. https://llrjournal.com/index.php/11/article/view/34

Akudo, F. U., Igbokwe, I. C., & Oparaji, I. C. (2021). SCHOOL MAPPING AS THE DETERMINANT OF THE PROVISION OF EDUCATION RESOURCES IN PUBLIC SECONDARY SCHOOLS. *European Journal of Education Studies*, *8*(3). Advance online publication. DOI: 10.46827/EJES.V8I3.3644

Anselin, L. (2024). An Introduction to Spatial Data Science with GeoDa: Volume 1 - Exploring Spatial Data. *An Introduction to Spatial Data Science with GeoDa: Volume 1 - Exploring Spatial Data*, 1–424. https://doi.org//DOI: 10.1201/9781003274919

Anselin, L., & Rey, S. J. (2022). Open Source Software for Spatial Data Science. *Geographical Analysis*, *54*(3), 429–438. DOI: 10.1111/GEAN.12339

Burke, M., Driscoll, A., Lobell, D. B., & Ermon, S. (2021). Using satellite imagery to understand and promote sustainable development. *Science*, *371*(6535). Advance online publication. DOI: 10.1126/SCIENCE.ABE8628 PMID: 33737462

Caquard, S., & Dimitrovas, S. (2017). Story Maps & Co. The state of the art of online narrative cartography. Http://Journals.Openedition.Org/Mappemonde, *121*. https://doi.org/DOI: 10.4000/MAPPEMONDE.3386

Carniel, A. C., & Schneider, M. (2021). A Survey of Fuzzy Approaches in Spatial Data Science. *IEEE International Conference on Fuzzy Systems, 2021-July*. https://doi.org/DOI: 10.1109/FUZZ45933.2021.9494437

Chen, C., Guo, Z., & Judge, J. (2024). A QGIS Plugin for GIS-based Multicriteria Decision Analysis: An Application of Developing Alternative Future Land-Use Scenarios in Ghana. *Applied Spatial Analysis and Policy*, *17*(2), 779–797. DOI: 10.1007/S12061-024-09566-X

Couillard, B. K., Foote, C. L., Gandhi, K., Meara, E., & Skinner, J. (2021). Rising Geographic Disparities in US Mortality. *The Journal of Economic Perspectives*, *35*(4), 123–146. DOI: 10.1257/JEP.35.4.123 PMID: 35079197

Gedamu, W. T., Plank-Wiedenbeck, U., & Wodajo, B. T. (2024). A spatial autocorrelation analysis of road traffic crash by severity using Moran's I spatial statistics: A comparative study of Addis Ababa and Berlin cities. *Accident; Analysis and Prevention*, *200*, 107535. DOI: 10.1016/J.AAP.2024.107535 PMID: 38489942

Helfenbein, R. J. (2021). Critical geographies of education: Space, place, and curriculum inquiry. *Critical Geographies of Education: Space, Place, and Curriculum Inquiry*, 1–110. https://doi.org//DOI: 10.4324/9781003178590

Janowicz, K. (2023). Philosophical Foundations of GeoAI: Exploring Sustainability, Diversity, and Bias in GeoAI and Spatial Data Science. *Handbook of Geospatial Artificial Intelligence*, 26–42. https://doi.org/DOI: 10.1201/9781003308423-3

Karelkhan, N., Kadirbek, A., & Schmidt, P. (2023). Setting Up and Implementing ArcGIS to Work with Maps and Geospatial Data with Python for Teaching Geoinformation Systems in Higher Education. *International Journal of Emerging Technologies in Learning*, *18*(14). Advance online publication. DOI: 10.3991/ijet.v18i14.39833

Kolhe, N. P., Dhote, K. K., & Parihar, A. (2023). *Mapping the Access of Internet Facility to Schedule Tribe Population—An Approach Towards Digital Education*. 1–20. https://doi.org/DOI: 10.1007/978-981-19-8967-4_1

Lee, H., Chae, M. S., Park, J. Y., Lim, K. J., & Park, Y. S. (2022). Development and Application of a QGIS-Based Model to Estimate Monthly Streamflow. *ISPRS International Journal of Geo-Information*, *11*(1). Advance online publication. DOI: 10.3390/ijgi11010040

Li, Z., & Ning, H. (2023). Autonomous GIS: The next-generation AI-powered GIS. *International Journal of Digital Earth*, *16*(2), 4668–4686. DOI: 10.1080/17538947.2023.2278895

Madanipour, A., Shucksmith, M., & Brooks, E. (2022). The concept of spatial justice and the European Union's territorial cohesion. *European Planning Studies*, *30*(5), 807–824. DOI: 10.1080/09654313.2021.1928040

Martin, R., Martinelli, F., & Clifton, J. (2022). Rethinking spatial policy in an era of multiple crises. *Cambridge Journal of Regions, Economy and Society*, *15*(1), 3–21. DOI: 10.1093/CJRES/RSAB037

Moraga, P. (2023). Spatial Statistics for Data Science: Theory and Practice with R. *Spatial Statistics for Data Science: Theory and Practice with R*, 1–279. https://doi.org//DOI: 10.1201/9781032641522

Pebesma, E., & Bivand, R. (2023). Spatial Data Science: With Applications in R. In *Spatial Data Science: With Applications in R.* https://doi.org/DOI: 10.1201/9780429459016

Pereira, G. W., Valente, D. S. M., de Queiroz, D. M., Coelho, A. L. de F., Costa, M. M., & Grift, T. (2022). Smart-Map: An Open-Source QGIS Plugin for Digital Mapping Using Machine Learning Techniques and Ordinary Kriging. *Agronomy 2022, Vol. 12, Page 1350, 12*(6), 1350. https://doi.org/DOI: 10.3390/AGRONOMY12061350

Rawat, A. K., Dahiya, M., & Khushpal. (2025). Comparative study of Sondh village through Geospatial data analytics using QGIS, Tableau and GeoPandas. *Progressive Computational Intelligence, Information Technology and Networking*, 474–480. https://doi.org//DOI: 10.1201/9781003650010-78

Sarker, I. H. (2021). Data Science and Analytics: An Overview from Data-Driven Smart Computing, Decision-Making and Applications Perspective. *SN Computer Science, 2*(5), 1–22. DOI: 10.1007/S42979-021-00765-8 PMID: 34278328

Shi, Y. (2022). Advances in Big Data Analytics: Theory, Algorithms and Practices. *Advances in Big Data Analytics: Theory, Algorithms and Practices*, 1–728. https://doi.org//DOI: 10.1007/978-981-16-3607-3

Titti, G., Sarretta, A., Lombardo, L., Crema, S., Pasuto, A., & Borgatti, L. (2022). Mapping Susceptibility With Open-Source Tools: A New Plugin for QGIS. *Frontiers of Earth Science, 10*, 842425. DOI: 10.3389/FEART.2022.842425

Vaz, E. (2024). Innovations in Spatial Analysis: The Impact of GIS and Python in Knowledge Societies. *Regional Knowledge Economies*, 73–85. https://doi.org/DOI: 10.1007/978-3-031-76906-1_6

Venkatesan, R. G., & Mappillairaju, B. (2023). Detection of hotspots of school dropouts in India: A spatial clustering approach. *PLoS ONE, 18*(1 January). https://doi.org/DOI: 10.1371/journal.pone.0280034

Vojteková, J., Žoncová, M., Tirpáková, A., & Vojtek, M. (2022). Evaluation of story maps by future geography teachers. *Journal of Geography in Higher Education, 46*(3), 360–382. DOI: 10.1080/03098265.2021.1902958

Walker, K. (2023). Analyzing US census data: Methods, maps, and models in R. *Analyzing US Census Data: Methods, Maps, and Models in R*, 1–368. https://doi.org//DOI: 10.1201/9780203711415

Wong, C. (2022). Spatial thinking and policymaking in the UK: A spatial planning perspective. *Space and Polity, 26*(2), 135–142. DOI: 10.1080/13562576.2022.2090060

Zhao, Q., Yu, L., Du, Z., Peng, D., Hao, P., Zhang, Y., & Gong, P. (2022). An Overview of the Applications of Earth Observation Satellite Data: Impacts and Future Trends. In *Remote Sensing* (Vol. 14, Issue 8). https://doi.org/DOI: 10.3390/rs14081863

Chapter 3
Prompt Engineering in Higher Education: Perceptions, Practices, and Pedagogical Potentials

Seçil Tümen Akyıldız
https://orcid.org/0000-0003-4116-7344
Fırat Üniversitesi, Turkey

ABSTRACT

This study examines how university instructors in Eastern Türkiye perceive and use prompt engineering in higher education. Using an interpretivist/constructivist stance, a generic qualitative design and reflexive thematic analysis were employed. Fifteen instructors from five state universities were interviewed until saturation. Four perception areas emerged: a practical, instruction-focused view; recognition of student-centered potential; challenges from lack of training; and varying motivation. In practice, prompts supported material design, assessment, and critical thinking, while research use was limited to idea generation, summaries, and tool drafting. Ethical concerns were stronger among senior staff, while early-career academics were more confident. The study suggests tailored professional development, collaboration with computing units, and clear AI policies. Though region- and interview-based, findings indicate prompt engineering can become a key pedagogical and methodological skill in universities.

1. INTRODUCTION

Higher education institutions (HEIs) today are under growing pressure to remain competitive and relevant in an increasingly dynamic academic landscape. University

DOI: 10.4018/979-8-3373-8805-2.ch003

leadership and instructors continuously seek innovative ways to attract prospective students, retain current ones, increase their academic motivation, and offer them a more engaging and meaningful learning experience. One of the main strategies in this regard is to improve the overall satisfaction of students, not only with the academic content but also with the quality of services and support they receive throughout their education. Traditionally, HEIs are expected to fulfill three core functions: teaching, research, and community engagement (Waghid, 2002). Through teaching, institutions aim to develop students' academic and practical skills, preparing them for professional life (Srikanthan & Dalrymple, 2002). Research activities generate new knowledge and address societal challenges, while community service initiatives promote collaboration between universities and local stakeholders, contributing to social development (Kearney, 2009; Marginson, 2011).

In recent years, Artificial Intelligence (AI) has started to play a more visible role in enhancing these institutional missions. AI-powered tools are now widely used in various fields to support intellectual and creative tasks, and education is no exception (Elmessiry & Elmessiry, 2024). In the context of higher education, AI applications are being explored for multiple purposes, including the personalization of learning paths, increasing student engagement, expanding access to educational resources (Tonbuloğlu, 2023, Balaquiao, 2024, Çayak, 2024), predicting academic achievement (Gaftandzhieva et al., 2022), and automating both instructional and administrative duties (Harry, 2023). AI-supported systems are also used to improve decision-making and assessment processes, especially in online learning environments (Ouatik et al., 2021, Karadağ, 2023).

Beyond teaching, research is also one of the main functions of higher education and in recent years the integration of artificial intelligence (AI) into research processes is changing the way knowledge is discovered, organized and produced. The use of AI tools gives opportunities for scholars to explore, analyse and innovate in different disciplines and in this way it can expand the frontiers of knowledge. In higher education context, it is possible to see four main areas where AI is supporting research: literature review, hypothesis generation, experiment optimization and also data analysis. For example, AI-based systems are able to summarise the related articles, show important trends and also find the gaps in the literature which helps the researchers to make their reviews more complete and effective (Khurana, 2024). These tools can also give valuable insights about new patterns in a field and in this way guide the scholars to create new research questions (Kacena et al., 2024). When it comes to hypothesis generation, AI has the ability to suggest new hypotheses by analysing the available data, literature and the trends, so it can support creativity and sometimes show the connections that maybe human observation will miss (Extance, 2018). Another contribution is in the optimization of experiments, because AI can help to plan the use of resources and variables in a more effective way, which makes the research design stronger. By analysing complex experimental parameters, AI can create optimized models that increase the reliability of the results especially in research areas that require detailed planning (Liu et al., 2021). Finally, AI algorithms are very important in analysing large-scale data quickly and with high precision, they can show patterns and correlations that make the findings more valid and rich in detail (Atalay & Çelik, 2017). All these points show that AI is not only a technical support but also it is becoming an important driver of academic research and innovation in today's world.

Building on the broader integration of AI in teaching and research, a more recent and specific area of interest has emerged in higher education: prompt engineering. As educators and researchers increasingly engage with generative AI tools, the way they interact with these systems, particularly through well-crafted prompts, has started to shape both instructional design and scholarly inquiry. Based on these developments, it is important to understand how faculty members perceive and apply prompt engineering in their academic practices. Despite its growing relevance, there is still limited empirical research examining the role of prompt engineering in real-world educational settings, particularly in the context of higher education in Türkiye. This study aims to explore how university instructors from Eastern Türkiye define and make use of prompt engineering in their teaching and research activities. The research also seeks to identify potential challenges, opportunities, and institutional dynamics that shape their engagement with this emerging digital skill. In line with this perspective, the following sections will first examine the general foundations of prompt engineering, followed by its specific applications in the field of education. The chapter will then present the methodology, findings, and interpretation of a qualitative study conducted with university instructors. Finally, the discussion and conclusion sections will highlight key implications for higher education practice and future research.

1.2. Prompt Engineering

As artificial intelligence continues to expand its role in academic life, the ability to ask meaningful and well-structured questions is becoming a fundamental skill in this new AI-driven landscape. Öncü and his colleagues (2023) stated that it is essential for chatbots to understand questions as clearly as possible and to provide appropriate responses based on the data set. Tools such as ChatGPT are highly effective in answering different types of questions; however, they still show limitations in producing uniquely creative responses (Zhang, Zhou, Wu, Xie, & He, 2024). Therefore, improving the quality of prompts and instructions given to AI systems is now considered essential for generating deeper and more insightful outputs. In the near future, especially in higher education and related industries, the competence to formulate good questions and improve upon generated answers is expected to become more valuable than simply knowing the correct answer (Zhang et al., 2024). Prompt engineering, in this sense, has emerged as a promising approach that focuses on preparing effective prompts and guiding AI in ways that lead to better performance. The practice involves adjusting and rephrasing user queries to help AI systems understand the intention more clearly and respond more effectively (Zhang et al., 2024). As machine learning and deep learning technologies advance, prompt engineering is gaining recognition as a crucial tool for interacting with AI in a more dynamic and context-sensitive way. In today's educational settings, where AI is increasingly integrated, prompt engineering has become an essential element that not only improves response quality but also makes AI tools more accessible and functional. The selection and structure of the prompt largely determine the relevance and accuracy of the AI's output (O'Connor et al., 2024), which underlines the growing importance of prompt engineering in the evolving relationship between humans and machines.

1.2.1. Prompt Engineering and Large Language Models

Recent improvements in computational capacity and AI technologies have increased the power and the quality of conversational systems in a remarkable way. In the centre of this development there are Large Language Models (LLMs) which are the main structure behind many generative AI tools that are now used for education and also for research purposes (Wang et al., 2024). Prompt engineering has become an important technique which is helping the users to communicate more effectively with these models. If the prompts are written carefully, LLMs can produce outputs that are more relevant, more accurate and also more aware of the context, so this situation makes them more useful in academic environments (Feng et al., 2023). Instead of depending only on the technical capacity of the AI tools, prompt engineering gives the users a chance to affect the results by giving more intentional and well-prepared inputs. For this reason, knowing how these models are working and how the prompt design is shaping the output is very important for educators and researchers who want to use AI tools in a meaningful way in their academic works.

As the use of LLMs becomes more common across various platforms, the demand for precise and well-structured inputs has also increased. Prompt engineering has emerged as a response to this need, focusing on how to design and improve user inputs in order to optimize the performance of tools like ChatGPT or other AI-based systems (Strobelt et al., 2022). The process involves not only the careful choice of words but also the organization and clarity of the overall prompt structure. Although LLMs have been applied successfully in areas such as chatbots, machine translation, text generation, and voice assistants (Kotei & Thirunavukarasu, 2023), their effectiveness still depends heavily on the quality of the prompts they receive. If the prompt is vague, overly simple, or poorly formulated, the AI model may fail to produce relevant or useful output, leading to time loss and reduced efficiency. Despite its potential, prompt engineering is not without its complexities and challenges. Crafting effective prompts often requires a deep understanding of language, subject matter, and the capabilities and limitations of the LLM AI. Moreover, it often involves an iterative process of refining and testing the prompts based on the AI's responses. These complexities and challenges matter because they influence the effectiveness of LLM AI. For example, if the prompts are too vague, the AI's responses might be too broad or off-topic. If they are too specific, the AI might not generate a diverse range of responses. Striking the right balance is key to harnessing the full potential of LLM AI, and this balance is better achieved through effective prompt engineering (Cain, 2024).

With the continued spread of LLM applications, prompt engineering is now considered a valuable and necessary skill across professional domains—including healthcare, finance, education, retail, and media—where professionals increasingly rely on AI to process large volumes of data and extract meaningful insights. In this context, prompt engineers are gaining recognition as key figures who "translate" human goals into effective AI instructions, guiding the models with precision and intention (Wahidur et al., 2024). Given this growing importance, it is essential to understand not only how prompt engineering operates in general AI applications, but also how it is specifically applied within educational contexts. As more instructors and students begin to interact with AI tools, developing prompt engineering skills becomes increasingly relevant for teaching, learning, and academic productivity. The following section will explore the role of prompt engineering in education, with a particular focus on its pedagogical value and practical implications for classroom use.

1.2.2. Prompt Engineering in Educational Contexts

At its simplest, prompt engineering means writing clear and organized instructions so that natural language generation tools can give better and more useful answers (White et al., 2023). In educational settings, this becomes more important because both teachers and students now use AI tools in their learning activities, creating content, or doing academic tasks. According to Liu et al. (2021), prompts can be grouped into two main types: cloze prompts, where the AI fills in missing parts, and prefix prompts, where the AI continues a given text. Still, making prompts that work well is not always easy, especially for people who are not very experienced with AI. As Dang et al. (2022) mention, writing a good prompt often takes trying several versions until one works well. Oppenlaender et al. (2023) also point out that prompt engineering is not something you know immediately—it's a skill that improves with time and practice. To get better results from AI tools, Reynolds and McDonell (2021) suggest some useful strategies like explaining clearly what you want, giving examples, using comparisons, and setting some specific limits in the prompt. These techniques help not only with improving the answers but also with making them more creative and related to the topic. In education, a good prompt should be direct and understandable, so the tool can give the right response. If the prompt is not clear or has too many meanings, the answers may not be helpful. The prompt should focus on one clear topic and tell the AI exactly what is expected in a simple way (Giray, 2023). How the prompt is written—its structure and wording—really changes the quality of the answer. If it is written badly, the tool might give answers that are too general or not correct, which reduces its usefulness in learning. But if it is written well, the output becomes more correct, useful, and even more creative. For this reason, prompt engineering has become an important skill that both teachers and students should try to learn and use when working with AI tools (Shin et al., 2020; Heston, 2023). Looking ahead, prompt engineering practices are also expected to act as a catalyst for educational transformation. As AI tools become more deeply embedded in classroom environments, they may significantly impact not only the way teachers design activities but also broader pedagogical approaches, curriculum structures, and assessment methods. According to Mollick and Mollick (2022), such developments could support a shift away from conventional, didactic teaching methods toward more interactive, student-centered learning experiences, which may promote higher levels of engagement and the development of critical thinking skills. Similarly, curriculum design could become more flexible and adaptive, enabling personalized learning at scale. Prompt-engineered assessments, meanwhile, offer the possibility of delivering real-time feedback, fostering self-assessment habits, and supporting continuous learning among students (Cain, 2024). These evolving possibilities indicate that prompt engineering is not only a technical skill but also a pedagogical enabler that aligns with the goals of 21st-century education. Furthermore, the integration of human-AI cognitive partnerships—such as prompt engineering with LLMs—has the potential to disrupt the limitations of traditional education by enabling uniquely personalized learning experiences tailored to individual needs and preferences. Conventional challenges like one-size-fits-all instruction, lack of individualized attention, and high student-to-teacher ratios could be addressed more effectively. As Cain (2024) suggests, if LLMs are skillfully guided through prompt engineering to align with specific learning objectives, we may witness improved engagement, deeper comprehension, and broader access to personalized learning at scale.

Finally, the full potential of prompt engineering in education can only be realized through the active involvement of all stakeholders. Students can take on the role of prompt engineers by engaging in self-directed learning, shaping their educational journeys through curiosity, critical thinking, and personalized content interaction. Instructors, in turn, may utilize prompt engineering not only to diversify their teaching but also to support students in designing prompts that align with specific learning goals, thus shifting their roles from content providers to facilitators of learning experiences. Beyond the classroom, administrators and policymakers also have a role to play. Prompt engineering, when supported institutionally, could lead to more effective instructional design, improved student outcomes, and better-informed educational decisions. The integration of LLM-based AI into educational programs, combined with strategic data use, holds the potential to make personalized and scalable learning a reality (Cain, 2024). These developments suggest a need to explore how educators are currently engaging with prompt engineering and how their experiences may inform future practices.

Based on these recent discussions, it has become necessary to examine how university instructors currently perceive and use prompt engineering in higher education. This study specifically focuses on universities located in the Eastern Anatolia region of Türkiye, a region that is still not well represented in the academic literature on prompt engineering. Although universities in this area have access to similar technological resources and AI tools like those in other parts of the country, there has not been much research on how instructors from this region actually engage with AI-based practices. For this reason, studying their experiences may help us understand how prompt engineering is approached in different academic and institutional environments. The participants of the current study were selected from faculties of education and social sciences. These departments were preferred because they play an important role in both teaching and academic research, and they often focus on communication, human interaction, and instructional design. Choosing instructors from these fields also helps to explore how people with different levels of digital knowledge and AI experience apply prompt engineering in their professional lives. In this sense, the study not only adds to the limited research on AI in higher education but also offers useful ideas for universities to support instructors through professional development programs and training related to AI literacy and prompt engineering.

This study, therefore, aims to explore instructors' perceptions and practices regarding prompt engineering and to identify potential challenges and opportunities associated with its use in academic work. In line with this aim, the study addresses the following research questions:

RQ1: How do university instructors in Eastern Türkiye perceive the concept of prompt engineering in the context of higher education?

RQ2: In what ways do instructors apply prompt engineering in their teaching practices?

RQ3: In what ways do instructors utilize prompt engineering in their academic research activities?

2. METHODOLOGY

2.1. Research Design

This study is framed within an interpretivist and also constructivist paradigm, because the aim was to explore in detail how university instructors make sense of prompt engineering in their own teaching and research context. In this view, reality is seen as socially constructed and knowledge is produced through interaction and interpretation (Creswell & Poth, 2018; Guba & Lincoln, 1994). A generic qualitative design was preferred here, as it allows the researcher to focus on the "what" and "how" questions without the strict procedures of a specific qualitative tradition (Merriam & Tisdell, 2016). This design was considered appropriate for answering the three research questions, which deal with perceptions, practices, and challenges. For analysing the data, I followed the reflexive thematic analysis steps of Braun and Clarke (2006), because this method is flexible enough to identify and organise patterns of meaning across different participants and still keep the voice of each one visible. The choice of this approach is also related to my own position as a language education scholar who is familiar with both the pedagogical and technological sides of the topic. This position made it possible to understand not only the literal words of the participants but also the professional context behind them, although I was careful to keep an audit trail and peer feedback to reduce personal bias. The main idea in this design was to capture the variety of experiences, but the focus was more on finding cross-case patterns and shared meanings rather than doing a full phenomenological analysis.

2.2. Data Collection Process

The data for this study were collected through semi-structured interviews that were prepared according to the research questions and related literature. Before starting the main data collection, a pilot study was carried out with two instructors to check the clarity and suitability of the questions. After making some small adjustments, the actual interviews were conducted between 20 July 2025 and 1 August 2025. Three of the interviews were done face-to-face, while the rest were conducted online because of participants' availability. All interviews were conducted in Turkish, then translated into English by the researcher, who is also a native-level English language expert. The average duration of each interview was around 20 minutes. With the permission of the participants, all interviews were audio-recorded, and some field notes were taken during the sessions. A total of 15 instructors from faculties of education and social sciences participated in the study. Data saturation was considered to be reached at the seventh interview, as no new codes were emerging and the themes identified were being repeated across participants. Additional interviews were still conducted to confirm the stability of these patterns and to ensure that no significant perspectives were overlooked.

2.3. Participants

The study involved a total of 15 university instructors, three from each of five different universities in Eastern Türkiye. Among the participants, seven were male and eight were female. Their professional experience ranged from 7 to 25 years. Seven of them were working in faculties of education, while eight were affiliated with faculties of social sciences. In terms of academic titles, the sample included two research assistants, four assistant professors, five associate professors, and four full professors. For anonymity, participants were assigned codes showing their interview order, years of professional experience, and academic title. For example, the code 1(7) (Res. Asst.) refers to Participant 1, who has 7 years of experience and holds the position of research assistant. These demographic details are presented more clearly in Table 1.

Table 1. Participant Demographics

Participant Code	University Code	University Type	Faculty	Academic Title	Years of Experience	Gender
1 (7) Res. Asst.	University A	State	Education	Research Assistant	7	Female
2 (10) Res. Asst.	University B	State	Social Sciences	Research Assistant	10	Male
3 (10) Asst. Prof.	University C	State	Education	Assistant Professor	10	Female
4 (12) Asst. Prof.	University D	State	Social Sciences	Assistant Professor	12	Male
5 (11) Asst. Prof.	University E	State	Education	Assistant Professor	11	Female
6 (14) Asst. Prof.	University A	State	Social Sciences	Assistant Professor	14	Male
7 (14) Assoc.	University B	State	Education	Associate Professor	14	Female

continued on following page

Table 1. Continued

Participant Code	University Code	University Type	Faculty	Academic Title	Years of Experience	Gender
8 (17) Assoc.	University C	State	Social Sciences	Associate Professor	17	Male
9 (15) Assoc.	University D	State	Education	Associate Professor	15	Female
10 (18) Assoc.	University E	State	Social Sciences	Associate Professor	18	Male
11 (15) Assoc.	University A	State	Education	Associate Professor	15	Female
12 (19) Prof.	University B	State	Social Sciences	Professor	19	Male
13 (20) Prof.	University C	State	Education	Professor	20	Female
14 (25) Prof.	University D	State	Social Sciences	Professor	25	Male
15(18)Prof.	University D	State	Social Sciences	Professor	18	Female

Participants were chosen purposefully from the faculties of education and social sciences because they are the ones who usually deal with teaching and research activities where AI tools can be used more actively. The idea was not to make statistical generalization but to get a deeper understanding of how instructors make sense of prompt engineering in their own work. Still, since the sample was small and from one region, the results should be taken as exploratory and limited to this specific context.

2.4. Data Analysis

In this study, thematic analysis was used to examine the interview data because this method gives a chance to explore the participants' experiences and perceptions in a rich and detailed way (Braun & Clarke, 2006; Nowell et al., 2017). The main reason for choosing thematic analysis was not only to see what ideas repeat but also to go deeper and understand the meanings and the context behind how instructors engage with prompt engineering.

The process followed Braun and Clarke's (2006) six steps:

(1) Familiarization with the data by reading the transcripts many times, both in Turkish and after their English translation.
(2) Generating initial codes directly from the data without forcing pre-set categories.
(3) Searching for themes by bringing together related codes.

(4) Reviewing themes to check the consistency and the relationship between codes and data.
(5) Defining and naming themes clearly so that each one covers a specific idea.
(6) Producing the final report with direct quotations from different participants to reflect various perspectives.

Codes and themes were created inductively, using the exact words of participants when possible, but also interpreted according to the research questions. For ensuring trustworthiness, I followed Lincoln and Guba's (1985) criteria – credibility, transferability, dependability, and confirmability. I used peer debriefing, member checks, and also kept an audit trail to make the process more transparent (Nowell et al., 2017).

2.5. Ethical Considerations and Trustworthiness

All participants were informed about the aim of the study and assured that their personal information will be kept confidential. They were told that participation is voluntary and they can withdraw any time without giving a reason. Verbal consent was taken before the interviews. Trustworthiness of the study was ensured through Lincoln and Guba's (1985) criteria. For credibility, member checking was used by sharing some excerpts from transcripts and interpretations with participants to confirm accuracy. For transferability, thick description was provided about the context, participants, and process to help readers judge whether the findings can apply to other settings. For dependability, detailed notes were kept of the data collection and analysis steps. For confirmability, personal bias was reduced by seeking peer feedback and maintaining an audit trail. These strategies contributed to making the findings more transparent and reliable (Nowell et al., 2017).

All the interviews were made in Turkish and later translated into English by the researcher since she has a high level in English. To avoid possible bias in the translation, for some important quotations she asked an independent bilingual colleague to translate them back into Turkish, so it is caught if the meaning is same. Also, another academic who is expert in English language teaching and qualitative research checked the translated parts for clarity and correctness. If there was any difference in wording or meaning, they discussed and agreed on the final form. An audit trail was also kept, including coding notes, theme development memos and the decisions made during translation, so the process can be seen more transparently.

As the researcher, she is an EFL academic working in the same higher education context with the participants, so she has an insider knowledge about the pedagogical and institutional situation in Eastern Türkiye. This position helped her to understand better some expressions or examples that the instructors gave, but at the same time she was aware that such closeness to the topic could influence how the data was coded and interpreted. To reduce this effect, she carried out peer debriefing with a colleague who has a more neutral view about AI in education, and also kept analytic memos to reflect on her own assumptions during the analysis. These steps helped her to use the insider position as an advantage, while still keeping a distance in interpretation.

3. FINDINGS

The findings of this study are presented in line with the three research questions. The analysis followed the thematic analysis approach, and themes were supported with direct quotations from participants to reflect their perspectives in their own words. In all excerpts, participant codes indicate the order, years of experience, and academic rank (e.g., 3 (10) Asst. Prof. refers to the third participant, with 10 years of academic experience at the rank of Assistant Professor).

3.1. RQ1: How do university instructors in Eastern Türkiye perceive the concept of prompt engineering in the context of higher education?

The analysis of the data revealed four main themes: Conceptual Understanding of Prompt Engineering, Perceived Educational Potential, Perceived Challenges and Limitations, and Personal Interest and Motivation.

3.1.1. Conceptual Understanding of Prompt Engineering

Most participants described prompt engineering as the ability to prepare clear and structured instructions that enable AI tools, especially LLM-based systems, to produce more relevant and accurate outputs. Instructors with fewer years of experience tended to provide more detailed and practical definitions, often drawing on their own trial-and-error experiences. Senior professors, in contrast, tended to describe the concept more generally and without technical details.

> *"It's like telling AI exactly what you want so it can give you a better answer. You just need to be clear about it." (1 (7) Res. Asst.)*
>
> *"I think of it as a way to talk to AI in an organized way. But to be honest, I don't really know much about the technical part." (14 (25) Prof.)*

3.1.2. Perceived Educational Potential

Participants, particularly from faculties of education, saw prompt engineering as a valuable tool for enhancing interactive learning, promoting critical thinking, and supporting student engagement. They emphasized its potential to make lessons more tailored to students' needs, especially when prompts were carefully prepared.

> *"When I prepare the prompts well, I can design activities that really match what my students need. For example, I once asked AI to create debate topics for my class, and it came up with ideas that perfectly fit their level. It's like having a teaching assistant who works instantly." (5 (11) Asst. Prof.)*
>
> *"If we guide students to ask the right kind of questions, AI can actually push them to think more critically. For instance, I sometimes make them refine their prompts step by step, and they start to see how changing just a few words can make a big difference." (8 (17) Assoc.)*

3.1.3. Perceived Challenges and Limitations

Some instructors expressed that mastering prompt engineering was not easy, mainly because of the absence of formal training opportunities. For them, learning was largely through experimentation, which could be time-consuming and at times frustrating. This challenge was more evident among senior faculty members who had limited direct engagement with AI tools.

> *"Sometimes I give it a try, but the answers don't quite fit what I'm looking for. For example, I once asked it to prepare reading comprehension questions, and half of them were either too easy or off-topic. I guess I'm still not very good at writing the right prompts." (10 (18) Assoc.)*
>
> *"The biggest problem is that we don't get any official training on this. We're just figuring it out by trial and error. For instance, I learned how to get better results only after trying the same prompt in three different ways." (2 (10) Res. Asst.)*

3.1.4. Personal Interest and Motivation

The level of interest in learning and applying prompt engineering varied considerably among participants. Younger instructors and those at the early stages of their academic careers (research assistants and assistant professors) generally expressed more enthusiasm and perceived it as an important skill for professional growth. Among professors, only one with 19 years of experience showed strong motivation to develop AI-related skills.

"I really want to get better at this because I'm sure it's going to be important for my future projects and publications. For example, I can already imagine using it to refine survey questions or draft article outlines." (3 (10) Asst. Prof.)

"I'm curious about it, but I just can't spend much time on it right now. Maybe once I finish my current book chapter, I'll be able to explore it more." (13 (20) Prof.)

Overall, these findings for the first question show that there is a visible difference according to academic seniority. The instructors who are in the earlier stages of their careers usually have more practical and concrete understanding about prompt engineering, and they can give more specific examples from their teaching or research. They also seem more willing to try and improve themselves, because they believe it will be useful for their future academic works. On the other hand, senior faculty members mostly accept that it is important, but they do not go deep into the technical or practical sides. They often say that they have no time, or too many responsibilities, or that they never had a formal training. This situation shows there is a kind of generation and career stage difference in how prompt engineering is used and understood in higher education.

3.2. RQ2: In what ways do instructors apply prompt engineering in their teaching practices?

The data analysis revealed three main themes: Designing Course Content and Materials, Supporting Assessment and Feedback, and Enhancing Student Engagement and Skills. Across all themes, the examples shared by participants reflected different levels of familiarity and creativity in using prompt engineering for teaching.

3.2.1. Designing Course Content and Materials

Many instructors, especially younger ones from the Faculty of Education, reported that they use prompt engineering to prepare lesson plans, activity sheets, and discussion questions more efficiently. They mentioned that AI tools helped them adapt content to different student levels and save preparation time.

"When I have to teach a new topic, I sometimes write a detailed prompt to create examples and exercises. For example, I once asked AI to prepare a short story with certain vocabulary for intermediate students, and it gave me something I could use directly." (1 (7) Res. Asst.)

"It is like having another colleague in your office. I can ask it to generate debate topics, role-play scenarios, or comprehension questions, and then I just adjust them for my class." (5 (11) Asst. Prof.)

Some senior academics also reported using prompt engineering for lecture preparation, but their approach was more occasional and less experimental.

"If I am short on time, I may ask AI to create some examples for my slides, but I still prefer to prepare most things myself." (14 (25) Prof.)

3.2.2. Supporting Assessment and Feedback

Several participants explained that prompt engineering was particularly useful for creating exam questions and answer keys. They valued the ability to quickly produce a variety of question types, especially for formative assessments.

"Before the midterm, I asked AI to write ten multiple-choice questions and five open-ended ones on the topics we covered. It saved me hours. I also told it to make an answer key, so I could check consistency." (8 (17) Assoc.)

"Sometimes I prepare the questions myself but use AI to generate model answers, especially for essay-type questions. It helps me see different possible responses before grading." (3 (10) Asst. Prof.)

One instructor pointed out that the key was in the way the prompt was written.

"If you just say 'write questions,' it gives very general ones. But if you say 'write five higher-order thinking questions on X topic for advanced students with answers,' it becomes much more useful." (2 (10) Res. Asst.)

3.2.3. Enhancing Student Engagement and Skills

Some participants integrated prompt engineering directly into classroom activities, using it as a tool to improve students' questioning skills, critical thinking, and creativity.

"I sometimes let students write their own prompts to get AI to produce an essay or a dialogue, and then we compare which prompts gave better outputs. They really see how wording changes the result." (6 (14) Asst. Prof.)

"Once I made students work in groups to refine a prompt step by step. At first, they wrote something very general, and the AI gave a boring answer. By the third try, they learned to add context, length, and difficulty level, and the results were much better." (7 (14) Assoc.)

These findings show that instructors apply prompt engineering in different ways depending on their teaching style, subject area, and familiarity with AI tools. While younger academics tend to explore more interactive and creative uses, senior ones often focus on practical and time-saving applications.

3.3. RQ3: In what ways do instructors utilize prompt engineering in their academic research activities?

The analysis revealed three main themes: Using AI for Research Support, Concerns about Ethics and Academic Integrity, and Need for Training and Skill Development. While most professors recognized the potential of prompt engineering in research, their actual use was limited, often due to ethical concerns or unfamiliarity with the technical side. In contrast, younger academics and those at early career stages used it more frequently, though often without clear strategies for crafting effective prompts.

3.3.1. Using AI for Research Support

Participants reported using prompt engineering for different stages of the research process, including idea generation, literature summaries, and drafting research instruments. However, the depth of usage varied greatly.

"I sometimes ask AI to summarize an article quickly, especially when I am checking if it's relevant to my work. It's like having an assistant who reads faster than me." (12 (19) Prof.)

"When I was preparing my last project proposal, I asked it to give me possible research questions based on my topic. Some of them were not usable, but a few gave me new angles to think about." (3 (10) Asst. Prof.)

Several younger instructors noted that AI could speed up certain research tasks, but only if the prompt was written with enough detail.

"If you just say 'summarize this,' it gives something very general. I learned to write like: 'Summarize this in 150 words focusing on methodology and key findings.' That way it is much more useful for me." (1 (7) Res. Asst.)

3.3.2. Concerns about Ethics and Academic Integrity

Professors, in particular, expressed caution about over-reliance on AI for research, worrying that it might undermine academic integrity or blur the line between original work and AI-generated content.

"I don't want my work to be questioned later for being AI-produced. In academia, our reputation is built over years, and I don't want to risk it for speed." (14 (25) Prof.)

"I think we need clear institutional policies. If I use AI to write a literature review section, how much of that is still mine? I don't want to cross a line without realizing it." (13 (20) Prof.)

Some younger academics shared similar worries, but often focused more on whether reviewers or colleagues could detect AI involvement.

"My fear is that if it looks like AI wrote it, it might be rejected, even if I revised it a lot. So, I try to use it more for brainstorming than writing final texts." (2 (10) Res. Asst.)

3.3.3. Need for Training and Skill Development

A recurring point across participants was the need for structured training on how to write prompts for research purposes. Some even suggested inviting colleagues from computer science or software engineering to give workshops.

"We are all learning by trial and error. It would be great to have a short course, maybe from software engineering faculty, on how to get the best out of these tools for academic writing." (5 (11) Asst. Prof.)

"I think I am wasting time sometimes because I don't know how to ask it properly. If I could learn better strategies, I could use it for more complex things like analyzing qualitative data." (8 (17) Assoc.)

"If someone shows me how to make it write code for my data analysis, that would save me weeks. But right now, I don't know how to ask it in the right way." (7 (14) Assoc.)

These findings suggest that while prompt engineering is starting to enter academic research practices, its use is uneven. Early-career academics engage with it more frequently, mainly to save time and generate ideas, whereas senior academics remain cautious, often due to ethical and reputational concerns. Across all groups, there is a shared recognition that training—especially from experts in AI and software engineering—could help make its use more effective and responsible.

All in all, when the answers to the three research questions are considered together, it becomes clear that academic seniority creates a visible difference in how prompt engineering is perceived and used. Early-career academics, especially research assistants and assistant professors, tend to use it more frequently and creatively in both teaching and research, seeing it as an important skill for their future academic productivity. In contrast, senior faculty members acknowledge its potential but engage less with its technical and practical aspects, often due to time limitations or ethical concerns. A common point across all groups is the need for structured training to ensure its effective and responsible use. This situation shows that in both teaching and research, there is a necessity for institutional steps and policies to make the use of prompt engineering more systematic and beneficial.

4. DISCUSSION

The findings of the present study show that the way university instructors in Eastern Türkiye perceive and use prompt engineering is closely connected to the points already discussed in the literature. In line with Zhang et al. (2024), most participants defined prompt engineering as the ability to give clear and structured instructions so that AI tools can generate more relevant and useful answers. However, while the literature often presents this skill in a rather technical way, our participants—especially the less experienced ones—tended to describe it through their own classroom or research experiences, often with examples of trial-and-error attempts. This is similar to what Oppenlaender et al. (2023) emphasise: prompt engineering is not something that is mastered immediately but rather improves with repeated practice.

The study also confirms the view of Reynolds and McDonell (2021) and Giray (2023) that the quality of a prompt directly influences the quality of AI output. Participants who gave detailed, context-rich prompts—sometimes including constraints or examples—reported receiving more accurate and level-appropriate results. For example, one instructor's experience in preparing debate topics matched Mollick and Mollick's (2022) point that prompt engineering can help create more interactive and student-centred activities. This supports the idea that, when used consciously, prompt engineering can act as a pedagogical enabler rather than just a technical tool.

Regarding teaching applications (RQ2), the results align with Cain's (2024) argument that prompt engineering can make assessment and instructional design more flexible and adaptive. Some participants shared that they used AI to create exam questions, prepare answer keys, or design differentiated activities for students with different needs. These uses clearly resonate with the broader claim in the literature that AI, when guided by well-prepared prompts, can enhance both efficiency and personalization in higher education (Balaquiao, 2024; White et al., 2023). Interestingly, in our study, the ability to prepare effective prompts for teaching seemed to be more developed among younger instructors, possibly because of their greater openness to experimenting with new tools. These results are also in line with the findings of Lin, Li, and Li (2025), who compared AI-generated and standard textbook questions in the context of surgical nursing. Their study showed that AI-generated questions tended to be more case-based and aimed at developing higher-order thinking skills, while standard questions were often more concise and procedural. Similar to our participants' use of prompt engineering for creating exam questions and differentiated classroom activities, Lin et al. (2025) emphasized that although AI outputs can offer richer scenarios and greater complexity, they may also require refinement to ensure accuracy, clarity, and alignment with learning objectives. This reinforces our finding that well-prepared prompts can enhance both the depth and variety of instructional materials, but conscious editing and adaptation by the instructor remain essential.

Similar patterns were reported by Lee et al. (2024) in the field of English education, where a structured AI-assisted question generation framework helped teachers produce a wider range of question types, but also revealed technical limitations that required expert review and refinement. As in our study, their findings highlight that while AI can significantly broaden the scope and depth of instructional materials, the process still demands careful prompt design, iterative testing, and conscious adaptation by the instructor to ensure accuracy, clarity, and pedagogical relevance. This reinforces our finding that well-prepared prompts can enhance both the depth and variety of instructional materials, but conscious editing and adaptation by the instructor remain essential.

In a K-12 STEM education context, Li (2024) similarly showed that prompt engineering can be used to create interactive, personalized tutoring experiences. By integrating pre-designed prompts into an AI-enabled "personal tutor" tool, Li was able to guide students through content explanations, quizzes, and simplified reviews tailored to their grade level and learning pace. This mirrors our finding that prompt engineering can enhance both the depth and variety of instructional materials, but also reinforces that conscious editing and adaptation by the instructor—or guided system design—remains essential to ensure alignment with learning objectives and to avoid misuse.

While some researchers emphasize that prompt engineering is a transferable digital skill that should be systematically taught to higher education students (Bozkurt & Sharma, 2023), others caution that it may not remain a priority in the long term, as advances in large language models could make such skills less critical (Acar, 2023). However, emerging studies indicate that advanced techniques—such as incorporating structured reasoning steps, selection-inference, and chain-of-thought prompting—can substantially improve the quality of AI outputs (Kleesiek et al., 2023; Sivarajkumar et al., 2023). Our findings also point to the value of such training, as participants who had more developed prompting strategies were able to design richer and more context-appropriate AI outputs for teaching and assessment purposes. In this transitional stage, providing educators and learners with targeted instruction in prompt engineering could therefore be valuable, not only to enhance their effective engagement with generative AI but also to reduce potential digital inequities by addressing gaps in AI-related knowledge and skills (O'Connor et al., 2023).

For research applications (RQ3), the findings partly confirm Khurana's (2024) and Kacena et al.'s (2024) views on AI's contribution to literature review and hypothesis generation. Several instructors reported using AI—sometimes with only moderate success—for drafting article outlines, refining survey questions, or generating research ideas. Yet, in contrast to the more optimistic tone in Extance

(2018) or Liu et al. (2021), our data suggest that many instructors, especially senior professors, do not yet fully benefit from AI's research-related potentials. Their usage is often occasional and exploratory rather than systematic. Moreover, ethical concerns—such as the fear of being seen as "relying too much" on AI—were most pronounced among these senior participants, echoing White et al.'s (2023) reminder that institutional and cultural attitudes play an important role in AI adoption. In terms of research practices, our findings reflect the increasing scholarly attention to prompt engineering in recent years, particularly after the release of ChatGPT. This is not surprising given the broader publication trends reported by Leal, Capetillo, and Castorena (2025), whose bibliometric analysis showed an exponential rise in research on prompting and AI since 2022. Their results also highlighted that while computer science leads the field, social sciences—including education—hold the second position, with engineering following closely. This suggests that the prompt phenomenon is no longer confined to technical disciplines but is becoming a relevant subject of inquiry across domains, including language education. Similar to the trend noted in their review, our study contributes to this growing body of literature by examining prompt engineering from a pedagogical perspective and offering qualitative evidence on how it is being integrated into higher education teaching practices. This alignment reinforces the idea that the expansion of prompt engineering research is accompanied by an increasing interest in its application for instructional innovation and professional development in educational contexts. In terms of research practices, our findings also resonate with emerging literature showing how systematic prompt design can shape the quality and efficiency of LLM-assisted academic tasks. For example, Colangelo et al. (2025) demonstrated in a biomedical context that translating structured criteria such as PICO into actionable prompts can significantly affect recall, precision, and overall screening performance in systematic reviews. Their distinction between "soft" prompts, which maximise recall, and "strict" prompts, which require explicit evidence for inclusion, parallels the variation we observed among our participants in framing their prompts for research-related purposes. Similar to their conclusion that expert oversight remains essential to ensure the reliability of AI outputs, our participants also stressed the need to critically review and adapt AI-generated content rather than accepting it uncritically. These insights further support our argument that well-crafted prompt engineering is not only a pedagogical tool but also an emerging methodological skill in academic research, with potential to streamline complex processes while maintaining quality standards.

The study also highlights a clear experience-based difference. Younger academics, particularly those still in the process of academic promotion, tend to use prompt engineering more frequently and with more confidence. This may be related to what Shin et al. (2020) describe as the importance of early-career exposure to digital skills, which shapes long-term technology integration habits. On the other hand, senior academics expressed more hesitation and often lacked confidence in knowing "how to write a good prompt," a point that Cain (2024) associates with the absence of structured training. This gap is important because, as Strobelt et al. (2022) note, the effectiveness of LLMs is highly dependent on the clarity and precision of user input.

Finally, the expressed need for formal training in prompt engineering, sometimes even in collaboration with software engineering departments, strongly supports the call in O'Connor et al. (2024) and Wahidur et al. (2024) for interdisciplinary capacity building. Eke (2024) also support the idea of implementing comprehensive training and professional development programs for instructors focusing on the practical implementation of AI-powered educational tools. According to him this will enhance their confidence, competence, and ability to effectively integrate these technologies into their teaching practices. Without such support, instructors risk underusing AI tools despite recognizing their potential. In our context, this was clear: even those who valued prompt engineering admitted they learned mostly by trial and error, and that more structured opportunities to learn from experts could greatly improve their confidence and output quality.

Overall, the discussion suggests that while the literature presents prompt engineering as both a technical and pedagogical skill, its actual adoption in Eastern Türkiye is still uneven, shaped by generational differences, institutional culture, and the absence of formal training structures. The integration of these findings with previous research reinforces the idea that, for prompt engineering to fully deliver its pedagogical and research-related potentials, targeted professional development and institutional encouragement will be necessary.

5. IMPLICATIONS

The findings of this study have several implications for higher education practice and policy, particularly in regions where the integration of AI into academic work is still at an early stage. First, there is a clear need for structured professional development on prompt engineering, designed for instructors from different career stages and disciplines. Such training should not only focus on technical aspects but also on pedagogical applications, ethical considerations, and discipline-specific adaptation. Instructors could benefit from practical workshops where they design, test, and refine prompts for their own teaching and research needs.

Second, the differences between younger and senior academics suggest that training programmes may need to be differentiated. Early-career academics might benefit from advanced techniques and creative uses, while senior academics may require more foundational guidance and confidence-building in AI-related skills.

Third, interdisciplinary collaboration should be encouraged, especially between education faculties and computer or software engineering departments, to ensure that both the pedagogical and technical dimensions of prompt engineering are addressed. Such collaborations could also help in developing shared resources and repositories of well-designed prompts.

Finally, institutional policies should provide clear guidelines on the ethical and responsible use of AI in both teaching and research. This would address the concerns expressed by some participants and create a supportive environment where instructors can integrate AI tools without uncertainty about academic integrity. By investing in capacity building and policy clarity, universities can help instructors use prompt engineering not only as a technical skill but as a driver of innovation and quality in higher education.

6. CONCLUSION

This study examined how university instructors in Eastern Türkiye perceive and use prompt engineering in their teaching and research activities. The results show that while many recognize its potential, the actual adoption is uneven and shaped by career stage, institutional culture, and the lack of structured training. Younger academics tend to experiment more and use prompt engineering creatively, while senior academics are more cautious, often because of ethical concerns or limited familiarity with AI tools. These findings confirm that prompt engineering can be both a pedagogical and methodological skill, but to reach its full potential it needs institutional encouragement and targeted capacity building.

Future Research Directions

In future research, it would be useful to include a larger and more diverse group of participants from different universities and disciplines, because this can show how the understanding and use of prompt engineering may change across academic fields. Studies that combine qualitative interviews with surveys or small experimental designs could give a clearer picture of how instructors' attitudes, experiences, and actual practices are connected. In addition, longitudinal and mixed-method studies are important, since both AI technologies and institutional policies are developing very fast. Such studies could follow the changes in instructors' perceptions and practices over time and help to understand how universities adapt to this new situation.

Limitations

This study was conducted with a relatively small group of instructors from five state universities in Eastern Türkiye, which may limit the transferability of the findings to other regions or contexts. Data were collected only through interviews, so the results rely on self-reported practices and perceptions. In future studies, it would be better to use more than one method, for example by combining interviews with small surveys, some prompt examples, or usage records. In this way, the results can be checked from different sides and not depend only on what participants say.

REFERENCES

Acar, O. A. (2023, June 9). *AI prompt engineering isn't the future. Harvard Business Review*. https://hbr.org/2023/06/ai-prompt-engineering-isnt-the-future

Atalay, M., & Çelik, E. (2017). Büyük veri analizinde yapay zekâ ve makine öğrenmesi uygulamaları - Artificial intelligence and machine learning applications in big data analysis. *Mehmet Akif Ersoy Üniversitesi Sosyal Bilimler Enstitüsü Dergisi*, *9*(22), 155–172.

Balaquiao, E. (2024). Optimizing students' performance through Artificial Intelligence (AI) technology: A gamified approach to smart learning environment. *Journal of Pedagogy and Education Science*, *3*(02), 104–114.

Bozkurt, A., & Sharma, R. C. 2023. Generative AI and prompt engineering: the art of whispering to let the genie out of the algorithmic world. *Asian J. Distance Educ. 18* (2), 1–6. http://asianjde.com/ojs/index.php/AsianJDE/article/view/749

Braun, V., & Clarke, V. (2006). Using thematic analysis in psychology. *Qualitative Research in Psychology*, *3*(2), 77–101.

Cain, W. (2024). Prompting change: Exploring prompt engineering in large language model AI and its potential to transform education. *TechTrends*, *68*(1), 47–57. DOI: 10.1007/s11528-023-00896-0

Çayak, S. (2024). Investigating the relationship between teachers' attitudes toward artificial intelligence and their artificial intelligence literacy. *Journal of Educational Technology & Online Learning*, *7*(4), 367–383.

Colangelo, M. T., Guizzardi, S., Meleti, M., Calciolari, E., & Galli, C. (2025). How to write effective prompts for screening biomedical literature using large language models. *BioMedInformatics*, *5*(1), 15. DOI: 10.3390/biomedinformatics5010015

Creswell, J. W., & Poth, C. N. (2018). *Qualitative inquiry and research design: Choosing among five approaches* (4th ed.). SAGE Publications.

Dang, H., Mecke, L., Lehmann, F., Goller, S., & Buschek, D. (2022). *How to prompt? Opportunities and challenges of zero-and few-shot learning for human–AI interaction in creative applications of generative models*. https://arxiv.org/abs/2209.01390

Eke, O. E. (2024). Assessing the readiness and attitudes of Nigerian teacher educators towards adoption of artificial intelligence in educational settings. *Journal of Educational Technology & Online Learning*, *7*(4), 473–487.

Elmessiry, A., & Elmessiry, M. (2024). Navigating the evolution of Artificial Intelligence: Towards education-specific retrieval augmented generative AI (ES-RAG-AI). In *INTED2024 Proceedings* (pp. 7692–7697).

Extance, A. (2018). How AI technology can tame the scientific literature. *Nature, 561*(7722), 273–275. PMID: 30202054

Feng, Y., Wang, X., Wong, K. K., Wang, S., Lu, Y., Zhu, M., & Chen, W. (2023). Promptmagician: Interactive prompt engineering for text-to-image creation. *IEEE Transactions on Visualization and Computer Graphics*, *30*(1), 1–11. DOI: 10.1109/tvcg.2023.3327168 PMID: 37878445

Gaftandzhieva, S., Talukder, A., Gohain, N., Hussain, S., Theodorou, P., Salal, Y., & Doneva, R. (2022). Exploring online activities to predict the final grade of student. *Mathematics*, *10*(20), 3758. DOI: 10.3390/math10203758

Guba, E. G., & Lincoln, Y. S. (1994). *Competing paradigms in qualitative research*. In N. K.

Harry, A. (2023). Role of AI in education. *Interdisciplinary Journal and Humanity*, *2*(3), 260–268.

Kacena, M. A., Plotkin, L. I., & Fehrenbacher, J. C. (2024). The use of artificial intelligence in writing scientific review articles. *Current Osteoporosis Reports*, •••, 1–7. PMID: 38227177

Karadağ, N. (2023). The impact of artificial intelligence on online assessment: A preliminary review. *Journal of Educational Technology & Online Learning*, *6*(4), 822–837.

Kearney, M.-L. (2009). Higher education, research and innovation: Charting the course of the changing dynamics of the knowledge society. In Meek, V. L., Teichler, U., & Kearney, M.-L. (Eds.), *Higher education, research and innovation: Changing dynamics* (pp. 7–23). INCHER and UNESCO.

Khurana, V. (2024). Accelerating pace of scientific discovery and innovation through big data enabled artificial intelligence and deep learning. *Emerging Trends in Machine Intelligence and Big Data*, *16*(1), 38–53.

Kleesiek, J., Wu, Y., Stiglic, G., Egger, J., & Bian, J. (2023). An opinion on ChatGPT in health care—Written by humans only. *Journal of Nuclear Medicine*, *64*(5), 701–703. DOI: 10.2967/jnumed.123.265687 PMID: 37055219

Kotei, E., & Thirunavukarasu, R. (2023). A systematic review of transformer-based pre-trained language models through self-supervised learning. *Information (Basel)*, *14*(3), 187. DOI: 10.3390/info14030187

Leal, D. C., Capetillo, A., & Castorena, D. G. (2025, January 28). *Prompting literature review: The impact of Transformer models and ChatGPT on prompt engineering and AI research publications*. In *2025 Institute for the Future of Education Conference (IFE)* (pp. 1–7). IEEE. doi:DOI: 10.1109/IFE62519.2025.1234567

Lee, U., Jung, H., Jeon, Y., Sohn, Y., Hwang, W., Moon, J., & Kim, H. (2024). Few-shot is enough: Exploring ChatGPT prompt engineering method for automatic question generation in English education. *Education and Information Technologies*, *29*, 11483–11515. DOI: 10.1007/s10639-023-12249-8

Li, M. Z. (2024, March 9). *Using prompt engineering to enhance STEM education*. In *2024 IEEE Integrated STEM Education Conference (ISEC)* (pp. 262–267). IEEE. https://doi.org/DOI: 10.1109/ISEC61299.2024.10664775

Lin, Y., Li, C., & Li, H. (2025). Comparing AI-generated and traditional text-book multiple-choice questions in nursing education: A prompt engineering-based Delphi study. *Medical Teacher*. Advance online publication. DOI: 10.1080/0142159X.2025.2533401 PMID: 40684326

Lincoln, Y. S., & Guba, E. G. (1985). *Naturalistic inquiry*. Sage Publications.

Liu, P., Yuan, W., Fu, J., Jiang, Z., Hayashi, H., & Neubig, G. (2021). Pre-train, prompt, and predict: A systematic survey ofprompting methods in natural language processing. arXiv: 2107.13586.

Liu, T., Gao, Z., & Guan, H. (2021). Educational information system optimization for artificial intelligence teaching strategies. *Complexity*, ●●●, 1–13.

Marginson, S. (2011). Higher education and public good. *Higher Education Quarterly*, *65*, 411–433.

Merriam, S. B., & Tisdell, E. J. (2016). *Qualitative research: A guide to design and implementation* (4th ed.). Jossey-Bass.

Mollick, E. R., & Mollick, L. (2022). New modes of learning enabled by AI chatbots: Three methods and assignments. (SSRN *Scholarly Paper* 4300783). 10.2139/ssrn.4300783

Nowell, L. S., Norris, J. M., White, D. E., & Moules, N. J. (2017). Thematic analysis: Striving to meet the trustworthiness criteria. *International Journal of Qualitative Methods*, *16*, 1–13.

O'Connor, S., Peltonen, L. M., Topaz, M., Chen, L. Y. A., Michalowski, M., Ronquillo, C., & Denis-Lalonde, D. (2024). Prompt engineering when using generative AI in nursing education. *Nurse Education in Practice*, *74*, 103825. DOI: 10.1016/j.nepr.2023.103825 PMID: 37957062

O'Connor, S., Permana, A., Neville, S., & Denis-Lalonde, D. (2023). Artificial intelligence in nursing education 2: Opportunities and threats. *Nursing Times*, *119*(11). https://www.nursingtimes.net/roles/nurse-educators/artificial-intelligence-in-nursing-education-2-opportunities-and-threats-09-10-2023/

Öncü, S. E., Gevher, M., & Erdoğdu, E. (2025). Exploring the potential use of generative AI for learner support in ODL at scale. *Journal of Educational Technology & Online Learning*, *8*(1), 80–99.

Oppenlaender, J., Linder, R., & Silvennoinen, J. (2023). Prompting AI art: An investigation into the creative skill of promptengineering. arXiv. Doi:10.48550/arXiv.2303.13534

Ouatik, F., Ouatik, F., Fadli, H., Elgorari, A., Mohadab, M. E. L., & Raoufi, M. (2021). E-learning & decision-making system for automate students assessment using remote laboratory and machine learning. *Journal of E-Learning and Knowledge Society*, *17*(1), 90–100.

Reynolds, L., & McDonell, K. (2021). Prompt programming for large language models: Beyond the few-shot paradigm. arXiv: 2102.07350. doi:10.48550/arXiv.2102.07350

Sivarajkumar, S., Kelley, M., Samolyk-Mazzanti, A., Visweswaran, S., & Wang, Y. (2023). An empirical evaluation of prompting strategies for large language models in zero-shot clinical natural language processing. *arXiv*. https://arxiv.org/abs/2309.08008

Srikanthan, G., & Dalrymple, J. (2002). Developing a holistic model for quality in higher education. *Quality in Higher Education*, *8*(3), 215–224.

Strobelt, H., Webson, A., Sanh, V., Hoover, B., Beyer, J., Pfister, H., & Rush, A. M. (2022). *Interactive and visual prompt engineering for ad-hoc task adaptation with large language models*. IEEE.

Tonbuloğlu, B. (2023). An evaluation of the use of artificial intelligence applications in online education. *Journal of Educational Technology & Online Learning*, *6*(4), 866–884.

Waghid, Y. (2002). Knowledge production and higher education transformation in South Africa: Towards reflexivity in university teaching, research and community service. *Higher Education*, *43*(4), 457–488. DOI: 10.1023/A:1015211718131

Wahidur, R. S., Tashdeed, I., Kaur, M., & Lee, H.-N. (2024). Enhancing zero-shot crypto sentiment with fine-tuned language model and prompt engineering. *IEEE Access : Practical Innovations, Open Solutions*, *12*, 10146–10159. DOI: 10.1109/access.2024.3350638

Wang, L., Bi, W., Zhao, S., Ma, Y., Lv, L., Meng, C., & Lv, H. (2024). Investigating the impact of prompt engineering on the performance of large language models for standardizing obstetric diagnosis text: Comparative study. *JMIR Formative Research*, *8*(1), e53216. DOI: 10.2196/53216 PMID: 38329787

White, J., Fu, Q., Hays, S., Sandborn, M., Olea, C., Gilbert, H., Elnashar, A., Spencer-Smith, J., & Schmidt, D. C. (2023). Aprompt pattern catalog to enhance prompt engineering with ChatGPT. https://arxiv.org/abs/2302.11382

Zhang, K., Zhou, F., Wu, L., Xie, N., & He, Z. (2024). Semantic understanding and prompt engineering for large-scale traffic data imputation. *Information Fusion*, *102*, 102038. DOI: 10.1016/j.inffus.2023.102038

Chapter 4
Enhanced Framework for Automated University Questionnaire Creation

Satwik Jambula
https://orcid.org/0009-0002-7184-8319
Lamar University, USA

ABSTRACT

This chapter presents an enhanced framework for automated university questionnaire creation using generative artificial intelligence technologies. The authors propose a comprehensive system integrating AI capabilities with inclusive educational practices, universal design principles, and rigorous survey methodology. The framework addresses growing demand for scalable, personalized, and ethically sound assessment solutions in higher education through four core components: intelligent question generation systems, adaptive response mechanisms, inclusive design protocols, and comprehensive evaluation metrics. Implementation strategies and illustrative case studies demonstrate practical applications across diverse academic contexts. This resource guides educators, administrators, and technology professionals in implementing automated questionnaire systems that enhance educational equity while maintaining academic rigor and institutional integrity.

INTRODUCTION

The landscape of higher education assessment has undergone profound transformation in recent years, accelerated by technological advances and evolving pedagogical understanding (Ouyang et al., 2022). The emergence of generative artificial intelligence tools has catalyzed unprecedented changes in how educational

DOI: 10.4018/979-8-3373-8805-2.ch004

institutions approach data collection, student evaluation, and learning analytics (Jin et al., 2024). Universities worldwide face mounting pressure to efficiently gather meaningful data about student experiences, learning outcomes, and institutional effectiveness while simultaneously ensuring accessibility and inclusiveness for diverse student populations (National Centre for AI, 2024).

Traditional questionnaire design in university settings has long been characterized by manual processes that are both time-intensive and resource-demanding (Dillman et al., 2014). Faculty members and administrators typically invest substantial effort in crafting assessment instruments, often without specialized training in survey methodology or accessibility considerations (Fowler, 2013). This conventional approach frequently results in questionnaires that may inadvertently exclude certain student populations, contain biased language, or fail to capture the nuanced experiences of diverse learners (Biesta, 2010).

Recent studies have demonstrated significant evolution in ChatGPT applications in education from 2022 to 2024, with research shifting towards integrating AI in specific educational tasks, particularly assessments (Khlaif et al., 2024). Current data indicates that 92% of students now use AI in some form, up from 66% in 2024, with 88% having used generative AI for assessments (HEPI, 2025). This rapid adoption necessitates institutional responses that harness AI capabilities while maintaining educational integrity and promoting inclusive practices.

The concept of automated questionnaire creation represents a convergence of several technological and pedagogical developments. Contemporary AI survey tools like QuestionPro AI and SurveyMonkey's Build with AI demonstrate the practical feasibility of conversational interfaces that generate comprehensive questionnaires within seconds (QuestionPro, 2024). These platforms leverage natural language processing and machine learning algorithms to interpret user requirements and generate contextually appropriate questions, response options, and survey logic (Kaival, 2025).

However, existing automated survey tools primarily target commercial and general research applications, with limited consideration for the unique requirements of higher education environments. Universities require questionnaire systems that address specific institutional needs including academic integrity, diverse learning styles, accessibility compliance, multilingual support, and integration with existing learning management systems (Hurix Digital, 2025). Additionally, university questionnaires must often comply with educational research ethics standards and institutional review board requirements that may not apply to commercial survey applications.

The framework presented in this chapter addresses these specialized requirements by proposing a comprehensive system specifically designed for university contexts. This framework integrates cutting-edge generative AI technologies with established principles of inclusive education (CAST, 2018), universal design for learning (Rose & Meyer, 2002), and rigorous survey methodology (Dillman et al., 2014; Fowler, 2013). The resulting system promises to enhance both the efficiency and effectiveness of university questionnaire creation while ensuring compliance with accessibility standards and promoting educational equity.

LITERATURE REVIEW AND THEORETICAL FOUNDATION

Generative AI in Educational Assessment

The integration of generative artificial intelligence in educational assessment represents a paradigmatic shift from traditional evaluation methods toward more dynamic, personalized, and scalable approaches. Recent systematic reviews indicate that assessment and evaluation constitute the most common application of AI in higher education, with automatic assessment being implemented in 26 of 138 reviewed studies (Ouyang et al., 2022). This widespread adoption reflects both the practical benefits and transformative potential of AI-enhanced assessment systems.

Contemporary research on ChatGPT-4 in educational evaluation demonstrates promising capabilities for assessing university students' open-ended written examination responses, showing good consistency with teacher grading when proper prompting techniques are employed (Isiaku et al., 2024). These developments suggest that large language models possess sufficient sophistication to understand and evaluate complex academic content across diverse disciplines. Research emphasizes that AI applications can be utilized for a wide range of purposes in addressing indicators of effective online education, including personalized learning experiences, learning content creation, and comprehensive evaluation systems (Tonbuloğlu, 2023).

The evolution of AI assessment tools has progressed from simple multiple-choice question generators to sophisticated systems capable of creating complex, contextually appropriate questionnaires that adapt to specific educational objectives. Studies demonstrate that generative AI can create detailed, context-specific surveys efficiently, with particular benefits in generating comprehensive questionnaires tailored to various industries and educational needs (Kaival, 2025). The development of comprehensive AI assessment frameworks has become essential for ethical integration of AI tools in educational evaluation, ensuring better learning outcomes while upholding academic integrity (Kılınç, 2024).

Inclusive Education and Universal Design Principles

Inclusive education encompasses pedagogical approaches and technological implementations that ensure equitable access to learning opportunities for all students, regardless of their individual characteristics, backgrounds, or learning needs. The framework of inclusive excellence in higher education emphasizes accessibility, identity, and epistemology as three critical lenses through which educational technologies should be evaluated (National Centre for AI, 2024).

Universal Design for Learning principles provide structured guidelines for creating educational experiences that accommodate diverse learning styles and abilities (CAST, 2018; Rose & Meyer, 2002). When applied to questionnaire design, UDL principles suggest that assessment instruments should offer multiple means of representation, engagement, and expression to ensure that all students can effectively participate in data collection activities.

Recent research emphasizes that AI technologies can provide various forms of support for neurodiverse and students with special educational needs, including personalized learning experiences, adaptive assessments, and assistive technologies (National Centre for AI, 2024). This capability aligns with institutional commitments to creating inclusive educational environments that support student success across diverse populations.

The intersection of AI technology and inclusive education presents both opportunities and challenges. AI tools hold remarkable promise for providing more accessible, equitable, and inclusive learning experiences for students with disabilities (University of Pittsburgh Teaching Center, 2024), though implementation requires careful consideration of potential barriers and unintended consequences.

Survey Methodology and Questionnaire Design

Effective questionnaire design requires systematic attention to multiple methodological considerations including question construction, response format selection, survey logic implementation, and validation processes (Dillman et al., 2014; Fowler, 2013). Established frameworks for questionnaire development emphasize seven essential steps: determining aims, operationalizing variables, designing questions, selecting response formats, organizing content, pretesting instruments, and conducting validation studies.

Contemporary best practices in questionnaire design recommend wording items as questions rather than statements, avoiding agree-disagree response options to minimize acquiescence bias, and maintaining equal spacing between response options to reduce measurement error (Fowler, 2013). These principles become particularly important when designing automated systems that must generate methodologically sound questionnaires without direct researcher oversight.

Classification frameworks for automated feedback systems identify four main components essential for effective implementation: architecture, feedback mechanisms, educational context considerations, and evaluation protocols. These components provide structural guidance for developing automated questionnaire systems that maintain scientific rigor while accommodating diverse educational requirements.

The challenge of creating valid and reliable questionnaires through automated processes requires careful attention to established psychometric principles. Research emphasizes that questionnaire design lacks a unified theoretical foundation, making it more of an art than a science that relies heavily on empirical best practices developed through extensive research experience (Fowler, 2013).

Table 1. Synthesis of Literature Review Findings

Research Area	Key Studies	Main Findings	Implications for Framework
AI in Assessment	Ouyang et al. (2022); Isiaku et al. (2024)	AI widely adopted for assessment; GPT-4 shows consistency with teacher grading	AI capable of supporting educational questionnaire generation
Inclusive Education	CAST (2018); National Centre for AI (2024)	UDL principles essential; AI can support diverse learners	Framework must embed accessibility from design phase
Survey Methodology	Dillman et al. (2014); Fowler (2013)	Established best practices exist; design requires expertise	Automated systems must incorporate methodological rigor
AI Ethics	Floridi (2019); Noble (2018)	Bias concerns; need for transparency and fairness	Framework requires bias mitigation and ethical safeguards

ETHICAL CONSIDERATIONS AND DATA PRIVACY

Data Privacy and Security

The implementation of automated questionnaire systems in university settings raises significant data privacy and security concerns that require careful attention and proactive management (Floridi, 2019). Universities collect and maintain vast amounts of sensitive information about students, faculty, and institutional operations, making robust privacy protections essential for maintaining trust and compliance with applicable regulations.

Contemporary AI survey platforms emphasize that user data is not used to train AI models and implement various privacy protection measures (QuestionPro, 2024), establishing important precedents for educational implementations. However, university contexts require additional privacy considerations due to the sensitive nature of educational data and the potential for long-term impact on student outcomes and opportunities.

Data minimization principles require that automated questionnaire systems collect only information necessary for stated purposes while implementing appropriate retention and deletion policies (Floridi, 2019). Universities must establish clear policies regarding data usage, sharing, and retention that balance institutional needs with individual privacy rights and regulatory requirements.

Consent management becomes particularly complex in university settings where participation in assessment activities may be required for academic progression while privacy rights must be protected. Automated systems must implement sophisticated consent mechanisms that enable informed decision-making while accommodating different levels of participation and data sharing preferences.

International considerations add complexity to privacy management, particularly for universities with diverse international student populations or research collaborations. Systems must accommodate varying privacy regulations and cultural expectations regarding data collection and usage while maintaining consistent functionality and user experience.

Algorithmic Bias and Fairness

Automated questionnaire systems inherit potential biases from training data, algorithmic design decisions, and implementation choices that may systematically disadvantage certain groups or perspectives (Noble, 2018; O'Neil, 2016). Universities must implement proactive measures to identify, mitigate, and monitor bias to ensure that automated systems promote rather than hinder inclusive education objectives.

Research emphasizes that AI integration in education must address potential biases in algorithms and ensure equitable access to technology to avoid increasing existing divides (National Centre for AI, 2024). This concern becomes particularly acute in questionnaire systems that may influence institutional decision-making about resource allocation, policy development, and educational programming.

Training data bias represents a fundamental challenge for AI-powered questionnaire systems. Language models and question generation algorithms trained on historical survey data may perpetuate biases present in traditional assessment practices, potentially excluding or misrepresenting the experiences of marginalized groups (Noble, 2018). Universities must implement bias detection and correction mechanisms throughout the system development and deployment process.

Question generation bias may manifest in systematic preferences for certain question types, response formats, or content areas that reflect the characteristics of training data rather than optimal assessment practices. Regular audit procedures should examine generated questionnaires for evidence of systematic bias and implement corrective measures as needed.

Response interpretation bias may occur when AI systems analyze questionnaire responses using frameworks that do not adequately account for diverse cultural backgrounds, communication styles, or lived experiences (Selwyn, 2019). Universities must ensure that response analysis capabilities incorporate diverse perspectives and avoid imposing uniform interpretive frameworks on diverse populations.

Mitigation strategies should include diverse stakeholder involvement in system design and evaluation, regular bias auditing procedures, transparent algorithmic decision-making processes, and ongoing monitoring of system outcomes across different demographic groups (Floridi, 2019). Universities should also maintain human oversight mechanisms that enable identification and correction of biased outcomes.

Academic Integrity and Authenticity

The integration of AI-powered questionnaire systems raises complex questions about academic integrity, authenticity, and the appropriate role of automation in educational assessment. Universities must navigate these challenges while maintaining institutional values and ensuring that automated systems support rather than undermine educational objectives.

Research indicates that educators express significant concern about potential academic integrity issues associated with AI tool usage, with most instructors worrying that students will use AI for generating answers even when prohibited (Khlaif et al., 2024). The impact of AI on online assessment requires careful preliminary review and consideration of ethical implications (Karadağ, 2023), as these concerns extend to questionnaire contexts where AI assistance might compromise the authenticity of student responses or feedback.

Transparency requirements necessitate clear communication about AI involvement in questionnaire creation and administration. Students and other respondents should understand how AI systems contribute to assessment processes while maintaining confidence in the validity and utility of their participation (Floridi, 2019). Universities must balance transparency with maintaining natural response patterns that might be affected by excessive awareness of AI involvement.

Technological Dependence and Sustainability

Universities must carefully consider the implications of increased dependence on AI technologies for critical assessment functions while ensuring sustainable implementation approaches that maintain institutional autonomy and flexibility.

System reliability requirements become particularly critical when automated questionnaire systems support essential institutional functions such as accreditation reporting, program evaluation, and student support services. Universities must implement backup procedures, redundancy measures, and contingency plans that ensure continuity of assessment capabilities during system outages or technical failures.

Vendor dependence represents a strategic risk for universities that rely heavily on external AI service providers for questionnaire functionality. Implementation strategies should consider long-term sustainability, vendor stability, licensing terms, and potential migration requirements to avoid lock-in situations that could compromise institutional flexibility.

Cost sustainability requires careful analysis of long-term financial implications including licensing fees, infrastructure costs, training expenses, and ongoing maintenance requirements. Universities should develop cost-benefit analyses that consider both direct costs and indirect benefits such as efficiency gains and improved educational outcomes.

Technological evolution considerations require implementation approaches that accommodate rapid changes in AI capabilities and educational technology requirements. Universities should prioritize flexible architectures that enable incorporation of new AI developments while maintaining compatibility with existing institutional systems and practices.

ENHANCED FRAMEWORK FOR AUTOMATED UNIVERSITY QUESTIONNAIRE CREATION

Framework Overview

The Enhanced Framework for Automated University Questionnaire Creation represents a comprehensive system designed to address the unique requirements of higher education institutions while leveraging the capabilities of contemporary generative AI technologies. This framework consists of four interconnected components that work synergistically to produce high-quality, inclusive, and methodologically sound questionnaires for diverse university applications.

Figure 1. Overall Framework Architecture

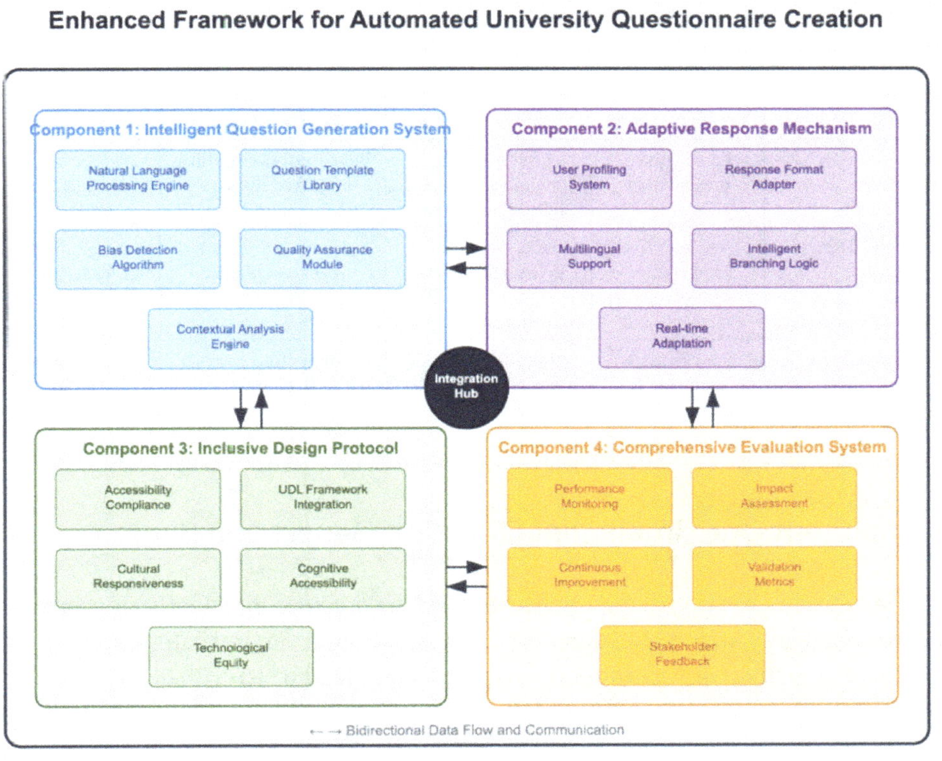

The framework adopts a holistic approach that integrates technological capabilities with pedagogical principles, accessibility standards, and institutional requirements. Rather than simply automating existing questionnaire creation processes, this framework reimagines how educational institutions can gather meaningful data about student experiences, learning outcomes, and institutional effectiveness through intelligent, adaptive, and inclusive assessment instruments.

The four core components of the framework include: the Intelligent Question Generation System, which utilizes advanced natural language processing and machine learning algorithms to create contextually appropriate questions; the Adaptive Response Mechanism, which personalizes questionnaire content and format based on individual user characteristics and preferences; the Inclusive Design Protocol, which ensures compliance with accessibility standards and universal design principles; and the Comprehensive Evaluation System, which provides ongoing assessment of questionnaire effectiveness and impact.

Table 2. Framework Components Synthesis

Component	Primary Function	Key Features	Expected Outcomes	Integration Points
Intelligent Question Generation System	AI-powered contextual question creation	NLP processing, validated templates, quality assurance	Methodologically sound questions; 60-70% time reduction	LMS, assessment databases
Adaptive Response Mechanism	Personalized presentation	User profiling, dynamic adjustment, multilingual support	Increased accessibility; improved response rates	Identity management, analytics
Inclusive Design Protocol	Accessibility and equity compliance	UDL principles, WCAG standards, cultural responsiveness	Equitable participation; legal compliance	Accessibility services, student support
Comprehensive Evaluation System	Performance monitoring and improvement	Multi-dimensional metrics, continuous feedback loops	System effectiveness; data-driven refinement	Data analytics, quality assurance

Component One: Intelligent Question Generation System

This system uses advanced generative AI to create contextually appropriate, methodologically sound questions for university questionnaires, aligning with educational objectives and institutional requirements (Isiaku et al., 2024). It processes input like educational context and target population, leveraging conversational interfaces for quick question generation (Kaival, 2025). The process begins with contextual analysis, ensuring alignment with educational best practices. The system uses NLP to avoid common pitfalls like leading language and bias (Fowler, 2013). It maintains extensive knowledge bases of validated question templates and survey logic, ensuring adherence to psychometric principles (Dillman et al., 2014). Quality assurance includes automated bias detection, accessibility compliance, and validity assessment. Feedback loops enable continuous improvement.

Component Two: Adaptive Response Mechanism

This sophisticated system personalizes questionnaire presentation based on individual user characteristics, preferences, and accessibility requirements (CAST, 2018; Rose & Meyer, 2002). It accommodates diverse learning styles and technological capabilities. AI tools provide customized support, including text-to-speech, speech-to-text, and automated translation (National Centre for AI, 2024). The mechanism uses dynamic user profiling (with consent) to adapt question formats, such as enhanced contrast or simplified language, for users with assistive technology needs (University of Pittsburgh Teaching Center, 2024). Intelligent branching logic personalizes questionnaire flow, and multilingual support ensures cultural sensitivity (Dillman et al., 2014). Real-time adaptation modifies presentation based on user behavior, maintaining motivation and data quality.

Component Three: Inclusive Design Protocol

This protocol establishes comprehensive standards for ensuring automated questionnaire systems promote accessibility, equity, and meaningful participation (CAST, 2018; Rose & Meyer, 2002). It integrates universal design principles and proactively embeds accessibility. The protocol covers physical, cognitive, linguistic, and cultural accessibility, as well as technological equity. It mandates compliance with accessibility standards (WCAG 2.1 AA), leveraging AI for enhanced audio descriptions and automatic captioning (University of Pittsburgh Teaching Center, 2024). Cognitive accessibility focuses on clear navigation, simplified language, and flexible pacing. Linguistic accessibility extends to cultural sensitivity and AI-powered translation. Cultural responsiveness guidelines ensure content reflects university diversity. Technological equity addresses disparities in device access and internet connectivity.

Component Four: Comprehensive Evaluation System

This system provides ongoing assessment of questionnaire effectiveness, impact, and alignment with institutional objectives and inclusive education principles. It evaluates technical performance (reliability, response time, accuracy), educational effectiveness (data utility, alignment with objectives), accessibility compliance, user satisfaction, and institutional impact. Technical evaluation aims for high accuracy rates. Educational effectiveness assesses data gathering and decision-making support (Ouyang et al., 2022). Accessibility compliance includes automated testing and user experience evaluation. User satisfaction gathers feedback from stakeholders. Institutional impact examines broader effects on efficiency, quality, and culture.

Table 3. Evaluation Metrics by Dimension

Evaluation Dimension	Specific Metrics	Data Sources	Assessment Frequency	Target Benchmarks
Technical Performance	System uptime, response time, error rates, AI accuracy	System logs, monitoring tools	Continuous/Real-time	99.5% uptime; <2s response time
Educational Effectiveness	Data quality, response rates, decision-making impact	Response data, usage analytics, case studies	Quarterly	>70% response rate; >4.0/5.0 data utility rating
Accessibility Compliance	WCAG conformance, AT compatibility, participation rates by disability status	Automated testing, user feedback, demographic data	Monthly	100% WCAG 2.1 AA; equitable participation rates
User Satisfaction	Interface usability, perceived value, recommendation likelihood	Surveys, interviews, focus groups	Semester	>4.0/5.0 satisfaction; >80% recommendation rate
Institutional Impact	Efficiency gains, cost savings, decision quality	Time studies, financial analysis, longitudinal studies	Annual	50-70% time reduction; positive ROI within 2 years

IMPLEMENTATION STRATEGIES AND TECHNICAL CONSIDERATIONS

Implementation Process Flow

The implementation of automated university questionnaire systems follows a systematic process that ensures quality, accessibility, and institutional alignment while leveraging advanced AI capabilities for optimal outcomes (Burns & Muscanell, 2024). This process encompasses four distinct phases that progress from initial requirements analysis through continuous evaluation and improvement.

Figure 2. Implementation Process Flow

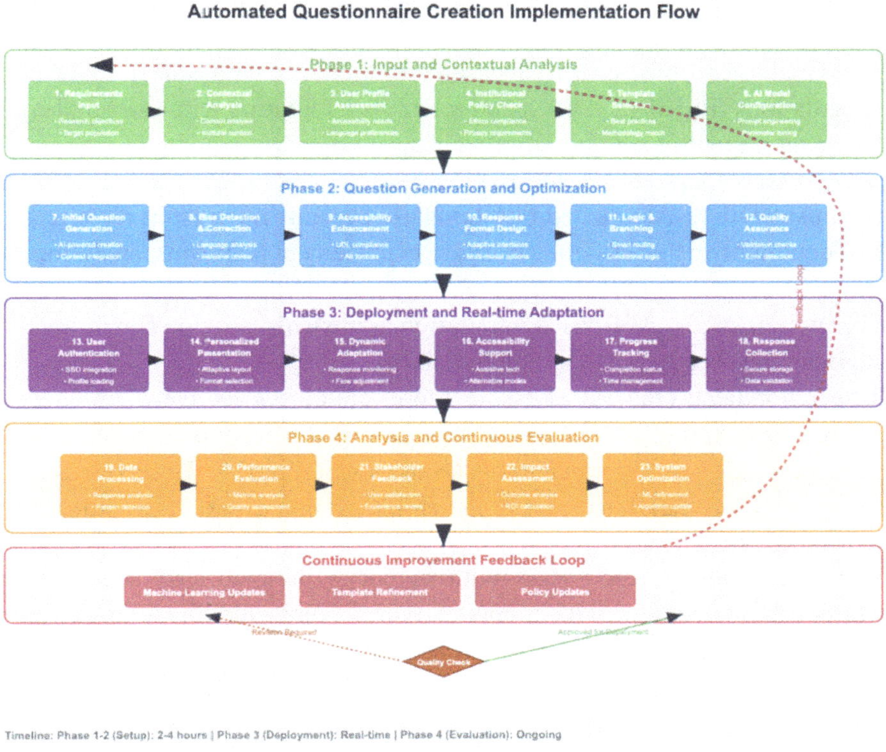

The implementation process begins with comprehensive requirements gathering and contextual analysis to understand specific institutional needs, target populations, and educational objectives (EDUCAUSE, 2024). This foundational phase ensures that automated questionnaire systems align with institutional values and educational goals while addressing unique organizational characteristics and constraints.

Infrastructure Requirements

Successful implementation of automated university questionnaire systems requires careful consideration of technological infrastructure, integration capabilities, and scalability requirements. Universities must evaluate existing technological capacity and develop implementation plans that align with institutional resources and strategic priorities (Burns & Muscanell, 2024).

Cloud-based architecture represents the preferred approach for automated questionnaire systems due to scalability advantages, maintenance efficiency, and integration capabilities. Modern survey platforms demonstrate the viability of cloud-based solutions that can handle unlimited surveys while maintaining security and performance standards (QuestionPro, 2024). Universities should prioritize solutions that offer robust security measures, compliance with educational data privacy regulations (FERPA, GDPR), and seamless integration with existing learning management systems.

Integration with university information systems constitutes a critical implementation consideration. Automated questionnaire systems must interface effectively with student information systems, learning management platforms, assessment databases, and analytics tools to maximize utility and minimize administrative burden (Hurix Digital, 2025). API-based integration approaches provide flexibility while maintaining data security and system reliability.

Research indicates that AI assessment tools are most effective when integrated smoothly with institutional learning management systems, enabling automated data transfer and grade syncing capabilities (Hurix Digital, 2025). Universities should prioritize solutions that demonstrate proven integration capabilities with their existing technological ecosystem.

Scalability planning must address both current institutional needs and anticipated growth in AI-powered assessment applications. Implementation strategies should incorporate capacity for increased usage volume, expanded functionality, and integration with emerging AI technologies. Universities should consider implementation approaches that enable gradual expansion while maintaining system stability and user experience quality.

Technical Architecture

The technical architecture for automated university questionnaire systems must balance sophisticated AI capabilities with reliability, security, and maintainability requirements. The recommended architecture employs a modular design that separates core AI functionality from institutional integration components, enabling flexible deployment and customization while maintaining system coherence.

Figure 3. Technical System Architecture

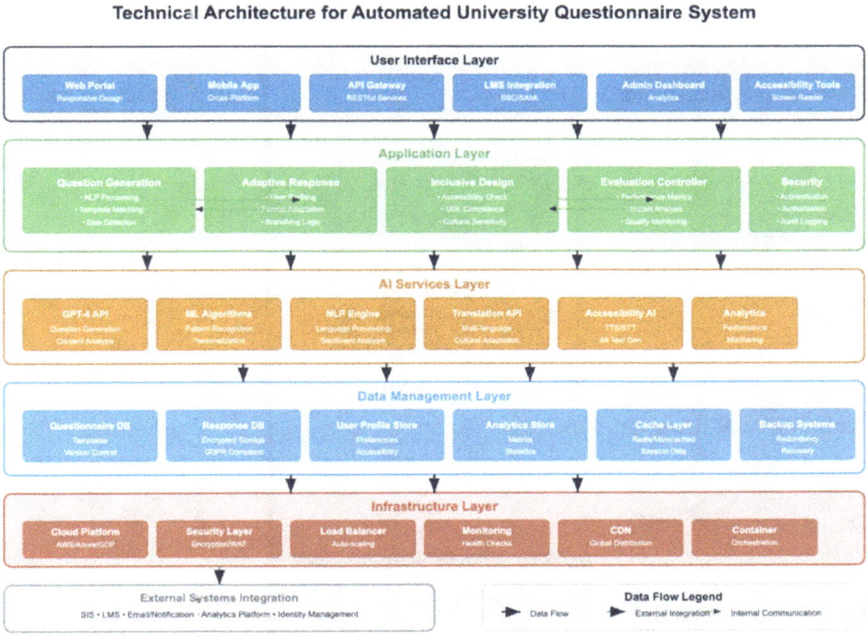

The natural language processing component serves as the foundation for question generation capabilities, requiring access to advanced language models trained on educational content and survey methodology principles. Recent developments in ChatGPT-based assessment systems demonstrate the feasibility of utilizing OpenAI's GPT models for educational applications through carefully engineered prompting strategies (Isiaku et al., 2024).

Database architecture must accommodate complex questionnaire structures, response data, user profiles, and evaluation metrics while maintaining performance and security standards. Universities should implement database solutions that support both structured and unstructured data types, enable efficient querying and analysis, and provide robust backup and recovery capabilities.

Figure 4. Data Flow and System Integration Architecture

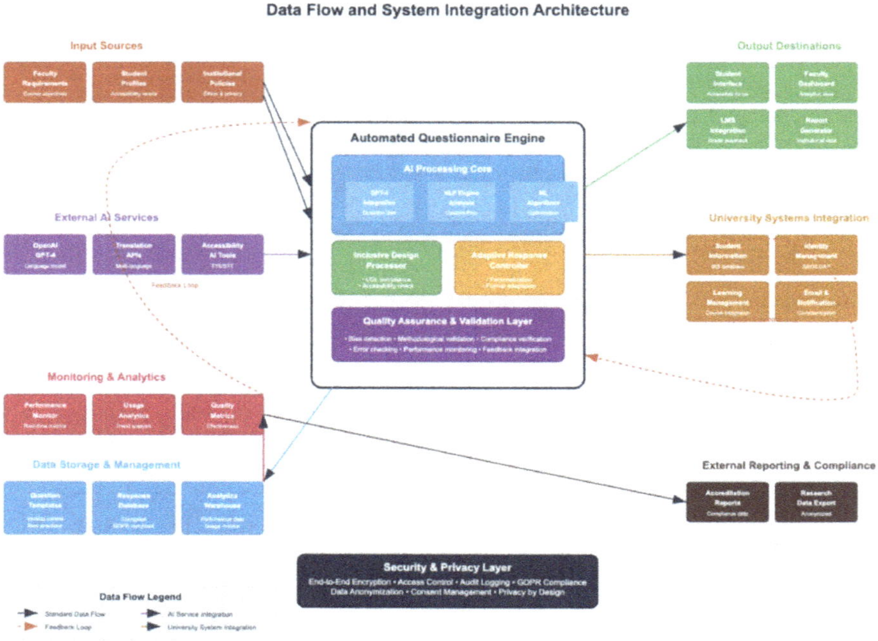

Security architecture must address multiple risk factors including data privacy, user authentication, system integrity, and compliance with educational regulations (Floridi, 2019). Implementation should incorporate encryption for data transmission and storage (AES-256, TLS 1.3), multi-factor authentication for system access, audit logging for compliance monitoring, and regular security assessment procedures.

API architecture should provide standardized interfaces for integration with existing university systems while enabling future expansion and customization. RESTful API design principles facilitate integration while maintaining system modularity and enabling third-party development of complementary tools and services.

Training and Professional Development

Successful implementation of automated questionnaire systems requires comprehensive training and professional development programs that prepare university personnel to effectively utilize new capabilities while maintaining educational quality and inclusive practices (Burns & Muscanell, 2024).

Faculty development programs must address both technical competencies and pedagogical considerations related to AI-enhanced assessment practices. Current research indicates that staff AI literacy has increased significantly, with 42% of students suggesting staff are well-equipped to help them with AI, compared with just 18% in 2024 (HEPI, 2025). However, continued professional development remains essential for ensuring effective implementation.

Training curricula should encompass AI capabilities and limitations, ethical considerations in automated assessment (Floridi, 2019), inclusive design principles (CAST, 2018), questionnaire methodology best practices (Dillman et al., 2014; Fowler, 2013), and practical system operation procedures. Professional development should adopt hands-on approaches that enable faculty to experiment with automated questionnaire creation while receiving guidance and support from educational technology specialists (EDUCAUSE, 2024).

Administrative training programs must prepare staff members to oversee system implementation, monitor performance, address technical issues, and ensure compliance with institutional policies and external regulations. This training should include project management competencies, technical troubleshooting capabilities, and understanding of evaluation metrics and improvement processes.

Student orientation programs should introduce learners to automated questionnaire systems while addressing concerns about privacy, data usage, and academic integrity. These programs should emphasize student agency in assessment processes while explaining how AI-enhanced questionnaires support educational improvement and institutional effectiveness.

CASE STUDIES AND APPLICATIONS

Illustrative Case Study One: Student Experience Assessment

Note: This case study describes a hypothetical implementation scenario for illustrative purposes to demonstrate framework application in practice.

A large public university implements the automated questionnaire framework to improve student experience assessment across its diverse population of 40,000 students. The institution seeks to gather frequent, detailed feedback while reducing administrative burden and improving response rates, particularly among underrepresented groups.

Implementation Approach: The institution begins with stakeholder consultation involving students, faculty, student affairs professionals, and disability services coordinators to identify assessment priorities and accessibility requirements. The Intelligent Question Generation System is configured with institutional priorities including academic support services, campus climate, co-curricular learning opportunities, student engagement initiatives, and wellness resources.

The Adaptive Response Mechanism accommodates diverse student populations including undergraduate and graduate students, international students (representing 15% of enrollment), students with disabilities (documented at 8%), and students from various socioeconomic backgrounds. The system provides multilingual support in the ten most common languages on campus, alternative response formats for students with disabilities, and flexible timing options for students balancing work and family responsibilities.

Expected Outcomes: Based on research demonstrating that AI-enhanced systems can improve response rates and data quality (Kaival, 2025), the institution anticipates response rate increase from current 35% to 55-65%, particularly among international students and students with disabilities; reduced questionnaire development time by 60-70%; enhanced data granularity enabling targeted interventions for specific student populations; improved accessibility compliance reducing legal risks; and greater faculty satisfaction due to reduced administrative burden.

The system generates culturally responsive questions that avoid common biases present in traditional assessment instruments while capturing nuanced experiences of diverse student populations (Noble, 2018). Real-time adaptive logic identifies students experiencing difficulties and provides appropriate support resource information integrated within the questionnaire completion process.

Illustrative Case Study Two: Course Evaluation Innovation

Note: This case study describes a hypothetical implementation scenario for illustrative purposes.

A private liberal arts college with 2,500 students utilizes the framework to transform traditional course evaluations, addressing persistent challenges including evaluation fatigue, potential bias in student feedback, and limited accessibility of standard evaluation forms. The institution's goal is creating engaging, inclusive evaluations that provide actionable feedback for faculty professional development.

Implementation Approach: The Intelligent Question Generation System is trained on the institution's educational philosophy emphasizing liberal arts learning objectives and faculty development priorities. The system generates questions aligned with institutional values including critical thinking development, interdisciplinary connections, and collaborative learning while accommodating variations in course characteristics (seminar versus lecture format), disciplinary requirements (laboratory versus discussion-based courses), and pedagogical approaches (traditional versus experiential learning).

The Adaptive Response Mechanism accommodates diverse learning styles and student preferences. Participants can choose from multiple response modalities including traditional rating scales, open-ended text responses, voice recordings for students who process verbally, and multimedia submissions for visual learners. The system automatically adjusts question complexity based on course level and student characteristics while maintaining consistency necessary for longitudinal faculty evaluation (Dillman et al., 2014).

Expected Outcomes: The college anticipates improved evaluation quality through reduced non-response bias, more thoughtful student feedback due to reduced cognitive burden, decreased evaluation fatigue through personalized pacing, enhanced accessibility for students with disabilities, and culturally responsive evaluation processes. Faculty receive richer qualitative feedback for professional development while maintaining quantitative data necessary for promotion and tenure decisions (Fowler, 2013).

Illustrative Case Study Three: Research Survey Development Support

Note: This case study describes a hypothetical implementation scenario for illustrative purposes

A research-intensive university implements the framework to support faculty and student researchers in developing survey instruments for educational research projects. The institutional research center seeks to improve research quality while reducing the time and expertise required for questionnaire development, particularly supporting novice researchers who may lack extensive survey methodology training.

Implementation Approach: The system is configured to incorporate educational research ethics standards, institutional review board (IRB) requirements, and disciplinary best practices from various fields represented within the university community. The Intelligent Question Generation System maintains knowledge bases covering research methodology, measurement theory, and domain-specific considerations for different academic disciplines (Dillman et al., 2014; Fowler, 2013).

Researchers interact with the system through a conversational interface, describing their research questions, target populations, theoretical frameworks, and methodological approaches (Kaival, 2025). The system generates appropriate questionnaire items, suggests validated scales from existing literature, identifies potential validity threats, and recommends pilot testing procedures consistent with established research standards.

RISK MANAGEMENT AND MITIGATION STRATEGIES

Technological Risk Assessment

Automated university questionnaire systems face technological risks including system reliability issues, integration challenges, security vulnerabilities, and vendor dependence concerns (Burns & Muscanell, 2024). System reliability risks include AI service failures, database corruption, network connectivity problems, and software bugs necessitating comprehensive backup and disaster recovery procedures. Integration challenges with existing university systems can cause data synchronization errors, workflow disruptions, and user experience inconsistencies. Security risks involve unauthorized access attempts, cyberattacks targeting educational data, and data breaches requiring secure infrastructure (Floridi, 2019). Vendor dependence risks include service disruptions or pricing changes, requiring careful vendor evaluation and contingency planning. Performance degradation due to increased usage loads or AI model limitations needs ongoing monitoring and optimization.

Table 4. Risk Mitigation Strategies

Risk Category	Specific Risks	Mitigation Strategies	Monitoring Approach
Technical Reliability	System downtime, AI failures, integration errors	Redundant systems, backup procedures, SLAs with vendors	Real-time monitoring, incident tracking, performance dashboards
Data Security	Unauthorized access, data breaches, privacy violations	Encryption (AES-256, TLS 1.3), multi-factor authentication, security audits	Continuous security scanning, penetration testing, compliance audits
Algorithmic Bias	Discriminatory outputs, exclusionary design	Bias auditing, diverse training data, human oversight, stakeholder involvement	Regular bias assessments, disaggregated outcome monitoring
Academic Integrity	AI misuse, response authenticity issues	Detection algorithms, verification protocols, educational guidance	Pattern analysis, spot auditing, behavioral analytics
Vendor Dependence	Service disruptions, vendor failure, price increases	Multi-vendor strategy, data portability provisions, exit planning	Vendor performance monitoring, contract reviews, market analysis

Data Security and Privacy Framework

Protecting sensitive educational data requires comprehensive security frameworks that comply with privacy regulations including FERPA and GDPR (Floridi, 2019). Encryption protocols must secure data during transmission, processing, and storage using industry-standard algorithms (AES-256 for stored data, TLS 1.3 for transmission) and secure key management practices. Access control systems should implement the principle of least privilege with role-based access for different user types (students, faculty, administrators, researchers), multi-factor authentication for sensitive operations, and comprehensive audit trails of all data access and modifications. Data anonymization procedures must protect individual privacy while preserving data utility for aggregate analysis and institutional research. Consent management systems need to provide transparent information about data collection purposes, granular control over data sharing preferences, easy withdrawal mechanisms, and clear communication about data retention policies. Incident response procedures are crucial for detecting security breaches, containing incidents, investigating root causes, recovering compromised data, and notifying affected parties according to regulatory requirements. Regular security auditing, including automated vulnerability monitoring and manual security reviews, is essential for identifying vulnerabilities and implementing improvements.

INTERNATIONAL PERSPECTIVES AND GLOBAL IMPLEMENTATION

Cross-cultural Design Considerations

Implementing automated questionnaire systems in international university contexts requires sophisticated understanding of cultural differences in communication patterns, educational expectations, assessment preferences, and technology usage patterns (Selwyn, 2019). These considerations ensure that automated systems promote rather than hinder cross-cultural understanding and inclusive participation.

Communication style variations across cultures affect question interpretation, response patterns, and engagement preferences in ways that automated systems must accommodate. High-context cultures (e.g., many East Asian and Middle Eastern societies) may prefer indirect communication approaches emphasizing relational harmony, while low-context cultures (e.g., North American and Northern European societies) favor explicit, direct questioning (Dillman et al., 2014). Automated systems require adaptive presentation capabilities that respect cultural communication norms without compromising data quality.

Educational tradition differences influence expectations about assessment format, response requirements, evaluation criteria, and feedback provision across different cultural contexts. With emerging technologies such as generative AI, we should be able to create theoretical, conceptual, and technological artifacts that can tackle these gaps, and provide strategies and tools ranging from policy to practice (Jin et al., 2024), emphasizing the need for culturally responsive technological solutions.

Power distance considerations affect how respondents from different cultures interact with institutional assessment systems, particularly regarding willingness to provide critical feedback or express disagreement with authority figures (Selwyn, 2019). Automated systems must accommodate these cultural variations through features such as anonymous response options, varied question framing that respects different power dynamics, and culturally appropriate feedback mechanisms, while ensuring meaningful data collection across diverse populations.

Collectivist versus individualist cultural orientations influence response patterns, with some cultures emphasizing group harmony and collective identity while others prioritize individual expression and personal achievement. Questionnaire systems must provide response options and formats that accommodate these different cultural orientations without introducing systematic bias (Noble, 2018).

Regulatory Compliance Across Jurisdictions

Universities operating across multiple jurisdictions face complex regulatory requirements for data protection, privacy rights, educational assessment, and technology usage that automated questionnaire systems must accommodate (Floridi, 2019). These requirements vary significantly across different countries and regions while evolving rapidly in response to technological developments.

European Union General Data Protection Regulation (GDPR) requirements establish comprehensive standards for data collection, processing, storage, and sharing that affect university questionnaire systems serving EU residents. Compliance requires explicit consent mechanisms, data minimization practices, right to erasure capabilities, and data portability features that may not be required in other jurisdictions.

United States educational privacy regulations including Family Educational Rights and Privacy Act (FERPA) requirements affect questionnaire systems that collect information about students while establishing specific protections for educational records and directory information. Compliance requires careful classification of questionnaire data, implementation of appropriate access controls, and documented disclosure procedures.

Regional and national data localization requirements may restrict where questionnaire data can be stored or processed while affecting choice of cloud service providers and system architecture decisions. Universities must evaluate data residency requirements across all jurisdictions where they operate while ensuring system functionality and performance (Burns & Muscanell, 2024).

COST-BENEFIT ANALYSIS AND RESOURCE PLANNING

Financial Impact Assessment

Universities considering automated questionnaire system implementation require comprehensive financial analysis that examines both direct costs and indirect benefits while accounting for long-term sustainability and return on investment considerations (Burns & Muscanell, 2024). This analysis provides essential information for institutional decision-making while supporting strategic planning for technology adoption and resource allocation.

Direct implementation costs include software licensing fees (typically ranging from $10,000-$100,000 annually depending on institution size and feature requirements), hardware infrastructure requirements (cloud services estimated at $5,000-$30,000 annually), integration development expenses (one-time costs of $20,000-$150,000), training program costs ($10,000-$50,000 for comprehensive programs), and ongoing maintenance and support expenses (typically 15-20% of initial implementation costs annually).

Personnel cost analysis examines changes in staffing requirements including potential reductions in questionnaire development time, shifts in skill requirements for assessment professionals toward data analysis and interpretation, and new training needs for faculty and support staff in AI-enhanced assessment practices. These changes may result in net cost savings while requiring investment in professional development and skill enhancement.

Efficiency benefits encompass time savings in questionnaire development, administration, and analysis processes that enable reallocation of human resources to higher-value activities such as data interpretation, educational improvement initiatives, and direct student support. Quality improvement benefits include enhanced data accuracy, increased response rates, improved accessibility compliance, and better alignment with institutional objectives that contribute to more effective institutional decision-making and educational outcomes.

Scalability economics examine how per-unit costs change with increased system usage while identifying optimal deployment strategies that maximize return on investment. Automated systems typically demonstrate favorable scalability characteristics with decreasing marginal costs as usage volume increases. Risk mitigation value encompasses the financial benefits of reduced exposure to compliance violations, data breaches, accessibility lawsuits, and other potential liabilities that automated systems help prevent through improved security, compliance monitoring, and accessibility features.

VALIDATION AND QUALITY CONTROL MECHANISMS

Comprehensive Testing Protocols

Rigorous validation of automated questionnaire systems requires systematic testing protocols that examine system functionality, output quality, user experience, and alignment with educational objectives across diverse implementation scenarios. These protocols ensure that automated systems meet institutional requirements while maintaining reliability and effectiveness.

Functional testing evaluates core system capabilities including question generation accuracy, adaptive response functionality, accessibility feature operation, and integration with university systems. Testing must encompass various usage scenarios, user types, and operational conditions to ensure robust performance across diverse implementation contexts.

Content validation examines the quality, appropriateness, and effectiveness of AI-generated questionnaire content through expert review, stakeholder feedback, and comparative analysis with manually developed alternatives. Research on GPT-4 generated content for educational applications demonstrates successful validation approaches for AI-generated educational content that can inform questionnaire system evaluation (Isiaku et al., 2024).

Usability testing involves systematic evaluation of user interface design, navigation effectiveness, accessibility compliance, and overall user experience across diverse user populations and device types. This testing identifies potential barriers to effective participation while informing interface improvements and accessibility enhancements (CAST, 2018).

Performance testing examines system responsiveness, scalability, reliability, and resource utilization under various load conditions while identifying optimal configuration parameters and potential bottlenecks. Performance testing ensures that systems can accommodate anticipated usage patterns while maintaining acceptable response times.

Security testing evaluates system vulnerability to various attack vectors, data protection effectiveness, access control functionality, and compliance with security requirements (Floridi, 2019). Security testing must encompass both automated vulnerability scanning and manual penetration testing while examining integration security with university systems.

Integration testing examines system compatibility and functionality when connected with various university systems including student information systems, learning management platforms, identity management services, and analytics tools. Integration testing ensures seamless operation while identifying potential compatibility issues or performance impacts.

Quality Metrics and Benchmarking

Establishing comprehensive quality metrics enables systematic evaluation of automated questionnaire system performance while providing benchmarks for comparison with alternative approaches and identification of improvement opportunities. These metrics must encompass multiple dimensions of system effectiveness while accommodating diverse institutional contexts and objectives.

Accuracy metrics examine the correctness and appropriateness of AI-generated questionnaire content through comparison with expert-developed alternatives, stakeholder evaluations, and outcome analysis. Efficiency metrics measure time savings in questionnaire development, administration, and analysis processes while examining resource utilization and productivity improvements.

Accessibility metrics assess system compliance with universal design principles, accommodation effectiveness, and participation rates across diverse user populations (CAST, 2018). User satisfaction metrics examine stakeholder experiences with automated questionnaire systems including interface usability, perceived value, recommendation likelihood, and overall satisfaction ratings. Data quality metrics evaluate the completeness, accuracy, and utility of questionnaire responses while examining response rates, completion patterns, and subsequent data usage effectiveness (Dillman et al., 2014).

System reliability metrics monitor uptime, error rates, performance consistency, and recovery capabilities while identifying potential improvements to system stability and user experience. Reliability metrics ensure that automated systems provide dependable service while maintaining institutional confidence and user trust.

Continuous Improvement Processes

Automated questionnaire systems require systematic improvement processes that enable ongoing enhancement based on user feedback, performance data, technological developments, and evolving institutional needs. These processes ensure that systems remain current, effective, and aligned with institutional objectives while adapting to changing educational environments.

Feedback collection mechanisms gather input from diverse stakeholders including students, faculty, administrators, and external users while providing systematic analysis of improvement suggestions and prioritization of enhancement opportunities. Effective feedback systems balance comprehensive input gathering with manageable analysis and response processes.

Performance monitoring systems continuously track key performance indicators while identifying trends, anomalies, and improvement opportunities through automated analysis and alert systems. Monitoring capabilities enable proactive system management while providing data for evidence-based decision-making about system enhancements.

User behavior analysis examines interaction patterns, completion behaviors, and usage trends to identify optimization opportunities and potential user experience improvements. This analysis can reveal insights about effective questionnaire design, optimal presentation approaches, and successful engagement strategies.

Technology update evaluation examines emerging AI capabilities, educational technology developments, and best practice evolution to identify opportunities for system enhancement and capability expansion. Regular technology review ensures that systems remain current with advancing capabilities while maintaining compatibility and reliability.

Iterative development processes enable systematic implementation of improvements through careful planning, testing, and deployment procedures that minimize disruption while enhancing system capabilities. These processes should incorporate user feedback, performance data, and strategic objectives while maintaining system stability and reliability.

ADVANCED FEATURES AND CAPABILITIES

Intelligent Personalization Systems

Contemporary automated questionnaire systems must incorporate sophisticated personalization capabilities that extend beyond basic demographic adaptations to encompass complex individual learning profiles, cultural backgrounds, and dynamic preference evolution (National Centre for AI, 2024; Tonbuloğlu, 2023). These systems leverage machine learning algorithms to continuously refine personalization approaches based on accumulated interaction data and outcome patterns.

The personalization engine operates through multi-dimensional user modeling that considers cognitive processing preferences, communication styles, technological comfort levels, and accessibility requirements. Research demonstrates that AI can provide various forms of support for neurodiverse and SEND students, including personalized learning experiences, adaptive assessments, assistive technologies, and behavioral support (National Centre for AI, 2024), highlighting the importance of comprehensive personalization approaches. AI applications enable the creation of personalized learning opportunities and well-designed instructional content with effective use of visuals, sounds, and interactive elements (Tonbuloğlu, 2023).

Advanced personalization incorporates temporal factors that recognize how user preferences and capabilities may evolve throughout academic terms, degree programs, and career development. The system maintains historical profiles while adapting to changing circumstances such as increased technological proficiency, evolving accessibility needs, or shifting cultural contexts for international students.

Cultural personalization represents a particularly complex dimension that requires understanding of diverse communication norms, educational expectations, and assessment preferences across different cultural backgrounds. Generative AI demonstrates potential for creating educational materials in multiple languages (National Centre for AI, 2024), demonstrating the technical capability for culturally responsive questionnaire design.

Real-time Adaptive Logic Systems

Modern automated questionnaire systems require sophisticated adaptive logic capabilities that enable dynamic modification of questionnaire flow, content presentation, and response collection based on real-time analysis of user behavior and response patterns. These systems represent significant advancement over traditional static survey instruments that provide identical experiences regardless of individual respondent characteristics or engagement patterns.

The adaptive logic engine continuously monitors multiple indicators including response completion time, answer quality metrics, engagement level indicators, and navigation patterns to assess optimal questionnaire modifications. Research indicates that AI assessment tools are most effective when integrated smoothly with institutional learning management systems, enabling automated data transfer and seamless user experiences (Hurix Digital, 2025), emphasizing the importance of seamless integration for adaptive functionality.

Intelligent branching algorithms determine optimal question sequencing based on response content analysis and user behavior patterns. These algorithms can identify when respondents may benefit from clarifying questions, alternative response formats, or simplified language options while maintaining survey validity and reliability requirements (Dillman et al., 2014).

Multilingual and Cross-cultural Adaptation

Universities serving diverse international populations require automated questionnaire systems that provide sophisticated multilingual support extending beyond simple translation to encompass cultural adaptation, contextual relevance, and linguistic accessibility for non-native speakers. These capabilities ensure meaningful participation across diverse cultural and linguistic backgrounds while maintaining measurement validity (Dillman et al., 2014).

Advanced translation systems incorporate contextual understanding that preserves meaning and cultural appropriateness across different languages and cultural contexts. Generative AI tools can generate bilingual content tailored to specific learning needs (National Centre for AI, 2024), demonstrating the technical feasibility of sophisticated multilingual content generation.

Cultural adaptation algorithms analyze questionnaire content for potential cultural bias, inappropriate examples, or concepts that may not translate effectively across different cultural contexts. These algorithms can suggest alternative phrasings, culturally appropriate examples, or modified response formats that maintain questionnaire validity while improving cultural relevance.

Cross-cultural validation protocols ensure that translated and adapted questionnaires maintain measurement equivalence across different cultural and linguistic groups (Dillman et al., 2014). These protocols incorporate statistical analysis of response patterns, cultural expert review, and ongoing validation studies to maintain scientific rigor in diverse implementation contexts.

FUTURE DIRECTIONS AND EMERGING TECHNOLOGIES

Advanced AI Capabilities

The rapid evolution of artificial intelligence technologies presents opportunities for enhancing automated questionnaire systems beyond current capabilities while raising new challenges for implementation and oversight (Selwyn, 2019). Universities must remain informed about emerging AI developments while carefully evaluating their potential benefits and risks for educational assessment applications.

Multimodal AI capabilities promise to expand questionnaire possibilities beyond traditional text-based formats to include voice interactions enabling hands-free questionnaire completion, visual elements supporting diverse learning preferences, video responses capturing richer qualitative feedback, and gesture-based interfaces accommodating physical disabilities. While current large language models remain primarily text-based, emerging capabilities for multimedia processing offer potential for more engaging and accessible assessment experiences (Isiaku et al., 2024).

Advanced personalization algorithms may enable questionnaire systems to adapt not only to stated user preferences but also to learned patterns of engagement, comprehension indicators, response quality signals, and evolving user needs over time. These capabilities could optimize questionnaire experiences for individual users while maintaining standardization necessary for meaningful data aggregation and analysis.

Predictive analytics integration could enable questionnaire systems to anticipate assessment needs, identify potential challenges before they emerge, recommend proactive interventions, and optimize institutional decision-making based on historical patterns and real-time indicators (Ouyang et al., 2022). These capabilities might support early warning systems for student support services or predictive models for educational outcome improvement.

Integration with Learning Analytics

The convergence of automated questionnaire systems with comprehensive learning analytics platforms presents opportunities for creating a more holistic understanding of student experiences and educational effectiveness (Ouyang et al., 2022). This integration requires careful consideration of data architecture, privacy implications, and analytical methodologies.

Real-time assessment integration could enable questionnaire systems to automatically generate assessment instruments based on learning analytics data, course activity patterns, and student performance indicators. This capability might support more responsive and targeted data collection that addresses emerging issues and opportunities as they develop (Hurix Digital, 2025).

Longitudinal data integration could connect questionnaire responses with long-term student outcome data to validate assessment effectiveness and identify factors that contribute to student success. This longitudinal approach requires robust data management capabilities and sophisticated analytical methodologies that respect privacy while generating actionable insights (Dillman et al., 2014).

Emerging Assessment Paradigms

Automated questionnaire systems may contribute to fundamental shifts in educational assessment paradigms that move beyond traditional survey approaches toward more dynamic, interactive, and responsive data collection methods (Biesta, 2010; Selwyn, 2019).

Research on AI-resistant assessments suggests that future evaluation methods will increasingly focus on higher-order thinking skills such as critical analysis, creativity, ethical reasoning, and complex problem-solving that cannot be easily replicated by AI systems (Khlaif et al., 2024). Automated questionnaire systems must evolve to support these sophisticated assessment approaches while maintaining accessibility and efficiency.

Adaptive assessment paradigms enabled by AI technologies might create questionnaire experiences that continuously adjust based on response patterns, ensuring optimal challenge levels and engagement while gathering comprehensive data about student capabilities and experiences (CAST, 2018; Rose & Meyer, 2002).

IMPLEMENTATION RECOMMENDATIONS

Institutional Readiness Assessment

Universities considering implementation of automated questionnaire systems should conduct comprehensive readiness assessments that examine technological capacity, organizational culture, stakeholder preparedness, and strategic alignment (EDUCAUSE, 2024). These assessments provide foundation for successful implementation while identifying potential challenges and resource requirements.

Educational institutions can utilize AI readiness assessment frameworks that examine strategy, governance, technology, workforce, and teaching and learning dimensions to evaluate preparedness for AI initiatives (EDUCAUSE, 2024). These frameworks provide structured approaches for institutional self-assessment and improvement planning.

Technological readiness assessment should examine existing infrastructure capabilities, integration requirements with current systems, security provisions and compliance capabilities, scalability potential for anticipated growth, and staff technical expertise and support capacity. Organizational readiness assessment should consider institutional culture regarding technology adoption, change management capabilities, stakeholder support and potential resistance factors, resource availability for implementation and ongoing operation, and strategic alignment with institutional priorities.

Phased Implementation Strategy

Universities should adopt phased implementation approaches that enable gradual system deployment while maintaining institutional stability and allowing for learning and adjustment throughout the process (Burns & Muscanell, 2024). Phased strategies reduce implementation risks while providing opportunities for stakeholder feedback and system refinement.

Pilot phase implementation should focus on limited applications with carefully selected stakeholders who can provide detailed feedback about system performance and user experience. Expansion phase implementation should gradually increase system usage scope while maintaining careful monitoring of performance, user satisfaction, and educational outcomes. Full deployment should occur only after successful completion of pilot and expansion phases with demonstrated system reliability, user acceptance, and educational effectiveness.

Stakeholder Engagement Strategies

Successful implementation of automated questionnaire systems requires active engagement and collaboration among diverse institutional stakeholders including students, faculty, administrators, technology professionals, and external partners (Burns & Muscanell, 2024). Engagement strategies should recognize the diverse perspectives and interests of different stakeholder groups while building consensus around implementation objectives and approaches.

Student engagement should emphasize transparency about system capabilities and limitations while soliciting feedback about user experience preferences and accessibility requirements. Research emphasizes the importance of consulting students when designing questionnaires, as they possess detailed insights into issues valued by student communities (HEPI, 2025).

Faculty engagement should address both pedagogical and practical considerations related to automated questionnaire implementation. Faculty members require understanding of how AI-enhanced assessment tools can support their educational objectives while maintaining academic freedom and professional judgment (Khlaif et al., 2024).

CONCLUSION

The Enhanced Framework for Automated University Questionnaire Creation represents a significant advancement in educational assessment by integrating generative AI with established principles of survey methodology (Dillman et al., 2014; Fowler, 2013), Universal Design for Learning (CAST, 2018; Rose & Meyer, 2002), and inclusive education (National Centre for AI, 2024). This comprehensive framework addresses critical challenges facing higher education institutions including efficiency demands, accessibility requirements, cultural responsiveness needs, and data quality expectations.

The four-component framework—Intelligent Question Generation System, Adaptive Response Mechanism, Inclusive Design Protocol, and Comprehensive Evaluation System—provides a structured approach for universities to implement AI-enhanced questionnaire systems while maintaining methodological rigor, ethical standards, and educational quality (Isiaku et al., 2024). The hypothetical case applications demonstrate potential for improved response rates, enhanced data quality, reduced administrative burden, and increased accessibility across diverse student populations.

However, successful implementation requires addressing significant challenges including data privacy protection (Floridi, 2019), algorithmic bias mitigation

(Noble, 2018; O'Neil, 2016), academic integrity preservation (Khlaif et al., 2024), and sustainable resource management (Burns & Muscanell, 2024). Universities must approach AI adoption thoughtfully, considering implications for accessibility, identity, and epistemology while maintaining commitment to inclusive excellence (National Centre for AI, 2024).

The ethical imperative for thoughtful AI integration in educational assessment cannot be overstated. As Floridi (2019) argues, AI systems must be designed and deployed in ways that promote human flourishing, respect autonomy, ensure fairness, and prevent harm. Selwyn's (2019) critical perspective reminds us that educational technology adoption must account for power relations, social contexts, and potential unintended consequences rather than assuming technological solutions automatically improve educational outcomes.

Future advancements in AI technologies, including improved natural language processing, enhanced personalization capabilities, and multimodal interaction possibilities, will further transform automated questionnaire systems (Hurix Digital, 2025; Isiaku et al., 2024). However, technological capabilities must be balanced with ethical considerations, pedagogical principles, and practical implementation realities.

Universities seeking to implement automated questionnaire systems should adopt phased approaches that begin with comprehensive readiness assessment (EDUCAUSE, 2024), proceed through carefully designed pilot implementations, and scale gradually based on evidence of effectiveness and stakeholder feedback. Success hinges on sustained commitment to inclusive design (CAST, 2018; Rose & Meyer, 2002), active stakeholder engagement (Burns & Muscanell, 2024), continuous improvement mechanisms, and ethical technology use (Floridi, 2019).

The framework offers universities a practical pathway toward more efficient, effective, and inclusive assessment practices that support institutional missions while promoting educational equity. However, implementation requires careful attention to institutional context, adequate resource allocation, comprehensive training programs, and ongoing evaluation to ensure systems achieve intended benefits while avoiding potential harms (Selwyn, 2019).

As generative AI continues transforming higher education, universities must thoughtfully consider how these technologies can enhance rather than replace human judgment, promote rather than hinder educational equity, and support rather than undermine academic integrity (Khlaif et al., 2024). The Enhanced Framework for Automated University Questionnaire Creation provides one model for achieving these objectives through systematic integration of technological capabilities with educational principles, ethical standards, and inclusive practices.

Ongoing research, professional collaboration, and institutional learning will be essential for realizing the full potential of AI-enhanced questionnaire systems while addressing challenges and avoiding pitfalls. By maintaining commitment to educational quality, ethical technology use, and inclusive excellence, universities can harness AI capabilities to create more effective assessment practices that serve diverse student populations and support institutional missions (National Centre for AI, 2024).

The path forward requires vigilance regarding potential risks, openness to innovation, commitment to equity, and sustained attention to the human dimensions of educational assessment that technology can support but never fully replace (Biesta, 2010; Selwyn, 2019).

REFERENCES

Biesta, G. (2010). *Good education in an age of measurement: Ethics, politics, democracy*. Routledge., DOI: 10.4324/9781315634319

Burns, S., & Muscanell, N. (2024). EDUCAUSE QuickPoll results: A growing need for generative AI strategy. *EDUCAUSE Review*. https://er.educause.edu/articles/2024/4/educause-quickpoll-results-a-growing-need-for-generative-ai-strategy

CAST. (2018). *Universal Design for Learning Guidelines version 2.2*. Retrieved from http://udlguidelines.cast.org

Dillman, D. A., Smyth, J. D., & Christian, L. M. (2014). *Internet, phone, mail, and mixed-mode surveys: The tailored design method* (4th ed.). John Wiley & Sons.

EDUCAUSE. (2024). Higher education generative AI readiness assessment. *EDUCAUSE Library*. Retrieved from https://library.educause.edu/resources/2024/4/higher-education-generative-ai-readiness-assessment

Floridi, L. (2019). Establishing the rules for building trustworthy AI. *Nature Machine Intelligence*, *1*(6), 261–262. DOI: 10.1038/s42256-019-0055-y

Fowler, F. J. (2013). *Survey research methods* (5th ed.). SAGE Publications.

HEPI. (2025). Student generative AI survey 2025. *Higher Education Policy Institute*. Retrieved from https://www.hepi.ac.uk/2025/02/26/student-generative-ai-survey-2025/

Hurix Digital. (2025). AI-enabled assessment: Redefining evaluation in education. Retrieved from https://www.hurix.com/blogs/ai-enabled-assessment-redefining-evaluation-in-education/

Isiaku, L., Muhammad, A. S., Kefas, H. I., & Ukaegbu, F. C. (2024). Enhancing technological sustainability in academia: Leveraging ChatGPT for teaching, learning and evaluation. *Quality Education for All*, *1*(1), 385–416. DOI: 10.1108/QEA-07-2024-0055

Jin, Y., Yan, L., Echeverria, V., Gašević, D., & Martinez-Maldonado, R. (2024). Generative AI in higher education: A global perspective of institutional adoption policies and guidelines. *arXiv preprint arXiv:2405.11800*. https://doi.org//arXiv.2405.11800DOI: 10.48550

Kaival. (2025). Enhancing survey creation with generative AI: A guide to dynamic and customized questionnaires. *Medium*. Retrieved from https://medium.com/@Neopric/enhancing-survey-creation-with-generative-ai-a-guide-to-dynamic-and-customized-questionnaires-91dc8961d854

Karadağ, N. (2023). The impact of artificial intelligence on online assessment: A preliminary review. *Journal of Educational Technology and Online Learning*, *6*(4), 822–837. DOI: 10.31681/jetol.1351548

Khlaif, Z. N., Ayyoub, A., Hamamra, B., Bensalem, E., Mitwally, M. A., Ayyoub, A., Mogannam, B., Sanmugam, M., Joma, A. I., Itmazi, J., Shaqour, A. Z., & Tairab, H. (2024). University teachers' views on the adoption and integration of generative AI tools for student assessment in higher education. *Education Sciences*, *14*(10), 1090. DOI: 10.3390/educsci14101090

Kılınç, S. (2024). Comprehensive AI assessment framework: Enhancing educational evaluation with ethical AI integration. *Journal of Educational Technology and Online Learning*, *7*(4), 521–540. DOI: 10.31681/jetol.1492695

National Centre for AI. (2024). AI: Empowering inclusive education - Supporting special needs and tackling language barriers. Retrieved from https://nationalcentreforai.jiscinvolve.org/wp/2024/01/09/ai-empowering-inclusive-education/

Noble, S. U. (2018). *Algorithms of oppression: How search engines reinforce racism*. NYU Press.

O'Neil, C. (2016). *Weapons of math destruction: How big data increases inequality and threatens democracy*. Crown.

Ouyang, F., Zheng, L., & Jiao, P. (2022). Artificial intelligence in online higher education: A systematic review of empirical research from 2011 to 2020. *Education and Information Technologies*, *27*(6), 7893–7925. DOI: 10.1007/s10639-022-10925-9

QuestionPro. (2024). QuestionPro AI: Build surveys using artificial intelligence. Retrieved from https://www.questionpro.com/features/qxbot.html

Rose, D. H., & Meyer, A. (2002). *Teaching every student in the digital age: Universal Design for Learning*. Association for Supervision and Curriculum Development.

Selwyn, N. (2019). *Should robots replace teachers? AI and the future of education*. Polity Press.

Tonbuloğlu, B. (2023). An evaluation of the use of artificial intelligence applications in online education. *Journal of Educational Technology and Online Learning*, *6*(4), 866–884. DOI: 10.31681/jetol.1335906

University of Pittsburgh Teaching Center. (2024). Using generative AI to create more accessible student learning experiences. Retrieved from https://teaching.pitt.edu/resources/using-generative-ai-to-create-more-accessible-student-learning-experiences/

Chapter 5
AI-Based Adaptive Learning Systems for Developing Writing Skills in Primary Education:
A Model Proposal

Güliz Şahin
https://orcid.org/0000-0003-4487-5258
Balikesir University, Turkey

ABSTRACT

This chapter explores the potential of artificial intelligence (AI)-based adaptive learning systems in supporting the development of writing skills among primary school students. Building on theoretical foundations such as Vygotsky's Zone of Proximal Development, Bruner's stages of cognitive growth, and process-based writing instruction, the chapter introduces the AI-Assisted Adaptive Writing Instruction with Teacher Scaffolding (AAWIT) Model. The model integrates real-time AI feedback with teacher guidance, aiming to enhance cognitive, affective, and social learning outcomes while ensuring inclusivity and educational equity. The chapter discusses the stages of the model, highlights the dual roles of teachers and digital systems, and outlines potential benefits such as improved metacognitive awareness, personalized learning, and systematic monitoring of student progress. Limitations related to developmental appropriateness, teacher competence, digital inequality, and ethical data use are critically examined, followed by recommendations for future research and implementation.

DOI: 10.4018/979-8-3373-8805-2.ch005

INTRODUCTION

The digital transformation of the 21st century is redefining education not only through technical tools but also through innovative pedagogical approaches. In an era that calls for flexible and personalized learning experiences sensitive to students' individual differences, the role of educational technologies has become more critical than ever. One of the most remarkable aspects of this transformation is the emergence of artificial intelligence based adaptive learning systems (AI-ALS). By offering content tailored to learners' individual needs, these systems hold the potential to make the learning process not only more effective but also more inclusive and sustainable (Holmes et al., 2019; Luckin et al., 2016). At the level of primary education, where literacy skills are acquired, this process is particularly crucial as it directly shapes not only cognitive development but also students' social and emotional growth. Among these skills, writing emerges as a multidimensional competence that holistically supports linguistic development as well as creative thinking, emotional expression, and cognitive organization (Graham & Harris, 2005). Yet, the acquisition of writing skills often varies greatly from student to student. Hokanson (2022) emphasizes that educational technologies are not only tools that support learning but also the driving force behind digital transformation on a global scale. Similarly, in this study, artificial intelligence-based adaptive learning systems are considered a dynamic structure at the center of educational transformation.

Writing is a multilayered ability encompassing not only linguistic but also cognitive, affective, and socio-cultural domains. For this reason, teaching writing goes beyond teaching spelling or grammar; it is also about planning, structuring, and expressing thought effectively. The process-based approach to writing instruction deepens learning by positioning writing within a cycle of drafting, feedback, revision, and reproduction (Graves, 1983; Flower & Hayes, 1981). In this approach, supporting students' individual writing processes fosters metacognitive awareness and positive attitudes toward writing. In primary schools, however, writing instruction is often product-oriented and focused on accuracy, while structured guidance for the writing process remains limited (Akyol, 2019). The initial literacy stage represents the child's first encounter with written language, and this experience significantly influences future academic life.

In Turkey, mother tongue education is structured around a phonics-based approach, organized in letter groups. Within this process, writing skills are introduced through line-drawing exercises, letter formation, and short sentences, with instruction emphasizing fundamental technical skills (MEB, 2024). It is observed that teacher guidance in students' writing processes largely relies on classroom observation and the evaluation of written products; however, digital technologies—particularly AI-supported personalized learning systems—have not yet been widely integrated into the writing process. This situation also brings about the problem of failing to utilize the potential of technology effectively from a pedagogical perspective. In contrast, countries such as Finland, Canada, and Australia adopt meaning-centered models built on children's experiences, emphasizing meaning-making through multimodal and play-based practices. In these contexts, students are introduced to supportive technologies from early ages to foster writing production (Neuman & Roskos, 2007).

Where do artificial intelligence and adaptive learning systems fit into this process? AI, with its ability to collect and analyze data on learners' cognitive processes and deliver personalized content based on these analyses, holds transformative potential in education. Adaptive learning systems, in particular, dynamically shape the learning process according to students' learning pace, response accuracy, content preferences, and error types (Luckin et al., 2016). In the context of writing skills, these systems can analyze a student's text in terms of grammar, lexical variety, coherence, and content, providing immediate feedback. They may also recommend supplementary materials in areas where the student struggles. Tools such as Grammarly, Quillionz, and Write & Improve are among the pioneering applications that guide users in the writing process through text analysis. However, most of these systems primarily target adults or advanced learners, and their pedagogical adaptation to early childhood or primary education remains underdeveloped (Zawacki-Richter et al., 2019).

A study on the effectiveness of automated writing evaluation system was also conducted by Koh (2017). He presented an experimental example of how to effectively implement an Automated Writing Evaluation (AWE) system within a process-based writing pedagogy in his research. He investigated the effective application of instantaneous feedback from AWE systems within the framework of process-based writing instruction. The study compared the relative effects of two types of interventions (continuous and intermittent feedback), varying in frequency of access to AWE feedback, on the writing performance of Korean EFL students. The findings revealed that, contrary to concerns about process-based approaches, the group receiving continuous feedback performed significantly better on content and grammar dimensions. Furthermore, the students exhibited a positive attitude toward instantaneous AWE feedback, suggesting a demand for language-related support at an early stage. This research aimed to provide empirical evidence on when and how the AWE system should be implemented to maximize its pedagogical value. Such adaptive learning systems can also provide dynamic feedback appropriate to the cognitive and emotional needs of students by personalizing the learning process (Tonbuloğlu, 2023).

In countries such as the United States and China, AI-supported writing applications are increasingly integrated into school curricula, both in academic and creative writing. Systems like IBM Watson Education and Squirrel AI, for instance, function as digital coaching tools that collaborate with teachers. Estonia, a pioneer in digitalization, has introduced AI-based learning platforms from the early grades, tailoring them to students' individual needs.

In Turkey, however, the use of AI-based applications at the primary and secondary school levels remains quite limited. Kaldırım and Tavşanlı (2021), in their thematic analysis research, found that digital tools in Turkish language teaching generally remain at a technical level and are not sufficiently integrated with pedagogical foundations. This situation highlights the need to restructure AI-supported systems in line with pedagogical design principles. OkusFocus, a new initiative in Türkiye, is an educational platform powered by artificial intelligence technology that measures the oral reading performance of primary and secondary school students in seconds. It's an innovative system designed to improve students' reading skills through AI-powered reading analysis. The system first prompts the student to read aloud, and the OkusFocus AI-powered system records their reading. Advanced AI algorithms analyze reading performance. Comprehensible, comprehensive reports are generated for teachers and parents. Finally, personalized development recommendations are provided for each student's needs. However, OkusFocus, currently available only for institutional purchases, has not been made available for use outside of institutions (OkusFocus, 2025). Focusing solely on reading performance, this initiative is planned to be expanded in the coming years to support effective native language use.

Students' learning is shaped by a variety of factors, such as their pace, interests, prior experiences, motivation, the level of family support for learning, and the overall quality of instruction (Tompkins, 2012). Consequently, the need for individualized and dynamic learning environments in writing instruction is becoming increasingly evident. At this point, AI-ALS offer promising solutions to overcome the limitations of traditional teaching methods. These systems are digital learning platforms capable of tailoring content, pace, feedback, and support according to learners' individual needs.

By analyzing students' performance, learning styles, mistakes, and progression speed, these systems personalize the learning process. In the context of writing, they can monitor text production in real time, detecting spelling errors, grammatical structures, clarity of expression, and content coherence. Based on this analysis, they provide learners with personalized suggestions appropriate to their level, thereby guiding them through the writing process (Roscoe et al., 2017). This perspective allows writing instruction to be understood not merely as a product-oriented outcome, but as a process-oriented developmental journey. Moreover, when considered within the framework of Vygotsky's theory of the zone of proximal development, these systems can serve as a form of "digital scaffolding" that helps students move beyond their current potential.

In the existing literature, AI-supported writing systems have predominantly focused on second language learning (L2), academic writing, or applications at the high school and university levels (Zawacki-Richter et al., 2019; Wilson & Roscoe, 2020). However, their adaptation to the primary school level remains an underexplored area, particularly in terms of pedagogical sensitivity and developmental appropriateness. Yet, supporting writing skills at an early age provides long-term benefits not only for language learning but also for self-efficacy, confidence, and attitudes toward learning (Puranik & Lonigan, 2014). In this context, the development and implementation of AI-assisted systems that can guide children in the writing process while providing both instructive and motivating feedback is of critical importance.

For these technologies to be effectively implemented at the primary school level, it is not sufficient to rely solely on digital tools; the systematic integration of teacher guidance into the process is equally essential. The teacher is not merely a user of technology but also a mentor who ensures that technology is directed in ways most conducive to the child's development. Therefore, enhancing teachers' pedagogical and technological competencies is indispensable for the effective use of such systems (Ertmer & Ottenbreit-Leftwich, 2010). In the evolving landscape of AI-supported adaptive learning environments, teachers are no longer passive users of technology but *pedagogical designers* who make informed, ethical, and context-sensitive decisions about its integration. The Technological Pedagogical Content Knowledge (TPACK) framework developed by Mishra and Koehler (2006) continues to provide a robust foundation for understanding how teachers balance the intersection of technology, pedagogy, and disciplinary content. Within this model, effective technology integration requires teachers to go beyond technical proficiency, developing the ability to design learning experiences where digital tools serve clearly defined pedagogical goals (Koehler, Mishra, & Cain, 2013).

Recent studies have extended this framework to the field of Artificial Intelligence in Education (AIED), introducing the notion of *AI Pedagogical Knowledge* (AI-PK), which emphasizes educators' capacity to interpret, adapt, and critically evaluate AI-driven systems (Holmes, Bialik, & Fadel, 2019). Teachers must understand not only how AI functions but also how it mediates learning, data, and ethics. AI literacy for teachers entails reflective judgment about data privacy, algorithmic transparency, and human-AI collaboration in the classroom. In this context, TPACK evolves into a dynamic and ethically aware model that equips teachers to orchestrate meaningful learning experiences in AI-enhanced contexts. It is also known that teachers with high TPACK confidence can more effectively facilitate technology-supported learning environments and provide personalized guidance to students (Kaşcı, & Selçuk, 2021). According to Özen and Kurtuluş (2023), teachers' effective integration of technology within the TPACK framework enhances not only instructional design but also their capacity to provide adaptive feedback through digital tools. The findings of Kıyıcı and Dikkartın Övez (2021) show that teachers with higher TPACK proficiency accept technology more readily and demonstrate more effective digital pedagogical practices.

Therefore, fostering teachers' TPACK competence in alignment with AI literacy is essential to ensure that intelligent systems serve human learning rather than replace human agency. Professional development should aim to empower teachers as *critical interpreters and co-designers* of AI in education—bridging technological potential with human-centered pedagogy and ensuring that the integration of AI remains pedagogically sound, equitable, and sustainable.

In this study, proposed the AI-Assisted Adaptive Writing Instruction Model with Teacher Scaffolding (AAWIT Model) to enhance primary school students' writing skills through personalized AI feedback integrated with teacher guidance. This model adopts a holistic approach that not only considers students' digital writing development but also emphasizes how teachers can actively guide and enrich this process. As is known, teachers' technology integration competencies are closely related to their adoption of innovative teaching approaches (Eskici, 2023). Within this framework, the current literature has been reviewed, existing applications analyzed, and a pedagogically grounded adaptation model developed.

PROBLEM STATEMENT

Writing skills contribute to students' ability to communicate effectively at every stage of their education by enhancing their capacity to express ideas, structure knowledge, and engage in creative production. At the primary school level, writing instruction not only forms the foundation of academic success but also supports self-confidence, language use, and social-emotional development (Graham & Perin, 2007). However, writing is defined as one of the most complex language skills to teach and assess, and students' individual differences and attitudes toward writing further complicate teachers' tasks. In crowded classrooms, it is often difficult to provide each student with feedback tailored to their writing process.

In this context, the need for technological solutions that go beyond the limitations of traditional methods and provide individualized support is steadily increasing. AI-ALS have the potential to address this need by analyzing students' written work, providing instant feedback, identifying areas of difficulty, and suggesting appropriate content. Such systems support active student participation in the writing process, encouraging them to recognize and correct their own mistakes and monitor their progress more autonomously (Roscoe et al., 2017). Yet, most existing AI-assisted systems are designed for high school or older learners. There is still a limited number of AI tools that are pedagogically appropriate, developmentally sensitive, and feasible for integration into primary education.

Moreover, the effective integration of technological tools into educational contexts depends not only on the quality of the software but also on the guiding role of the teacher. For AI-supported systems to truly benefit students, teachers must consciously incorporate them into pedagogical practice (Ertmer & Ottenbreit-Leftwich, 2010). Teacher support is particularly critical at the primary level, where students require guidance, emotional encouragement, and developmental monitoring. For this reason, structuring adaptive learning systems under the guidance of classroom teachers should be considered not merely a technological option but also a pedagogical necessity.

AAWIT MODEL: AI-ASSISTED WRITING INSTRUCTION WITH TEACHER SCAFFOLDING

Theoretical Foundations of the Model

The AAWIT Model offers an AI-supported learning environment design integrated with teacher support to develop writing skills at the elementary school level. Before presenting the proposed model in detail in this section, it is appropriate to summarize its theoretical foundations. This framework model is based on Vygotsky's Zone of Proximal Development (ZPD), the socio-cultural approach, Bruner's principles of cognitive development, and the process-based writing model, respectively, which form the theoretical foundations of the model.

Vygotsky's Theory of the Zone of Proximal Development (ZPD)

Vygotsky, one of the most influential cognitive psychologists, argued that direct one-to-one instruction and teaching practices that foster interaction between children, peers, and adults play a critical role in cognitive development. In this context, the core concept of Vygotsky's theory is the zone of proximal development (ZPD), which he defined as the distance between a child's "actual developmental level," determined by independent problem solving, and the "potential developmental level," determined through problem solving under adult guidance or in collaboration with more capable peers (Bağlı, 2004). The ZPD thus represents the very space where learning occurs (Yurdakul, 2010). The concept of ZPD has been widely applied in educational research, including mathematics, science, and second language teaching (Dunn & Lantolf, 1998; Lantolf & Pavlenko, 1995), moral education (Tappan, 1998), education for gifted and preschool children (Smith, 1993), and teacher training (Jones, Rua, & Carter, 1998; Torres, 1996).

Vygotsky conceptualized the ZPD as "the distance between the actual developmental level determined by independent problem solving and the level of potential development determined through problem solving under adult guidance or in collaboration with more capable peers.” The essence of this approach lies in offering the learner opportunities slightly beyond their current level. In contemporary contexts, AI-assisted adaptive learning systems can serve as a “digital scaffold,” providing real-time, individualized feedback and thereby supporting students’ cognitive development in line with the principles of ZPD.

The Socio-Cultural Approach and the Mediating Role of Artificial Intelligence

The socio-cultural approach to learning argues that knowledge is not constructed in isolation within the individual's mind, but rather through social interaction and cultural tools. This view emphasizes that learning is not only an individual cognitive activity but also a process of social and cultural participation (Vygotsky, 1978; Wertsch, 1991; Rogoff, 2003). In this context, teaching is approached as a network of interactions that supports the student in constructing meaning within their own cultural context. The concept of the ZPD, proposed by Vygotsky (1978), forms the core of socio-cultural theory. This zone represents the distance between an individual's current competence and their potential development, and learning occurs within this distance. For learning to occur, the individual needs the support of a more experienced guide—this could be a teacher, peer, or digital system. Cole (1996) emphasizes that cultural tools—language, symbols, technologies—serve as mediators in the learning process; the interaction the individual establishes with their environment gains meaning through these tools.

From this perspective, AI-ALS can be considered a new cultural mediator in contemporary education. Like language, artificial intelligence mediates the individual's cognitive processes; it structures, interprets, and transforms the student's interaction with the outside world. These systems guide the meaning-making process by analyzing the student's written expressions; they also provide dynamic digital scaffolding that increases the student's cognitive awareness. Thus, artificial intelligence transforms learning from a purely individual cognitive activity into a socially shaped meaning-building process mediated by technology. Rogoff (2003) states that learning takes place within a “participatory community.” From this perspective, AI- ALS becomes a digital extension of the learning community by creating a continuous flow of interaction between the student, teacher, and system. The teacher, as the cultural mediator of this process, enables the student to experience technology in a meaningful context; they blend the data coming from the system with cultural and pedagogical knowledge. As Wertsch (1991) states, human actions are mediated by cultural tools; therefore, the quality of learning is directly dependent on the quality of the tool used. For AI- ALS to be effective, it must be structured not only technically but also culturally in a meaningful way.

Consequently, the socio-cultural learning approach strengthens the pedagogical foundation of the AAWIT Model. In this model, AI is not merely software; it is a learning agent that supports the student's cognitive development, social interaction, and cultural meaning production. Thus, technology transforms into a collaborative space that centers the human being in the learning process.

Bruner's Principles of Cognitive Development

Bruner theoretically supports the use of digital systems that prioritize the active participation of learners. He viewed cognitive development as a lifelong process and divided it into three stages: enactive, iconic, and symbolic (Senemoğlu, 2012). During the enactive phase, knowledge is acquired directly through actions and experiences. In AI-supported learning environments, this stage occurs through interactions such as drag-and-drop, voice response, and writing practice. Iconic representation involves constructing meaning through visuals, shapes, and mental images. Supporting students with visual representations during this period (e.g., dynamic writing screens provided by artificial intelligence systems, example sentence maps, visual feedback symbols) reinforces Bruner's principle of "transition from concrete to abstract." In the symbolic stage, learning reaches the level of abstraction through language and symbols; students organize and internalize their thoughts through writing (Bruner, 1973; Wood, Bruner & Ross, 1976). Designing learning activities in alignment with these principles greatly facilitates the learning process.

For instance, during the iconic stage, incorporating computer-based activities can help concretize abstract concepts through simulations and models, while allowing learners to progress at their own pace. By integrating multimedia techniques such as images, videos, audio, and animations, computer-assisted instruction not only makes learning more engaging and enjoyable but also addresses individual differences among learners (Güven & Sülün, 2012). Such approaches can encourage students to reflect deeply on concepts, make sense of complex ideas more effectively, and positively influence their writing production processes.

Bruner also developed the concept of "scaffolding" (cognitive support), shifting the teacher's role from that of a "knowledge transmitter" to that of a "guide." In this respect, Bruner's views are complementary to Vygotsky's theory of the ZPD. Bruner's principle of "discovery learning" aligns directly with students learning writing strategies by experimenting in artificial intelligence environments. In this process, the teacher is responsible for lightening the student's cognitive load, guiding them with the right questions, and creating meaningful contexts (Bruner, 1996). AI supported writing systems transfer Bruner's representational stages to the digital plane: The student takes action (produces text), the system provides visual feedback (color, symbol, audio alert), and then symbolically reorganizes the text. Thus, learning becomes not just the acquisition of information, but a continuous cycle of interaction and restructuring. In this context, Bruner's principles of cognitive development strengthen the pedagogical foundation of the AAWIT Model, revealing the potential of AI- ALS to transform children's ways of thinking.

The Process-Based Approach to Writing Instruction

The process-based writing model approaches written expression not as a final product but as a process, focusing on teaching the stages involved in that process (Türkben, 2021; Hyland, 2003). This model aims to help students manage their own writing processes while developing self-regulation skills. As a student-centered approach grounded in constructivist theory, it seeks to organize writing processes with the cognitive support of teachers (Kaldırım, 2014). Writing is thus regarded as an activity in which students can explore and investigate their ideas to construct meaning. It fosters critical thinking by enhancing awareness, independent learning, decision-making, problem-solving, and planning skills (Duman, 2004).

In contrast to traditional product-oriented methods, the process-based model acknowledges that no text is ever truly perfect. Rather, it emphasizes that through generating ideas, reflecting, and revising successive drafts, writers can gradually approach improvement. The guiding principle is that a strong product is the outcome of a strong process (Sun & Feng, 2009). Instead of focusing solely on the final text, this approach highlights the act of writing itself -idea generation, planning, drafting, reviewing, and revising. Brookes and Grundy (1999) defined writing as an activity involving various stages such as considering what to write and arranging ideas into sentences and paragraphs, noting that writing requires sufficient time to complete these steps. How each student develops awareness at these stages, however, varies individually.

Studies indicate that this model generally consists of five non-linear stages, allowing movement back and forth between phases (Johnson, 2008; Zeng, 2005). The first stage is pre-writing, which plays a vital role in constructing written expression. At this stage, students generate ideas about the topic, prepare themselves psychologically and mentally for writing, and determine the purpose, audience, and genre of their text. Techniques such as clustering and brainstorming are employed to develop ideas and organize information. Although often neglected, Murray (1982) argued that 70% of writing time should be devoted to this phase.

The second stage is drafting. The aim here is to transfer the ideas gathered in the pre-writing stage onto paper without focusing on formal issues such as grammar and punctuation; linguistic accuracy is considered secondary (Widodo, 2008). Students should be reminded that what they write is not a final product but a draft open to revision (Akyol, 2008). At this stage, the main structure of the text is planned with an introduction, body, and conclusion. The third stage is reviewing/revision. Drafts are reread and content-based revisions are made. Students receive feedback from teachers or peers, with peer review playing a crucial role. The focus is not on surface-level features like spelling or punctuation but on meaning, coherence, and organization. Based on feedback, ideas may be added, removed, or reorganized.

The fourth stage is editing. Once content revisions are complete, attention shifts to form. The text is checked for spelling, punctuation, formatting, grammar, and word choice. The aim is to refine the work so that it is accurate and polished before being shared with the target audience. According to Widodo (2008), this phase helps students produce well-written texts by correcting formal and grammatical errors prior to submission or presentation. The final stage is publishing/sharing. At this point, students present their completed work to an audience -through oral reading in class, posting on bulletin boards, or publishing in school newspapers, magazines, or even on social media. This stage highlights writing as an effective means of communication and motivates students to engage in the writing process.

These stages are taught with the goal of helping students develop as strategic writers, enabling them to plan, evaluate, and organize their own thoughts (Tompkins, 2004). In this process-oriented approach, teacher and student roles differ significantly from traditional models. The teacher acts as a facilitator, motivator, feedback provider, and guide throughout the writing process, rather than simply evaluating the final product. Meanwhile, the student takes on a more active role, gaining the ability to plan, evaluate, and organize their own ideas while managing their writing process independently from start to finish.

Writing is not merely a linguistic production process; it is a complex cognitive activity in which thought is structured, planned, and transformed. Therefore, writing instruction should aim to develop not only the student's grammatical accuracy but also their cognitive organization skills. The Cognitive Process Model developed by Flower and Hayes (1981) approaches writing as a dynamic problem-solving activity consisting of interconnected sub-processes such as planning, text production, and revision. This model is based on the concept of a "cognitive field" in which the writer continuously stores, recalls, and transforms information in their memory. When writing, students do not merely create text; they also mentally manage their target audience, their goals, and the coherence of the text.

Bereiter and Scardamalia (2013) explained the writing process at two levels: knowledge-telling and knowledge-transforming. Beginner-level students generally remain at the knowledge-telling stage; that is, they list what they know but struggle to construct a deep web of meaning. Transitioning to the knowledge-transforming level requires interacting with the text, evaluating feedback, and restructuring. In this context, AI-supported adaptive systems not only evaluate the student's writing process but also enhance their cognitive awareness through immediate suggestions, guiding them toward the knowledge-transforming stage. Kellogg (1994) emphasizes that writing relies on the simultaneous interaction of multiple cognitive systems: planning, formulation, review, and motor control processes constantly influence each other. This multitasking structure is cognitively quite challenging, especially for younger students. AI systems reduce this cognitive load, allowing students to focus more on higher-order thinking skills. For example, AI-powered language models can automatically detect spelling errors, redirecting the student's attention from formal accuracy to semantic coherence. This frees up the student's cognitive resources for strategic thinking and creative expression during text production.

By adopting this approach, the AAWIT Model transforms the student's writing process from being "product"-focused to a "cognitive development" process. With personalized feedback from the system, students recognize their own writing strategies, restructure their text, and develop self-regulation skills. Teachers can observe this process to monitor students' cognitive progress and plan pedagogical interventions based on data. Thus, writing becomes a process of constructing meaning, transforming ideas, and generating insight with teacher guidance and AI support.

Adaptive Learning Systems (AI- ALS)

The effective integration of AI-ALS into primary education requires careful consideration of children's cognitive, affective, social, and linguistic developmental characteristics. At this stage, as children have not yet fully reached the level of abstract thinking, learning materials and systems must be concrete, gamified, and structured under teacher guidance (Piaget, 1972; Vygotsky, 1978). Since primary school students are more receptive to visual learning, the user interfaces of AI-ALS platforms should be designed with large icons, visually supported instructions, and auditory feedback. Such designs help reduce cognitive load and enhance interaction with the system (Mayer, 2005). The complexity of the content should be automatically adjusted to the child's age, grade level, and individual pace of progress. For example, first graders might receive short sentences with fewer words and audio reading support, while fourth graders could be provided with longer texts and creative writing prompts (Anderson & Krathwohl, 2001).

Motivation in primary education is often driven by play. Therefore, AI systems can maintain students' attention through gamification elements such as digital badges, character development, or story completion tasks (Gee, 2003). Additionally, AI capable of analyzing emotional states—such as facial expressions, voice tone, or emotional cues in written language—can monitor children's engagement and stress levels, offering appropriate guidance in response (D'Mello & Graesser, 2013). Since digital literacy skills are not yet fully developed at this age, these systems must be used under teacher supervision. Rather than replacing the teacher, AI functions as a supportive tool, continuously providing feedback that informs and guides the teacher (Luckin et al., 2016). Moreover, systems designed for children must be tailored to those under the age of 13 and comply with national and international regulations on data privacy. The explainability of AI (XAI) also plays a key role in ensuring transparency and accountability in these systems (Floridi et al., 2018).

The Role of Teacher Scaffolding

Within the proposed model, teacher roles differ from those in traditional writing instruction, aligning instead with the principles of the process-based approach. Adaptive learning systems analyze student performance and provide personalized content and suggestions, taking on roles such as evaluating written products, offering feedback during the writing process, and providing resources for text production. However, the effective integration of AI-ALS into classrooms depends on structuring these systems not merely as tools, but as supportive partners that complement teachers' pedagogical guidance (Luckin et al., 2016). In this context, the classroom teacher shifts from being an "instructor" to becoming a "facilitator of learning." By providing both real-time and historical data on students' writing processes, AI systems enable teachers to better understand learners. Teachers can then analyze this data to design individualized instructional strategies (Koehler, Mishra, & Cain, 2013). The teacher's role here is not only to receive data, but to interpret it through pedagogical expertise and translate it into meaningful action.

For primary school students, creating safe, supportive, and meaningful learning environments remains a fundamental responsibility of the teacher. While AI systems address students' cognitive needs, teachers safeguard their emotional well-being. Thus, empathy, emotional awareness, and social support emerge as critical teacher roles (Wang & Johnson, 2021). Teachers must also continuously monitor the pedagogical integrity and ethical appropriateness of the digital systems being used, and remain vigilant to any negative behavioral patterns in students' interaction with technology (Selwyn, 2019). Particularly in expressive domains such as writing, teachers are expected to encourage originality. AI systems are most effective when developed not solely by engineers but also with teachers' input. Teachers enhance the educational quality of these systems by contributing to content development, proposing example activities, and providing feedback on user interfaces (Holmes et al., 2019). At the same time, according to the research findings of Önal and Önal (2023), in artificial intelligence-supported learning environments, the teacher's guiding role must be restructured in an integrated manner with digital systems.

Because teachers' roles evolve in AI-supported learning environments, their digital pedagogical competencies also need to be redefined. Teachers should not only be capable of using technology but must also understand how to integrate it into pedagogy with clear purpose and intent (Mishra & Koehler, 2006; Ertmer & Ottenbreit-Leftwich, 2010). This brings forward an important question: *What should teacher-system interaction look like?* Such interaction must be framed within a collaborative AI approach (Holmes et al., 2022). That is, teachers use the data provided by the system to inform their decisions, while the system provides insights into students' learning processes. Several principles are essential here:

- The system must be transparent, clearly explaining what data it processes and how (principle of transparency).
- Teachers must retain the right to modify or override system suggestions (principle of flexibility).
- Information flow must be bidirectional—from the system to the teacher and from the teacher back to the system (feedback loop).
- Finally, the system must not replace teachers' decisions but complement and enrich them, functioning as supportive AI.

Önal and Önal (2023) noted that teacher candidates experience significant difficulties in maintaining student engagement and providing guidance in online teaching applications. This finding highlights the need to restructure the teacher's guidance role in AI-supported learning environments in an integrated manner with digital systems.

Stages of the AAWIT Model

The AAWIT Model structures the teaching of writing as a dynamic cycle of assessment, guidance, practice, feedback, revision, and sharing. Within this cycle, the roles of the digital system and the teacher are clearly distinguished yet complementary. The digital system is primarily responsible for providing real-time analysis, technical feedback, and adaptive suggestions tailored to students' individual needs. It evaluates aspects such as grammar, vocabulary, coherence, and content development, offering personalized pathways for improvement. The teacher, on the other hand, plays a central role as a pedagogical and emotional guide. Teachers interpret the system's data through their professional expertise, contextualize feedback, and provide motivational and social-emotional support to students. They ensure that digital guidance is aligned with educational goals, ethical standards, and the holistic development of learners. By integrating these dual roles, the model ensures that technology does not replace teachers but rather strengthens their capacity to deliver inclusive, process-oriented, and student-centered writing instruction. The stages of the model are presented with explanations in Table 1 below.

Table 1. Roles of Teachers and Digital Systems in AI-Assisted Adaptive Writing Instruction

Stage	Content	Digital System Role	Teacher Role
1. Initial Assessment	Determining students' writing proficiency with a sample text	Analyzes text (word count, grammar, coherence, vocabulary)	Complements system data with classroom observations and contextual insights
2. Pre-Writing and Guidance	Generating ideas, setting goals, identifying audience and text type	Provides prompts, graphic organizers, brainstorming tools	Motivates students, scaffolds idea development, clarifies purpose
3. Writing Process	Drafting the text without focusing on form	Offers real-time guidance (e.g., "add more details," "check sentence clarity")	Provides motivational and emotional support, ensures student engagement
4. Feedback and Revision	Reviewing and revising drafts	Compares versions, highlights changes, suggests improvements	Interprets system data pedagogically, guides revision strategies, fosters reflection
5. Editing and Improvement	Correcting grammar, spelling, punctuation, word choice, formatting	Detects linguistic and formal errors, provides micro-feedback	Ensures corrections align with meaning and communicative intent
6. Publishing and Sharing	Presenting the final text (classroom, bulletin board, school magazine, digital platforms)	Offers publishing formats, digital portfolios, peer sharing options	Encourages originality, celebrates effort, builds confidence in writing

Table 1 above compares the roles of teachers and digital systems in the six fundamental stages of the writing process within the AAWIT Model. The process begins with determining the student's writing level and concludes with the publication of the text. The digital system provides data analysis, guidance, feedback, and correction support at each stage, while the teacher completes the process by providing pedagogical interpretation, motivation, emotional support, and observing student development. The system responds to the student's individual needs with text analysis, real-time suggestions, and micro-feedback, while the teacher guides the process in terms of meaningful learning, originality, communicative purpose, and critical thinking. Thus, the model offers a holistic approach that strengthens writing skills both cognitively and affectively, focusing on the interaction between technology and pedagogy. Figure 1 is presented to visualize the cyclical nature of this model. This diagram illustrates the interactive and sequential relationship between the digital system and teacher roles across six instructional stages of the AAWIT model.

Figure 1. Conceptual process flow diagram of the AAWIT Model

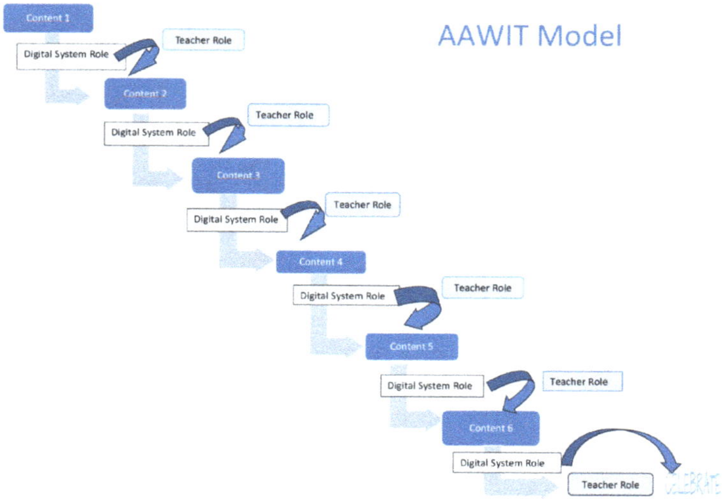

Practical Classroom Scenario for Implementing the AAWIT Model

In this section, a six-step sample scenario is presented to illustrate how the Artificial Intelligence–Supported Adaptive Writing Instruction Model (AAWIT) operates in a classroom context. Each step focuses on a distinct aspect of writing instruction at the primary school level and demonstrates the dynamic interaction among the teacher, student, and artificial intelligence system.

Scenario.

At the beginning of the writing process (initial assessment), students are asked to write a short sample text to determine their writing skill level. The AI-based system analyzes these texts in terms of vocabulary richness, sentence length, grammatical accuracy, and textual consistency. The data obtained is presented to the teacher in the form of a summary report showing the students' strengths and areas for improvement. For example, if the system determines that a student frequently uses short sentences and has weak conjunction usage, the teacher provides more support to this student in "sentence expansion" activities in the following weeks. This stage is the starting point of the personalized writing process.

Then, the second stage, pre-writing and guidance, begins. In this stage, fourth-grade students are asked to write a short story titled "A Day in Nature." The artificial intelligence system monitors the student's writing process in real time and provides guidance tips for content creation. When a student completes the story with only three sentences, the system provides feedback as follows: "Can you describe what happened in your story in a little more detail? Try adding what the characters felt." The teacher uses the system's analysis report to ask additional questions to help the student develop the plot and enrich the emotional expressions. This scenario represents the preparation and guidance phase, which combines the teacher's guidance with micro-feedback from artificial intelligence.

The next stage is the writing process stage. It aims to support vocabulary enrichment. Writing exercises with synonyms are conducted with students. In this stage, students are asked to write a short paragraph and enrich repetitive words. When a student writes the sentences, "The forest was big. The trees were big. The animals were big too," the system intervenes as follows: "You can express the word 'big' with different words. For example: 'huge,' 'massive,' or 'enormous.'" The teacher guides students in classifying the suggested words according to their different meanings. In this stage, artificial intelligence supports linguistic diversity, while the teacher fosters semantic awareness by discussing the contextual appropriateness of words. Thus, the writing process develops in terms of both vocabulary and stylistic richness.

Another example can be given for a student's descriptive writing assignment. In this example, the student is expected to reflect the use of opposites in the writing process with antonyms. This section exemplifies the next stage, feedback and revision. In the descriptive writing activity, students are asked to describe a scene using contrasting characteristics (e.g., "night–day," "quiet–noisy"). One student writes: "The room was dark, but the window was darker." The AI detects that the contrast in the text is weak and makes a suggestion: "Would you like to use an antonym? Writing bright instead of dark could strengthen the narrative. Let's try again!" The student revises their text based on this feedback. The teacher also provides feedback supporting the AI's suggestion. During this process, the teacher can work one-on-one with students who feel they need support in terms of motivation. They can encourage them in their writing and mention their previous writing successes. In this way, the student's ability to edit their own text is developed.

Another writing process aims to support linguistic accuracy and expressive variety skills by facilitating the teaching of the cultural dimension of language. In this process, students are asked to use a proverb or idiom in their writing. One student writes: "He was hitting two birds with one stick." Artificial intelligence detects that the idiom is incorrect and offers a correction: "The correct expression is "kill two birds with one stone." This idiom describes achieving two results with a single effort." The teacher turns this situation into an opportunity to explain the meaning, origin, and contextual use of idioms.

Once the writing process is complete, the final stage, publishing and sharing, begins. At the end of the writing process, students upload their revised texts to their digital portfolios. The system displays the student's progress with visual graphics, showing their improvement in writing performance. The teacher reviews the portfolios and evaluates the student's progress both qualitatively and quantitatively. Additionally, students provide constructive feedback on each other's work in an online environment. This stage transforms the writing process from an individual activity into community-based learning.

The sample scenario presented here with the six-stage writing process demonstrates how the AAWIT Model integrates micro-level artificial intelligence feedback with macro-level teacher guidance. While artificial intelligence provides instant personalized feedback, the teacher continues to play the role of providing emotional support, pedagogical interpretation, and holistic guidance. This collaboration creates an adaptive learning ecosystem that supports writing instruction in its cognitive, affective, and cultural dimensions.

Application Challenges and Educational Requirements from the Teacher's Perspective

Effectively integrating the AAWIT Model into the classroom environment requires not only technological competence but also pedagogical awareness and ethical sensitivity. Artificial intelligence systems are not structures that replace teachers; they are cognitive tools that enhance teacher guidance. However, establishing this balance brings certain challenges, especially at the elementary school level.

First, most teachers vary in their level of pedagogical technology knowledge (TPACK) regarding AI-based learning systems. Some teachers use technology only as a "digital tool" and struggle to structure cognitive support embedded in the student's writing process. This situation requires teacher training to focus not only on technical skills but also on adaptive writing pedagogy. It is important that teacher candidates in education programs are equipped with skills such as interactive teaching design with artificial intelligence, real-time data interpretation, ethical decision-making, and using student data for pedagogical purposes (Mishra & Koehler, 2006; Holmes et al., 2022).

Second, in classroom practice, teachers are observed to experience difficulties in time management, technological infrastructure deficiencies, and providing simultaneous guidance to students of different levels. While artificial intelligence systems support teachers in terms of data analysis and providing individual feedback, adapting the system's suggestions to the pedagogical context remains the teacher's responsibility. This necessitates teachers to develop their critical digital literacy and data interpretation skills.

Finally, teachers need to gain awareness on data privacy, children's rights, and artificial intelligence transparency in order to manage such systems within ethical boundaries. The sustainability of the AAWIT Model is only possible if teachers are positioned as pedagogical decision-makers and ethical guides rather than as "users" of technology. Therefore, teacher training is not merely a complementary element but a decisive factor in the success of this model.

Outcomes Targeted by the AAWIT Model

The AAWIT Model not only supports the development of students' writing skills but also aims to foster multilayered growth based on technology-enhanced personalization, teacher scaffolding, and student autonomy. The key outcomes of this model can be grouped under five main categories: cognitive outcomes, affective and social outcomes, pedagogical outcomes, technical and operational outcomes, and educational equity and inclusivity.

From a cognitive perspective, the model enhances students' metacognitive awareness of the writing process. Students internalize strategies such as planning, evaluating, and revising. During the process of text production, learners improve in linguistic accuracy, coherence, consistency, and textual organization. Through AI-supported suggestions, students expand their vocabulary, strengthen conceptual learning, and diversify sentence structures and expression.

From an affective and social perspective, the provision of immediate feedback during the writing process fosters positive attitudes toward writing, self-confidence, and a sense of ownership. The ability to track their written products in a digital portfolio provides students with a tangible sense of progress and satisfaction. Applications enriched with peer feedback further strengthen empathy, critical evaluation, and social learning.

Pedagogical outcomes are primarily linked to teachers. The model allows teachers to monitor students not only through their written products but also throughout the writing process, enabling them to analyze strengths and areas for growth based on data. In crowded public school classrooms, where individualized attention is difficult, the provision of learning analytics reports for both typically developing and struggling learners is a significant advantage. Thus, integrating the teacher's pedagogical role with the digital system transforms the teacher into an "intelligent guide."

From a technical and operational perspective, the model makes writing processes data-driven, trackable, and comparable, thereby making student development more tangible. Systematically generated revision suggestions help students build a lasting habit of improving their texts, while also offering school leaders and policymakers cumulative insights into writing performance at the classroom and school levels.

Finally, the model strengthens educational equity and inclusivity by providing adaptive support for students with diverse learning styles, those who struggle with written expression, or those whose first language is not the language of instruction. In doing so, it ensures a fairer and more inclusive learning environment responsive to individual differences. For students with special educational needs, simplified interfaces, auditory guidance, and multiple modes of expression foster active participation, thereby putting the principle of accessibility into practice. Importantly, these outcomes extend beyond the individual level: they align with Sustainable Development Goal 4 (Quality Education) by reinforcing inclusivity in education. In this way, the AAWIT Model guarantees equitable access to writing skills while contributing to a sustainable and just vision of education.

Artificial Intelligence Ethics and Human Autonomy

The integration of artificial intelligence in education raises fundamental questions not only in terms of efficiency and personalization, but also in terms of ethics, autonomy, and human dimensions. The increasing role of artificial intelligence systems in decision-making mechanisms in teaching processes brings with it serious debates on issues such as data privacy, algorithmic bias, transparency, and the protection of human autonomy. Floridi and colleagues (2018) emphasize that artificial intelligence in education should be conducted within the framework of the principles of beneficence, non-maleficence, autonomy, and justice. These principles ensure that intelligent systems develop human potential rather than limiting it. The ethical implications of AI-supported adaptive systems become even more critical in primary school, when cognitive and emotional development is particularly sensitive. UNESCO (2021) states that AI designs in education should be based on human-centered values and that applications that do not protect children's rights or reinforce existing social or linguistic inequalities should be avoided. In this context, teachers are not merely technology users in the digital classroom, but also ethical agents who interpret the meaning of AI outputs, contextualize data, and provide empathetic guidance. Furthermore, Williamson and Eynon (2020) discuss a risk termed the automation of pedagogy. In this case, algorithmic decision-making processes can overshadow teachers' pedagogical intuition and human judgment. Therefore, AI-supported systems must be designed as tools that empower teachers' professional capacity, supporting rather than directing them. Transparent data policies, explainable decision mechanisms, and culturally sensitive algorithms should be an integral part of ethical design.

Ultimately, ethical AI integration is not a technical issue, but a profoundly pedagogical one. The AAWIT Model positions the teacher at the center of the process, treating them as an ethical subject who guides the responsible use of technology. This ensures that ethical awareness is preserved in adaptive learning environments, allowing artificial intelligence to be a tool for inclusivity, justice, and empowerment rather than a control mechanism.

Limitations of the Model

Although the AAWIT Model offers an innovative, inclusive, and digitally enhanced learning environment designed to support primary school students' writing skills, it faces several limitations both in theoretical and practical dimensions. Critically addressing these limitations not only strengthens the model's validity but also provides guidance for future research in this field.

First, primary school children are still in the early stages of cognitive and emotional development. The emotional support, role modeling, and face-to-face feedback required during the writing process may not be fully met by AI systems. To prevent AI-based feedback from causing emotional vulnerability or feelings of learned helplessness, the system's language and approach must be designed with great care. Thus, grounding the model not solely in digital solutions but in the indispensability of teacher scaffolding is a pedagogical necessity. Online teaching experiences during the COVID-19 pandemic have shown that pedagogical guidance in digital environments is not as effective as face-to-face teaching (Önal & Önal, 2023). This situation confirms the need for adaptable systems that strengthen teacher guidance in digital environments, as proposed by the AAWIT Model.

Second, AI systems are typically developed with a technical engineering mindset, which may not fully capture pedagogical or didactic depth. For instance, a "problem of expression" in a student's writing may involve not only syntax but also meaning, context, and communicative intent. In such cases, system-generated suggestions risk remaining superficial. Therefore, stronger collaboration between educators and software developers is essential for advancing the model.

Third, in some countries, access to digital learning environments is still constrained by socio-economic inequalities. If implemented, the model may face challenges in rural schools with insufficient hardware, poor internet infrastructure, or limited teacher digital competence. To address this, the model should also be adaptable to hybrid use and mobile systems that function offline. Fourth, AI systems that analyze student writing inherently collect personal data, leading to ethical risks such as student profiling and digital surveillance. It is critical that data processing procedures be explicitly defined within the framework of national data protection laws and international child rights conventions. Transparency and maximum data security must be ensured.

Finally, if AI systems assume a decision-making role, the teacher's pedagogical intuition, emotional guidance, and ability to recognize students as individuals may be overshadowed. The model must therefore position the teacher not as a mere "user" of the system but as the pedagogical decision-maker and ethical guide. Future research should thus focus on developing models that balance AI systems with teacher scaffolding.

CONCLUSION AND RECOMMENDATIONS FOR FUTURE RESEARCH

The role of artificial intelligence in education is no longer an optional opportunity but an integral part of an inevitable transformation. However, when the human and pedagogical dimensions of this transformation are neglected, education risks being dominated by technology as a technical mechanism rather than as a developmental and instructional tool. Therefore, AI-supported systems must be shaped by models that address children's development holistically, maintain the teacher at the center, and prioritize educational equity.

Hokanson (2022) also states that digital transformation requires not only technological change but also an ethical and pedagogical restructuring of teaching culture. This perspective aligns with the AAWIT Model's goal of human-centered AI integration guided by teachers. This study has explored the potential of AI-assisted adaptive learning systems in developing primary school students' writing skills through the proposal of a theoretical model. Writing, from early childhood onward, is considered not only a foundation for academic success but also a key pillar of cognitive, affective, and social development. Yet in traditional classrooms—particularly those with large student numbers—it becomes increasingly difficult to provide each learner with individualized support for their writing process. At this point, AI's capacity for personalization, combined with holistic models grounded in teacher scaffolding, offers important opportunities for promoting educational equity and making writing development more trackable. Eskici (2023) states in his study that teachers' self-efficacy regarding technology integration is evaluated together with innovative teacher characteristics. This result indicates that the role of the teacher in AI-based learning environments needs to be redefined not only as an implementer but also as a pedagogical designer and learning process leader.

The proposed AAWIT Model integrates an AI system that delivers real-time feedback on the writing process with teacher scaffolding, thus presenting a robust framework that is both technological and pedagogical. By treating writing instruction as a process rather than a product, the model supports students' self-regulation skills, digital writing portfolios, and meaning-making capacities. It also empowers teachers with classroom-level learning analytics, enabling them to make pedagogical decisions in a data-informed manner. Nevertheless, careful implementation is required, given the model's multilayered limitations related to developmental appropriateness, teacher competence, digital inequalities, and ethical data use.

Beyond writing, future research could explore how the principles of the AAWIT Model can be extended to support **speaking and oral communication skills**. Integrating adaptive AI systems into speech-based tasks could enable real-time feedback on pronunciation, coherence, and fluency, thereby promoting multimodal literacy development. Such an expansion would align with current trends emphasizing the integration of writing and speaking as complementary modes of language expression. Furthermore, investigating how teacher scaffolding functions in AI-assisted speaking environments could provide valuable insights into designing holistic, language-rich learning ecosystems for primary education.

REFERENCES

Akyol, H. (2008). *Yeni programa uygun Türkçe öğretim yöntemleri*. Kök Yayıncılık.

Akyol, H. (2019). *Türkçe öğretimi: Okuma-yazma öğretimi*. Pegem Akademi Yayıncılık.

Anderson, L. W., & Krathwohl, D. D. (Eds.). (2001). *A taxonomy for learning, teaching, and assessing: A revision of Bloom's taxonomy of educational objectives*. Longman.

Bağlı, M. T. (2004). Oyun, Bilişsel gelişim ve toplumsal dünya: Piaget, Vygotsky ve sonrası. *Ankara Üniversitesi Eğitim Bilimleri Fakültesi Dergisi*, *37*(2), 137–169.

Bereiter, C., & Scardamalia, M. (2013). *The psychology of written composition*. Routledge.

Brookes, A., & Grundy, P. (1999). *Beginning to write: Writing activities for elementary and intermediate learners*. Cambridge University Press.

Bruner, J. S. (1960). *The Process of Education*. Harvard University Press.

Bruner, J. S. (1973). *Going Beyond the Information Given*. Norton.

Bruner, J. S. (1997). The culture of education. In *The culture of education*. Harvard University Press.

Bruner, J. S. (2009). *Actual minds, possible worlds*. Harvard University Press.

Cole, M. (1996). *Cultural psychology: A once and future discipline*. Harvard University Press.

D'mello, S., & Graesser, A. (2013). AutoTutor and affective AutoTutor: Learning by talking with cognitively and emotionally intelligent computers that talk back. [TiiS]. *ACM Transactions on Interactive Intelligent Systems*, *2*(4), 1–39.

Duman, B. (2004). *Learning-teaching theories and process-based education*. Ani Publishing.

Dunn, W. E., & Lantolf, J. P. (1998). Vygotsky's zone of proximal development and Krashen's i+ 1: Incommensurable constructs; incommensurable theories. *Language Learning*, *48*(3), 411–442.

Ertmer, P. A., & Ottenbreit-Leftwich, A. T. (2010). Teacher technology change: How knowledge, confidence, beliefs, and culture intersect. *Journal of Research on Technology in Education*, *42*(3), 255–284.

Eskici, M., & Çayak, S. (2023). The Relationship between Teachers' Technology Proficiencies and their Levels of Integrating Technology into their Lessons. *Journal of Educational Technology and Online Learning*, *6*(4), 808–821.

Floridi, L., Cowls, J., & Beltrametti, M.. (2018). AI4People—An ethical framework for a good AI society. *Minds and Machines*, *28*(4), 689–707. PMID: 30930541

Flower, L., & Hayes, J. R. (1981). A cognitive process theory of writing. *College Composition and Communication*, *32*(4), 365–387.

Gee, J. P. (2003). *What video games have to teach us about learning and literacy*. Palgrave Macmillan.

Graham, S., & Harris, K. R. (2005). Improving the writing performance of young struggling writers: Theoretical and programmatic research from the Center on Accelerating Student Learning. *The Journal of Special Education*, *39*(1), 19–33.

Graham, S., & Perin, D. (2007). A meta-analysis of writing instruction for adolescent students. *Journal of Educational Psychology*, *99*(3), 445.

Graves, D. H. (1983). *Writing: Teachers and children at work*. Heinemann.

Güven, G., & Sülün, Y. (2012). Bilgisayar destekli öğretimin 8. sınıf fen ve teknoloji dersindeki akademik başarıya ve öğrencilerin derse karşı tutumlarına etkisi. *Journal of Turkish Science Education*, *9*(1), 68–79.

Hokanson, B. (2022). New approaches on education technologies: A global perspective for digital transformation. *JETOL*, *5*(4), 775–780.

Holmes, W.. (2022). *AI and education: Guidance for policymakers*. UNESCO.

Holmes, W., Bialik, M., & Fadel, C. (2019). *Artificial intelligence in education: Promises and implications for teaching and learning*. Center for Curriculum Redesign.

Hyland, K. (2003). Genre-based pedagogies: A social response to process. *Journal of Second Language Writing*, *12*(1), 17–29.

Johnson, A. P. (2008). *Teaching reading and writing: A guidebook for tutoring and remediating students*. Rowman and Littlefield Education.

Jones, M. G., Rua, M. J., & Carter, G. (1998). Science teachers' conceptual growth within Vygotsky's zone of proximal development. *Journal of Research in Science Teaching: The Official Journal of the National Association for Research in Science Teaching*, *35*(9), 967–985.

Kaldırım, A. (2014). The effect of 6+1 analytical writing and evaluation model on the sixth-grade students' writing expression skills (Unpublished master's thesis). Kütahya Dumlupınar University, Graduate School of Educational Sciences.

Kaldırım, A., & Tavşanlı, Ö. F. (2021). A thematic review of using digital teaching technologies in Turkish language teaching. *Journal of Educational Technology and Online Learning*, *4*(2), 70–95. DOI: 10.31681/jetol.898014

Kaşcı, T., & Selçuk, G. (2021). Examination of classroom teachers' technological pedagogical content knowledge and teacher self-efficacy beliefs. *Journal of Educational Technology and Online Learning*, *4*(4), 774–792. DOI: 10.31681/jetol.1018879

Kellogg, R. T. (1994). *The psychology of writing*. Oxford University Press.

Kıyıcı, O. D., & Dikkartın Övez, F. T. (2021). Examination of technology acceptance and TPACK competencies ofmathematics teachers who are involved in distance education practices during the pandemic process. *Journal of Educational Technology and Online Learning*, *4*(4), 805–821.

Koehler, M. J., Mishra, P., & Cain, W. (2013). What is technological pedagogical content knowledge (TPACK)? *Journal of Education*, *193*(3), 13–19.

Koh, W. Y. (2017). Effective applications of automated writing feedback in process-based writing instruction. *English Teaching*, *72*(3), 91–118.

Lantolf, J. P., & Pavlenko, A. (1995). Sociocultural theory and second language acquisition. *Annual Review of Applied Linguistics*, *15*, 108–124.

Luckin, R., Holmes, W., Griffiths, M., & Forcier, L. B. (2016). *Intelligence unleashed: An argument for AI in education*. Pearson Education.

Mayer, R. E. (2005). *The Cambridge handbook of multimedia learning*. Cambridge University Press.

MEB. (2024). *Eğitimde kullanılabilecek yapay zekâ araçları rehberi*. Yenilik ve Eğitim Teknolojileri Genel Müdürlüğü.

Mishra, P., & Koehler, M. J. (2006). Technological pedagogical content knowledge: A framework for integrating technology in teacher knowledge. *Teachers College Record*, *108*(6), 1017–1054.

Murray, D. M. (1982). Teaching the other self: The writer's first reader. *College Composition and Communication*, *33*(1), 140–147.

Neuman, S. B., & Roskos, K. (2007). Literacy knowledge in practice: Contexts of participation for young writers and readers. *Early Childhood Research Quarterly*, *22*(1), 27–43.

OkusFocus. (2025). AI-Powered Reading Analysis. https://www.okusfokus.com/

Özen, E., & Kurtuluş, A. (2023). A study on mathematics teachers' technological pedagogical content knowledge (TPACK) and frequency of use of educational information network (EBA) assessment tools. *Journal of Educational Technology and Online Learning*, *6*(4), 1009–1026.

Piaget, J. (1972). *The psychology of the child.* Basic Books.

Puranik, C. S., & Lonigan, C. J. (2014). Emergent writing in preschoolers: Preliminary evidence for a theoretical framework. *Reading Research Quarterly*, *49*(4), 453–467. PMID: 25316955

Rogoff, B. (2003). *The cultural nature of human development.* Oxford University Press.

Roscoe, R. D., Varner, L. K., Crossley, S. A., & McNamara, D. S. (2017). Unlocking the potential of automated writing evaluation: Feedback, coaching, and revision. *Educational Psychology Review*, *29*(1), 139–165.

Selwyn, N. (2019). *Should robots replace teachers? AI and the future of education.* Polity Press.

Senemoğlu, N. (2012). *Gelişim öğrenme ve öğretim: Kuramdan uygulamaya.* Pegem Akademi.

Smith, A. B. (1993). Early childhood educare: Seeking a theoretical framework in Vygotsky's work. *International Journal of Early Years Education*, *1*(1), 47–62.

Sun, C., & Feng, G. (2009). Process approach to teaching writing applied in different teaching models. *English Language Teaching*, *2*(1), 150–155.

Tanık Önal, N., & Önal, N. (2023). Online learning and teaching experiences of preservice science teachers during Covid-19 pandemic. *Journal of Educational Technology and Online Learning*, *6*(2), 295–314.

Tappan, M. B. (1998). Moral education in the zone of proximal development. *Journal of Moral Education*, *27*(2), 141–160.

Tompkins, G. E. (2004). *Teaching writing: Balancing product and process* (4th ed.). Merrill/Prentice Hall.

Tompkins, G. E. (2012). Teaching writing: Balancing process and product. Pearson Higher Ed.

Tonbuloğlu, B. (2023). An Evaluation of the Use of Artificial Intelligence Applications in Online Education. *Journal of Educational Technology and Online Learning*, *6*(4), 866–884.

Torres, M. N. (1996). *Teacher-Researchers in the" Zone of Proximal Development*. Insights for Teacher Education.

Türkben, T. (2021). Examination of classroom writing practices in the context of process-based approach to teaching writing. *Journal of Language and Linguistic Studies*, *17*(SI-1), 619–644.

UNESCO. (2021). AI and education: Guidance for policy-makers. Paris: United Nations Educational, Scientific and Cultural Organization (UNESCO).

Vygotsky, L. S. (1978). *Mind in society: The development of higher psychological processes* (Cole, M., John-Steiner, V., Scribner, S., & Souberman, E., Eds.). Harvard University Press.

Wang, Y., & Johnson, T. E. (2021). Emotion regulation and learning engagement in intelligent tutoring systems. *Computers & Education*, *165*, 104148.

Wertsch, J. V. (1991). *Voices of the mind: A sociocultural approach to mediated action*. Harvard University Press.

Widodo, H. P. (2008). Process-based academic essay writing instruction in an EFL context. *Bahasa dan Seni*. *Tahun*, *36*(1), 101–111.

Williamson, B., & Eynon, R. (2020). Historical threads, missing links, and future directions in AI in education. *Learning, Media and Technology*, *45*(3), 223–235.

Wilson, J. A., & Roscoe, R. D. (2020). Adaptive learning systems and writing instruction. In *Adaptive educational technologies for literacy instruction* (pp. 75–96). Routledge.

Wood, D., Bruner, J. S., & Ross, G. (1976). The role of tutoring in problem solving. *Journal of Child Psychology and Psychiatry, and Allied Disciplines*, *17*(2), 89–100. PMID: 932126

Yurdakul, B. (2010). Yapılandırmacılık. In *Eğitimde Yeni Yönelimler, Editör: Özcan Demirel* (pp. 39–65). Pegem Akademi Yayıncılık.

Zawacki-Richter, O., Marín, V. I., Bond, M., & Gouverneur, F. (2019). Systematic review of research on artificial intelligence applications in higher education – Where are the educators? *International Journal of Educational Technology in Higher Education*, *16*(1), 1–27.

Zeng, D. (2005). The process-oriented approach to ESL/EFL writing instruction and research. *Teaching English in China*, *28*(5), 67–72.

Chapter 6
Artificial Intelligence Project-Based Learning English for Specific Purposes Nexus:
Advancing Language Learning and Communication

Jean Mathieu Tsoumou
https://orcid.org/0000-0002-4651-9161
Universidad Europea de Madrid, Spain

ABSTRACT

The aim of this paper is to demonstrate how PBL and AI can be implemented in English for Specific Purposes (ESP) classrooms. The primary goal is to encourage students to develop critical thinking, problem-solving, collaboration, and communication skills while applying knowledge and concepts from various disciplines. If there is a need to ensure that students use AI responsibly, PBL stands out as an effective alternative approach in ESP classrooms. PBL enables students to (re) negotiate their learning. In a PBL context, the final product no longer has to be a traditional written essay or paper but rather a solution to a real-life problem. For instance, students might develop an app or a computer program that is beneficial not only for the fields of physics and aerospace engineering but also for society at large.

DOI: 10.4018/979-8-3373-8805-2.ch006

1. INTRODUCTION

Two trends have become prominent in higher education worldwide. On the one hand, globalization has favoured the expansion and influence of the English language in higher education systems. On the other hand, AI has brought about transformative changes and challenges affecting teaching and learning processes in higher education. While these developments have increasingly attracted the attention of scholars (Pali ă 2023, Macías 2023; Romadhon 2024; Du 2024; Li et al. 2025; Ruiz Viruel et al. 2025), little attention has been given to how AI can transform and improve language teaching and learning at La Universidad Europea de Madrid (UEM).

The ESP-AI-PBL Nexus research project aims to explore the intersection between English for Specific Purposes (ESP), Artificial Intelligence (AI), and Project-Based Learning (PBL) to enhance language learning, communication, and specialized domain knowledge acquisition. This project seeks to develop AI-driven solutions that address the diverse needs of learners in specialized fields—including aerospace engineering, medicine, physics, marketing, business administration, and law—fostering effective communication and proficiency in domain-specific English.

Specifically, this paper aims to demonstrate how PBL and AI can be implemented in ESP classrooms. This stems from my hands-on experience teaching ESP. During the 2024/2025 academic year, I initiated and successfully implemented PBL for the first time in English for Physics and English for Aerospace Engineering. Driven by the need to address challenges related to the inappropriate and irresponsible use of ChatGPT in writing assignments, PBL emerged as a more effective approach to both enhancing English learning and mitigating the misuse of AI tools. In the wake of AI advancements, it is crucial for educators to continuously reflect on how teachers and students engage both in and outside the classroom.

The remainder of this paper is organized as follows: Section Two reviews the literature on PBL and AI, Section Three describes the methodology, Section Four presents the case study, and Section Five provides concluding remarks along with the implications of this proposal for university teaching practices.

2. LITERATURE REVIEW ON PBL AND ESP

The use of PBL in the ESP context stems from the idea that active methodologies are alternatives to linear, traditional, and uniform approaches. These methodologies encourage reflection, motivation, and creativity (Macías 2023; Ngo, 2025). As a student-centered approach, PBL not only enables students to develop and improve communicative skills such as fluency and accuracy but also allows them to build personal and interpersonal qualities, as well as develop skills such as confidence, problem-solving, decision-making, and collaboration (Lundstrom 1996; Stoller 2006; Xiaofan 2025).

PBL is a teaching and learning approach that emphasizes student engagement and active participation through the completion of a project. In a PBL context, students work on a project over an extended period, investigating and responding to a complex question, problem, or challenge. This approach encourages students to develop critical thinking, problem-solving, collaboration, and communication skills while applying knowledge and concepts from various disciplines (Lundstrom 1996; Musikhin 2016).

PBL has thus long been championed in language education for its capacity to situate authentic communicative tasks in domain-specific contexts. When combined with ESP, PBL supports the development of genre-appropriate discourse, workplace interactional routines, and discipline-specific lexical resources. Recent literature highlights that AI —especially conversational agents, automated feedback systems, and generative large language models (LLMs)—is rapidly transforming how PBL can be designed and enacted in ESP courses by providing scalable simulation, individualized scaffolding, and rapid formative feedback (Du 2024; Li et al. 2025; Ruiz Viruel et al. 2025).

Empirical and review literature from 2023 to 2025 identifies three principal affordances of AI for ESP-oriented PBL. First, AI chatbots and conversational agents create low-stakes, repeatable simulations of professional interactions—such as client meetings, patient handovers, or technical briefings—allowing learners to rehearse pragmatic routines and specialized terminology at scale. Systematic reviews report consistent gains in speaking confidence and increased opportunities for disciplinary interactional practice when chatbots are integrated into curricula (Cao et al. 2025; Du 2024; Davar 2025; Lee et al. 2025). Second, AI-driven formative assessment tools, such as automated scoring engines, pronunciation analyzers, and genre-aware feedback systems, accelerate iterative drafting cycles central to PBL. These tools help students refine domain texts (e.g., reports or proposals) while freeing instructors to focus on higher-order feedback and professional communication strategies. Studies emphasize measurable improvements in task-specific writing and revision processes when these analytics are embedded within project workflows (Ruiz Viruel et al. 2025). Third, generative AI functions as a co-designer and content generator, useful for brainstorming project prompts, producing case scenarios, or generating model texts for analysis. However, researchers caution that generative outputs must be critically evaluated for domain accuracy and ethical reliability (Li et al. 2025; Lee et al. 2025).

Despite promising affordances, the literature points to persistent challenges. A major concern is domain accuracy: LLM-generated content can appear persuasive while containing factual or disciplinary errors, which in high-stakes ESP contexts may propagate misunderstandings. Teacher oversight and domain-expert validation are therefore essential (Kitila 2023; Lee et al. 2025). Closely related is academic integrity and overreliance. For example, students have been reported to have the tendencies to offload cognitive work to AI tools, prompting calls for explicit AI-literacy instruction and process-oriented assessment strategies in PBL tasks (Davar et al. 2025). Moreover, it is undeniable, for example, that traditional approaches, such as assigning writing tasks to be completed at home, may tempt students to use ChatGPT or other AI programs. If students are not carefully monitored, AI tools can become an easy shortcut. This could ultimately lead to AI tools losing their effectiveness as powerful learning tools. In this context, teachers are increasingly concerned that AI tools are being used uncontrollably by students as shortcuts to avoid challenging tasks in the learning process. In other words, the downside of AI tools is that students may no longer hesitate to cheat using tools like ChatGPT. Institutional equity and teacher readiness—particularly access to AI tools and training—are additional barriers.

Emerging design patterns for effective AI-enhanced ESP-PBL converge on three pedagogical principles. First, teacher-in-the-loop models emphasize that AI should support but not replace human pedagogical judgment (Ruiz Viruel et al. 2025). Second, process accountability frameworks require students to document decisions, evaluate AI outputs, and justify revisions (Du and Daniel 2024). Third, domain validation encourages collaboration with subject-matter experts or validated corpora to verify AI-generated content (Li et al. 2025). Studies testing LLMs inside short PBL modules reports increased engagement and task completion, but scholars call for longitudinal, domain-validated studies to demonstrate sustained gains in professional communicative competence (Lee et al. 2025). AI is thus positioned as a powerful scaffold for ESP-oriented PBL, capable of magnifying opportunities for rehearsal, feedback, and content creation. Yet safe, equitable, and pedagogically sound adoption depends on strong teacher mediation, AI literacy education, and rigorous checks on domain accuracy—priorities that future research and curriculum design must continue to address (Li et al. 2025; Ruiz Viruel et al. 2025). This is why, in this paper, I argue that PBL is an effective approach to counter the misuse of AI tools in ESP classrooms. When properly applied, both AI tools and PBL have the potential to make learning more engaging for students and emphasize the acquisition of skills essential for success in the modern workplace.

3. METHOD

The research adopted a qualitative case study design situated within an exploratory and action-oriented pedagogical framework. This design was selected to gain an in-depth understanding of how AI and PBL interact to enhance ESP instruction at *La Universidad Europea de Madrid* (UEM). The study focused on English for Physics and English for Aerospace Engineering courses during the 2024–2025 academic year, comprising a total of 28 students (11 physics and 17 aerospace engineering). The overarching aim was to examine how integrating AI into a PBL framework could promote students' language development, professional communication, and higher-order cognitive skills while mitigating the misuse of AI tools such as ChatGPT in academic writing.

The case study approach was particularly suitable because it enabled the researcher to explore real-life classroom practices, contextualize findings within authentic learning environments, and document the iterative implementation of PBL. The design aligns with interpretivist paradigms that prioritize participants' perceptions, experiences, and reflections as sources of data. Within this framework, the instructor acted as both teacher and researcher, observing how AI-enhanced PBL reshaped learner engagement, collaboration, and motivation over a semester-long course.

Data collection relied primarily on a student survey instrument administered online at the end of the semester, following the completion of the PBL project. The survey was developed to elicit students' reflections on their learning processes and experiences. It consisted of open-ended questions and short-answer prompts, allowing for qualitative depth and flexibility in responses. The instrument was structured around five key thematic dimensions: (1) improvement in English communication and technical vocabulary; (2) development of higher-order skills such as problem-solving, analytical reasoning, teamwork, and critical thinking; (3) motivation and engagement through collaborative PBL activities; (4) experiences and perceptions regarding AI tools (e.g., ChatGPT, MATLAB, DALL·E) and their educational value; and (5) overall satisfaction with PBL as a learning approach compared to traditional methods. Each question was designed to encourage self-reflection and descriptive responses rather than evaluative or yes/no answers. The inclusion of multiple questions across these domains provided triangulation within the data source, enhancing the trustworthiness of the findings.

The data analysis procedures followed a qualitative content analysis approach grounded in thematic coding. After collecting the responses, all data were anonymized and manually coded. Initial open coding identified descriptive categories such as *communication improvement*, *teamwork*, *motivation*, *AI relevance*, and *ethical concerns*. Subsequently, axial coding was applied to cluster related ideas into broader analytical themes—for example, merging *teamwork*, *collaboration*, and *peer assessment* under the theme of *collaborative learning*. Through selective coding, key themes were refined to interpret how students perceived the pedagogical interplay between AI and PBL.

Descriptive summaries and frequency counts were presented in tables to illustrate the distribution of dominant themes across participants. This mixed qualitative-quantitative presentation allowed for a clearer visualization of trends without reducing the interpretive depth of individual responses. The final stage involved a theory-driven interpretation, connecting emergent patterns with constructs from the literature on AI-mediated PBL and ESP. This analytical process ensured that findings were not only grounded in empirical classroom realities but also conceptually aligned with broader theoretical perspectives in applied linguistics, educational technology, and experiential learning.

4. CASE STUDY: DESIGN AND IMPLEMENTATION OF PBL FOR PHYSICS AND AEROSPACE ENGINEERING STUDENTS

The design of a PBL applied to ESP is a fundamental phase. An essential aspect of the project design is the acronym *SMART*, which stands for Specific, Measurable, Achievable, Relevant, and Timely (Xiaofan 2025). The goals of any PBL must be specific, measurable, achievable, relevant, and timely. For example, in designing PBL for physics and aerospace engineering students, it is important to ensure that the PBL is tailored to students' needs and aspirations. In other words, the features of the project must be specifically linked to physics/aerospace engineering and their respective job opportunities.

Additionally, all the tasks involved in the project development must yield physical evidence that allows the teacher to measure students' dedication, progress, uptake, and retention. For instance, all groups must hold their meetings on Teams, which the teacher will monitor to ensure evidence of their work. All of this was both achievable and relevant to the learning needs and the students' aspirations. Finally, the project was designed to be carried out in a timely fashion. Every detail of the project was clearly explained in a document provided to the students as a handout on Canvas. In this process, the role of artificial intelligence, especially ChatGPT, was significantly important in both the project development and the students' language development.

For a PBL to be successful, it must be implemented rationally. Students should be aware of what is expected of them from the very beginning of the course. For example, in the first week of class, students were introduced to the PBL approach. The content and different phases of the project were clearly explained. On the first day, students were informed that, alongside traditional subject content, they would be working on PBL throughout the semester. Similarly, the definition and phases of PBL were thoroughly explained to the students. Lastly, the role of AI and the reasons why it should be used in the project's development were emphasized. To support this, a list of 10 suggested topics was provided to the students, allowing them to choose a topic that suited their aspirations.

4.1. Phases of PBL

This project was structured into five different phases, described as follows.

4.1.1. Phase 1

Phase 1 is referred to as group creation. In this phase, students voluntarily and freely create or join groups. The choice of group is critical to the success of a PBL, as the success of the project depends on students' motivation and their willingness to work with peers they feel comfortable with. Therefore, the selection of group members was left to the students. They were given two business weeks to create or join groups of four members. By week 3 of the course, the project was underway.

4.1.2. Phase 2

In Phase 2, the students' task is to select an appropriate topic for their team. Once the topic is selected, students must conduct research and prepare for the first evaluative assessment, called the Elevator Pitch, in Phase 3. An elevator pitch is a brief description of an idea, product, or company that explains the concept in a way that any listener can understand in a short period of time.

Figure 1. Possible topics

1. Possible topics

Here are some project-based topics in physics that you can consider:

1.	**Projectile motion analysis**: Investigate and in schematic form, describe the factors that affect the trajectory of a projectile, such as launch angle, initial velocity, and air resistance.
2.	**Electric circuits**: Build and analyze various electrical circuits, such as series and parallel circuits, and investigate concepts like resistance, voltage, and current.
3.	**Optics and light**: Build a simple telescope or microscope and explore concepts like refraction, reflection, and magnification. Investigate how different lenses affect the behavior of light
4.	**Renewable energy sources**: Design and build a small-scale model of a renewable energy system, such as a wind turbine or a solar-powered device. Measure and analyze its efficiency.
5.	**Thermodynamics and heat transfer**: Investigate heat transfer mechanisms, such as conduction, convection, and radiation. Build a calorimeter to measure specific heat capacities of different materials.
6.	**Fluid dynamics**: Explore the behavior of fluids by designing experiments to investigate concepts like Bernoulli's principle, viscosity, and fluid pressure.
7.	**Quantum mechanics**: Explore the principles of quantum mechanics by conducting experiments related to quantum phenomena, such as wave-particle duality or quantum entanglement.
8.	**Magnetic fields and electromagnetism**: Build an electromagnet and investigate the factors affecting its strength, such as the number of wires turns or the amount of current flowing through it.
9.	**Astrophysics**: Investigate astronomical phenomena, such as the properties of stars, planetary motion, or the behavior of black holes. Use data analysis and simulations to understand these phenomena.
10.	**Nuclear physics**: Explore the properties of radioactive materials and their decay processes. Investigate concepts like half-life, radiation shielding, and nuclear reactions.

These topics are suggested choices. However, students have the option to work on any other topic of their choosing, provided the choice receives the teacher's approval.

From the outset, students are provided with guidance on the use of AI in the classroom. Following the AI usage protocol established by La UEM, students are informed about the role of AI in both the development and evaluation of the project, as it pertains to the different phases. For instance, while students are allowed to use chatbots in the design of the elevator pitch, the evaluation of the elevator pitch focuses primarily on the students' abilities to communicate and explain complex concepts in a clear and convincing way.

In addition, while the project is underway, two AI workshops are scheduled and included in the syllabus. The first workshop is scheduled for mid-September, and the second for mid-November. These workshops are designed to give students a clear understanding of both the strengths and weaknesses of AI in academic settings. It is important to emphasize the role of these workshops not only in the development of the project but also in the students' broader language development.

For example, the workshops are structured to teach students the best strategies and practices for creating effective, specific, and engaging prompts to extract the right information and data from chatbots. Additionally, while students learn proper ways to use AI, exercises and activities focused specifically on language and linguistic development are also included in these workshops. Exercises such as discourse analysis, text analysis, grammar analysis, and spelling analysis are key components of these workshops. In this way, AI workshops in ESP contexts serve as an innovative approach to teaching language through chatbots while enhancing technological abilities and skills.

4.1.3. Phase 3

Phase 3 is referred to as the Elevator Pitch phase, in which students are required to conduct research on the topic their group has selected (see Appendix 1). The students must identify a research gap that allows them to narrow down their project and prepare a presentation in the form of an elevator pitch. This preliminary research should enable students to prepare a short presentation in which they describe the reason for choosing a particular topic, its relevance within the fields of physics and aerospace engineering, and the job opportunities the topic offers.

As explained earlier, an elevator pitch is a brief description of an idea, product, or company that conveys the concept in a way that any listener can understand within a short period of time. This phase lasts for one month. In this case, Phase 3 runs from September 20 to October 20. On October 20, students will make group oral presentations.

The difference between Phase 2 and Phase 3 is that whereas Phase 2 involved no assessment, the elevator pitch in Phase 2 is considered an assessable task. What is required and expected from the students is their ability to convey a clear and concise message to the audience. These presentations are designed to help students develop not only communication skills but also confidence in public speaking, while encouraging teamwork and collaboration.

It is important to note that both physics and aerospace engineering, being predominantly project-based fields, require teamwork, collaboration, communication skills, and public speaking for success. Developing these skills in an academic setting helps prepare students to face potential professional challenges inherent in both fields. To this end, students are given clear and specific instructions listed as follows:

General Instructions for Graded Task 1:

- Choose a specific topic for your group (see the document on Project-based Learning).
- Design a graph that will support your elevator pitch.
- Distribute tasks fairly among group members.
- Submit the graph in its final form on Canvas the day before the presentation.
- Practice your work before giving the presentation.

Specific Instructions:

- Identify the problem based on the selected topic (i.e., why did you choose this topic?).
- Identify the gap and design the solution to the problem (i.e., what has been done before, and what do you want to accomplish with your project?).
- Design your workplan to achieve that solution (i.e., how will you work together to achieve the goal of your project? How will tasks be distributed among members? Who will do what?).
- Describe the value of your work (i.e., what value will you add once you complete your project? What impact will it have on society, the world, or the environment?).

These instructions require a literature review and careful decision-making to deliver an effective elevator pitch. This phase is rooted in the principle of learning through practical actions with a real purpose. One of the most important skills needed by experts in physics and/or aerospace engineering is the ability to communicate complex ideas and concepts fluently and effectively. Accordingly, the students' elevator pitches will be assessed based on the grammatical and lexical resources used, how students manage their discourse, how well words are pronounced, and their abilities to respond to and maintain interactive communication with audience members who may ask questions.

The use of a rubric for evaluation helps keep students focused on the task (see Appendix 2). This ensures students are self-conscious and mindful of language use, especially in terms of grammar, spelling, discourse, pronunciation, and interactive communication. All these elements are crucial for making strong presentations and for language development.

4.1.4. Phase 4

This phase assumes that the students have worked hard enough to produce the final product of their project. After four months of collaborative work, Phase 5 provides an opportunity for the students to showcase the physical evidence of their ideas. This phase must derive from and be clearly linked to previous phases, especially Phases 2 and 3. It is divided into Part A and Part B. While Part A represents the written project, Part B draws from Part A and translates it into the oral presentation of the final project.

Part A represents an original piece of work produced by students in an academic manner[1]. In this part, students must demonstrate communication skills appropriate for upper-intermediate and advanced English levels. They should show a strong ability to organize ideas and use specific physics and aerospace engineering vocabulary both appropriately and accurately. In the final phase of the project, students should clearly define what the project was about, the problem they aimed to solve, and how they solved it. If they have developed or designed a specific product, they should describe its functioning in detail and its impact not only in the fields of physics and aerospace engineering but, more importantly, in society at large. Students should also clearly demonstrate how the developed product works and who can use it.

In case the students opt for mainly written report, the length of the written project will be between 500 and 650 words, excluding the cover page, annexes, and reference list (the latter should be in APA format).

Part A of Phase 5 (see Appendix 3) is evaluated based on four criteria: content, communicative achievement, organization, and language. It is important to note that while students carry out the project as an out-of-class assignment, in-class teaching activities should focus on enabling students to not only prepare the different phases of the project but, more importantly, to integrate both content and language. Therefore, students will be taught various techniques (such as scanning, skimming, note-taking, summarizing, paraphrasing, interjecting, source assessment, formal and informal styles, academic expression, etc.) to develop their reading, listening, speaking, and writing competencies based on physics content.

As is the case for every evaluative phase, the rubric for evaluation must be clear and analytical. The aim of this analytical rubric is to ensure that students use language according to the demands of their professional aspirations. The written project should therefore be composed with precision, coherence, and conciseness, requiring students to possess language skills that interact with both the content and the background underlying physics.

Part B, the oral presentation of the written project, requires students to design a PowerPoint based on the written project (see Appendix 4). The specific instructions require students to:

1. Provide an overview of their project (For example: "Our project is about xxx."),
2. Clearly explain the aim/purpose/objective of the study (For example: "Our purpose in this study was to explain the role of xxx."),
3. Present the points/findings considered to answer/respond to the research question (For example: "Our research question found its scientific answer through the following points...."),
4. Provide the most important concluding remarks from the findings (For example: "The most important conclusion of my project is that...").
5. For the oral presentation, students are required to present within a time limit. Each group will have 10 minutes: 8 minutes for the presentation and 2 minutes for questions from the audience and answers from the presenting group.

The analytical rubric for this phase allows the teacher to evaluate the students' oral production. To meet the rubric's expectations, the teacher should adopt a communicative language approach during in-class teaching. The focus should be on learning to communicate by interacting in the language being learned. The benefits of a communicative language approach include its ability to: (1) help learners become familiar with the texts typically used in the target situation, (2) give learners the opportunity to focus on language and manage their learning process, (3) improve students' personal and professional experiences, leading to better performance in the classroom, and (4) increase awareness of how what is learned in the classroom can be applied to real-life contexts outside it (Musikhin, 2016).

4.1.5. Phase 5: Peer Review Assessment

Since the project is carried out in groups, students are given the opportunity to assess their groupmates based on the criteria described below: collaboration, input, commitment, and leadership. At this stage, they are required to anonymously rate the dedication, involvement, and commitment of each group member. The assessment of collaboration consists of determining whether the groupmates have collaborated fully or partially. Very active and proactive members score the highest points (2.5 pts), regular members score 1, and absent members score 0 (null points).

It is important for students to assess the input of each group member. Within this criterion, any student who has substantially participated scores 2.5 pts, a regular participant scores 1, and a student with low participation scores 0. Commitment to the group is also assessed based on whether the groupmates were all committed to the success of the group. The highest score (2.5 pts) is attributed to the highly committed member, whereas the lowest score is attributed to the non-committed member (0 pts).

Finally, peer assessment also includes an evaluation of the students' leadership skills. Working collaboratively requires each group member to take responsibility for the success of the project. Therefore, any student who is considered by their peers as a very good leader scores 2.5 pts.

This peer review assessment aims to evaluate individual contributions to the group project and provide constructive feedback to improve teamwork and collaboration skills. Each group member will assess the contributions of their peers in the semester-long project. The feedback should reflect each member's effort, quality of work, and teamwork. This peer review will also give students an opportunity to reflect on their own contributions as well (see Appendix 5). The responses of the peer review must remain anonymous. The instructor will aggregate and review the feedback to ensure fairness. Finally, each member must include at least 2-3 sentences of constructive feedback that address both strengths and areas for improvement for their peers.

In the ChatGPT era, assessment in a PBL context refers to diagnosing the student's learning to help them improve, if necessary. Each phase of the PBL is equally important. This process is normally ongoing, and it allows the teacher to evaluate how well the student's performance aligns with expectations. The three main steps of assessment are (a) the establishment of goals and objectives, (b) the collection of information on the students' performance, and (c) the interpretation of such information. The different rubrics used in the various phases of the PBL allow the teacher to achieve the specific objectives set for each phase. The goal of the assessment is to ensure that the teaching/learning process enables the student to improve their skills, better understand scientific discourse, and develop critical thinking. It is evident that understanding writing patterns in science and critical thinking are two aspects that must be complemented with communication skills for scientists whose mother tongue is not English, as English is the lingua franca of this field.

Table 1 summarizes the different phases of the project along with the evaluation system inherent to each phase.

Table 1. PBL phrases

Phases		**Includes a grading scale**	**Includes rubric of evaluation**
Phase 1: Group creation		X	X
Phase 2: Topic selection		X	X
Phase 3: Elevator pitch		✓	✓
Phase 4: Final product	Part A	✓	✓
	Part B	✓	✓
Phase 5: Peer review		✓	✓

4.2. The Role of the Teacher

Throughout the progress of the project, the teacher shall be available to the students. The groups created on Teams shall be supervised continuously. This supervision in no way implies participation in the ongoing chats among the students. The deadline for each phase must be clearly set at the beginning of the semester, and modifications should be avoided.

Although the teacher's role in the students' PBL is limited to providing guidance, feedback and feedforward, it is very important that the teacher considers how they will work with their students to help them not only attain their goals but also connect the knowledge acquired in the classroom with the different phases and objectives of the project. The students are the main agents in the PBL. They shall collaboratively work towards common goals in a responsible manner. They make a deliberate choice of the topic based on their interests and professional aspirations. To help the teacher keep track of the students' out-of-classroom progress, the students are required to conduct periodic meetings within their respective groups created on Teams and leave evidence of their work. While the teacher can access the students' meetings, chats, and documents shared on Teams, they do not intervene in any way.

5. THE STUDENTS' UPTAKE

Upon completion, the students shall reflect on the experience of working in groups, not just to produce the final product, but also to learn English through collaboration, commitment, and common goals. This subsection examines the students' uptake by analysing their comments and responses to the survey. To begin with, the effectiveness of PBL will be explored. Second, the students' engagement, motivation, and satisfaction will be analysed. Finally, the comments on the relevance of AI will be examined.

a. PBL approach in the development of both English language proficiency and technical communication skills

It must be argued that an ESP program should emphasize the development of interpersonal communication skills in students who are preparing for graduate work in engineering (Faheem 2016; Lee et al. 2025). This is because communication skills are not only at the heart of what is expected from students in the market, but also play a tremendous role in representing the physical evidence of language learning. Tailoring language instructions to meet the needs of learners in a specific context through PBL makes professionally based communication skills achievable. Considering this, students' experiences with PBL in ESP classes are overwhelmingly positive. In the data presented in Table 2, nearly every student reported having a good experience learning ESP through PBL. In other words, learning ESP through PBL satisfies and fulfils the students' learning needs and expectations.

The effectiveness of PBL in an ESP context stems from its numerous benefits, which extend beyond improving communication skills and fostering the ability to use language effectively in specific contexts. These benefits include boosting confidence in language learning, understanding the importance of non-verbal communication in oral production, enhancing technical and subject-specific vocabulary, refining report-writing skills, and increasing overall English proficiency. In a competitive world where collaboration and efficiency are paramount, the skills and abilities developed through PBL in ESP classes equip students with higher-order competencies, effectively preparing them to face the challenges of the professional world.

Table 2. PBL and communication skills development

	How has the PBL approach improved your English communication skills (e.g., technical vocabulary, report writing, presentations)?
1	Being more confident
2	I got more comfortable speaking in front of people and using new skills like walking around/making eye contact while presenting
3	Not much
4	In report writtting vocabulary and presentation ability.
5	helped to review the grammar
6	I have learned more vocabulary related to aerospace engineering.
7	It has been useful because it has helped me to talk in public and prepare more serious presentations.
8	little to non at all. I am a native English speaker, therefore, it was very basic for me
9	It has improved my English skills because it forced me to talk, present and communicate with others in English and using technical vocabulary.
10	By making student's understand and apply terminology in different contexts.
11	The PBL approach has significantly improved my English communication skills by providing opportunities to use technical vocabulary in realistic moments
12	presentations cause it help me how to talk in front of audience
13	It helped me to get to know a lot of aerospace engineering vocabulary
14	It has mainly improved my report writing skills through team work and allowing me to understand how other people approach their writing process, taking the positives from many of them and applying them to strengthen my own writing.
15	A lot, I feel that my english is more fluent than ever.
16	While working in groups and having to discuss some topics.
17	Yes
18	It hasn't
19	A lot, I lost the nervousness to speak in English.
20	I learn a lot of vocabulary and presentations
21	not much because I already had a very good English before starting the course
22	A lot
23	The PBL approach has improved my English communication skills by enhancing my technical vocabulary, refining my report-writing abilities, and boosting my confidence in delivering clear and professional presentations.
24	The technical parts mostly.
25	Not at all as i am a proficient english speaker
26	I consider that my pronunciation and presentation of projects has improved.
27	Very little, as physics is pretty similar between Spanish and English
28	Anything.

English may be internationally known as the language of technology, science, and engineering, but it is undeniable that it only fulfils these roles when communication skills—whether written or spoken—are well developed and actively used by its users. The merit of PBL is that it provides learners with the opportunity to develop not only communication skills but also other critical professional and organizational abilities, such as critical thinking and problem-solving, among many others. These skills, by their nature as higher-order thinking skills, are essential for evaluating information, making decisions, and solving complex problems.

However, despite the effectiveness of PBL in developing both English language proficiency and technical communication skills, not all students report achieving proficiency through PBL. For instance, comment 28 suggests that the student did not experience significant language development in this PBL context. Similarly, comment 25 implies that the student's proficiency in English prevented them from learning more than what they already knew. As revealed in the comments, highly proficient English learners may have different experiences or perspectives.

Table 3. PBL and high-order skills development

	Which language skills (critical thinking, problem-solving, analytical skill, teamwork) improved the most through the PBL approach? Please explain.
1	My analytical skill has improved a lot
2	Teamwork, I got to collaborate with my peers.
3	teamwork. I have developed this skill by working in groups in the different fases of the project
4	Team work and team organization
5	analytical skill
6	Maybe it can be teamwork skill because we had to perform in groups.
7	speaking in public
8	teamwork and critical thinking, due to having to read and analyze different academic articles
9	I think teamwork and problem-solving were the skills that we worked the most.
10	Collaboration because of the numerous projects and activities that we completed both in class and at home.
11	Teamwork improved the most through the PBL approach because it required constant collaboration
12	teamwork cause in a project we must collaporate to have a bright ideas and a good project
13	Teamwork
14	The project based learning was most influential in improving my teamwork ability as well as my problem solving when I assumed more managerial positons in a group setting where I was faced with complex problems to solve as well as asigning people accordingly and trying to meet everyones wants.
15	I think that understanding what they want to tell me.
16	The language skill that I have improved the most has been the English oral comprenhension.
17	There was not problem-solving and too much critical thinking but I improve teamwork
18	Teamwork
19	Teamwork, because we had to collaborate to finish the project.
20	Teamwork, because i need a team to made projects
21	Teamwork
22	Express myself
23	Teamwork improved the most through the PBL approach because collaborating on projects required effective communication, idea-sharing, and resolving challenges together, fostering a supportive and productive learning environment.
24	Problem-solving
25	Teamwork as it is always something I can improve on no matter the level of english
26	I Thunderbolt the team working.
27	I don't know
28	Any of them. I learned all of those things in Bachiller.

Implementing PBL in ESP classes is an effective way to instil in students (a) cognitive skills, such as reasoning, evaluating, and synthesizing information, (b) 21st-century skills, which are crucial for success in modern professional and academic environments, and (c) employability skills that are essential for effective decision-making across industries. For instance, when asked about specific skills developed through PBL, students reported gaining one or more of these skill sets. The first student, for example, mentions an improvement in their analytical skills, while students 2 and 3 highlight teamwork as the primary skill developed through their PBL experience. In other words, PBL facilitates the integration of higher-order skills through context-driven, interactive, and real-world tasks that align with students' professional fields. As student 23 succinctly puts it: "Teamwork improved the most through the PBL approach because collaborating on projects required effective communication, idea-sharing, and resolving challenges together, fostering a supportive and productive learning environment."

Zhai and Wibowo (2023: 13) emphasize that "by effectively integrating AI technologies, students can develop essential skills such as critical and creative thinking, collaboration, communication, and problem-solving, which are vital for success in the 21st century. Therefore, incorporating technology is crucial in enhancing student learning and success." Table 4 below illustrates students' positive uptake of the collaborative nature of PBL, which has been highly rated.

Table 4. PBL and students' motivation

	Did the collaborative nature of PBL activities motivate you to participate more actively? Why or why not?
1	Yes to be more effective and time efficient
2	Yes because I didnt want to be behind or slacking in my group
3	It may have done so, as the subject makes us verbally engage in daily class
4	yes
5	yes as it is interactive and more enjoyable
6	Yes because we were on a similar project before and it did help us to participate on it more actively
7	yes because I enjoyed the process
8	yes, because it forces me to engage directly with the source material
9	Yes because it crates a commitment to work with our partners.
10	Yes, not only because the activities where quite interesting, but also because participating felt productive.
11	Yes, as it was necesary to be constantly learning new things
12	yes this is because the teamwork and presentations skills
13	Yes, of course
14	It mostly did, except when certain people would take managerial roles and be to authoritarian without considering anyone else's imput.
15	Yes, because I need to talk more.
16	Yes, due to the teacher encouraging everyone to speak.
17	Sometimes when i need them for real problems
18	Not entirely, but you are forced to.
19	Yes, because we needed to work as a team to achieve the goals.
20	No. I prefere doing individual activities
21	yes because of the teamwork
22	Yes, because of group engagement
23	Yes, collaboration in PBL boosts motivation by fostering teamwork, diverse perspectives, and practical problem-solving, making learning more engaging and relevant.
24	Yes, but only with a few persons. The people in the class made me reconsider the use
25	Yes because each team member had a specifically defined job
26	Not enough because I am someone who is quite reclusive and I feel that I have a much lower level.
27	Not really, I think there wasn't much communication in my team
28	Yes,

As can be seen, virtually all students have had positive experiences collaborating with their classmates. As argued earlier, both physics and aerospace engineering are fields in which teamwork is crucial to the success or failure of work-related projects, as collaboration involves two or more people working together to achieve a common goal.

What is particularly noteworthy are the reasons students provide for why collaboration in PBL is important. For example, while student 1 in Table 4 highlights that collaboration enhances effectiveness and efficiency in time management, comment 2 emphasizes its role in motivating their contribution and pace (e.g., *"Yes, because I didn't want to be behind or slacking in my group"*). However, it is also important to consider the reasons given by students (comments 18, 20, 26, and 27) who did not find collaboration beneficial for the project's development. Comment 18, for instance, expresses dissatisfaction with the collaborative nature of PBL, stating that they felt forced to collaborate. Similarly, comment 20 attributes their response to self-sufficiency, implying they prefer working independently (Ngo 2025). Interestingly, the negative response from comment 27 stems from poor communication within their group—suggesting that, had communication been more effective, they might have had a more positive experience. Overall, beyond merely completing the group project, collaboration enables students to develop essential skills such as problem-solving (comment 23), commitment to group success (comment 9), and productivity (comment 10).

b. Students' engagement, motivation, and satisfaction with the integration of PBL in the ESP course

Classroom engagement, motivation, and satisfaction are key outcomes of students' positive experiences with a given teaching and learning approach. Positive experiences are rooted in high engagement, which stems from strong motivation and ultimately leads to high satisfaction. As shown in Table 5 below, virtually every student reported a positive experience with PBL. From Comment 1 to Comment 28, the most frequently used adjective to describe students' experiences with PBL is "good."

The favourability of these experiences supports the argument that teaching ESP through PBL helps students meet their expectations and enjoy the teaching and learning process. It is also important to note that the positive experiences resulting from the implementation of PBL stem from each student's individual motives or reasons. For some, these positive experiences arise from the autonomy PBL provides, such as the ability to choose their own topics (e.g., Comment 3: "A good experience because we had free election about the topic."). For others, satisfaction comes from the collaborative and hands-on nature of PBL (e.g., Comment 9: "I think project-based learning is a good tool to teach students how to work in groups effectively. Overall, in my case, the experience was good and profitable."). Additionally, some students value the absence of traditional theoretical tests, which are common in traditional ESP classes (e.g., Comment 15: "To be honest, I prefer doing projects rather than exams. For example, in this lesson, in my opinion, projects are better.").

Table 5. Students' overall experience with PBL

	How would you describe your overall experience with the project-based learning (PBL) approach in this course?
1	Great
2	Useful and engaging
3	Satisfactory and progressive learning, really good for me
4	A good experience because we had free election about the topic
5	Normal
6	Usefull if you have a good project in mind, it can help a lot to make you carry out it and don't stay just with the idea.
7	I find it is a good method of learning because it gives us a freedom of topic to work on, therefore you can work on what you like whilst we learn more.
8	It was good
9	I think the project based learning is a good tool to teach students how to work in groups effectively. Overall, in my case the experience was good and profetable.
10	It was good and helpful to develop more practical skills as well as improve overall collaboration.
11	It provided general knowledge and time-management
12	its very useful and it gave me a valuable experience
13	Very good
14	it was great and very dynamic
15	To be honest, I prefer doing projects rather than exams. For example on this lesson, in my opinion, projects are way better.
16	My overall experience with the PBL has been very pleasant and comfortable.
17	My overall experience has been positive. It allowed me to apply theoretical concepts to real-world problems and dynamics, which made the learning process more practical.
18	Good idea, but makes you sacrifice too much time.
19	Normal
20	My experience in this kind of learning it´s good
21	very good(I am Javi)
22	Interesting
23	My overall experience with the project-based learning (PBL) approach has been positive. It provided hands-on opportunities to apply concepts, encouraged collaboration, and made learning more engaging and practical
24	I find it a more comfortable and interactive method than the traditional examination method.
25	It is more interactive and potentially more effective for more people than more conventional teaching methods
26	Very good, I consider it to be something necessary and very useful for the future of work.
27	I think it was interesting, but I have had issues about the main objective of the project
28	Good

In terms of engagement, similar patterns can be observed in students' experiences. In other words, not only do virtually all students find the implementation of PBL in ESP classes more engaging compared to traditional teaching and learning approaches, but the reasons for their engagement vary from student to student. Zhai and Wibowo (2023: 12) note that "learner engagement is a measure of the quantity and quality of a learner's involvement in their learning." In this study, students' involvement depends on different attributes. For some students, the emphasis on collaboration makes PBL more engaging (e.g., Comment 2: *"More engaging, I worked more with my peers and did interactive activities to solidify my learning."*). For others, engagement stems from the fact that PBL allows both the learning process and the final product to be evaluated (e.g., Comment 12: *"I did find it more satisfactory, as with this method, the work throughout the whole course is evaluated rather than just one or two exams."*). Additionally, some students appreciate that PBL focuses on their professional and personal interests (e.g., Comment 14: *"Yes, because the group setting and emphasis on research and our personal learning journeys allowed for a more engaging and interest-based learning."*). Finally, for others, learning through PBL changes the course's dynamics and focus, allowing students not only to learn grammar and vocabulary but, more importantly, to connect abstract content with practical and professional contexts (e.g., Comment 27: *"I find it as engaging as other projects in my career, but I find the PBL approach more useful than grammar and vocabulary classes."*).

Table 6. PBL versus traditional learning approaches

	Did you find the PBL approach more engaging compared to traditional methods of learning? Why or why not?
1	Yes, its better than doing power points all class
2	More engaging. I worked more with my peers and did interactive activities to solidify my learning
3	I did find it more satisfactory, as with this method the work throughout the whole course is evaluated rather than just one or two exams.
4	Yes, because we chose the topic an this is very interesant.
5	yes but I think that it could be done better
6	Yes, because it as I said on the other question it helps you to perform it more.
7	I do, it gives a different approach to what students are used to do on class which makes it enjoyable.
8	yes, because i was able to engage with the materiel we were learning in class in a more hand on approach allowing me to see it more clearly
9	It's more engaging because we learn from other and at the same time we are able to teach things to our partners. This allows us to reinforce and clarify our language.
10	Yes, because it actually requires the student's participation and engagement
11	yes, because it involved active learning
12	yes,cause it gave me precious skills
13	I personally like it more as a learning method because it makes you work in groups to solve stuff
14	Yes, because the group setting and emphasis on research and our personal learning journeys allowed for a more engaging and interest based learning
15	Yes, because you talk more in class, you see useful applications of science and its less stressing
16	Yes, I have find the PBL approach more engaging due to being a whole different idea, also the experience of group work has been very ambitious.
17	Yes, because it emphasized active participation and problem-solving rather than passive memorization. Working on projects related to aerospace engineering helped me stay motivated, as I could see the direct application of what I was learning.
18	Yes, it basically forces you to be active.
19	Yes, because it's more practical
20	I think that it´s have some benefit such us learning to make presentations, but i don´t preffere
21	yes because we did a lot of presentations
22	Yes, it prompts us to do deep researchs while we learn
23	Yes, I found the PBL approach more engaging than traditional methods because it involved active problem-solving, collaboration, and real-world applications, making learning more interactive and meaningful.
24	Yes, I found it more engaging. Firstly because of the dynamism, it is much more fluid, secondly, because of its lightness. It is more comfortable to do a project for a week than to study a closed syllabus for a month.
25	Yes because it gives the student a greater degree of freedom in their learning
26	Yes, because I consider that in a project you can learn more than in simple written tests.
27	I find it as engaging as other projects in the career, but I find the PBL approach more useful than grammar and vocabulary classes
28	I find it very intense.

Compared to traditional teaching and learning approaches, PBL is overwhelmingly valued and positively received by students. For example, Comment 16 in Table 6 highlights that PBL is not only engaging but also fosters a sense of collective purpose through group learning (e.g., *"Yes, I have found the PBL approach more engaging due to it being a completely different concept. Additionally, the experience of group work has been highly ambitious"*).

Similarly, Comment 24 emphasizes the dynamism of PBL, stating that it is more meaningful and valuable to their learning than following a rigid syllabus for a month (e.g., *"Yes, I found it more engaging. Firstly, because of its dynamism—it is much more fluid. Secondly, because of its lightness. It is more comfortable to complete a project in a week than to study a fixed syllabus for a month."*).

C. Relevance and impact of AI tools in/on the success and learning outcomes of the projects

Zhai and Wibowo (2023: 12) explain that *"technological integration in language learning is the use of technology to improve students' learning experience. Technology enhances students' opportunities for authentic connection with native speakers and other language learners of varying proficiency levels, both within and outside of the classroom."* Accordingly, when used appropriately, AI can serve as an immensely useful learning tool and resource for students. To explore its implications in the development of PBL in ESP classes, students were asked whether they used AI tools and how helpful these tools were in executing their projects. As shown in Table 7, most students utilized various AI tools for different purposes. The most frequently used tools were ChatGPT, DALL·E, and MATLAB. Among other applications, these tools were used to (a) generate ideas, (b) proofread grammar and vocabulary, (c) learn new content, (d) generate images and compare information, (e) enhance content understanding, (f) summarize ideas, and (g) solve problems.

A closer examination of students' reasons for using AI in project execution reveals not only their engagement and desire to extend learning beyond the classroom but also that AI tools provide additional opportunities to organize and develop projects from multiple perspectives.

Table 7. AI tools and their utilities

	Which AI tools did you use during the project, and how helpful were they? (e.g., ChatGPT, MATLAB, data visualization tools)
1	Chat GPT
2	I used chatGPT to generate ideas/pictures for projects or help me explore new perspectives about a writing task
3	We haven't used much AI
4	no a lot
5	gramarrly and after for vocabulary I used thesaurus
6	Maybe to learn some things that we didn't knew we used a little bit of ChatGPT, but we haven't use it that much
7	I did not use roughly any of them because most of the information is only known by the Lilium company member which provided us the information.
8	chat gpt was helpful for research and finding sources to read
9	Mainly ChatGPT and DALL-E
10	ChatCPT helped me in some cases to further understand a topic and come up with ideas for activities.
11	Specially Chat GPT, it was reaaly useful to generate images and contrast information
12	chatGPT as its not 100 percent correct but it give me guidlines or hints to find what i want
13	None
14	I used ChatGPT sometimes in order to evaluate my own ideas or sumarize certain texts, but I didn't use AI that often in general.
15	Chat gpt in order to search useful pages for information.
16	No AI tools at all.
17	Image generator IA, Matlab
18	ChatGPT
19	I used ChatGPT and MATLAB; they were very useful for solving problems and generating ideas.
20	Chatgpt
21	chatgpt and Matlab
22	ChatGPT
23	I used AI tools like ChatGPT for research and drafting content, and data visualization tools for creating clear, informative charts. These tools were extremely helpful in streamlining complex tasks and enhancing project quality.
24	MATLAB and CHAT GPT
25	ChatGPT to condense highly technical research
26	ChatGPT
27	ChatGPT, Python
28	ChatGPT

Noticeably, ChatGPT is the most used AI tool. This is understandable, given its popularity. However, what is particularly interesting is that the variety of AI tools used by students suggests that teaching best practices for AI integration in the classroom enables them to understand and purposefully utilize these tools. For example, Comment 23 explicitly outlines the reason for using AI: *"I used AI tools like ChatGPT for research and drafting content, and data visualization tools for creating clear, informative charts. These tools were extremely helpful in streamlining complex tasks and enhancing project quality."* Comment 23 highlights key components of both language development and higher-order thinking skills. This underscores the importance of AI in education. Table 8 below presents students' perspectives on the relevance of AI in supporting learning and development in physics and aerospace engineering.

Table 8. AI and its role in supporting learning and development

	How relevant do you think AI is for supporting learning and development in aerospace engineering and/or physics?
1	Extremely relevant
2	Very relevant, AI is useful to explain every step of the process making it very useful for math/science applications
3	I think it downplays the efforts and work of the student
4	IA in this topics have some failures
5	helps a lot to understand new concepts and is much easier to learn
6	If you use it the right way it can be so usefull
7	it is a tool more that we have but not important or necessary.
8	very relevant
9	It's very reelevant because it can do the easy boring job and leave us time for the most analytical and complex tasks.
10	It is relevant seeing as it can give clear and easy to understand explanations.
11	It is very important although it can be mistaken
12	yes AI supports in development and supporting learning in aerospace engineering
13	Very relevant
14	It was mainly relevant in making my learning more time eficient
15	It is crucial, it can be used in a hundred ways in the sector.
16	Very relevant.
17	Is very important for the vocabulary, gramar, structure, analysis
18	Very
19	It is very relevant because it accelerates learning and helps solve problems faster.
20	It will become so important
21	very relevant, it helps you to remember details
22	Very important
23	AI is highly relevant for supporting learning in aerospace engineering and physics, as it enhances simulations, data analysis, and optimization, helping students grasp complex concepts, solve problems faster, and explore new solutions more effectively.
24	Very relevant
25	Somewhat relevant but not vital
26	I think it is important since it is a very useful tool.
27	Really important, as it is the future of experimentation
28	It's a supporting tool.

The transformation brought about by AI in language teaching and learning is undeniable. A closer look at students' responses regarding the relevance of AI tools in their projects reveals that these tools can be categorized based on their ability to (a) allow students to explore new horizons (see Comment 5), (b) help them track project progress (see Comment 21), (c) accelerate language learning, problem-solving, and time management(see Comments 12, 14, and 23), and

(d) support vocabulary acquisition, grammar comprehension, and the development of well-structured projects.

These self-reported benefits suggest that AI tools can effectively complement ESP courses, significantly enhancing learning objectives and outcomes. The comments in Table 8 indicate that AI provides personalized, efficient, and relevant learning experiences. The integration of AI in PBL promotes learner autonomy, real-world applicability, and linguistic proficiency, making it an indispensable tool in modern ESP instruction.

The key argument is that incorporating AI into project-based learning for ESP enhances personalization, fosters real-world engagement, streamlines research and writing, and encourages collaboration. By leveraging AI-driven tools, students not only improve their language proficiency but also develop industry-specific communication skills essential for their careers. As AI continues to evolve, its role in ESP education will become even more critical, transforming how professionals communicate in specialized fields.

For instance, Table 9 below highlights the specific skills students have developed through AI tools. Notably, almost every student acknowledges that AI integration in the classroom has helped them enhance various skills and abilities, including structuring projects (Comments 1, 7, and 17), improving writing (Comments 2 and 3), finding relevant information and data (Comments 9 and 13), and learning how to conduct research and summarize texts (Comments 26 and 27).

Table 9. What IA tools bring to the students learning project

	How did the use of AI enhance or hinder your ability to complete the project? Please elaborate
1	To structurice the proyect
2	AI helped me get broader ideas to improve my writing
3	not much
4	i dont used the IA
5	improve in language skills and writting skills.
6	To ask for kind of information related to how other countries use the project we are on.
7	It helped to structure the document and know what points to focus on
8	it enhanced it by making it easier to find information, using it as a search tool
9	It enhanced it because it saves time in searching for information relevant to our project.
10	It sligtly enhanced my ability, but it was just an additional help rather than something crucial to understand a complete the activities.
11	It motivated me to continue when I felt stuck, as it was a solution
12	AI enhance me to have a good project
13	I didn't use them
14	AI helped me take time off of some tidious tasks
15	Using AI brings you the possibility of doing the job really well. This doesent means that it does everything, but if you know how to use it, it is very powerful.
16	I did not use the AI.
17	ChatGpt has a more coherent structure while writing about something and sometimes analyzes deeply what you want.
18	Selecting the themes to talk about
19	It improved the project by simplifying complex tasks, but sometimes it was hard to use advanced features.
20	The AI make the projects easier
21	for the structure
22	Yes, plot group ideas in terms of design
23	The use of AI enhanced my ability to complete the project by providing quick access to information, automating complex calculations, and supporting data analysis. It streamlined workflows and allowed me to focus on critical thinking and problem-solving.
24	It made it both more difficult and better, the ease and access to a lot of previously inaccessible information. This is both an advantage and a disadvantage.
25	It made research slightly easier and more efficient
26	For cohesion or summarizing very long or complex documents, AI has helped me a lot.
27	To seafch for relevant papersand to create the 3D model
28	It didn't enhance or hinder my ability because I barely used it.

Notably, the students' comments on the PBL experience in the ESP classroom are mostly positive. What is particularly interesting is how each student emphasizes a different aspect of the PBL experience that they valued most. For instance, in the first and third comments, the students highlight the usefulness of the elevator pitch, which represents phase 3 of the project. For these students, the elevator pitch (and the project in general) allows them to develop valuable skills and communicative abilities, helping them confidently present their ideas. The second comment emphasizes the importance of the ESP content learned for the student's future professional career.

Comment 23 draws attention to the benefits of AI, outlining how the use of AI enhanced the student's learning: *"The use of AI enhanced my ability to complete the project by providing quick access to information, automating complex calculations, and supporting data analysis. It streamlined workflows and allowed me to focus on critical thinking and problem-solving."* For a physics or aerospace engineering student, conducting complex calculations in English indicates that PBL has enhanced both their language skills and their comprehensive understanding of what is required of students in these fields today.

The experience of collaborating with peers and conducting experiments is regarded as a valuable outcome of PBL in English for physics students. What is particularly noteworthy about these comments is that, overall, they are well-written. This suggests that PBL has helped students not only develop their competence in communication in English but also acquire the knowledge necessary to continue learning independently and enhancing their communicative skills.

5. DISCUSSION

The findings in this paper provide strong empirical support for the theoretical premise that PBL, when augmented with AI, can significantly enhance ESP learning by integrating language development, disciplinary knowledge, and 21st-century competencies. In line with Ruiz Viruel et al. (2025) and Li et al. (2025), the project demonstrates that AI–PBL integration creates a learning ecosystem where learners engage in authentic, domain-relevant communication tasks while leveraging AI for feedback, research, and creative output. This aligns with constructivist and socio-constructivist theories that position learners as active co-constructors of knowledge within socially mediated and technologically supported environments (Stoller 2006).

The students' overwhelmingly positive responses—particularly regarding enhanced teamwork, confidence in communication, and professional vocabulary acquisition—mirror what Du and Daniel (2024) identify as the principal pedagogical affordances of AI-enhanced language learning: interactivity, personalization, and immediacy of feedback. From a theoretical perspective, these outcomes can be interpreted through Vygotsky's (1978) concept of the Zone of Proximal Development (ZPD), where AI functions as a dynamic scaffold mediating between the learner's current competence and potential development. In this case, AI tools such as ChatGPT and MATLAB served as "cognitive apprentices" that supported students' problem-solving processes without supplanting human agency—a central tenet of teacher-in-the-loop design models (Ruiz Viruel et al. 2025).

The data further reveal that PBL provided the necessary structure to counteract the risk of AI misuse, as the iterative and collaborative nature of projects required students to demonstrate original thinking, critical evaluation of AI-generated content, and sustained engagement. This finding substantiates recent warnings in the literature about academic overreliance on AI (Davar et al. 2025) and illustrates how structured, process-oriented assessment within PBL can restore academic integrity and promote ethical AI use. In theoretical terms, this reflects an integrative model of autonomy and regulation, where AI functions as a mediational tool within a regulated, socially accountable learning environment (Chiu et al. 2023; Stein-Smit 2023).

Moreover, students' appreciation of collaboration and motivation corroborates the claim that AI–PBL fosters situated learning (Lave & Wenger 1991), wherein knowledge is constructed through participation in authentic communities of practice. ESP, by definition, thrives on such authenticity—linking linguistic competence to real-world professional communication. The project's outcomes, especially the development of technical vocabulary and confidence in public speaking, illustrate how AI-supported PBL situates language learning within meaningful disciplinary discourse communities.

Nevertheless, the data also indicate variability among advanced learners, some of whom reported limited linguistic gains. This resonates with the literature's observation that AI–PBL's impact may plateau for learners already near target proficiency (Li et al. 2025). It also suggests a need for differentiated AI scaffolding and personalized project design—an approach consistent with adaptive learning theories emphasizing the calibration of challenge and support (Cao et al. 2025; Wang 2025).

Theoretically, this study advances a model of AI-mediated experiential learning for ESP, in which PBL acts as the macro-structure for experiential engagement, AI provides the micro-level cognitive and linguistic scaffolds, and teacher mediation ensures ethical, domain-accurate application. This triadic model echoes the AI–PBL–ESP nexus described in recent research: a dynamic, human-centered interaction among technology, pedagogy, and disciplinary language.

The findings substantiate contemporary theory suggesting that AI, when embedded in PBL, transforms ESP from a knowledge-delivery paradigm into a knowledge-construction ecology. Learners become co-designers of meaning, teachers become facilitators and curators of AI literacy, and language learning becomes an interdisciplinary, technologically mediated act of professional communication.

6. CONCLUSIONS AND IMPLICATIONS

The aim of the present paper was to demonstrate how PBL and AI can be implemented in ESP classrooms. In the wake of AI, especially ChatGPT, language teaching is facing challenges that need to be addressed through the adoption of new teaching and learning strategies. Since the pandemic, higher education systems worldwide have been transforming and evolving daily. However, what is clearly lacking in this transformation, or rather in the efforts to transform these systems, is a clear understanding of the roles of both the teacher and the students. Believe it or not, technological transformation has also redefined the traditional ways in which teachers present themselves to students and vice versa. This paper offers a closer look at what it means to be a teacher or student in the wake of the transformation brought about by the AI revolution.

What has been described in this paper is, in a sense, a teaching approach that revolves around offering students an integral learning experience. For example, the various investigative activities involved in the execution of PBL allow the teaching/ learning process to become more data driven. illustratively, conducting experiments in the lab using English is an effective way to help physics students become more aware of what is required of a physicist in society.

If there is a need to guide students in using AI responsibly, PBL stands out as a strong alternative approach in the ESP classroom. PBL enables students to (re) negotiate their learning. As shown in this paper, the final product no longer must be a traditional written essay or paper. It could, for example, be a project in which students develop an app or computer program that is useful for both the physics field and society at large. In terms of assessment, the teaching process shifts from evaluating traditional writing and speaking skills to assessing students' oral and written productions on-site.

It is important to note that the PBL, AI, and ESP nexus can also benefit substantially if it is tailored to the students' needs through a needs analysis conducted before the project begins. Whenever time permits, it is advisable to understand students' expectations, needs, and English levels before launching the project. This is because if there were a significant gap in English proficiency levels, some students (i.e., those with higher proficiency) might lose interest, potentially leading to the project's failure.

REFERENCES

Cao, S., Chen, Y., & Zhang, L. (2025). An empirical study of an AI-driven platform in blended learning: Effects on Business English proficiency and engagement. *Language Testing in Asia*, *15*(1), 2–25.

Chiu, T. K. F., Xia, Q., Zhou, X., Chai, C. S., & Cheng, M. (2023). Systematic literature review on opportunities, challenges, and future research recommendations of artificial intelligence in education. *Computers and Education: Artificial Intelligence*, *4*, 1–15. DOI: 10.1016/j.caeai.2022.100118

Davar, N. F., Dewan, M. A. A., & Zhang, X. (2025). AI Chatbots in Education: Challenges and Opportunities. *Information (Basel)*, *16*(3), 2–25. DOI: 10.3390/info16030235

Du, J., & Daniel, B. K. (2024). Transforming language education: A systematic review of AI-powered chatbots for English as a foreign language speaking practice. *Comput. Educ. Artif. Intell.*, *6*, 100230.

Faheem, S. (2016). ESP Learners and the Language Based Activities. *Information Journal of English Language. Literature and Humanities*, *4*(1), 58–65.

Kitila, F. (2023). The Impact of Writing Through Integrated Skills Intervention on English Students' Writing Skills: Focus on Vocabulary and Grammar. *Journal of Language Teaching and Research*, *14*(2), 297–303.

Lave, J., & Wenger, E. (1991). *Situated learning: Legitimate peripheral participation*. Cambridge University Press.

Lee, S., Choe, H., Zou, D., & Jeon, J. (2025). Generative AI (GenAI) in the language classroom: A systematic review. *Interactive Learning Environments*, •••, 1–25. DOI: 10.1080/10494820.2025.2498537

Li, B., Lily Tan, Y., Wang, C., & Lowell, V. (2025). Two years of innovation: A systematic review of empirical generative AI research in language learning and teaching. *Computers and Education: Artificial Intelligence*, *9*, 1–27.

Lundstrom, P. (1996). Task-based language teaching in a learner-centered ESP setting: A case study. *Revista de Lenguas para Fines Específicos*, *3*, 199–213.

Macías, M. (2023). English for specific purposes in Spain: Project based learning classroom proposal in vocational education. *International Journal of Professional Development. Learners and Learning*, *5*(1), 1–9.

Musikhin, I. (2016). English for specific purposes: Teaching English for science and technology. *ISPRS Annals of the Photogrammetry, Remote Sensing and Spatial Information Sciences*, *III-6*, 29–35. DOI: 10.5194/isprs-annals-III-6-29-2016

Ngo, T. N. (2025). Artificial intelligence for academic purposes (AIAP): Conceptualizing AI literacy and educational practices. *Educational Research Review*, *28*, 102–118.

Pali ă, E. (2023). Teaching English in the artificial intelligence context. *Research and Science Today*, *2*(26), 56–62.

Romadhon, R. (2024). AI in language learning: English for specific purposes perceptions toward ChatGPT. *Lingua Journal*, *2024*(4), 120–135.

Ruiz Viruel, S., Sánchez Rivas, E., & Ruiz Palmero, J. (2025). The Role of Artificial Intelligence in Project-Based Learning: Teacher Perceptions and Pedagogical Implications. *Education Sciences*, *15*(2), 1–18.

Stein-Smit, K. 2023. The Independent Self-Directed Language Learner and the Role of the Language Educator — Expanding Access and Opportunity. *Journal of Language Teaching and Research*, Vol. 14 (2), 269-277.

Stoller, F. (2006). Establishing a Theoretical Foundation for Project-Based Learning in Second and Foreign Language Contexts. In Beckett, G. H., & Miller, P. C. (Eds.), *Project-Based Second and Foreign Language Education: Past, Present, and Future* (pp. 19–40). Information Age.

Tang, J., Zhang, P., & Li, R. (2023). Artificial intelligence–based needs analysis for English for specific purposes. *Journal of Applied Linguistics*, *44*, 210–229.

Vygotsky, L. S. (1978). *Mind in society: The development of higher psychological processes*. Harvard University Press.

Wang, Y. (2025). A scoping review of empirical studies on generative AI in language education (2022–2024). *Journal of Educational Technology & Society*, *28*(2), 1–22.

Xiaofan, W. (2025). Investigating the use of AI tools in English language learning: A phenomenological approach. *Contemporary Educational Technology*, *16*(4), 301–320.

ENDNOTES

1 This work can take various forms, including software programs, business plans, potential future airport designs, solutions to fuel efficiency issues, and space exploration ships. The teacher should encourage students to innovate and explore potential ways to address modern-day challenges. In this context, the final product may be a written report, a physical apparatus, or a graphic design. In the case of the latter, the final product should be accompanied by a description of the apparatus or a graphic design.

Chapter 7

Young Adults' Attitudes Toward Generative Artificial Intelligence and Its Role in STEM Education

Merve Çolakoğlu
https://orcid.org/0000-0001-5102-0528
Independent Researcher, Turkey

Semiral Öncü
https://orcid.org/0000-0001-8549-094X
Balikesir University, Turkey

Hüseyin Colak
https://orcid.org/0009-0009-5826-9567
Northeastern Illinois University, USA

ABSTRACT

Using artificial intelligence (AI) tools in education is a contemporary method that enhances the evaluation, transformation, and promotion of learning and teaching processes. Integrating AI tools into the learning process in STEM fields contributes to the development of students' metacognitive abilities. This study aims to learn and evaluate adolescents' opinions and insights regarding the use of AI tools in STEM fields. Our research examines students' attitudes, confidence, and perceptions towards using AI tools and their perspectives on current global issues. Their views on the use of digital AI tools to solve these problems are also explored. Face-to-face

DOI: 10.4018/979-8-3373-8805-2.ch007

interviews were conducted with eight participants for the study. The collected data were analyzed using content analysis methods. A review of the relevant literature revealed no studies similar to the methodology of this study. In this regard, we believe that the results of our study will benefit researchers conducting studies on the use of AI tools in education especially towards STEM education.

INTRODUCTION

The use of artificial intelligence (AI) in education varies significantly between adolescents and college students. In higher education, AI is primarily a collaborative tool, a means to enhance projects, refine ideas, locate relevant sources, and receive feedback before submission. College students tend to use AI as an augmentative partner, integrating it into research and creative processes to extend their own analytical and problem-solving capabilities. Integration of AI can also help instructors to evaluate student work, provide feedback, and analyze student progress quickly and timely (Smith et al., 2019). In addition, AI has the potential to expand access to quality education, provide personalized learning experiences, support data-driven decision-making processes, and thus contribute to overcoming educational challenges and fostering the development of a sustainable education system (Çayak, 2024).

In contrast, middle and high school students often engage with AI in a more guided and immediate way. They rely on AI-supported tools to check their answers, receive instant explanations, and reinforce classroom learning. For them, AI functions as an interactive tutor, providing quick feedback and motivation within structured learning environments.

Across all levels, the central aim of education remains constant: to prepare students for the evolving demands of the twenty-first-century workforce. That preparation requires more than factual knowledge, it calls for the ability to construct knowledge through self-learning (Aleven et al., 2016), effective decision making, adapt to new situations, persist through challenges, and remain intellectually agile in a world of continuous change (Hwang et al., 2020). All these skills are needed to become active learners rather than being a passive receiver of knowledge. Yannier et al. (2020) stated that a mixed-reality AI system supported with computational algorithms helps children's active learning so that it bridges the physical and virtual worlds to improve children's inquiry-based science, technology, engineering, and mathematics (STEM) learning. The effective use of AI in STEM education is possible through the selection and implementation of appropriate AI techniques that holistically evaluate the interaction among elements such as teachers, students, knowledge, environment, and context, in order to provide personalized learning experiences tailored to students' individual needs and learning styles (Alabdulhadi & Faisal, 2021; Xu & Ouyang, 2022a).

Teachers need to be trained to effectively use AI-powered tools in their classroom settings. Teachers are the main agents to facilitate AI-based activities and train students about how they will benefit from AI. The goal is to enhance students' learning. Yağci and Çevik, (2019) proposed AI-based algorithm models to predict students' academic achievements in science courses (physics, chemistry, and biology) and put forward suggestions to facilitate students' successful learning. To prepare students for the future job market and skills, AI-directed education is necessary in middle and high schools (Ouyang et al., 2022). Park et al. (2023) found that teachers' perceptions of integrating AI into science lessons in terms of the connection between AI and science, implementation challenges, and suggestions for improvement. Teachers stated that AI and science share similarities in developing accurate models with quality data and employing simplified reasoning, while they also play complementary roles in solving scientific problems. The main challenges were identified as a lack of confidence in content mastery and difficulties in gaining teachers' acceptance for curriculum adaptation. Therefore, it was recommended that comprehensive AI resources be provided to teachers and that such lesson packages could be effectively used in after-school science enrichment programs. To prepare students for the future job market — as an increasing number of industries become integrated with AI, and this trend is expected to continue — some researchers argue that AI education should be considered a fundamental literacy skill, similar to reading and writing (Casal-Otero et al., 2023; Kandlhofer et al., 2016).

Generative artificial intelligence (GenAI) has become an integral part of people's daily lives, appearing in everything from smartphones to smart homes and autonomous cars. Integrating GenAI into education has been argued to improve teaching and learning by automating tasks, personalizing instruction and expanding the accessibility of educational resources (Adiguzel et al., 2023; Chan & Hu, 2023; Ciampa et al., 2023; Wood & Moss, 2024). STEM education has also made significant progress by integrating GenAI. AI is transforming STEM education by creating unprecedented opportunities to address diverse challenges (Ouyang et al., 2022). The traditional assessment of collaborations in teams is self-reported, in-group peer assessment (Gueldenzoph & May, 2002), as students' success in specific STEM courses, such as physics, chemistry, and biology, is highly dependent on team projects and the quality of teamwork (Nixon et al., 2024).The higher-order thinking that STEM education imparts to students has been crucial in redefining educational paradigms with a focus on developing critical thinking, problem-solving skills and practical applications of scientific knowledge (Nixon et al., 2024; Wood & Moss, 2024). In the digital age we live in, the role of the teacher is evolving from teaching knowledge to facilitating the learning experience, guiding students towards problem solving and creativity (Chiu & Li, 2023). In this context, student engagement stands out as one of the most significant indicators of academic achievement, motivation, and learning outcomes (Öncü et al., 2024, 2025). Students must be active, learn by doing with the teacher, and construct knowledge. Educators need to understand their new role and leverage these technologies to improve learning outcomes (Chiu, 2023). In the studies reviewed, student outcomes include twenty-first century skills, motivation and engagement, academic performance and non-cognitive aspects (Chiu et al., 2023). Research should focus on optimizing AI integration in STEM education to meet and complement the needs emerging from traditional teaching methodologies while preparing students for a technology-centered future. AI's important educational role is not just about automating existing processes; it represents a fundamental shift in how education is delivered and experienced. By leveraging AI's capabilities in data interpretation, personalized learning, adaptive strategies and project assistance, educators can create more engaging and effective learning environments that prepare students for the complexities of the digital age (Katiyar et al., 2024; Silva et al., 2024).

Inspired by the capabilities of AI, this study aims to explore the transformative impact of AI tools, such as ChatGPT and Bing AI, on STEM education among adolescents, a group uniquely positioned to experience significant effects due to their pervasive interaction with AI in both academic practices and everyday leisure activities.

THEORETICAL FRAMEWORK

AI in education has evolved through a series of paradigmatic shifts in research, pedagogy, and technology that mirror broader educational theories (Ouyang & Jiao, 2021). The first paradigm, which can be referred to as AI-directed/programmed education, emerged from behaviorist learning theory (Skinner, 1958). In this stage, preprogrammed machines functioned as an instructor, delivering structured content to students who practiced pre-defined sequences of knowledge and skills. Early systems such as Stat Lady, Cognitive Tutors, and ASSISTment Builder (Razzaq et al., 2009) exemplify this model, emphasizing repetitive learning and mastery through feedback.

The second paradigm, AI-supported education, aligns with cognitive and social constructivism, positioning the learner as an active collaborator. Here, AI acts as a learning partner, providing adaptive feedback, scaffolding, and interactive problem-solving opportunities. Systems such as Dialogue-Based Tutoring Systems (Pai et al., 2021) and Explanatory Learner Models (Rosé et al., 2019) illustrate how AI fosters learner agency, exploration, and shared inquiry.

The third paradigm, AI-empowered education, reflects a shift toward complex adaptive systems theory, emphasizing learner autonomy and human–AI co-agency. In this model, AI functions as a dynamic collaborator, continuously adapting to students' needs and supporting self-directed, reflective learning. Emerging approaches such as human-centered AI (Riedl, 2019), human-AI collaboration (Hwang et al., 2020), and human-centered Artificial Intelligence in Education (AIEd) (Yang et al., 2021) embody this transformation.

Collectively, these paradigms trace a clear trajectory from teacher-directed to student-centered learning in STEM education. The field has progressively shifted toward AI-supported and AI-empowered approaches, highlighting a growing focus on collaborative, adaptive, and creative learning ecosystems that integrate human ingenuity with AI's analytical capabilities.

Accordingly AI, with its ease of use and interactive features, has increased students' interest in technology. In this context, as introduced so far, AIEd has emerged as an interdisciplinary field that employs AI technologies to promote, evaluate, transform, and design teaching and learning processes (Chen et al., 2020; Hwang et al., 2020; Smith-Mutegi et al., 2025; Xu & Ouyang, 2022b). In this evolving educational environment, it is essential to recognize the necessity of AI-based digital tools not only as repositories of knowledge but also as dynamic partners in the learning process. The growing integration of AI in education has led to increased research on its impact across various fields, aiming to enhance educational practices. These AI applications include robotics, e-learning platforms, virtual reality, online self-learning environments, and chatbots.

On the one hand, AI has the potential to transform education by increasing student engagement, adapting to individual learning needs, and supporting decision-making through data-driven insights (Buluş & Elmas, 2024). Such adaptive capabilities enable personalized learning experiences that foster academic growth and efficiency (Ifraheem et al., 2024). On the other hand, the reliance on AI raises some concerns. Overdependence on AI tools may hinder cognitive development by diminishing opportunities for critical thinking and problem-solving, skills essential for human creativity and intellectual growth (Chan & Hu, 2023). Moreover, excessive automation in education could undermine students' ability to process complex information independently, creating a passive learning environment (Jie & Kamrozzaman, 2024). The limited potential of GenAI algorithms also raises issues of data privacy, ethics, plagiarism and academic integrity. In terms of writing academic publications, AI-generated content was found to contain inappropriate references and failed to provide a personal perspective, despite being original content on the subject (Hs Kumar, 2023). It poses a challenge for language learners as it requires a certain level of language skills and may also jeopardize the development of individuals in terms of writing proficiency (Warschauer et al., 2023). In addition, GenAI tools cannot evaluate the content produced and check whether it contains inaccurate information, so human moderation is required in this case (Lubowitz, 2023). It is difficult to determine that work that cannot be checked by a plagiarism checker is the original work of an author (Peres et al., 2023), compromising the assessment of written assignments by text-generating applications such as ChatGPT (Zhai, 2022). Balancing these advantages and disadvantages is crucial to leveraging AI's transformative potential while safeguarding the developmental needs of learners.

STEM education is an educational model aimed at helping students achieve their goals in real life. AI's ability to make dynamic changes in academic programs aids the advancement of learning in STEM fields (Taylor et al., 2021). AI enables individuals to access materials more efficiently. AI applications are being integrated into STEM education to help students learn and solve problems (Botzees, 2022). The integration of AI into educational environments is crucial because it complements both Industry 4.0 and Education 4.0 (Tominc & Rožman, 2023). Moreover, the rapid growth of AI applications and the innovative results they produce significantly enhance students' learning experiences. Additionally, AI has the potential to develop educational materials and create a revolution by moving beyond traditional educational approaches (İçen, 2022). Integrating AI into education brings forth a new interdisciplinary approach that applies AI technologies to transform the teaching and learning process and motivate learners (Xu & Ouyang, 2022b). For students, connecting with emerging technologies and developing their skills is an indispensable part of STEM education environments (Chiu & Li, 2023). Students should be able to use emerging technologies to solve contemporary everyday problems within the context of STEM education (Chiu & Li, 2023), thus enhancing their knowledge and skills. Students' engagement, learning process, and interest in learning require using AI tools to advance STEM education successfully in every dimension of the teaching-learning process.

Integrating AI into STEM education presents a transformative opportunity (Bhose, 2024; KIDSPARK, 2024). By analyzing a student's performance data, AI can identify their strengths and weaknesses and offer customized resources to address gaps. Furthermore, AI can facilitate interdisciplinary learning by integrating STEM subjects with other fields such as computer science and data analytics (Bhose, 2024).

AI chatbots have the potential to assist in positive progress in both learning and teaching in education (Labadze et al., 2023). They offer students beneficial experiences in areas such as learning success, retaining information, quick access to information, and instant help, but studies in the literature indicate that they may have mixed effects on skills like critical thinking and motivation (Deng & Yu, 2023; Okonkwo & Ade-Ibijola, 2021; Wollny et al., 2021). While students find AI to be a useful tool for providing instant learning support (Chan & Hu, 2023), they are also aware of issues regarding the accuracy of information, ethical concerns (Ding et al., 2023), and its potential impact on their future careers (Bisdas et al., 2021; Buabbas et al., 2023).

Among students, ChatGPT is widely adopted in STEM subjects, especially biology courses, as a tool that supports the understanding of concepts (Valeri et al., 2025). Building on this trend, Chan and Hu (2023) examined higher education students' perceptions of integrating AI tools such as ChatGPT, focusing on their familiarity, willingness to participate, and perceived benefits and challenges. Their findings suggest that strategies aligned with students' concerns can support the responsible and effective use of generative AI in enhancing teaching and learning in higher education.

According to (Khallaf & Alqerafi, 2024), AI offers great potential in combating global warming, but challenges such as data quality, system integration, ethical issues and economic barriers need to be overcome to realize this potential. Furthermore, they argue that AI plays an important role in the development of effective climate adaptation strategies. This can help communities and ecosystems adapt to changing environmental conditions with solutions such as early warning systems for natural disasters, optimizing resource allocation and developing resilient infrastructure.

The integration of GenAI into STEM education can provide personalized learning environments and resources, support instructors in analyzing learning behavior patterns, and enable automated assessment of STEM performance (Nixon et al., 2024; Xu & Ouyang, 2022b). However, since STEM education functions as a system of interdependent elements —including knowledge, context, subject matter, frameworks, and social-pedagogical factors— achieving high-quality education requires considering these dimensions rather than relying solely on AI technologies (Krasovskiy, 2020; Xu & Ouyang, 2022a). The holistic perspective of STEM is vital for addressing complex environmental challenges and fostering innovative solutions (Maspul, 2024).

According to Maspul (2024), integrating STEM education with real-world problems such as climate change provides significant contributions to both the academic and social development of students. Through fieldwork and community-based activities, students not only enhance essential skills such as critical thinking, problem-solving, data analysis, and collaboration, but also develop environmental responsibility and sustainability awareness. Extending STEM projects beyond the classroom and grounding them in local community engagement positions students not merely as knowledge receivers but as "change agents" who generate solutions and contribute to society. Overall, Maspul emphasizes that combining STEM education with real-world challenges strengthens academic achievements while also enhancing students' capacity to cope with global issues, thereby preparing them to become more conscious and responsible individuals.

Integrating AI into STEM is also emerging as a strategy to cultivate a generation capable of combating climate change and advancing sustainability (Kalkan, 2024). Applying STEM principles to local issues not only helps students grasp scientific concepts but also enables them to contribute to their communities in meaningful ways (Maspul, 2024). By combining AI's capabilities with a strong STEM curriculum, educators can design engaging and personalized learning experiences that prepare students to become informed global citizens ready to drive positive change. For instance, learning about renewable energy technologies or sustainable agricultural practices equips future leaders with the skills to build a more sustainable world (Kalkan, 2024).

Although recent years have seen a growing body of research on GenAI, there is a notable gap in studies that specifically explore adolescents' perspectives through in-depth interviews. Adolescents, as digital natives, interact with AI technologies in unique ways that shape their learning experiences and future readiness. To address this gap, this study seeks to provide a comprehensive understanding of adolescents' views on AI integration in STEM education by answering the following research questions:

- RQ1: What are adolescents' perceptions of artificial intelligence, its potential impact on their career goals, and the support they need to foster their interest in this field?
- RQ2: How do adolescents perceive the role of artificial intelligence in addressing societal and global challenges such as climate change, sustainability, agriculture, health, and international collaboration?
- RQ3: From adolescents' perspectives, what opportunities and challenges do the integration of artificial intelligence into science, technology, engineering, and mathematics (STEM) education present, and how can this process contribute to preparing students for global challenges?

METHODOLOGY

In this study, a case study approach involving the examination of qualitative data has been employed. Case study methodology is preferred for understanding the characteristics of a particular situation or phenomenon within a specific context (Stake, 2024; Yin, 1994). It is an effective research method that involves a detailed examination of a single case over time. It is preferred when the researcher has minimal impact on the activities. The focus is on existing phenomena in a real environment (Yin, 1994). We aim to learn the genuine views of adolescents with a certain level of awareness about AI concepts and technologies regarding AI and the future without intervening in their real working environments. To this end, face-to-face interviews were conducted with eight adolescents aged between 14 and 18 with essential experience with AI. A semi-structured interview form created by the researchers was used during the interviews. After being drafted based on a literature review, the interview form was submitted for expert review and finalized according to feedback from five expert faculty members. Parental consent was obtained via a "parental consent form," and adolescents who voluntarily agreed to participate were included in the study.

The participants' data were transcribed and subjected to content analysis. Content analysis is conducted to identify concepts (themes) that can explain the collected data and the relationships between these concepts. It generally involves codes and coding that enable the organization, selection, and summarization of the data collected in the research (Miles & Huberman, 1994).

Content analysis is typically carried out in several stages (Erlingsson & Brysiewicz, 2017): Qualitative data is first read repeatedly to understand it. Then, the data is divided into meaning units. Each meaning unit is a unique piece of text that can simply be a sentence, a series of sentences with a single meaning, or a word that interweaves an idea and reflects its meaning when re-read. An evaluator divides each participant's responses to the questions into one or more meaning units. Similar meaning units are grouped and classified into themes through discussion. These themes are then organized under headings and presented in the Results section.

In this study, all processes of separating and classifying qualitative data are carried out using a spreadsheet program, Microsoft Excel. A total of 714 idea units were identified by a rater. Then, two raters independently coded about 30% of the idea units into sub-themes where research questions framed the main themes. They achieved 70.28% agreement as the interrater reliability. After they resolved the disagreements through discussion, one of the raters continued and completed the coding alone. The idea units that appeared equal to or less than five times or the ones that did not directly fit any of the identified sub-themes were coded as "other."

RESULTS

Our content analysis identified several sub-themes organized under 3 main themes corresponding to the research questions that encapsulate the participants' perspectives on the integration of generative AI into STEM education. Under each of these themes, several sub-themes emerged. They are presented below, organized according to the research questions guiding this study.

The results demonstrate that students perceive AI as a means of supporting personal development, enhancing individual competencies, and facilitating their learning processes. At the same time, they exhibit an awareness of the potential negative consequences of AI, particularly regarding ethical concerns, safety issues, and dependency risks. Moreover, sub-themes such as interest and curiosity, education, definition, problem-solving processes, technology use, and impact reveal that students critically reflect on the conceptual appeal of AI, its functionality within learning environments, and its broader individual and societal implications. Additionally, sub-themes including purposes of use, sustainability, cultural barriers, international communication, career planning, metaphors, information, and benefit suggest that, although their perspectives may be limited in scope, students hold a multidimensional understanding of AI's applications across diverse contexts.

The study first explored how adolescents conceptualize AI, the ways they anticipate it might shape their career trajectories, and the kinds of support they believe could foster their interest in the field. Analysis revealed 12 sub-themes. Based on the findings from the participants' responses, the most prominent sub-theme naturally was "definition." Participants described AI as "being able to think like a human," "being able to make decisions like a human," "attempts to create artificial intelligence," or "being able to answer everything asked." This demonstrates that students define AI primarily through its resemblance to human thinking abilities, while at the same time emphasizing its "artificial" nature. Such duality highlights both a closeness to and a distance from human intelligence. Another frequently emphasized sub-theme was "artificial intelligence-focused career planning." In this regard, students expressed views such as "thinking that they could advance as an artificial intelligence developer," "choosing a field where artificial intelligence could support them in making their work easier in the future," or "preferring professions that make artificial intelligence more accessible and easier to use." Another noteworthy sub-theme was "impact." Within this sub-theme, students emphasized the positive aspects of AI, such as "our work is becoming easier," its negative aspects, such as "AI seems to eliminate the need for thinking," as well as its broader influence in many areas, including education. This dual perception reflects an ambivalence: while AI is seen as a facilitator of efficiency and productivity, it is also regarded as a potential threat to human cognitive abilities and independence.

The second research question focused on how adolescents envision the role of AI in addressing global and societal challenges, including environmental sustainability, health, agriculture, and international collaboration. Participants' perceptions in this regard were shaped around 14 sub-themes. The most frequently mentioned sub-theme was "suggestions/benefit" (26%), indicating that students primarily perceive AI as a tool for problem-solving and generating useful outcomes. Within this sub-theme, references to areas such as agriculture and healthcare highlight their awareness of practical applications in everyday contexts, demonstrating signs of creative thinking and the ability to envision effective solutions when AI is integrated with technology.

The second most emphasized sub-theme was “sustainability and carbon footprint” (13%), reflecting a strong awareness of environmental issues. Students mentioned topics such as water usage, energy transformation, resource monitoring, and climate research, which point to their sense of environmental responsibility as well as key 21st-century competencies, including systems thinking and global citizenship. The third most frequent sub-theme, “overcoming language and cultural barriers” (10%), shows that students view AI as a facilitator of intercultural communication. They envisioned AI as a bridge between people from different linguistic backgrounds and even referred to real-world tools, such as ChatGPT’s voice capabilities, illustrating not only their awareness of current technologies but also their ability to imagine realistic applications that support mobility and communication needs. Taken together, these prominent three sub-themes demonstrate that students perceive AI not only as a technical tool but also as a social, environmental, and communicative facilitator.

The third research question examined adolescents’ perspectives on the integration of AI into STEM education, the opportunities and challenges this entails, and its potential to prepare students for global challenges. Based on the responses, participants’ views on AI were categorized into 11 different sub-themes, indicating diverse perspectives on the topic. The most frequently mentioned sub-themes included use of technology (18%), education and awareness (14%), recommendation/benefit (13%), solution process (9%), and form/purpose of use (6%). These findings suggest that students primarily evaluate AI in terms of its educational and practical dimensions. Under the use of technology sub-theme, students emphasized the need for technological infrastructure (such as computers and internet access) in order to benefit from AI. They also highlighted the frequent use of digital platforms like YouTube to support learning, reflecting the development of digital literacy skills and an awareness of the dependency on technology when engaging with AI-based learning tools. Within the education and awareness sub-theme, students noted the lack of formal education on AI and proposed integrating AI into the curriculum. Their suggestions included adding AI-related topics to science and mathematics courses and providing structured STEM and AI education. These ideas reveal not only students’ desire to become more informed and engaged with future-oriented learning but also their ability to reflect on and critique educational policies. For the solution process sub-theme, students presented creative and application-oriented ideas regarding AI. Examples included robotics, raising awareness to generate solutions, and interactive design experiences such as creating holographic objects through AI. These responses illustrate students’ capacity for innovative thinking and their potential to envision both practical and futuristic applications of AI, positioning them as active problem-solvers.

Overall, the findings demonstrate that students perceive AI not only as a technical tool but also as an educational, practical, and innovative learning resource. At the same time, they hold ambivalent views that balance optimism about AI's capacity to ease life, generate solutions, and foster global communication with concerns about its risks, such as diminishing human thinking, creating dependency, or leading to ethical and ecological challenges. This multidimensional perception suggests that students are developing both critical awareness and creative imagination in their engagement with AI, reflecting its role as both an opportunity and a challenge in 21st-century learning contexts.

The rapid entry of GenAI tools into today's social life and the education sector is unmistakable. In this sense, the capacity for using GenAI technologies already demonstrates the strength of their widespread impact. Since our study aims to examine adolescents' perceptions of GenAI, it also benefits from this potential widespread impact.

The results indicate a generally positive perception of GenAI among participants, with a particular emphasis on its potential to ease and enhance learning and career planning. Participants highlighted the ease and efficiency GenAI brings, its ability to mimic human thinking, and its role in education. They also expressed a need for more educational resources and support to explore GenAI further.

Participants were optimistic about the integration of AI in STEM education, believing it would facilitate better understanding and engagement. However, some noted potential short-term challenges, especially for those less familiar with AI technologies.

Participants also recognized GenAI's potential in developing critical skills such as problem-solving, communication, and critical thinking, although there were differing views on its effectiveness in enhancing human-like thinking and emotions.

When students were asked their foremost opinions about the term "generative artificial intelligence," two students thought of "making our work easier," and two students thought of "ChatGPT and similar chat tools." Three students said that they could describe AI to someone who had never heard of it as a tool that makes their work easier or a teacher that facilitates their tasks. Three students identified "YouTube videos" as resources they use to improve themselves about the use of GenAI. They mentioned that AI could benefit them in STEM-related courses by providing visual recognition capabilities and detailed explanations of topics.

Regarding skill development, they believed that GenAI could mostly help people with problem solving but two students thought that AI cannot think, thus limiting its ability to foster thinking and emotional development in humans. Finally, all students agreed that AI tools would make working in STEM fields easier for them.

CONCLUSION

This research aims not only to highlight the previously underemphasized relationship between AI and STEM education in the literature but also to address and explain this relationship from adolescent's perspective. In this context, the study provides an in-depth perspective on adolescents' general attitudes toward GenAI and their unique views regarding its tangible contributions to STEM education. The qualitative data obtained through face-to-face interviews contributes to the fulfillment of this rich information need. Understanding the use of GenAI in education among Turkey's younger generation can play a critical role in shaping educational policies and cultivating future technology leaders. In this sense, the unique value of this study lies in how the data obtained from this participant perspective will guide the design of more effective GenAI-supported STEM education and better prepare students for the future.

Furthermore, our research has revealed that while there are studies focused on university students' perceptions, there are very few AI-themed studies involving adolescents. Moreover, those AI-themed studies are not directly related to our research. For instance, Krullaars et al. (2023) offer recommendations to AI companies based on data collected from high school students during a short-term workshop. In our study, not only are STEM and AI considered together, but student views on current and ongoing global issues of worldwide concern are also highlighted.

This research highlights the substantial potential of GenAI to reshape education and career planning, as reflected in young adults' diverse perceptions. The findings indicate that they primarily view AI as a tool for problem solving, learning enhancement, and career development, while also recognizing its role in sustainability and intercultural communication. They emphasized both the need for technological infrastructure and the importance of integrating AI education into school curricula, which shows their awareness of current gaps and their forward-looking perspective on future learning. Furthermore, their creative suggestions, such as applications in robotics, healthcare, agriculture, and even holographic design, demonstrate their capacity to imagine innovative uses of AI beyond conventional boundaries. These insights align with previous research, which has shown that the integration of AI technologies in STEM education not only enhances students' engagement but also develops their problem-solving and design skills (Xu & Ouyang, 2022b).

At the same time, concerns regarding AI's limitations in fostering human-like thinking and emotions point to the necessity of providing ethical guidance and critical thinking support. These findings resonate with Zawacki-Richter et al. (2019), who identified that while students and educators acknowledge AI's potential to personalize learning and improve efficiency, they also express apprehension about ethical and privacy challenges. Similarly, Zhang and Aslan (2021) underscores both the opportunities and risks of AI integration in education, highlighting its promise in fostering innovation and individualized learning while warning against issues of equity, ethics, and overreliance. Taken together, these studies and the present findings suggest that young adults' views on AI are marked by a tension between optimism about its transformative role in education and society, and caution regarding its ethical, cognitive, and social implications.

AI has the potential to transform STEM education by reducing teacher workloads, personalizing instruction, and reshaping the roles of both teachers and students. Through automation — such as automatic assessment, translation, and adaptive tutoring systems — AI allows educators to focus on higher-level pedagogical tasks while offering students more tailored and flexible learning experiences (Holstein et al., 2019; Hwang et al., 2020; Xu & Ouyang, 2022a). In addition, AI-powered analytics, wearable technologies, and data tracking enhance the learning process by predicting student performance and monitoring engagement (Yağci & Çevik, 2019). AIEd has been argued to enhance student engagement through practices such as personalized resource recommendations, adaptive teaching systems, and the identification of learning gaps, all aimed at supporting student-centered learning (Kose & Arslan, 2017; Liu et al., 2017).

This transformation represents a shift from teacher-directed instruction to student-centered learning, redefining teachers as facilitators and collaborators rather than traditional transmitters of knowledge. Despite these benefits, significant ethical and practical challenges remain, including ambiguity in AI accountability, overreliance on technology, algorithmic bias, data privacy concerns, and accessibility to AI tools. While AI can efficiently manage repetitive tasks, it lacks essential human capacities such as empathy, reflection, and motivational influence, qualities fundamental to meaningful teaching and learning (Gary, 2019; Selwyn, 2021). Educators must therefore employ AI intentionally, ensuring it complements rather than replaces human expertise and interaction.

Future advancements in AI for STEM education should aim to align AI systems with human values and foster ongoing collaboration among teachers, students, and intelligent technologies (Segal, 2019). Research suggests three key directions: utilizing AI to analyze diverse learning data for improved personalization; integrating augmented and virtual reality (AR/VR) to visualize abstract STEM concepts and provide real-time feedback (Mystakidis et al., 2022; Riegler et al., 2019); and developing inclusive AI models that recognize social identity differences and support equitable, collaborative learning environments.

Ultimately, the future of AI in STEM education depends on balancing technological innovation with ethical responsibility, creating systems that empower both teachers and learners while promoting inclusion, transparency, and human-centered collaboration. By addressing these needs and challenges, educational institutions can better prepare students to leverage AI effectively and responsibly. Future research should further explore how AI can be integrated into different learning contexts and how its long-term impact on students' skills, career trajectories, and global awareness can be maximized.

REFERENCES

Adiguzel, T., Kaya, M. H., & Cansu, F. K. (2023). Revolutionizing education with AI: Exploring the transformative potential of ChatGPT. *Contemporary Educational Technology*, *15*(3), ep429. DOI: 10.30935/cedtech/13152

Alabdulhadi, A., & Faisal, M. (2021). Systematic literature review of STEM self-study related ITSs. *Education and Information Technologies*, *26*(2), 1549–1588. DOI: 10.1007/s10639-020-10315-z

Aleven, V., McLaughlin, E. A., Glenn, R. A., & Koedinger, K. R. (2017). Instruction based on adaptive learning technologies. In Mayer, R. E., & Alexander, P. A. (Eds.), *Handbook of research on learning and instruction* (2nd ed., pp. 522–560). Routledge., DOI: 10.4324/9781315736419-36

Bhose, M. (2024, August 23). *AI In STEM Education: Transforming Learning*. eLearning Industry. https://elearningindustry.com/ai-in-stem-education-transforming-learning

Bisdas, S., Topriceanu, C.-C., Zakrzewska, Z., Irimia, A.-V., Shakallis, L., Subhash, J., Casapu, M.-M., Leon-Rojas, J., Pinto Dos Santos, D., Andrews, D. M., Zeicu, C., Bouhuwaish, A. M., Lestari, A. N., Abu-Ismail, L., Sadiq, A. S., Khamees, A., Mohammed, K. M. G., Williams, E., Omran, A. I., & Ebrahim, E. H. (2021). Artificial Intelligence in Medicine: A Multinational Multi-Center Survey on the Medical and Dental Students' Perception. *Frontiers in Public Health*, *9*, 795284. DOI: 10.3389/fpubh.2021.795284 PMID: 35004598

Botzees. (2022, May 30). *Top 6 Trends in Stem Education in June 2022*. Botzees Toys. https://botzeestoys.com/blogs/news/top-trends-in-stem-education

Buabbas, A. J., Miskin, B., Alnaqi, A. A., Ayed, A. K., Shehab, A. A., Syed-Abdul, S., & Uddin, M. (2023). Investigating Students' Perceptions towards Artificial Intelligence in Medical Education. *Health Care*, *11*(9), 1298. DOI: 10.3390/healthcare11091298 PMID: 37174840

Buluş, B., & Elmas, R. (2024). Yapay Zeka Uygulamalarının Kimya Eğitiminde Kullanımı Alternatif Araçlar. *Turkiye Kimya Dernegi Dergisi Kısım C. Kimya Egitimi*, *9*(1), 1–28. DOI: 10.37995/jotcsc.1366999

Casal-Otero, L., Catala, A., Fernández-Morante, C., Taboada, M., Cebreiro, B., & Barro, S. (2023). AI literacy in K-12: A systematic literature review. *International Journal of STEM Education*, *10*(1), 29. DOI: 10.1186/s40594-023-00418-7

Çayak, S. (2024). Investigating the relationship between teachers' attitudes toward artificial intelligence and their artificial intelligence literacy. *Journal of Educational Technology and Online Learning, 7*(4-ICETOL 2024 Special Issue), 367–383. DOI: 10.31681/jetol.1490307

Chan, C. K. Y., & Hu, W. (2023). Students' voices on generative AI: Perceptions, benefits, and challenges in higher education. *International Journal of Educational Technology in Higher Education, 20*(1), 43. DOI: 10.1186/s41239-023-00411-8

Chen, L., Chen, P., & Lin, Z. (2020). Artificial Intelligence in Education: A Review. *IEEE Access : Practical Innovations, Open Solutions, 8*, 75264–75278. DOI: 10.1109/ACCESS.2020.2988510

Chiu, T. K. F. (2024). The impact of Generative AI (GenAI) on practices, policies and research direction in education: A case of ChatGPT and Midjourney. *Interactive Learning Environments, 32*(10), 6187–6203. DOI: 10.1080/10494820.2023.2253861

Chiu, T. K. F., & Li, Y. (2023). How Can Emerging Technologies Impact STEM Education? *Journal for STEM Education Research, 6*(3), 375–384. DOI: 10.1007/s41979-023-00113-w

Chiu, T. K. F., Xia, Q., Zhou, X., Chai, C. S., & Cheng, M. (2023). Systematic literature review on opportunities, challenges, and future research recommendations of artificial intelligence in education. *Computers and Education: Artificial Intelligence, 4*, 100118. DOI: 10.1016/j.caeai.2022.100118

Ciampa, K., Wolfe, Z. M., & Bronstein, B. (2023). ChatGPT in education: Transforming digital literacy practices. *Journal of Adolescent & Adult Literacy, 67*(3), 186–195. DOI: 10.1002/jaal.1310

Deng, X., & Yu, Z. (2023). A Meta-Analysis and Systematic Review of the Effect of Chatbot Technology Use in Sustainable Education. *Sustainability, 15*(4), 2940. DOI: 10.3390/su15042940

Ding, L., Li, T., Jiang, S., & Gapud, A. (2023). Students' perceptions of using ChatGPT in a physics class as a virtual tutor. *International Journal of Educational Technology in Higher Education, 20*(1), 63. DOI: 10.1186/s41239-023-00434-1

Erlingsson, C., & Brysiewicz, P. (2017). A hands-on guide to doing content analysis. *African Journal of Emergency Medicine : Revue Africaine de la Médecine d'Urgence, 7*(3), 93–99. DOI: 10.1016/j.afjem.2017.08.001 PMID: 30456117

Gary, K. (2019). Pragmatic Standards versus Saturated Phenomenon: Cultivating a Love of Learning. *Journal of Philosophy of Education, 53*(3), 477–490. DOI: 10.1111/1467-9752.12377

Gueldenzoph, L. E., & May, G. L. (2002). Collaborative Peer Evaluation: Best Practices for Group Member Assessments. *Business Communication Quarterly*, *65*(1), 9–20. DOI: 10.1177/108056990206500102

Holstein, K., McLaren, B. M., & Aleven, V. (2019). Co-Designing a Real-Time Classroom Orchestration Tool to Support Teacher–AI Complementarity. *Journal of Learning Analytics*, *6*(2), 27–52. DOI: 10.18608/jla.2019.62.3

Hs Kumar, A. (2023). Analysis of ChatGPT Tool to Assess the Potential of its Utility for Academic Writing in Biomedical Domain. *Biology, Engineering. Medicine and Science Reports*, *9*(1), 24–30. DOI: 10.5530/bems.9.1.5

Hwang, G.-J., Xie, H., Wah, B. W., & Gašević, D. (2020). Vision, challenges, roles and research issues of Artificial Intelligence in Education. *Computers and Education: Artificial Intelligence*, *1*, 100001. DOI: 10.1016/j.caeai.2020.100001

İçen, M. (2022). The future of education utilizing artificial intelligence in Turkey. *Humanities & Social Sciences Communications*, *9*(1), 268. DOI: 10.1057/s41599-022-01284-4

Ifraheem, S., Rasheed, M., & Siddiqui, A. (2024). Transforming Education Through Artificial Intelligence: Personalization, Engagement and Predictive Analytics. *Journal of Asian Development Studies*, *13*(2), 250–266. DOI: 10.62345/jads.2024.13.2.22

Jie, A. L. X., & Kamrozzaman, N. A. (2024). The Challenges of Higher Education Students Face in Using Artificial Intelligence (AI) against Their Learning Experiences. *Open Journal of Social Sciences*, *12*(10), 362–387. DOI: 10.4236/jss.2024.1210025

Kalkan, Ç. (2024, June 5). What is the Importance of STEM Education in Climate Change and Sustainability Education for Children? - Scientix blog Sustainable Development Goals. *Scientix Blog*. https://blog.scientix.eu/2024/06/what-is-the-importance-of-stem-education-in-climate-change-and-sustainable-development-goals-for-children/

Kandlhofer, M., Steinbauer, G., Hirschmugl-Gaisch, S., & Huber, P. (2016). Artificial intelligence and computer science in education: From kindergarten to university. *2016 IEEE Frontiers in Education Conference (FIE)*, 1–9. DOI: 10.1109/FIE.2016.7757570

Katiyar, N., Awasthi, M. V. K., Pratap, R., Mishra, M. K., Shukla, M. N., Tiwari, M., & Singh, R. (2024). AI-driven personalized learning systems: Enhancing educational effectiveness. *Educational Administration: Theory and Practice*, *30*(5), 11514–11524.

Khallaf, A. N., & Alqerafi, M. (2024). Using Ai to Help Reduce the Effect of Global Warming. *Power System Technology*, *48*(1), 1927–1947. DOI: 10.52783/pst.464

KIDSPARK. (2024, July 16). *AI & STEM Education: Leveraging Technology to Teach STEM*. https://kidsparkeducation.org/blog/ai-stem-education-leveraging-technology-to-teach-stem

Kose, U., & Arslan, A. (2017). Optimization of self-learning in Computer Engineering courses: An intelligent software system supported by Artificial Neural Network and Vortex Optimization Algorithm. *Computer Applications in Engineering Education*, *25*(1), 142–156. DOI: 10.1002/cae.21787

Krasovskiy, D. (2020, October 30). *The Challenges and Benefits of Adopting AI in STEM Education*. https://upjourney.com/the-challenges-and-benefits-of-adopting-ai-in-stem-education

Krullaars, Z. H., Januardani, A., Zhou, L., & Jonkers, E. (2023). *Exploring Initial Interactions: High School Students and Generative AI Chatbots for Relationship Development*. DOI: 10.18420/MUC2023-MCI-SRC-415

Labadze, L., Grigolia, M., & Machaidze, L. (2023). Role of AI chatbots in education: Systematic literature review. *International Journal of Educational Technology in Higher Education*, *20*(1), 56. DOI: 10.1186/s41239-023-00426-1

Liu, M., Li, Y., Xu, W., & Liu, L. (2017). Automated Essay Feedback Generation and Its Impact on Revision. *IEEE Transactions on Learning Technologies*, *10*(4), 502–513. DOI: 10.1109/TLT.2016.2612659

Lubowitz, J. H. (2023). ChatGPT, An Artificial Intelligence Chatbot, Is Impacting Medical Literature. *Arthroscopy*, *39*(5), 1121–1122. DOI: 10.1016/j.arthro.2023.01.015 PMID: 36797148

Maspul, K. A. (2024). Exploring STEM Education for Real-World Climate Change Concerns to Empower Students as Change Agents. *Journal of Physics Education and Science*, *1*(2), 12. DOI: 10.47134/physics.v1i2.249

Miles, M. B., & Huberman, A. M. (1994). Qualitative Data Analysis: An Expanded Sourcebook. *Sage (Atlanta, Ga.)*.

Mystakidis, S., Christopoulos, A., & Pellas, N. (2022). A systematic mapping review of augmented reality applications to support STEM learning in higher education. *Education and Information Technologies*, *27*(2), 1883–1927. DOI: 10.1007/s10639-021-10682-1

Nixon, N., Lin, Y., & Snow, L. (2024). Catalyzing Equity in STEM Teams: Harnessing Generative AI for Inclusion and Diversity. *Policy Insights from the Behavioral and Brain Sciences*, *11*(1), 85–92. DOI: 10.1177/23727322231220356 PMID: 38516055

Okonkwo, C. W., & Ade-Ibijola, A. (2021). Chatbots applications in education: A systematic review. *Computers and Education: Artificial Intelligence*, *2*, 100033. DOI: 10.1016/j.caeai.2021.100033

Öncü, S., Çolakoğlu, M., & Cigdem, H. (2025). Leveraging AI-Managed Learning Analytics and Micro-Credentials for Enhanced Student Engagement. In *Integrating Micro-Credentials With AI in Open Education* (pp. 133–152). IGI Global Scientific Publishing. DOI: 10.4018/979-8-3693-5488-9.ch007

Öncü, S., Çolakoğlu, M., & Colak, H. (2024). Engagement dynamics in information technology education: A comparative analysis of online vs. face-to-face instruction. *Journal of Educational Technology and Online Learning*, *7*(3), 321–333. DOI: 10.31681/jetol.1508735

Ouyang, F., & Jiao, P. (2021). Artificial intelligence in education: The three paradigms. *Computers and Education: Artificial Intelligence*, *2*, 100020. DOI: 10.1016/j.caeai.2021.100020

Ouyang, F., Jiao, P., McLaren, B. M., & Alavi, A. H. (2022). *Artificial Intelligence in STEM Education: The Paradigmatic Shifts in Research, Education, and Technology*. CRC Press.

Pai, K.-C., Kuo, B.-C., Liao, C.-H., & Liu, Y.-M. (2021). An application of Chinese dialogue-based intelligent tutoring system in remedial instruction for mathematics learning. *Educational Psychology*, *41*(2), 137–152. DOI: 10.1080/01443410.2020.1731427

Park, J., Teo, T. W., Teo, A., Chang, J., Huang, J. S., & Koo, S. (2023). Integrating artificial intelligence into science lessons: Teachers' experiences and views. *International Journal of STEM Education*, *10*(1), 61. DOI: 10.1186/s40594-023-00454-3

Peres, R., Schreier, M., Schweidel, D., & Sorescu, A. (2023). On ChatGPT and beyond: How generative artificial intelligence may affect research, teaching, and practice. *International Journal of Research in Marketing*, *40*(2), 269–275. DOI: 10.1016/j.ijresmar.2023.03.001

Razzaq, L., Patvarczki, J., Almeida, S. F., Vartak, M., Feng, M., Heffernan, N. T., & Koedinger, K. R. (2009). The ASSISTment Builder: Supporting the Life Cycle of Tutoring System Content Creation. *IEEE Transactions on Learning Technologies*, *2*(2), 157–166. DOI: 10.1109/TLT.2009.23

Riegler, A., Wintersberger, P., Riener, A., & Holzmann, C. (2019). Augmented Reality Windshield Displays and Their Potential to Enhance User Experience in Automated Driving. *I-Com*, *18*(2), 127–149. DOI: 10.1515/icom-2018-0033

Rosé, C. P., McLaughlin, E. A., Liu, R., & Koedinger, K. R. (2019). Explanatory learner models: Why machine learning (alone) is not the answer. *British Journal of Educational Technology*, *50*(6), 2943–2958. DOI: 10.1111/bjet.12858

Segal, M. (2019). A more human approach to artificial intelligence. *Nature*, *571*(7766), S18–S18. PMID: 31341307

Selwyn, N. (2021). *Education and Technology: Key Issues and Debates*. Bloomsbury Publishing.

Silva, G., Godwin, G., & Jayanagara, O. (2024). The Impact of AI on Personalized Learning and Educational Analytics. [ITEE]. *International Transactions on Education Technology*, *3*(1), 36–46. DOI: 10.33050/itee.v3i1.669

Skinner, F. (1958). Teaching Machines: From the experimental study of learning come devices which arrange optimal conditions for self-instruction. *Science*, *128*(3330), 969–977. PMID: 13592277

Smith, A., Leeman-Munk, S., Shelton, A., Mott, B., Wiebe, E., & Lester, J. (2019). A Multimodal Assessment Framework for Integrating Student Writing and Drawing in Elementary Science Learning. *IEEE Transactions on Learning Technologies*, *12*(1), 3–15. DOI: 10.1109/TLT.2018.2799871

Smith-Mutegi, D., Mamo, Y., Kim, J., Crompton, H., & McConnell, M. (2025). Perceptions of STEM education and artificial intelligence: A Twitter (X) sentiment analysis. *International Journal of STEM Education*, *12*(1), 9. DOI: 10.1186/s40594-025-00527-5

Stake, R. E. (2024). *The Art of Case Study Research*. SAGE Publications Ltd. https://uk.sagepub.com/en-gb/eur/the-art-of-case-study-research/book4954

Taylor, D. L., Yeung, M., & Bashet, A. Z. (2021). Personalized and Adaptive Learning. In Ryoo, J., & Winkelmann, K. (Eds.), *Innovative Learning Environments in STEM Higher Education* (pp. 17–34). Springer International Publishing. DOI: 10.1007/978-3-030-58948-6_2

Tominc, P., & Rožman, M. (2023). Artificial Intelligence and Business Studies: Study Cycle Differences Regarding the Perceptions of the Key Future Competences. *Education Sciences*, *13*(6), 580. DOI: 10.3390/educsci13060580

Valeri, F., Nilsson, P., & Cederqvist, A.-M. (2025). Exploring students' experience of ChatGPT in STEM education. *Computers and Education: Artificial Intelligence*, *8*, 100360. DOI: 10.1016/j.caeai.2024.100360

Warschauer, M., Tseng, W., Yim, S., Webster, T., Jacob, S., Du, Q., & Tate, T. (2023). The Affordances and Contradictions of AI-Generated Text for Second Language Writers. SSRN *Electronic Journal*. DOI: 10.2139/ssrn.4404380

Wollny, S., Schneider, J., Di Mitri, D., Weidlich, J., Rittberger, M., & Drachsler, H. (2021). Are We There Yet? - A Systematic Literature Review on Chatbots in Education. *Frontiers in Artificial Intelligence*, *4*, 654924. DOI: 10.3389/frai.2021.654924 PMID: 34337392

Wood, D., & Moss, S. H. (2024). Evaluating the impact of students' generative AI use in educational contexts. *Journal of Research in Innovative Teaching & Learning*, *17*(2), 152–167. DOI: 10.1108/JRIT-06-2024-0151

Xu, W., & Ouyang, F. (2022a). A systematic review of AI role in the educational system based on a proposed conceptual framework. *Education and Information Technologies*, *27*(3), 4195–4223. DOI: 10.1007/s10639-021-10774-y

Xu, W., & Ouyang, F. (2022b). The application of AI technologies in STEM education: A systematic review from 2011 to 2021. *International Journal of STEM Education*, *9*(1), 59. DOI: 10.1186/s40594-022-00377-5

Yağci, A., & Çevik, M. (2019). Prediction of academic achievements of vocational and technical high school (VTS) students in science courses through artificial neural networks (comparison of Turkey and Malaysia). *Education and Information Technologies*, *24*(5), 2741–2761. DOI: 10.1007/s10639-019-09885-4

Yang, S. J. H., Ogata, H., Matsui, T., & Chen, N.-S. (2021). Human-centered artificial intelligence in education: Seeing the invisible through the visible. *Computers and Education: Artificial Intelligence*, *2*, 100008. DOI: 10.1016/j.caeai.2021.100008

Yannier, N., Hudson, S. E., & Koedinger, K. R. (2020). Active Learning is About More Than Hands-On: A Mixed-Reality AI System to Support STEM Education. *International Journal of Artificial Intelligence in Education*, *30*(1), 74–96. DOI: 10.1007/s40593-020-00194-3

Yin, R. K. (1994). Discovering the future of the case study method in evaluation research. *Evaluation Practice*, *15*(3), 283–290. DOI: 10.1016/0886-1633(94)90023-X

Zawacki-Richter, O., Marín, V. I., Bond, M., & Gouverneur, F. (2019). Systematic review of research on artificial intelligence applications in higher education – where are the educators? *International Journal of Educational Technology in Higher Education, 16*(1), 39. DOI: 10.1186/s41239-019-0171-0

Zhai, X. (2022). ChatGPT User Experience: Implications for Education. SSRN *Electronic Journal*. DOI: 10.2139/ssrn.4312418

Zhang, K., & Aslan, A. B. (2021). AI technologies for education: Recent research & future directions. *Computers and Education: Artificial Intelligence, 2*, 100025. DOI: 10.1016/j.caeai.2021.100025

Chapter 8
Predicting Student Success in Distance Learning Using Machine Learning and Explainable AI for LMS Data

Çağatay Bal
https://orcid.org/0000-0002-7823-2712
Muğla Sitki Koçman University, Turkey

Eralp Doğu
https://orcid.org/0000-0002-8256-7304
Muğla Sitki Koçman University, Turkey

Müge Adnan
Muğla Sitki Koçman University, Turkey

ABSTRACT

In the era of distance education, understanding student behaviours through learning analytics has become crucial for improving educational outcomes. This study analyses log data obtained from a Learning Management System (LMS) to explore the relationship between student engagement patterns and academic performance. Student's interaction with various activity contexts were extracted as features and evaluated through machine learning methods. A Random Forest model, supported with Local Interpretable Model-Agnostic Explanations (LIME) interpretability, was applied to classify outcomes. The model achieved an accuracy of 81.67%, revealing that attendance patterns and exam duration are critical factors influencing success.

DOI: 10.4018/979-8-3373-8805-2.ch008

Findings offer practical implications for instructors and supporting the design of targeted interventions, early warning systems, and personalised feedback mechanisms. Ultimately, the research demonstrates the potential of log-based analytics and Explainable Artificial Intelligence to deliver evidence-driven improvements in distance education and student support.

1. INTRODUCTION

The rapid expansion of Internet-based distance education in recent years has transformed the way learning is delivered and experienced. Online platforms and Learning Management Systems (LMS) have enabled greater flexibility, wider access, and new opportunities for students across diverse contexts. However, this growth has also introduced significant challenges, including the need to sustain student motivation, monitor engagement, and ensure successful learning outcomes in the absence of traditional face-to-face interactions (Goh, 2025; Pan et al., 2024, Sevim et al., 2023).

Traditional statistical methods have been applied to predict student success, but their explanatory power is often limited in capturing the complexity of online learning environments. These approaches usually rely on a narrow set of variables and cannot fully reflect the multifaceted nature of student interactions, such as weekly attendance patterns, material usage, assignment submissions, or exam performance. As a result, their predictive capacity remains insufficient for early intervention and effective support (Riestra-González et al., 2021).

To address these shortcomings, interpretable machine learning methods have emerged as a promising alternative in educational research. Machine learning can integrate a wide variety of behavioral and contextual features extracted from LMS logs, offering stronger predictive accuracy and the potential to uncover hidden patterns. At the same time, interpretability tools such as LIME (Local Interpretable Model-Agnostic Explanations) provide transparency, making complex models understandable to educators and administrators who require actionable insights rather than black-box predictions (Rodríguez-Ortiz et al., 2025; Swamy et al., 2022).

Nonetheless, from an instructional design perspective, effective learning analytics must translate technical predictions into pedagogically meaningful actions. This requires understanding not only *which* behaviors predict success, but *why* these behaviors matter for learning, and *how* instructional interventions can support their development (Gašević et al., 2016).

Despite the growing adoption of machine learning in educational data mining, existing approaches often fall short in bridging the gap between predictive power and interpretability. Many studies emphasize accuracy without adequately considering how results can be translated into meaningful interventions. Others overlook critical engagement patterns, especially those occurring in late-semester periods, which play a decisive role in academic outcomes.

The primary objective of this study is to develop interpretable machine learning models capable of predicting student success in online learning environments. By leveraging LMS interaction data, the research aims to identify the behavioral patterns most strongly associated with academic outcomes such as course completion and performance (Guo et al., 2022; Yuan et al., 2024).

The first research question focuses on algorithmic performance: *Which machine learning algorithms perform best when applied to LMS interaction data?* Addressing this question requires comparing multiple approaches ranging from traditional classifiers to ensemble methods, with the aim of balancing predictive accuracy and computational feasibility.

The second research question explores student behaviour: *What interaction patterns most strongly predict academic success or failure?* Identifying critical features such as late-semester attendance, course material engagement, and exam participation which can provide valuable insights for designing timely interventions and improving student performance (Choi et al., 2025).

The third research question addresses interpretability: *How can machine learning predictions be made understandable and actionable for educators?* This question underscores the importance of explainable AI techniques, such as LIME and SHAP, which allow both global and local explanations of model outputs, ensuring that stakeholders trust and effectively use the results (Lundberg et al., 2017; Nnadi et al., 2024; Ribeiro et al., 2016; Swamy et al., 2022).

This study bridges high-performing predictive modeling with transparent, actionable insights to enhance learning design, sustain engagement, and enable targeted support in online education by applying machine learning to LMS interaction data and prioritising interpretability via LIME. Beyond outperforming traditional statistical approaches in capturing complex, temporal engagement patterns, the framework delivers educator-facing explanations that balance accuracy with clarity in decision-making (Holstein & Doroudi, 2021; Nnadi et al., 2024). Practically, the identification of late-semester attendance patterns and final-exam duration as strong predictors pinpoints when and where interventions matter most, informing early-warning systems and personalized feedback strategies (Choi et al., 2025). More broadly, coupling performance with explainability offers a methodological blueprint for future research and supports scaling across institutions and contexts (Ghimire et al., 2024; Rodríguez-Ortiz et al., 2025).

Following the introduction, the chapter reviews prior research on student success prediction, machine learning applications in education, and explainable AI to establish the study's theoretical and methodological foundations. The methods outline data collection, feature engineering, preprocessing, model selection, evaluation metrics, and the integration of LIME to ensure transparency and reproducibility. Results highlight Random Forest as the top-performing model, supported by global feature importance and local interpretability analysis. Finally, the discussion interprets findings within the context of educational practice, addresses study limitations, and proposes future directions, underscoring how combining predictive performance with interpretability advances both research and practical implementation in distance learning analytics.

2. BACKGROUND

2.1 Student Success Prediction in Online Learning

Early research into student success prediction in online learning relied heavily on traditional statistical techniques, most commonly regression models. While these methods offered straightforward analyses, they were limited in their ability to capture the nonlinear and temporal dynamics of online learning behaviours. For instance, it has been demonstrated that linear regression models failed to predict outcomes reliably in the early weeks of a course, whereas neural networks achieved substantially better accuracy by dynamically incorporating weekly test performance (Lykourentzou et al., 2009). This work highlighted both the potential of machine learning to improve predictive accuracy and the limitations of earlier statistical approaches that could not adapt to evolving student behaviours.

Subsequent research further emphasised the role of behavioural, motivational, and contextual factors. Kauffman (2015) reviewed predictive factors of student success and satisfaction, noting that variables such as self-regulation, motivation, and interaction with course content were consistently significant. However, most prior studies used survey-based or regression analyses, producing correlations rather than reliable predictive power. This exposed a key limitation: while researchers could identify important factors, traditional methods offered little actionable insight into when and how these variables influenced outcomes (Kauffman, 2015).

Complementing this, Yukselturk and Bulut (2007) provided empirical evidence that self-regulation, computer self-efficacy, prior online experience, and time management were strong predictors of student achievement. Yet their reliance on regression techniques again constrained the explanatory scope, as complex interdependencies between predictors could not be modelled effectively. The study underscored that while traditional predictors are valuable, more sophisticated methods are needed to capture the full range of learner characteristics and their dynamic interactions (Yukselturk & Bulut, 2007).

More recent work has focused explicitly on modelling student interaction as a determinant of success. Shelton, Hung, and Lowenthal (2017) used time-series clustering and decision tree models to analyse asynchronous online course data, finding that the frequency and consistency of interactions, rather than the sheer volume, were decisive indicators of success. Their results improved predictive accuracy and allowed identification of at-risk students earlier in the semester compared to earlier aggregation-based approaches. Still, while such machine learning techniques advanced predictive performance, they remained opaque to educators, limiting their direct pedagogical usefulness (Shelton et al., 2017).

Taken together, these studies illustrate a clear trajectory from traditional statistical approaches to increasingly sophisticated machine learning models. Early methods were constrained by linearity and static assumptions, while later studies identified richer sets of predictors including self-regulation, motivation, prior experience, and interaction behaviours. The evolution to neural networks, clustering, and decision trees improved accuracy and timeliness, yet across all four works, a persistent limitation emerges: the lack of interpretability. Models often function as black boxes, making it difficult for educators to understand why certain students are flagged as at risk. This limitation directly motivates the current study, which advances the field by integrating explainable AI techniques such as LIME with robust predictive models. In doing so, it addresses both the accuracy demands highlighted by earlier research and the pressing need for actionable, transparent insights that can inform interventions in distance education.

Moreover, beyond technical modeling, research in the learning sciences has long emphasized that predictive analytics should be interpreted within pedagogical frameworks that consider motivation, self-regulated learning, and instructional design principles (Winne & Hadwin, 2008; Zimmerman, 2013). Incorporating such perspectives ensures that machine learning outcomes are translated into meaningful teaching practices rather than remaining purely algorithmic findings. Studies on course design and instructor feedback loops (Gašević et al., 2016) also demonstrate how data-driven insights can enhance learning effectiveness when aligned with pedagogical intent.

2.2 Machine Learning in Educational Data Mining

Supervised models have become central to Educational Data Mining (EDM), enabling early prediction of course completion, grades, or dropout risk from digital traces captured by learning environments. Studies consistently report that models such as logistic regression, support vector machines, decision trees, random forests, multilayer perceptrons, and gradient boosting are effective when trained on well-curated features derived from LMSs and assessment platforms (Arizmendi et al.,

2023; Romero & Ventura, 2020). Beyond raw accuracy, recent work emphasizes *when* predictions become reliable during a term, as timeliness is essential for interventions; time-aware designs and temporally sliced features therefore play a growing role in supervised pipelines (Arizmendi et al., 2023; Macfadyen & Dawson, 2010).

The most challenging and consequential stage is transforming heterogeneous LMS logs into meaningful features. Canonical LMS exports include event timestamps, user identifiers, activity contexts, components, event names, and free-text descriptions which must be normalized, and mapped to behaviours. Effective pipelines aggregate these primitives into multi-granular indicators: weekly activity counts content and tool-specific frequencies, latency/interval features (time between consecutive actions), regularity/consistency indices (variance of weekly activity), and assessment-linked metrics (e.g., *final exam duration in minutes*). Comparative evidence shows that engineered temporal patterns (e.g., week-by-week sequences, burstiness, or inactivity streaks) often outperform simple totals; moreover, wrapper/filter feature selection further boosts generalization by reducing redundancy and leakage (Al-Zawqari et al., 2022; Levin, 2021). In binary settings where the target is encoded as two classes (e.g., *successful* vs. *unsuccessful*), class balance checks, stratified splits, and cost-sensitive metrics (ROC-AUC, PR-AUC, balanced accuracy) are recommended to avoid optimistic accuracy under skew (Arizmendi et al., 2023; Romero & Ventura, 2020).

Cross-model evaluations typically find that tree-based ensembles (Random Forest, Gradient Boosting) and kernel methods (SVM) provide strong baselines, while neural networks can excel with larger samples and richer sequential features; nonetheless, performance differences shrink when feature engineering is rigorous and temporally aware (Ahmed, 2024; Arévalo-Cordovilla et al., 2024). Recent comparative studies using LMS data corroborate that incorporating *temporal structure* and *interaction heterogeneity* is more impactful than swapping among standard classifiers, and that transparent reporting of feature provenance is essential for reproducibility and adoption by instructors (Ahmed, 2024; Romero & Ventura, 2020). Yet a persistent limitation is interpretability: high-performing models are often black boxes. Consequently, many EDM pipelines now combine tree/boosting models with global feature importance and local post-hoc explainers (e.g., LIME) to provide actionable, sentence-level rationales for flags—aligning with this chapter's emphasis on explainable AI in distance learning (Al-Zawqari et al., 2022; Romero & Ventura, 2020).

2.3 Explainable AI in Educational Technology

One of the most persistent challenges in applying artificial intelligence to educational contexts is the interpretability of models. While black-box algorithms such as neural networks and ensemble methods often yield high predictive accuracy, their opacity limits their usefulness for instructors and administrators who require not only predictions but also actionable explanations for decision-making (Holstein & Doroudi, 2021). Without interpretability, stakeholders may distrust results or struggle to design effective interventions, reducing the practical impact of otherwise powerful models.

LIME (Local Interpretable Model-agnostic Explanations) has emerged as a prominent solution to this challenge. LIME approximates complex models with locally interpretable surrogates, often linear regressions, around individual predictions (Ribeiro et al., 2016). This allows researchers and educators to identify which specific features such as late-semester attendance, content engagement, or exam duration most strongly influenced a given classification outcome. In educational data mining, LIME bridges the gap between model accuracy and transparency by enabling both global insights (e.g., recurring influential variables) and local explanations (e.g., why a particular student was flagged as at risk). Such dual capacity makes it highly suitable for sensitive contexts like student success prediction, where fairness and interpretability are as crucial as accuracy (George et al., 2025).

Balancing performance with transparency remains a critical concern in explainable AI for education. High-performing models may obscure their decision-making, while inherently interpretable models (e.g., logistic regression, decision trees) often underperform on complex LMS data. The integration of post-hoc explainability methods such as LIME provides a pragmatic compromise: it preserves the predictive strength of black-box algorithms like Random Forest while producing human-readable explanations that facilitate trust, accountability, and pedagogical action (Nnadi et al., 2024). As a result, explainable AI tools offer not only methodological advancements but also practical pathways toward responsible adoption of machine learning in educational technology.

In addition to LIME, other explainable AI frameworks such as SHAP (SHapley Additive exPlanations) have recently gained prominence for their solid theoretical grounding in cooperative game theory (Lundberg & Lee, 2017). SHAP provides consistent global and local interpretability and is particularly useful for comparing the relative contributions of features across different models. A brief comparison of LIME and SHAP underscores that both serve complementary purposes which are LIME offering localized, intuitive explanations and SHAP providing model-wide consistency. Integrating a short note on SHAP ensures fairness and completeness in the discussion of explainability tools.

2.4 Research Gap and Positioning

Although significant progress has been made in predicting student success through both statistical and machine learning approaches, several gaps remain. Traditional regression-based methods have provided valuable descriptive insights but consistently underperform in predictive accuracy and timeliness, limiting their practical utility for early interventions (Kauffman, 2015; Yukselturk & Bulut, 2007). More recent machine learning studies such as those employing neural networks, decision trees, or clustering have improved accuracy, yet they largely function as black boxes, offering limited interpretability to educators (Lykourentzou et al., 2009; Shelton et al., 2017). This lack of transparency hinders the translation of predictions into pedagogically meaningful strategies.

Another important methodological distinction in student success prediction lies between early-warning and post-exam modeling. Early-warning systems rely on formative data from the initial or mid-semester weeks to identify at-risk students in time for intervention, while post-exam prediction focuses on summative or retrospective analysis (Arizmendi et al., 2023; Macfadyen & Dawson, 2010). Situating the present work within the early-warning tradition highlights its contribution to proactive learning support rather than reactive evaluation.In addition, much of the existing research has relied on limited or static sets of features, often neglecting the richness of LMS log data and the potential of temporal patterns to provide early-warning signals (Levin, 2021; Macfadyen & Dawson, 2010). Feature engineering remains an underdeveloped area, with many studies focusing on aggregate counts of activity rather than more nuanced temporal, behavioural, and contextual indicators. This gap underscores the importance of constructing comprehensive datasets that reflect not just frequency of engagement but also its timing, regularity, and connection to assessment outcomes.

Positioned against this background, the present study contributes to the field in three ways. First, it develops a carefully engineered LMS-based dataset, incorporating weekly activity patterns, assessment-linked variables, and course engagement metrics to capture the multifaceted nature of student behaviour. Second, it applies high-performing machine learning algorithms, most notably Random Forest, to achieve strong predictive accuracy while mitigating overfitting through feature selection. Most importantly, it integrates explainable AI methods particularly LIME to provide both global and local interpretability of model outcomes. In doing so, this research directly addresses the limitations of earlier black-box approaches and positions itself at the intersection of predictive performance and transparency, offering actionable insights for instructors and administrators in distance learning.

3. METHODS

3.1 Data Collection and Preprocessing

The data for this study were obtained from the institutional LMS, which is based on the open-source Moodle platform.

This study was conducted in compliance with institutional ethical standards and approved by the University Ethics Committee of Mugla Sitki Kocman University (Approval No: 220004). Log data were extracted using the LMS's native reporting tools, producing CSV/Excel outputs that included key attributes such as timestamp, user identifiers, event context, component, event name, and free-text descriptions of user actions. These raw data tables correspond closely to the structure of typical Moodle logs, with columns including *Time*, *Full Name*, *Affected User*, *Event Context*, *Component*, *Event Name*, *Description*, *Origin*, and *IP Address*. For the purpose of this research, identifying information (e.g., full names, IP addresses) was anonymised at the point of extraction. Only pseudonymised identifiers were retained for linking activity records across weeks (Akhanli et al., 2024; Keskin & Yurdugul, 2022; Quansah & Essiam, 2021).

The dataset comprised interaction logs from a single undergraduate course titled *Introduction to Information Technologies*, delivered through the Moodle-based institutional LMS. The course spanned a full 14-week academic semester, with weekly synchronous and asynchronous components. In total, 284 students were enrolled, generating over 35,000 individual log records. This scale provided sufficient granularity to capture weekly engagement fluctuations while remaining tractable for feature engineering and model interpretation.

The course structure consisted of weekly modules combining asynchronous content delivery through video lectures and readings, synchronous discussion sessions, and hands-on practice exercises. Assessment included formative quizzes (Weeks 3, 7, 11), one midterm project (Week 8), and a comprehensive final exam (Week 14). This design follows principles of distributed practice and retrieval-based learning.

The final raw dataset contained interaction logs for a full academic term, encompassing multiple types of student actions such as viewing course resources, participating in forums, attempting course materials, and submitting assignments. In total, several thousand log entries were recorded, covering dozens of students across 14 instructional weeks. These logs formed the basis for subsequent feature engineering, where weekly activity counts, resource-specific frequencies, and assessment-linked variables were derived for predictive modelling. By capturing fine-grained engagement data over time, the dataset enables both global analyses of behavioural trends and individualised temporal profiles necessary for early-warning models.

Transforming raw LMS logs into analytically meaningful features is a crucial step in predictive modelling for student success. In this study, feature engineering was performed to capture the breadth, depth, and temporal structure of student engagement across the semester. The process began by aggregating event-level data into weekly activity counts, generating variables that reflected the number of logins, resource views, forum interactions, and quiz attempts for each instructional week. This temporal granularity allowed us to model learning behaviour dynamically and detect critical periods of engagement or disengagement.

In addition to weekly counts, content-specific features were derived to capture interaction with different resource types (e.g., lecture slides, supplementary files, practice quizzes). These were encoded as frequency indicators, providing a detailed picture of which course components contributed most to student activity. Assessment-linked features were also constructed, including the number of assignment submissions, quiz scores, and final exam duration. Here, "exam duration" refers to the total time (in seconds) that each student remained active within the final exam session with allowed time as 20 minutes, as recorded in LMS logs. This variable capture test-taking behavior and persistence rather than score outcomes, serving as a behavioral proxy for engagement intensity during assessment.

Prior to modelling, all features were standardised to ensure comparability across scales. The resulting feature matrix preserved both global trends and individualised engagement profiles, forming the foundation for supervised classification into two target classes (*successful* vs. *unsuccessful* students). This structured representation enables downstream machine learning models to leverage not just total activity, but also its distribution and timing, which are critical for early-warning systems.

Prior to model training, several preprocessing steps were applied to prepare the dataset for supervised classification. Missing observations most commonly arising from students who did not participate in a particular activity during a given week were handled using zero-padding. This approach explicitly encodes non-engagement as an informative signal rather than treating it as missing-at-random, which aligns with best practices in educational data mining where non-participation is often predictive of poorer outcomes (Macfadyen & Dawson, 2010; Papamitsiou & Economides, 2014). Padding with zeros has been shown to be particularly effective in count-based feature spaces, as it preserves the interpretability of features and avoids introducing noise through mean or random-value imputation (Romero & Ventura, 2020).

Following imputation, all count-based features were scaled to improve comparability and model convergence. Weekly attendance metrics were normalised to a [0,1] range, where values closer to 1 indicated higher levels of participation relative to the cohort average. This min–max normalisation ensures that highly active and inactive students are distinguished without disproportionately weighting variables with larger numeric ranges (Han et al., 2022). Other count-based features, such as content views, assignment attempts, and quiz interactions, were standardised where appropriate to reduce skew and stabilise variance, particularly for ensemble methods like Random Forest and gradient boosting that benefit from balanced feature distributions.

To prepare the data for supervised learning, the dataset was partitioned into training and test subsets by fixed ratio as %70 and %30 respectively using stratified sampling to maintain the proportion of successful and unsuccessful students. This approach prevents class imbalance from biasing performance metrics and ensures that evaluation reflects real-world distributions. Additionally, feature matrices were inspected for multicollinearity, and highly redundant variables were removed to improve model efficiency. These preprocessing steps resulted in a clean, normalised dataset suitable for downstream classification, enabling models to learn not only from the presence of activity but also from its absence, which is a critical early-warning indicator in online learning environments.

Special care was taken to avoid potential data leakage, particularly regarding variables such as final exam duration that occur at the end of the semester. These assessment-linked features were used only in retrospective analyses and excluded from early-warning model variants, ensuring that predictive validity was not inflated by post-hoc information.**3.2 Machine Learning Pipeline Design**

To evaluate student success prediction, a range of supervised learning algorithms was implemented, balancing predictive power with interpretability. The chosen models include both traditional statistical classifiers and tree-based ensemble methods, providing a spectrum from highly interpretable "white-box" techniques to more complex but higher-capacity learners.

Logistic Regression was selected as a baseline because of its simplicity and transparency. It estimates the probability of success as a function of weighted input features, allowing direct interpretation of coefficients to determine whether specific behaviours (e.g., late-semester attendance) are positively or negatively associated with outcomes. Similarly, Linear Discriminant Analysis (LDA) and Quadratic Discriminant Analysis (QDA) provide parametric decision boundaries based on class-specific means and covariances, offering interpretable geometric separations in feature space.

Naive Bayes was included as a probabilistic white-box classifier that models conditional independence among features, producing easily explainable posterior probabilities. While it assumes independence, it remains computationally efficient and provides interpretable likelihood contributions for each feature (Maron, 1961).

To capture nonlinear interactions and hierarchical feature splits, Decision Trees were employed. Decision tree models are inherently interpretable, as they produce human-readable if–then rules that reveal which features dominate decision-making at various thresholds (Quinlan, 1993).

Finally, Random Forest was chosen as the primary high-capacity model due to its strong performance on tabular, count-based datasets typical of LMS logs. It aggregates multiple decision trees through bagging, improving generalisation and reducing overfitting (Breiman, 2001). Although Random Forest is less interpretable than single trees, feature importance scores can be extracted to provide global insights, and in the present study, post-hoc explainability was further enhanced through LIME to offer local, instance-level explanations.

Collectively, these models were selected to compare predictive performance across different complexity–interpretability trade-offs, ensuring that the final approach not only maximises accuracy but also delivers actionable, transparent insights for educators. This focus on explainability positions the study within the growing body of work advocating responsible and trustworthy AI in education (Holstein & Doroudi, 2021; George et al., 2025).

The performance of the predictive models was evaluated using a comprehensive set of metrics to ensure both overall accuracy and balanced assessment of model behavior across the two target classes (*successful* vs. *unsuccessful* students).

Model performance was evaluated using multiple metrics, including accuracy, precision, recall, F1-score, AUC-ROC, and specificity, to ensure a balanced and comprehensive assessment of classification effectiveness. This multifaceted evaluation framework supports the selection of the most appropriate predictive approach for deployment in educational contexts.

3.3 Explainable AI Implementation

Understanding which features drive model predictions is essential for both scientific insight and practical intervention design in education. In this study, global feature importance was first extracted from tree-based models such as Random Forest, which compute importance scores by measuring the average decrease in node impurity across all trees (Breiman, 2001). This approach provides a ranked list of predictors, enabling identification of the most influential variables such as late-semester attendance, content views, or final exam duration that contribute to class separation on a global scale.

While model-dependent methods like importance is straightforward and computationally efficient, it has limitations, including potential bias toward variables with higher cardinality or more splits (Strobl et al., 2007). To mitigate this, model-agnostic approach was also considered. Model-agnostic method measure the drop in predictive performance when a single feature's values are randomly shuffled, thus estimating importance independently of the internal mechanics of the model (Ribeiro et al., 2016).

Combining these approaches yields a more robust understanding of feature relevance. Model-dependent methods quickly provide insight into which variables dominate decision paths, while model-agnostic techniques offer a cross-model comparison that is especially valuable when using multiple classifiers integrity of global and local interpretations. This dual strategy ensures that interpretations are not biased by the idiosyncrasies of a single algorithm, thereby increasing trustworthiness and applicability. Differences between model-dependent and model-agnostic methods in Table 1 below.

Table 1. Comparison of Model-Dependent and Model-Agnostic Feature Importance Methods

Criterion	Model-Dependent	Model-Agnostic
Computation	Fast, derived during training	Slower, requires retraining or evaluation passes
Interpretability	Intuitive within a specific model	Consistent across models
Bias Risk	Can favour high-cardinality features	Less biased, but computationally intensive
Use Case	Quick model-specific insights	Comparative evaluation and validation
Limitation	Dependent on algorithm structure	May be unstable on small datasets

3.3.2 LIME Implementation

To enhance interpretability at the individual prediction level, Local Interpretable Model-agnostic Explanations (LIME) was integrated into the analysis pipeline. LIME operates by perturbing the input data around a single observation and fitting an interpretable surrogate model typically a sparse linear regression or ridge regression to approximate the complex classifier's local decision boundary (Ribeiro et al., 2016). LIME was applied in two complementary ways: first is for **individual-level explanations**, showing which features contributed most to each student's classification outcome; and second is for **aggregate consistency checks**, comparing local explanations with global feature importance derived from the Random Forest model. This dual use allowed us to validate model reasoning both at micro and macro levels. This method produces a ranked list of feature contributions, indicating which variables most strongly influenced the prediction for that particular student.

In this study, LIME was applied to the final Random Forest model to generate local explanations for both correctly and incorrectly classified instances. For example, in cases where a student was predicted to be "unsuccessful," LIME revealed whether low late-semester attendance, reduced resource engagement, or short exam duration were the primary risk drivers. Conversely, for successful students, the method highlighted protective factors such as steady participation and consistent assignment submission patterns. By visualising these feature contributions with positive and negative directional impacts, LIME enabled educators to understand *why* the model flagged a given student and which behaviors should be encouraged or remediated.

The use of LIME also served as a validation step, allowing comparison between local explanations and global feature importance rankings. Consistency between the two provided evidence of model reliability, while discrepancies offered insight into individual-specific deviations worth investigating further. This dual-layer interpretability, global and local, supports actionable decision-making and aligns with calls for transparent and fair AI in educational contexts (George et al., 2025; Nnadi et al., 2024). By combining LIME with feature importance analysis, the study moves beyond predictive accuracy to offer explainable, trustworthy insights that can inform targeted interventions and optimise student outcomes.

While several alternative explainability techniques exist such as SHAP, LIME was selected for this study due to its computational simplicity, model-agnostic nature, and ease of integration into MATLAB workflows. This choice ensured transparent and reproducible interpretation without extensive parameter tuning, aligning with the chapter's emphasis on clarity and methodological transparency.

3.4 Experimental Setup

All analyses in this study were conducted in a MATLAB environment, chosen for its robust statistical and machine learning toolboxes and its capacity to handle large, structured datasets efficiently. The end-to-end workflow began with a data engineering phase, where raw Moodle LMS logs were systematically converted into a structured dataset suitable for machine learning. This conversion step involved writing custom MATLAB functions to clean, normalise, and aggregate the log data into student-level records. As previous research has noted, the transition from raw log data to an analytically meaningful feature matrix is often the most challenging stage of educational data mining (Levin, 2021). In this study, this step was the most labour-intensive component, as it required sessionisation, feature aggregation, and integration of assessment-linked variables over 14 weeks of activity. The reliability of all downstream modelling results depended on the quality and consistency of this data engineering process, underscoring its central importance.

Hyperparameter optimisation was performed using a straightforward trial-and-error strategy, rather than formal grid search or Bayesian optimisation routines. Parameters such as tree depth (Decision Tree), number of estimators (Random Forest), and regularisation strength (Logistic Regression) were iteratively tuned by observing training performance and cross-validation metrics until convergence on a stable, well-generalising configuration was achieved. Although simple, this approach offered full transparency and avoided overfitting to validation data, aligning with recommendations for educational contexts where interpretability and methodological clarity are prioritised over marginal performance gains (Bengio, 2012).

Taken together, the combination of carefully engineered data pipelines, manually tuned hyperparameters, and deterministic modelling produced a methodologically transparent and fully reproducible experimental setup. This rigor ensures that other researchers or institutional stakeholders could replicate the workflow and obtain the same results when applied to similar LMS datasets, thereby increasing trust in both the process and its pedagogical recommendations.

4. RESULTS

4.1 Model Performance Comparison

The overall classification results across all six algorithms; Logistic Regression, LDA, QDA, Naive Bayes, Decision Tree, and Random Forest are summarised in Table 2. Each model was evaluated using accuracy, precision, recall, F1-score, specificity, and macro-averaged AUC to provide a comprehensive assessment of performance.

Table 2. Overall performance metrics for all six classifiers (accuracy, precision, recall, F1, specificity, macro AUC).

Model	TestAccuracy	MacroAUC	Precision	Recall (Sensitivity)	F1Score	Specificity
Logistic Regression	0.56667	0.59147	0.56507	0.55556	0.56473	0.57576
Linear Discriminant Analysis	0.5	0.45847	0.48352	0.33333	0.47917	0.48485
Quadratic Discriminant Analysis	0.58333	0.56061	0.57805	0.51852	0.57758	0.63636
Naïve Bayes	0.61667	0.67789	0.65	0.25926	0.55063	0.70909
Decision Tree	0.78333	0.83838	0.78125	0.77778	0.78182	0.78788
Random Forest	**0.81667**	**0.86644**	**0.81561**	**0.77778**	**0.81414**	**0.84848**

Random Forest achieved the highest performance among all classifiers, with an accuracy of 81.67% and a Macro AUC of 0.86644, indicating strong discriminatory ability across both classes. Decision Tree ranked second, performing competitively but with slightly lower recall, suggesting that some at-risk students were misclassified as successful. Logistic Regression, while slightly less accurate, offered fully interpretable coefficients, making it a valuable baseline for understanding feature effects. Overall, the table shows a consistent improvement from linear models to ensemble methods, underscoring the advantage of capturing nonlinear engagement patterns in LMS data.

These results demonstrate that ensemble methods can capture nonlinear relationships among LMS-derived features more effectively than parametric models, while still being amenable to post-hoc interpretation through global feature importance and LIME explanations.

A deeper analysis of performance metrics provides further insight into the comparative strengths of the evaluated models. Accuracy vs. AUC trade-offs were first examined to assess whether models that achieved higher accuracy also maintained consistent discriminative ability across decision thresholds.

Figure 1. AUC graph of Random Forest model

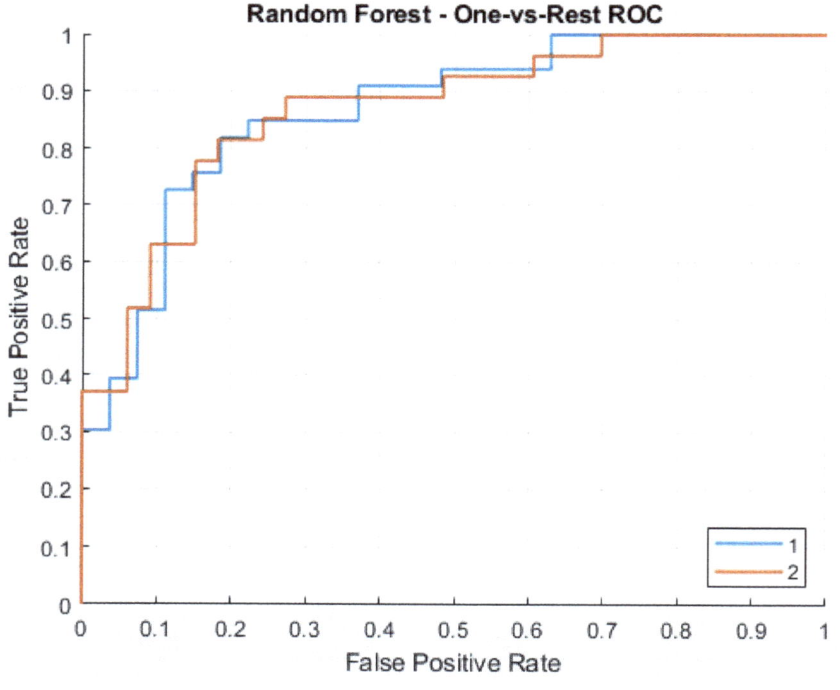

As illustrated in Figure 1 above, Random Forest achieved not only the highest accuracy but also the highest macro-averaged AUC (0.86644), indicating robust classification performance independent of threshold selection. By contrast, models such as Logistic Regression and Naive Bayes exhibited moderate accuracy but lower

AUC values, suggesting that their predictive probabilities were less well-calibrated across classes.

Precision and recall analysis highlights the ability of the models to balance false positives and false negatives, which is particularly critical for early-warning systems. Random Forest maintained the most favourable trade-off, achieving high recall minimising the number of at-risk students missed without sacrificing precision, thus avoiding unnecessary interventions. Decision Tree achieved similar recall but slightly lower precision, indicating a greater risk of failing to identify students who ultimately underperformed.

Finally, specificity was analysed to ensure that the models did not over-flag students as at risk. High specificity is essential to avoid overwhelming instructors with false alarms that could dilute the impact of targeted support. Random Forest again showed balanced behaviour, with a specificity level that correctly excluded the majority of successful students from risk alerts. This is especially important in scalable online learning environments, where limited resources must be directed toward those most in need.

Taken together, these metric-level analyses underscore that Random Forest not only excels in overall predictive accuracy but also achieves a desirable balance across multiple dimensions such as discrimination, sensitivity, precision, and specificity which making it well-suited as the foundation for explainability analyses and early-warning interventions.

4.2 Feature Importance and Critical Factors

The global feature importance analysis derived from the Random Forest model revealed several key predictors of student success.

Table 3. Feature importance list of Random Forest model.

Features	Description / Context
Week 9 Attendance	Weekly attendance count during Week 9
Week 11 Attendance	Weekly attendance count during Week 11
Week 12 Attendance	Weekly attendance count during Week 12
Week 13 Attendance	Weekly attendance count during Week 13
Week 2 Attendance	Weekly attendance count during Week 2
Final Exam Duration	Total time spent on the final exam (minutes)
Resource #10.1 "Formulas" Viewed	Course module view log for Formulas resource
Week 14 Attendance	Weekly attendance count during Week 14

continued on following page

Table 3. Continued

Features	Description / Context
Week 7 Attendance	Weekly attendance count during Week 7
Resource #13 "Charts" Viewed	Course module view log for Charts resource
Week 8 Attendance	Weekly attendance count during Week 8
Resource #12 "Working with Data" Viewed	Course module view log for Data exercise file
Resource "Section 4 – Technology and Lifelong Learning" Viewed	Module view log for the reading material
Week 10 Attendance	Weekly attendance count during Week 10
Resource #10.2 "Formula Writing Types" Viewed	Course module view log for Formula Types resource

Table 3 presents the list of features. Among all predictors, especially late-semester attendance and final exam duration emerged as the most influential variables, with strongly associated with successful course completion. This result suggests that students who devoted more attendance during last weeks and more time to the final assessment demonstrated greater engagement and mastery of the material, aligning with prior findings linking assessment behaviours to academic outcomes. These importance scores confirm that late-semester attendance variables dominate the model's decision process, highlighting the timing of engagement as a decisive factor.

Figure 2 below, illustrates the tree structure of Random Forest model.

Figure 2. Tree structure

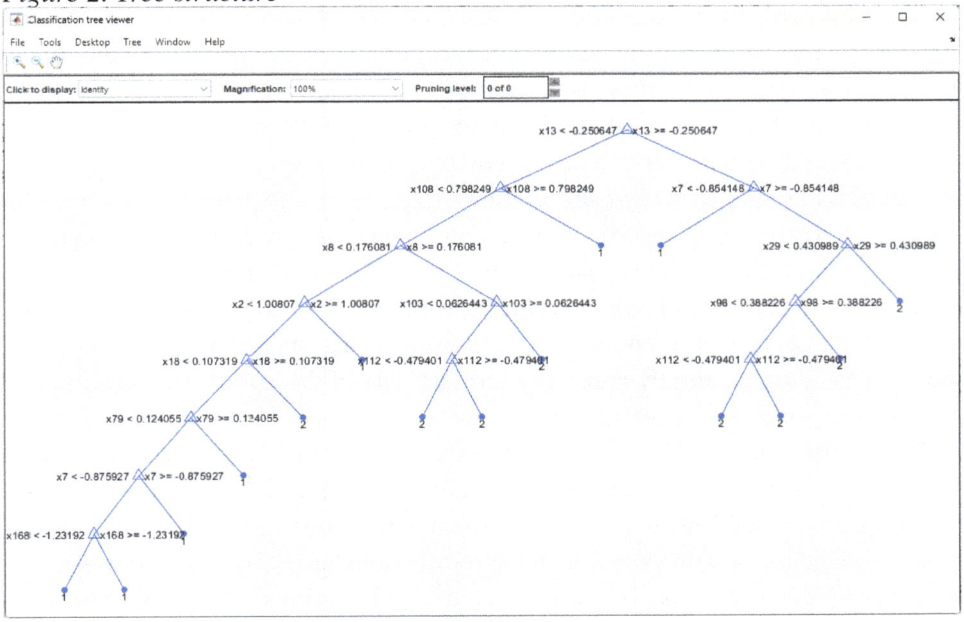

Weekly engagement variables also played a critical role, with Weeks 9, 11, 12, 13 and 2 showing the highest importance scores among temporal features. These weeks correspond to key instructional and assessment periods in the course schedule, including project deadlines and review sessions. The prominence of late-semester activity corroborates previous research emphasising the importance of sustained participation through the final stages of a course. Students with consistent engagement in these critical weeks were significantly more likely to be classified as successful, highlighting potential intervention windows for instructors.

In the decision tree visualisation, these temporal features appear as early splits: for example, x13 (< −0.250647) corresponds to Week 13 attendance, acting as the root node, and x108 (< 0.798249) represents one of the most discriminative resource interactions "Resource #13 Charts viewed", determining major left-branch separations. Similarly, x7 (< −0.854148) captures Week 7 attendance, and x168 (< −1.23192) represents the Final Exam Duration variable, both of which are decisive nodes that strongly influence classification outcomes. These mappings confirm that the model relies on a combination of late-week participation and critical resource usage events to split students into success/failure groups.

Content-related features, such as frequency of resource views and assignment submissions, also ranked highly, reinforcing the notion that active interaction with course materials is a strong predictor of achievement. Together, these results indicate that both cumulative engagement (final exam behaviour) and time-sensitive participation (critical weeks) are key determinants of performance. The global importance profile thus provides actionable guidance for course designers and instructors: emphasise continuous participation throughout the term, with targeted support around Weeks 9–14 to maximise retention and success rates.

Timing effects further amplify the predictive value of resource use. Engagement concentrated around late-semester windows (e.g., revision weeks and assessment periods) is particularly discriminative, consistent with evidence that week-by-week dynamics and sustained participation toward course end are strong signals of outcome trajectories. In practice, resources accessed during these critical weeks review documents, exam guides, and final project materials tend to co-vary with success labels more strongly than early-term activity of the same type, highlighting intervention windows for instructors.

Finally, document vs. URL engagement exhibits meaningful differences. Platform-hosted documents (PDFs, slide decks) usually benefit from richer, more reliable logging granularity (context, component, event name), whereas external URL clicks may introduce measurement noise due to redirections or incomplete return signals from third-party sites. Consequently, document interactions often yield more stable features for supervised models, while URL events may require aggregation or permutation-based robustness checks to mitigate over-interpretation. Together, these patterns support a feature-engineering strategy that prioritises assessment-linked, time-localised resource signals and treats external-link activity with additional caution during model interpretation.**4.3 Explainability Results**

To move beyond global feature rankings and provide actionable insights at the individual level, LIME was applied to the Random Forest classifier's predictions. Table 4 presents the ranked list of features for LIME.

Table 4. Feature importance list of Random Forest model.

Rank	Features	Description / Context
1	Final Exam Duration	Total time spent on the final exam (minutes)
2	Week 11 Attendance	Weekly attendance count during Week 11
3	**Week 6 Attendance**	**Weekly attendance count during Week 6**
4	Week 12 Attendance	Weekly attendance count during Week 12
5	Resource #11 "Functions" Viewed	Course module view log for Functions resource
6	Week 14 Attendance	Weekly attendance count during Week 14
7	Week 9 Attendance	Weekly attendance count during Week 9
8	Week 13 Attendance	Weekly attendance count during Week 13

continued on following page

Table 4. Continued

Rank	Features	Description / Context
9	Lecture Slides #1_1 “Basic Concepts” Viewed	Course module view log for introductory lecture slides
10	Week 10 Attendance	Weekly attendance count during Week 10
11	Lecture Notes #2 “Operating Systems and Computer Usage” Viewed	Course module view log for operating systems lecture notes
12	Resource #13 “Charts” Viewed	Course module view log for Charts resource
13	Resource #10.1 “Formulas” Viewed	Course module view log for Formulas resource
14	**URL: Course Syllabus Viewed**	**Accessed the course syllabus through an external URL**
15	Lecture Slides #8 Viewed	Course module view log for lecture slides covering Week 8 topics

Figure 3 illustrates representative features of local explanations for classified students.

Figure 3. LIME feature list

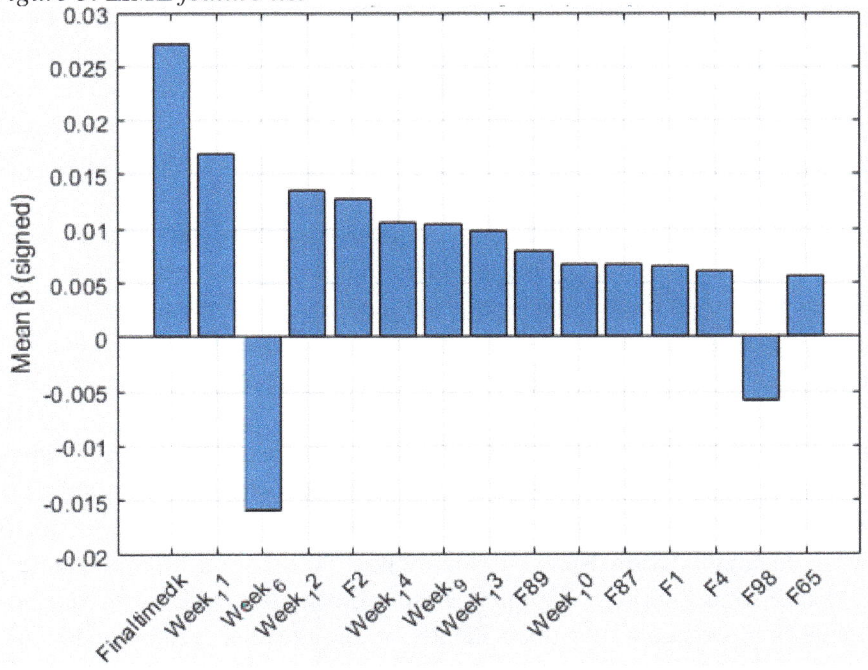

For students correctly classified as successful, positive contributions were dominated by primarily final exam duration and late-semester engagement features particularly high activity counts in Weeks 9–14. These variables collectively pushed the prediction toward the success class. In contrast, students predicted as at risk exhibited strong negative contributions from 6th week and corresponding course syllabus URL which can be seen from Table 4 and Figure 3. These negative features indicate the need for further investigation of the content for this specific week to alter the outcome for students' performance based on the Random Forest model. The ranked list illustrates how final exam duration and late-semester activity consistently shape individual predictions, supporting the model's internal consistency.

Importantly, LIME explanations proved useful even for misclassified cases. For example, a student who was actually successful but misclassified as unsuccessful displayed low early-week engagement but compensated later with high final exam duration. The local explanation highlighted the conflicting signals, suggesting that weighting late-semester behaviours more heavily could improve model calibration. These individual-level insights allow instructors to design interventions tailored to the specific deficits revealed by the model. The visual distribution of positive and negative contributions clarifies why specific students were classified as at risk or successful, helping instructors interpret individual cases.

To assess the reliability and trustworthiness of the model, global feature importance rankings were compared with aggregated local explanations. The top globally important variables final exam duration and activity in Weeks 9–14 consistently appeared among the highest-weighted features in local explanations for both success and failure cases. This alignment supports the internal consistency of the model and suggests that predictions are driven by stable, meaningful signals rather than spurious correlations.

Global–local consistency also served as a validation mechanism: when local explanations diverged significantly from global rankings, these instances were flagged for further inspection. In most cases, such divergences corresponded to edge cases with atypical participation patterns (e.g., students with very low engagement but perfect assessment performance), providing valuable feedback for iterative model refinement.

Overall, the combination of global importance analysis and LIME-based local explanations enhances the model's transparency and trustworthiness, fulfilling a key requirement for responsible AI deployment in education. By confirming that both population-level and individual-level reasoning point to the same critical features, the study demonstrates not only high predictive accuracy but also interpretive coherence, enabling educators to act confidently on the model's recommendations. These findings provide the empirical foundation for interpreting how engagement patterns and assessment behaviors relate to performance, which is discussed in the following section.

5. DISCUSSION AND CONCLUSION

Building upon these empirical results, the discussion interprets how these patterns can inform pedagogical and managerial strategies in distance learning environments. The results of this study highlight three key findings that contribute to both the methodological and practical understanding of student success prediction in online learning environments. First, Random Forest achieved superior predictive performance, reaching 81.67% accuracy and the highest macro AUC (0.86644) among all tested models. Its ensemble nature allowed for effective handling of nonlinear feature interactions and robust generalisation, confirming its suitability for heterogeneous LMS-derived datasets.

Second, the analysis revealed that late-semester attendance and final exam duration were critical predictors of course success. These variables consistently ranked at the top of the global feature importance list, underscoring the significance of sustained engagement through the final weeks of the course and adequate time investment in the culminating assessment. The identification of these temporal hotspots offers clear guidance for targeted interventions, suggesting that instructors may prioritise monitoring and support efforts during Weeks 9–14 to maximise student retention and achievement. The prominence of late-semester engagement aligns with research on desirable difficulties (Bjork, 1994) and suggests that students who persist through increasingly challenging material demonstrate deeper learning. Instructionally, this points to the need for enhanced scaffolding during Weeks 9-14.

Finally, LIME-based local explanations demonstrated strong alignment with global feature importance rankings, validating the reliability of the model's decision-making process. This consistency enhances the transparency of the predictive framework and provides educators with interpretable, actionable insights at both the cohort and individual student levels. By combining predictive performance with explainability, the study bridges the gap between algorithmic modelling and practical application, paving the way for trustworthy, data-driven interventions in online education.

The temporal analysis indicates that support efforts should be concentrated in Weeks 9–14, where engagement signals most strongly differentiate successful from unsuccessful trajectories. Targeted nudges, scaffolded practice, and deadline-aligned checkpoints in these windows can raise recall of at-risk students without inflating false alarms, as late-semester activity has repeatedly been shown to carry high predictive value in online courses.

Building on these findings, instructors and administrators can translate these signals into concrete pedagogical actions. For instance, reminder messages or motivational prompts during Weeks 9–14 may help sustain engagement when dropout risk typically increases. Short scaffolded review activities or formative quizzes can also be introduced during these weeks to maintain continuity and reinforce learning. Additionally, adaptive dashboards could alert teaching staff when a student's attendance or interaction drops below threshold levels, enabling timely support and personalised follow-up. Embedding such data-driven interventions into the regular instructional workflow would operationalize the predictive insights and turn analytics into meaningful educational practice (Gašević et al., 2016).

Engagement with assessment-proximal materials practice quizzes, worked examples, submission portals yields the most actionable signals for prediction and intervention; prioritising the curation and visibility of these resources is likely to improve outcomes. Platform-hosted documents (PDFs, slide decks) typically generate more reliable telemetry than external URLs, enabling stable features and clearer instructional decisions; instructors can therefore emphasise high-signal resources during critical weeks and streamline or aggregate low-signal link activity.

Embedding LIME at the point of use enables advisors and instructors to see *why* a student is flagged (e.g., low Week-11–14 activity, short final-exam duration) and to map each risk driver to a concrete action (reminders, review sessions, pacing support). Consistency between LIME's local attributions and global importance rankings strengthens trustworthiness and supports responsible adoption of predictive systems in educational settings.

Beyond predictive accuracy and interpretability, responsible use of educational data also demands attention to fairness and equity. Predictive models, even when explainable, may inadvertently reflect or amplify existing biases in participation, access, or prior achievement. Integrating fairness-aware evaluation and transparent reporting practices is therefore critical to ensure that interventions do not disadvantage underrepresented groups. Explainable AI methods such as LIME and SHAP further support ethical implementation by revealing how and why decisions are made, enabling educators to identify potential bias in feature attributions. This ethical lens aligns the technical framework with principles of responsible and equitable AI in education.

While the findings of this research provide valuable insights into student success prediction, several limitations must be acknowledged. First, the dataset was drawn from a single institution and a single course (Introductory Information Technologies), which may limit the generalisability of results to other institutional contexts, disciplines, or student populations. Second, the analysis focused on one academic term, meaning that temporal variability across multiple cohorts was not captured. Third, while the study engineered a rich set of features from LMS logs, it did not incorporate external factors such as demographic information, prior GPA, or psychosocial measures that could further improve prediction models (Papamitsiou & Economides, 2014). These constraints suggest that findings should be interpreted as course-specific evidence rather than universally applicable benchmarks.

Despite these limitations, the analytical framework proposed in this study has the potential to be adapted across different institutional and disciplinary contexts. The feature-engineering principles and interpretability design can be applied to a variety of LMS environments beyond Moodle with minor adjustments to event taxonomies and log structures. Moreover, disciplines with distinct engagement dynamics such as project-based STEM courses or discussion-heavy humanities courses can integrate the same approach by customizing feature definitions to reflect their pedagogical patterns. This adaptability underscores the generalizability of the framework and its potential to inform predictive analytics and intervention strategies across diverse educational ecosystems.

Several avenues exist for extending this work. First, automation of LMS data extraction and feature generation could streamline the pipeline, reducing manual overhead and allowing real-time or near real-time risk detection. Second, future research could explore dynamic feedback systems that provide weekly personalised recommendations to students based on predicted risk, integrating behavioural nudges or adaptive learning pathways. Third, the use of Deep Learning Architectures, may allow richer modelling of temporal dependencies in engagement data, provided that explainability layers (e.g., SHAP, attention visualisation) are incorporated to preserve interpretability (Rodríguez-Ortiz et al., 2025). Finally, cross-institutional validation studies are needed to assess the portability of both features and predictive models across different LMS platforms and academic disciplines, addressing concerns about generalisability and fairness.

Overall, these findings highlight that predictive accuracy must always be interpreted through the lens of educational meaning and institutional responsibility. The integration of explainable AI with pedagogical and managerial action thus represents not only a technical advance but also a step toward more inclusive, transparent, and data-informed education. Ultimately, this study demonstrates how explainable AI can transform distance learning analytics from retrospective evaluation into proactive educational innovation.

REFERENCES

Ahmed, E. (2024). Student performance prediction using machine learning algorithms. *Applied Computational Intelligence and Soft Computing*, *2024*(1), 4067721.

Al-Zawqari, A., Peumans, D., & Vandersteen, G. (2022). A flexible feature selection approach for predicting students' academic performance in online courses. *Computers and Education: Artificial Intelligence*, *3*, 100103.

Arévalo-Cordovilla, F. E., & Peña, M. (2024). Comparative analysis of machine learning models for predicting student success in online programming courses: A study based on LMS data and external factors. *Mathematics*, *12*(20), 3272.

Arizmendi, C. J., Bernacki, M. L., Raković, M., Plumley, R. D., Urban, C. J., Panter, A. T., & Gates, K. M. (2023). Predicting student outcomes using digital logs of learning behaviors: Review, current standards, and suggestions for future work. *Behavior Research Methods*, *55*(6), 3026–3054. PMID: 36018483

Bengio, Y. (2012). Practical recommendations for gradient-based training of deep architectures. In G. Montavon, G. B. Orr, & K.-R. Müller (Eds.), *Neural networks: Tricks of the trade: Second edition* (pp. 437–478). Springer.

Bjork, R. A. (1994). Memory and metamemory considerations in the training of human beings. In Metcalfe, J., & Shimamura, A. (Eds.), *Metacognition: Knowing about knowing* (pp. 185–205). MIT Press.

Breiman, L. (2001). Random forests. *Machine Learning*, *45*(1), 5–32.

Choi, W. C., Lam, C. T., Pang, P. C. I., & Mendes, A. J. (2025, June). A systematic literature review of explainable artificial intelligence (XAI) for interpreting student performance prediction in computer science and STEM education. In *Proceedings of the 30th ACM Conference on Innovation and Technology in Computer Science Education* V. 1 (pp. 221–227).

Gašević, D., Dawson, S., & Siemens, G. (2016). Let's not forget: Learning analytics are about learning. *TechTrends*, *59*(1), 64–71.

George, E. B., Senthilkumar, R., Al-junaibi, F., & Al-shuaibi, Z. (2025). Explainable AI methods for predicting student grades and improving academic success. *Journal of Information Systems Engineering & Management*, *10*(23s), 117–126.

Ghimire, S., Abdulla, S., Joseph, L. P., Prasad, S., Murphy, A., Devi, A., & Yaseen, Z. M. (2024). Explainable artificial intelligence–machine learning models to estimate overall scores in tertiary preparatory general science course. *Computers and Education: Artificial Intelligence*, *7*, 100331.

Goh, T. T. (2025). Learning management system log analytics: The role of persistence and consistency of engagement behaviour on academic success. *Journal of Computers in Education*, •••, 1–24.

Guo, Y., Gunay, C., Tangirala, S., Kerven, D., Jin, W., Savage, J. C., & Lee, S. (2022). Identifying critical LMS features for predicting at-risk students. *arXiv preprint arXiv:2204.13700.*

Han, J., Kamber, J., & Pei, J. (2022). *Data mining: Concepts and techniques* (4th ed.). Morgan Kaufmann.

Holstein, K., & Doroudi, S. (2021). Equity and artificial intelligence in education: Will "AIED" amplify or alleviate inequities in education? *arXiv preprint arXiv:2104.12920.*

Kauffman, H. (2015). A review of predictive factors of student success in and satisfaction with online learning. *Research in Learning Technology*, •••, 23.

Keskin, S., & Yurdugül, H. (2022). E-learning experience: Modeling students' e-learning interactions using log data. *Journal of Educational Technology and Online Learning*, *5*(1), 1–13.

Levin, N. A. (2021). Process mining combined with expert feature engineering to predict efficient use of time on high-stakes assessments. *Journal of Educational Data Mining*, *13*(2), 1–15.

Lundberg, S. M., & Lee, S. I. (2017). A unified approach to interpreting model predictions. *Advances in Neural Information Processing Systems*, •••, 30.

Lykourentzou, I., Giannoukos, I., Mpardis, G., Nikolopoulos, V., & Loumos, V. (2009). Early and dynamic student achievement prediction in e-learning courses using neural networks. *Journal of the American Society for Information Science and Technology*, *60*(2), 372–380.

Macfadyen, L. P., & Dawson, S. (2010). Mining LMS data to develop an "early warning system" for educators: A proof of concept. *Computers & Education*, *54*(2), 588–599.

Maron, M. E. (1961). Automatic indexing: An experimental inquiry. *Journal of the Association for Computing Machinery*, *8*(3), 404–417.

Nnadi, L. C., Watanobe, Y., Rahman, M. M., & John-Otumu, A. M. (2024). Prediction of students' adaptability using explainable AI in educational machine learning models. *Applied Sciences (Basel, Switzerland), 14*(12), 5141.

Pan, Z., Biegley, L., Taylor, A., & Zheng, H. (2024). A systematic review of learning analytics: Incorporated instructional interventions on learning management systems. *Journal of Learning Analytics, 11*(2), 52–72.

Papamitsiou, Z., & Economides, A. A. (2014). Learning analytics and educational data mining in practice: A systematic literature review of empirical evidence. *Journal of Educational Technology & Society, 17*(4), 49–64.

Quansah, R., & Essıam, C. (2021). The use of learning management system (LMS) moodle in the midst of covid-19 pandemic: Students' perspective. *Journal of Educational Technology and Online Learning, 4*(3), 418–431.

Quinlan, J. R. (1993). *C4.5: Programs for machine learning*. Morgan Kaufmann.

Ribeiro, M. T., Singh, S., & Guestrin, C. (2016, August). "Why should I trust you?" Explaining the predictions of any classifier. In *Proceedings of the 22nd ACM SIGKDD International Conference on Knowledge Discovery and Data Mining* (pp. 1135–1144).

Riestra-González, M., del Puerto Paule-Ruíz, M., & Ortin, F. (2021). Massive LMS log data analysis for the early prediction of course-agnostic student performance. *Computers & Education, 163*, 104108.

Rodríguez-Ortiz, M. Á., Santana-Mancilla, P. C., & Anido-Rifón, L. E. (2025). Machine learning and generative AI in learning analytics for higher education: A systematic review of models, trends, and challenges. *Applied Sciences (Basel, Switzerland), 15*(15), 8679.

Romero, C., & Ventura, S. (2020). Educational data mining and learning analytics: An updated survey. *Wiley Interdisciplinary Reviews. Data Mining and Knowledge Discovery, 10*(3), e1355.

Sevim, N., Erol, O., & Başer Gülsoy, V. G. (2023). Examination of the correlation between e-learning readiness and achievement goal orientation of college students. *Journal of Educational Technology and Online Learning, 6*(1), 184–201.

Shelton, B. E., Hung, J. L., & Lowenthal, P. R. (2017). Predicting student success by modeling student interaction in asynchronous online courses. *Distance Education, 38*(1), 59–69.

Strobl, C., Boulesteix, A. L., Zeileis, A., & Hothorn, T. (2007). Bias in random forest variable importance measures: Illustrations, sources and a solution. *BMC Bioinformatics*, *8*(1), 25. PMID: 17254353

Swamy, V., Radmehr, B., Krco, N., Marras, M., & Käser, T. (2022). Evaluating the explainers: Black-box explainable machine learning for student success prediction in MOOCs. *arXiv preprint arXiv:2207.00551.*

Winne, P. H., & Hadwin, A. F. (2008). The weave of motivation and self-regulated learning. In Schunk, D. H., & Zimmerman, B. (Eds.), *Motivation and self-regulated learning: Theory, research, and applications* (pp. 297–314).

Yuan, J., Qiu, X., Wu, J., Guo, J., Li, W., & Wang, Y. G. (2024). Integrating behavior analysis with machine learning to predict online learning performance: A scientometric review and empirical study. *arXiv preprint arXiv:2406.11847.*

Yukselturk, E., & Bulut, S. (2007). Predictors for student success in an online course. *Journal of Educational Technology & Society*, *10*(2), 71–83.

Zimmerman, B. J. (2013). From cognitive modeling to self-regulation: A social cognitive career path. *Educational Psychologist*, *48*(3), 135–147.

Chapter 9
An Analysis of AI Trends in Instructional Technology From a Bibliometric Perspective

Hamid Derviş
https://orcid.org/0000-0002-9069-571X
Kastamonu University, Turkey

ABSTRACT

Artificial intelligence (AI) has significantly impacted both conventional and online education, particularly the latter. Digital learning ecosystems now encompass a broad spectrum, from intelligent tutoring systems such as Cognitive Tutor developed at Carnegie Mellon University and AutoTutor at the University of Memphis, to contemporary AI-based tools like chatbots and adaptive learning platforms. On the other hand, bibliometric analysis offers a systematic and transparent approach to reviewing scholarly communication, identifying thematic clusters, and tracing the evolution of AI applications within instructional technology. This chapter analyzes AI and instructional technology trends using bibliometric methods, focusing on publication patterns, research hotspots, collaboration networks, and evolving methodologies. Beyond mapping scientific trends, the study also highlights the ethical implications of AI integration in education, emphasizing fairness, transparency, inclusivity, and accountability.

DOI: 10.4018/979-8-3373-8805-2.ch009

INTRODUCTION

Artificial intelligence (AI) has caused a drastic influence in instructional technology, reshaping how knowledge is delivered, assessed, and personalized. AI can be traced from early systems such as computer-assisted instruction: PLATO, and to more contemporary adaptive platforms like Khan Academy and generative systems like ChatGPT. AI's evolution in education reflects technological innovation and the development of pedagogical paradigms. As the field matures, researchers and practitioners increasingly need systematic approaches to assess how scholarship has developed, which topics dominate, and where opportunities for further exploration remain.

Moreover, bibliometrics is a systematic and objective process to analyse large scholarlycorpora, offering insights into publication trends, influential authors, and thematic developments in any period. Bibliometric analysis enables researchers to delve into documents or selective reviews quantitatively mapping how the field has evolved, whereby scholarly influence is concentrated, and what emerging patterns shape future directions, in the context of instructional technology and artificial intelligence. Bibliometric analysis tracks transparency, reproducibility, and scalability in the evaluation research realm, making it particularly valuable in rapidly expanding domains like AI in education (Donthu et al., 2021).

Applying bibliometric analysis to AI in instructional technology is particularly relevant because the field is characterized by rapid growth, rich interdisciplinary collaboration, and shifting research priorities. Conventional narrative reviews often struggle to capture this dynamism. Conversely, bibliometrics identifies the dominant research themes, evolving methodologies, and the complex cross-disciplinary linkages between education, computer science, and cognitive psychology. By systematically mapping the literature, bibliometric methods reveal the intellectual structure of the field and highlight research gaps and underexplored areas that can inform future innovation in AI-driven learning environments (Zupic & Čater, 2015).

Formed into three folds, the study (I) describes the historical and conceptual development in bibliometric analysis and AI landscape literature based on extracted data from Web of Science (WoS) in instructional technology, (II)uncovers the structural relationships—co-authorship, co-citation, and journal clusters exciting directions for future research, and (III) offers critical reflections on pedagogical implications, ethical challenges, and directions for future research. These sections provide a comprehensive account of how bibliometric methods can illuminate AI's past, present, and potential futures in instructional technology.

This chapter proceeds through a structured sequence of sections that together offer a comprehensive understanding of artificial intelligence within instructional technology from a bibliometric perspective. It begins by outlining the historical and conceptual background of bibliometrics, describing how the field emerged from early scientometric traditions and evolved with advances in digital databases and visualization tools. This provides the theoretical foundation for the subsequent bibliometric analysis. The next section examines global publication trends, authorship patterns, and thematic developments, identifying how AI research in instructional technology has expanded and diversified across disciplines. The methodological section follows, explaining the data retrieval process from the Web of Science, the inclusion criteria, and the analytical techniques employed to generate citation, co-authorship, and keyword networks. The results are then presented through a series of network and conceptual structure analyses, revealing patterns of collaboration, thematic evolution, and intellectual influence. The later sections move from empirical findings to critical reflection, discussing pedagogical, ethical, and practical implications of AI in education—particularly issues of equity, access, and AI literacy. The chapter also explores how AI has contributed to more inclusive and adaptive learning environments, including support for students with disabilities and equitable learning opportunities in pandemic and post-pandemic contexts. Finally, the discussion and conclusion synthesize the findings, highlight limitations, and propose directions for future research, emphasizing the need for responsible, sustainable, and human-centered integration of AI into instructional technology.

HISTORICAL DEVELOPMENT OF BIBLIOMETRICS

Bibliometrics can be traced to early studies by scientists to quantify scientific communication. For example, Alfred J. Lotka (1926) introduced Lotka's law, describing the frequency distribution of scientific productivity. Samuel C. Bradford (1934) formulated Bradford's law of scattering, which demonstrated how articles on a subject are dispersed across journals. George Kingsley Zipf (1949) contributed Zipf's law, describing word frequency distributions, which later influenced scientometric text analysis.Although previously mentioned, the scientist who laid the foundation for studying the scientific community, it was not until Alan Pritchard (1969) coined the term bibliometrics as "the application of mathematical and statistical methods to books and other media of communication." His contribution was pivotal in a unifying label that helped consolidate new quantitative approaches into a recognized scholarly domain.

Eugene Garfield (1955) pioneered the idea of citation indexing, which led to the creation of the *Science Citation Index* in the 1960s and subsequently the Web of Science database (now owned by Clarivate Analytics). The Web of Science enabled systematic citation tracking, which became the backbone of bibliometric studies. Price (1963) further articulated the exponential growth of science and highlighted cumulative advantage mechanisms in his seminal work *Little Science, Big Science*, and was instrumental in citation network analysis. Small (1973) introduced co-citation analysis, which became a fundamental method for mapping intellectual structures of science in the 1970s. This period also saw the development of co-word analysis and other content-based approaches to complement citation studies. During the 1980s and 1990s, bibliometric analysis expanded alongside the rise of digital databases and computational advances, supported by the growth of software applications allowing large-scale analyses of scholarly communication networks. With the advent of software environments such as Java and RStudio in the 2000s, bibliometrics became increasingly accessible. Packages like Bibliometrix in R (Aria & Cuccurullo, 2017) and visualization software such as VOSviewer (van Eck & Waltman, 2010) and CiteSpace (Chen, 2004, 2006) have empowered researchers to conduct sophisticated analyses with reproducible workflows. Today, bibliometrics is considered a central approach in scientometrics and research evaluation, widely applied in mapping scientific fields, evaluating research impact, university ranking, and identifying emerging scientific trends.

Table 1. Scientists Who Contributed to Bibliometrics as a Scientific Field

Year	Scholar(s)	Contribution
1926	Alfred J. Lotka	*Lotka's Law* of scientific productivity (distribution of authors' output).
1934	Samuel C. Bradford	*Bradford's Law of Scattering* (dispersion of articles across journals).
1949	George Kingsley Zipf	*Zipf's Law* on word frequency distributions, later applied in bibliometrics and text analysis.
1955	Eugene Garfield	*citation indexing* and later the *Science Citation Index*, foundational for citation-based studies.
1963	Derek J. de Solla Price	*Little Science, Big Science*, describing exponential growth of science and cumulative advantage.
1969	Alan Pritchard	the term *bibliometrics* and defined it as applying statistical/mathematical methods to scholarly communication.
1973	Henry Small	*co-citation analysis*, enabling mapping of scientific knowledge structures.
1980s–1990s	Diverse	Growth of computational power and digital databases expanded large-scale bibliometric analyses.
2000s–present	Aria & Cuccurullo (2017) van Eck, N. J., & Waltman, L. (2010); Chen, C. (2004)	Open-source tools like *Bibliometrix (R)*, VOSviewer, and CiteSpace made bibliometrics widely accessible and reproducible.

To sum up, bibliometrics introduces new search strategies. It connects quantitative and contextual understanding because it is reproducible and uses standardized databases, explicit search strings, and transparent criteria, unlike narrative reviews that depend on subjective selection. According to Donthu et al. (2021) and Aria & Cuccurullo (2017), bibliometrics makes the results replicable across researchers. Bibliometrics analysis quantifies and maps intellectual connections (co-citation, bibliographic coupling) and depicts thematic structures through co-word and topic modeling approaches. Opposite of narrative reviews, bibliometrics scales to thousands of records and reduces selection bias.

RECENT BIBLIOMETRIC WORKS ON AI IN INSTRUCTIONAL TECHNOLOGY

Bibliometric investigation of AI across different scientific domains enables practitioners to understand how artificial intelligence (AI) has developed and diversified within instructional technology. For instance, Keser et al.,(2025), in their investigation of 5,000 bibliographic data from WoS published between 1981 and 2024, revealed that 2023 was the highest number for scholarly communications; their findings showed that most publications were written in the English language. They found out that the most influential scholars are Hwang, Bond, and Zawacki-Richter, underscoring the intellectual anchors of the field. Their findings have indicated that publication volume and authorship trends indicate the consolidation of AI in education as a distinct research domain.

Similarly, Genç and Kocak (2024) extracted 869 papers in the context of science education using a compound query from 2019 to 2023, also from WoS. Their results indicated that the United States, China, and Australia are research leaders, with *Computers & Education* emerging as the most frequently cited journal. The salient keywords were "machine learning", "learning analytics", and "data science" in articles.

The thematic emphasis reverberates with the global perspectives and evolving research priorities highlighted in the bibliometric study approach, while also demonstrating the importance of domain-specific analyses for uncovering emerging disciplinary trends.Recently, AI has enriched many broad scientific spectra. Education studies are no exception. A study by Derinalp (2024) mapped the intellectual process of AI in education by tracing its roots and documenting its thematic evolution over time.

Other bibliometric research has foregrounded pedagogical and contextual concerns. Durak, Çankaya, Özdemir, and Can (2024) assessed AI's role in transforming teaching and learning, focusing on open and distributed education. Their findings provide that bibliometric evidence can illuminate the growth rate and pedagogical directions. Integrating AI into higher education is a challenging task. Ren and Wu (2025) examined the difficulties and challenges of integrating AI into higher education using a TPACK (Technological Pedagogical Content Knowledge) lens. This qualitative approach combines bibliometric evidence by highlighting teacher perspectives, identifying barriers to adoption, and the emerging professional role.

Teacher AI literacy is an issue raised by emerging research results. Emphasizing teacher preparation for AI literacy is prevalent. Kelley and Wenzel (2025) reported on professional partnerships in teacher education programs, indicating how collaborative investigation can build AI literacy among teacher candidates. It speaks directly with emphasis on future directions, particularly the need to prepare educators for a landscape in which AI literacy is essential.

In a recent technical study aimed at enhancing bibliometric analysis, Xu, Li, Tupayachi, Lian, and Omitaomu (2024) conducted a technical study to improve bibliometric analysis. They developed an AI system using transformers and vector databases to enhance research analysis in urban science and support better classification and understanding. In another study, Leibel and Bornmann (2024) demonstrated that bibliometric results can vary depending on the analysis method used, making it essential to test their reliability. They used multiverse analysis to see if small research teams produce more innovative work.

Table 2. Some Recent Studies Using Bibliometric Methods on AI and Education

# of the Articles	Method / Focus	Key Findings	Relevance to Folds
Keser Ateş, S., Kaleci, F., & Erdoğan, A. (2025). Artificial intelligence in education: A bibliometric analysis. *Ankara University Journal of Faculty of Educational Sciences, 58*(1), 95–132.	Bibliometric analysis of 4,935 studies (1981–2024) in WoS	2023 peak year, English dominant, most cited authors include Hwang, Bond, Zawacki-Richter	(Growth patterns, authorship trends, influential scholars)
Genç, H. N., & Kocak, N. (2024). Bibliometric analysis of studies on the artificial intelligence in science education. *Journal of Education in Science, Environment and Health, 10*(2), 132–152.	Analyzed 867 papers (2019–2023)	USA, China, Australia lead; Computers & Education top journal; keywords: "Machine Learning," "Learning Analytics," "Data Science"	Global perspectives, core journals, thematic evolution)
Derinalp, P. (2024). Past, present, and future of artificial intelligence in education: A bibliometric study. *Selçuk University Journal of Education Faculty, 48*(1), 35–58.	Longitudinal bibliometric mapping	Identifies intellectual roots and shifting themes; highlights transition to generative AI	(Historical foundations + thematic shifts)
Durak, G., Çankaya, S., Özdemir, D., & Can, S. (2024). Artificial intelligence in education: A bibliometric study on its role in transforming teaching and learning. *International Review of Research in Open and Distributed Learning, 25*(2), 120–139.	Bibliometric + thematic focus on open/distance learning	Highlights AI's transformative role in teaching/learning in distributed contexts	(Bibliometric insights + Pedagogical reflections)

continued on following page

Table 2. Continued

# of the Articles	Method / Focus	Key Findings	Relevance to Folds
TechTrends (2025). Examining teaching competencies and challenges while integrating AI in higher education. *TechTrends, 69*(1), 55–67.	Qualitative/TPACK framework	Identifies competencies needed, barriers to adoption in higher ed	(Pedagogical implications, teacher roles)
Kelley, J., & Wenzel, A. (2025). Advancing artificial intelligence literacy in teacher education through professional partnership inquiry. *Education Sciences, 15*(6), 659.	Case study of AI literacy in teacher education	Shows role of partnerships in developing AI competencies in teacher candidates	(Future directions: teacher prep, AI literacy)

HISTORICAL DEVELOPMENT OF AI

According to literature, the roots of AI in instructional technology extend back to the 1950s and 1960s, when at Dartmouth, the Dartmouth College Conference laid the foundation for AI. Ely(1999), although with his original paper published in BJET (British Journal of Educational Technology,1970), which discussed the early philosophical underpinnings of instructional technology, stated that the philosophy of instructional technology has long been viewed as an evolving, personal framework, shaped by beliefs, concepts, and attitudes. Instructional Technology was not established formally, with behavioral science providing the strongest theoretical foundation and technology as the primary organizing concept. These philosophical statements were always tentative, reflecting the field's ongoing development and the continuous refinement of its principles as scholars and practitioners gain experience and insight. In the early days, when hardware and software constraints and strict programming systems existed, they enabled the foundation for AI-supported learning environments by demonstrating that technology could deliver instruction at scale and adapt content presentation to some extent. Developing CAI (Computer-Assisted Instruction) into more advanced intelligent tutoring systems (ITS) signified a conceptual jump. Unlike CAI, which primarily delivered pre-programmed instruction, ITS incorporated elements of AI to model learners' knowledge, track their progress, and dynamically adjust instruction.

Carbonell's (1970) seminal work on "AI in CAI" integrated machine learning principles into tutoring systems as a new paradigm, setting a new paradigm in AI in the education environment. Asignificant shift occurred with Carbonell's (1970) work, which proposed that computers could function as adaptive "teachers," capable of assessing student understanding and adjusting instruction accordingly. This idea directly influenced the intelligent tutoring systems (ITS) movement of the late 1970s and early 1980s. Subsequent ITS, such as the SCHOLAR system, leveraged semantic networks and knowledge representations to provide adaptive, dialogue-based interactions with learners (Carbonell, 1970). This shift represented a move toward more personalized and context-sensitive instruction, laying the groundwork for contemporary adaptive learning platforms.

The development of AI in instructional technology has unfolded over several decades and has been shaped by both technological advances and evolving educational theories. In the 1950s and 1960s, early teaching machines and computer-assisted instruction (CAI) systems, including PLATO, focused mainly on delivering pre-programmed lessons with limited adaptability. According to the literature, PLATO (Programmed Logic for Automated Teaching Operations) was the first example of using computers for drill-and-practice exercises, tutorials, and basic simulations to support student learning (Suppes & Morningstar, 1969).

For instance, Sleeman and Brown (1982) set a framework that integrates student models, domain knowledge, and pedagogical strategies to provide individualized instruction for ITS design. AI gained momentum during the 1990s and significantly in the 2010s. AI and cognitive modeling improvements enabled more advanced adaptive learning environments, expanding ITS applications into higher education and professional training (Zawacki-Richter, Marín, Bond, & Gouverneur, 2019). By the 2010s, platforms such as MOOCs and adaptive systems like Knewton (Chen, Chen, & Lin, 2020) and Duolingo (Duolingo, n.d.) operationalized these ideas on a larger scale, making personalized learning more widely accessible (Chen, Chen, & Lin, 2020). From 2020, AI has introduced new functionality for dynamic content creation, such as images, sounds, and interactive learning experiences, relying on the foundational concepts introduced by Carbonell and subsequent researchers (Doroudi, 2023).

From the 1980s, ITS research had gained significant attention, whereby researchers were producing systems capable of diagnosing student misunderstandings, offering tailored feedback, and guiding learners through problem-solving processes (Anderson, Boyle, Corbett, & Lewis, 1990). These developments pushed the boundaries of AI applications in education and catalyzed an enduring research trajectory that continues to inform current advances in adaptive and generative AI. The heritage of CAI and ITS underscores the long-standing vision of leveraging intelligent systems to support human learning. This ambition remains pivotal to the present-day discourse on AI in instructional technology.

RESEARCH QUESTIONS AND OBJECTIVES

This study aims to provide a comprehensive yet summarized overview of the role of AI in education and the use of bibliometrics as a scientific method. The author strives to answer the following preliminary

1. How has the research volume on AI in instructional technology evolved?
2. Which authors and countries are the most productive in this field?
3. Which publications are the most cited and, therefore, the most influential?

DATA AND METHODS

Artificial intelligence, a groundbreaking technology that emulates the functions of the human brain, holds immense potential for the future. Bibliometrix, a user-friendly library package, seamlessly integrates with the RStudio software, making bibliometric analysis more accessible and efficient. The Web of Science core collections were selected for data sources because WoS is the most reliable reference database, with high ethics and standards. The terms used in the query were "artificial intelligence" and "educational technology" as topics in the Web of Science. Six hundred twenty articles, including their bibliographic data, were retrieved with no time restrictions, ensuring the study's inclusivity. A comprehensive analysis was conducted, with six hundred twenty records extracted using Bibliometrix, a powerful tool for bibliometric analysis, within RStudio version 2025.05.0. The bibliometrics analysis was created and mapped at the command line using the reference manual available at this address (www.bibliometrix.com).

BIBLIOMETRIC METHODS: CITATION ANALYSIS

Co-authorship networks, a type of social network where nodes represent authors and edges represent their relationships, have immense potential to understand the structure and evolution of scientific collaboration. To analyse social networks, researchers can identify collaboration patterns that are instrumental in disseminating knowledge among the scientific community and eventually shed light on the complex dynamics of scientific research(Bordons et al., 2015). As early as 1970s co-citation analysis plays a pivotal tool in evaluating research quality and credibility, maps the intellectual structure of scientific disciplines (Sullivan et al., 1977). This method identifies clusters of frequently cited papers, reflecting the cognitive frameworks within research specialties. By analyzing these clusters, researchers can gauge the development and coherence of scientific topics. More importantly, it provides profound insights into the current state of research and its evolution over time, sparking intrigue about its potential.

As early as the 1970s, co-citation analysis was a pivotal tool in evaluating research quality and credibility, and it maps the intellectual structure of scientific disciplines (Aksnes et al., 2019). Co-citation analysis determines clusters of frequently cited papers, which reflect the cognitive frameworks within research specialties. Researchers can track the development and themes of scientific topics by investigating clusters and the citation frequency among clusters. It leads to important and profound insights into the current state of research and its evolution over time, sparking intrigue about its potential. Tracks the most cited paired papers, which indicates the cognitive structure of the scientific field.

MAIN INFORMATION ABOUT DATA

A description of the data from 1987 to 2025 indicates a slow growth of publications; however, in 2017, it suddenly took a sharp turn, steadily rising to 260 by 2025. International collaborations account for about 23% of publications, indicating that collaborations are one factor in increasing publications (see Table. 3 and Figure 1).

Table 3. Descriptive data of bibliographic data from WoS on AI and Education

Period	1987-2025
Documents	12.21
Average citation per Docs	2023
Authors	109
Authors of single-authored docs	115
Single-authored docs	0.306
Doc per Author	3.66
Co-Authors per Docs	3.66
International co-authorships	22.74
Annual percentage growth rate	15.71

Table 3 summarizes the bibliometric attributes of 620 documents published from 1987 to 2025. The analysis reveals that the field has grown substantially, with an annual percentage growth rate of 15.71%, confirming the accelerating scholarly attention toward artificial intelligence in education. The average citation rate per document (12.21) shows a mild impact, comparable to similar bibliometric findings in educational technology research by Donthu et al. (2021). Authorship patterns highlight a strong culture of collaboration: 2,023 authors contributed to the dataset, averaging 3.66 co-authors per paper. However, individual contributions are increasingly rare since there is a relatively small share of single-authored documents (115 out of 620); this reflects the complexity and interdisciplinary of AI-related research. As a matter of fact, 22.74% of publications involve international collaboration, a figure slightly higher than the average in education research, where cross-border partnerships often range between 15–20% This demonstrates that AI in education is a local and global research priority, driven by transnational challenges and opportunities. Overall, the data show that a rapidly expanding, moderately cited, and highly collaborative research domain, echoing findings from similar bibliometric mappings of technology-enhanced learning and AI in education (Zawacki-Richter et al., 2019; Keser Ateş et al., 2025).

Figure 1. Annual Publications Based On "Artificial Intelligence" And "Educational Technology" Topic Keywords from 1987 to 2025 in Web of Science

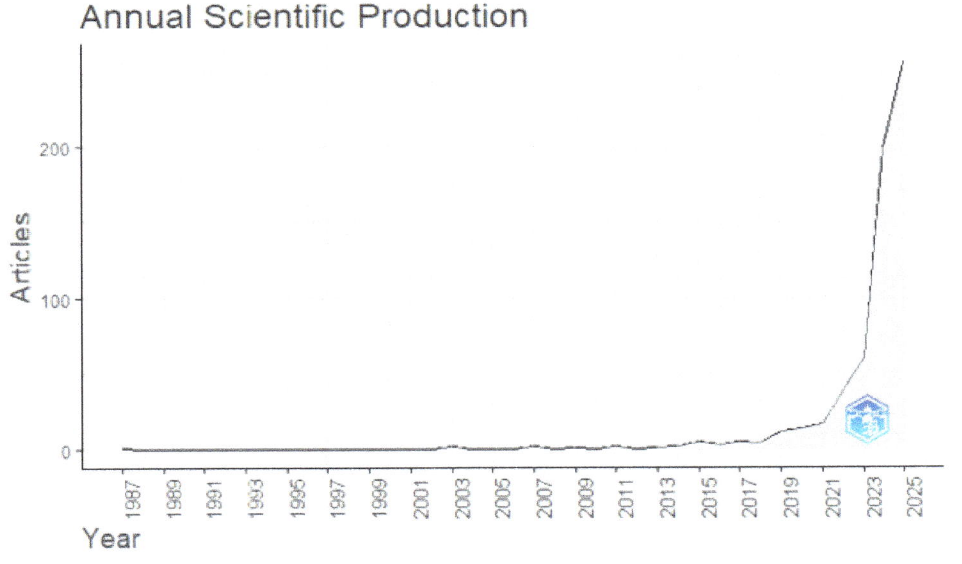

Table 1 and Figure 1 summarizes the bibliometric attributes of 620 documents published from 1987 to 2025. The analysis reveals that the field has grown substantially, with an annual percentage growth rate of 15.71%, confirming the accelerating scholarly attention toward artificial intelligence in education. The average citation rate per document (12.21) shows a mild impact, comparable to similar bibliometric findings in educational technology research by Donthu et al. (2021). Authorship patterns highlight a strong culture of collaboration: 2,023 authors contributed to the dataset, averaging 3.66 co-authors per paper. However, individual contributions are increasingly rare since there is a relatively small share of single-authored documents (115 out of 620); this reflects the complexity and interdisciplinary of AI-related research. As a matter of fact, 22.74% of publications involve international collaboration, a figure slightly higher than the average in education research, where cross-border partnerships often range between 15–20% This demonstrates that AI in education is a local and global research priority, driven by transnational challenges and opportunities.

Overall, the data show that a rapidly expanding, moderately cited, and highly collaborative research domain, echoing findings from similar bibliometric mappings of technology-enhanced learning and AI in education (Zawacki-Richter et al., 2019; Keser Ateş et al., 2025).

Figure 2. Co-Citation Network Structure of Co-Occurrence in AI and Instructional Technology (2010–2025)

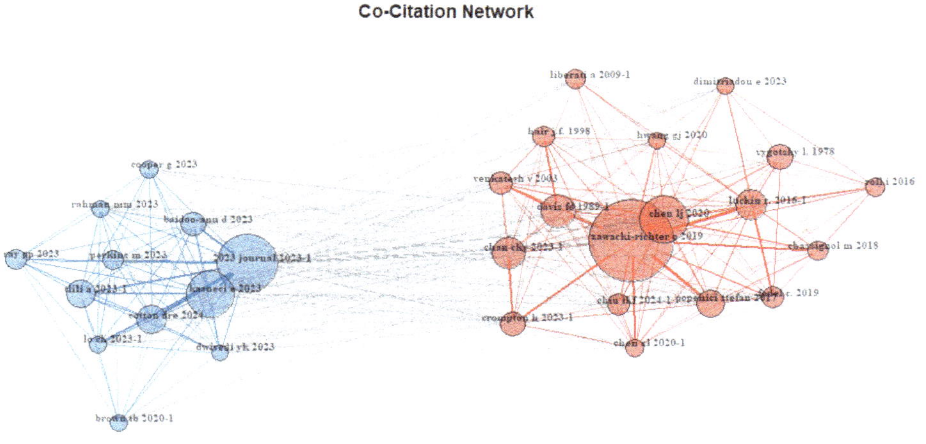

The map depicts of two main clusters: blue cluster (upper side) and red cluster (lower side), the blue cluster (upper side) contains foundation works, whereas the red cluster (lower side) encompasses the emerging works, for example, recent innovations like ChatGPT—the larger nodes located in the center of the cluster which are co-cited the most. The thicker the lines, the more they are cited together.

The blue cluster contains the classical studies on learning analytics, intelligent tutoring of AI in education, between the 1990s and the 2010s. Highly cited authors Zawacki-Richter et al, Siemens, and Koedinger, among others. The cluster illuminates pedagogical AI traditions such as ITS, LS/EDM, and NLP. Connections between clusters highlight how emerging studies build on established traditions while introducing new conceptual directions.

The graph depicts a dynamic of the field is not abandoning its conventional intellectual roots but adding new technological layers to pedagogical traditions. The result is a hybrid and evolving knowledge structure, whereby the past insights guide current debates, and emerging technologies reshape the future trajectory of AI in instructional technology.

Together, the blue and red clusters illustrate how the field of AI in instructional technology has developed along both continuity and transformation. Foundational contributions in the blue cluster — such as Koedinger et al.'s (1997) work on intelligent tutoring systems, Siemens and Baker's (2012) definition of learning analytics, and Zawacki-Richter et al.'s (2019) systematic review — established the methodological and pedagogical anchors of the field. These classical studies provided the theoretical and empirical frameworks that continue to inform current research practices. At the same time, the red cluster demonstrates how the rise of generative AI and ethical considerations has reframed these traditions. Studies such as Kasneci et al. (2023) and Rudolph et al. (2023) build on the foundations of pedelolgical data mining but to the extent that move toward the disruptive implications of large language models for assessment and instruction.

According to Reiser (2001), AI has evolved, starting with the visual aid and progressing to sophisticated intelligent tutoring systems. Instructional technology has consistently absorbed and adapted innovations that reshape how knowledge is accessed and transmitted (Reiser, 2001). AI represents the most transformative of these innovations, not merely as a tool but as a paradigm that redefines the interaction between learner, teacher, and content.

Mapping keyword clusters over time shows thematic shifts — e.g., from "expert systems" and "rule-based" in earlier decades to "machine learning", "deep learning", and "transformers" more recently. Tracking the emergence and decline of keywords gives a sense of topical life cycles and possible research saturation points. Clear thematic division between traditional education (red) and digital education (blue

CO-WORD AND KEYWORD NETWORK ANALYSIS

The network structure consists of two specific clusters of co-occurrence keywords. The network structure is categorized into educational research (red cluster) and digital technology (blue cluster) themes, with five bridge terms connecting both domains. Educational research (red cluster) and digital technology (blue cluster) themes are similar to the co-citation network, though the red cluster predominantly concentrates on research and academic themes. Conversely, the blue cluster primarily focuses on technology and digital education concepts. Co-word analysis (network of keywords or terms) helps chart latent topics and conceptual linkages. High-frequency keywords historically include "students" (central node), "education", "learning", "motivation", "feedback", "augmented reality", and partially visible/smaller nodes," classroom" "teaching", "technology"-bridge between clusters- "virtual", "research", "study", practice", an "learning" which appears multiple times (see Fig 3).

Figure 3. Keyword co-occurrence network in AI and instructional technology (2010–2025)

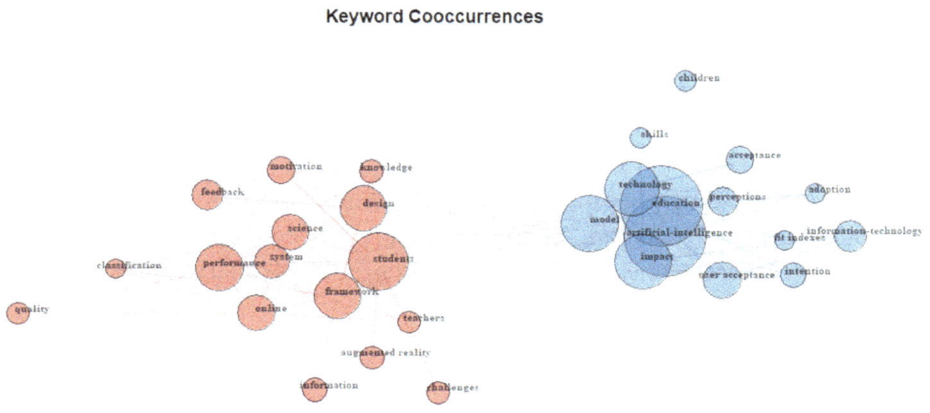

Bibliometrics provides a systematic and objective method to analyze large bodies of scholarly literature, offering insights into publication trends, influential authors, and thematic developments over time. In the context of instructional technology and artificial intelligence (AI), bibliometric analysis enables researchers to move beyond anecdotal accounts or selective reviews by quantitatively mapping how the field has evolved, where scholarly influence is concentrated, and what emerging patterns shape future directions. This approach ensures transparency, reproducibility, and scalability in evaluating research landscapes, making it particularly valuable in rapidly expanding domains like AI in education (Donthu et al., 2021).

THE SCIENTIFIC COLLABORATION

Figure 4 illustrates the most productive countries in artificial intelligence and education research, measured by the number of published documents indexed in the WoS database. China and the United States clearly dominate the landscape, with China leading in overall output and demonstrating strong participation in both single-country publications (SCP) and multiple-country collaborations (MCP). The United States follows China closely in co-authorship, followed by Spain, India, and Australia, showing a relatively high proportion of international representation in the second tier. Similarly, Germany and the United Kingdom maintain a notable but comparatively minor presence within European countries. Canada, Saudi Arabia, and Mexico indicate the collaborations in terms of diversity. While Smaller research communities often leverage international collaborations to enhance their visibility and impact, China and the United States are leaders in self-sustained scholarship, according to the balance between SCP and MCP across nations (see Fig. 4)

Figure 4. Number of publicans based on collaboration between countries

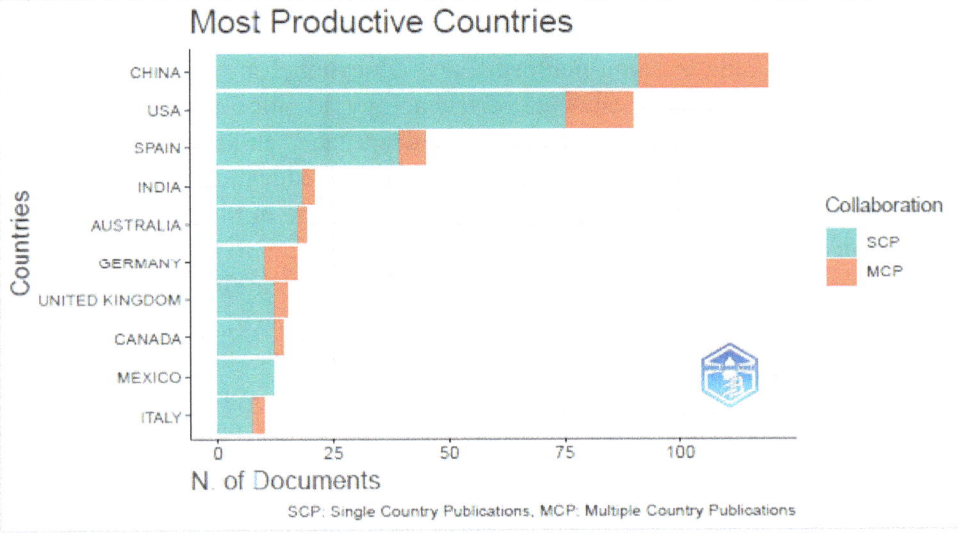

The conceptual structure map, a comprehensive visualization of the results of a Multiple Correspondence Analysis (MCA) embedded in the R package that examines relationships between various educational technology concepts and AI, is a testament to the clarity of the analysis. Using a two-dimensional coordinate system, the visualization effectively clusters related concepts based on statistical associations. The map visualizes the conceptual structure of academic research, likely focusing on educational technology or technology acceptance. The map visualizes the conceptual structure of academic research, likely focusing on educational technology or technology acceptance. The horizontal dimension (Dim 1), which explains a significant portion of the variance in the data (31.29%), appears to represent a continuum from internal, perceptual factors (mental processes and individual beliefs) to external, applied systems (tangible tools and measurable results). The high variance suggests that these factors are crucial in accepting and effectively using technological tools in educational settings. The substantial divergence indicates the broad spectrum of factors that prove the acceptance and effective use of technological tools in educational settings. On the left side of the graph, terms "concepts", "perceptions," "intention," and "self-efficacy" are used in the technology acceptance model describing the psychological and inner drivers of behavior.

On the other hand, the right side is dominated by concrete systems and outcomes, such as "training systems,"" learning analytics," "performance," and "frameworks," which represent the tangible tools and measurable results.The vertical dimension (Dim 2, 13.51%) contrasts theoretical constructs with specific user contexts and validation. The upper left of the graph contains several theoretical terms like "information technology," "adoption," and "model." The lower part of the coordinate focuses more specifically on the 'impact' within real-world environments, such as classrooms, online learning platforms, and educational institutions. The term "impact" refers to the developments of technology adoption and acceptance in educational environments, which includes "students" and "children," and concepts like "engagement," "validation," and "achievement." Education technology is a key study area connecting data-driven systems (right side of the graph) with user interaction and outcomes (bottom side).

The key terms surrounding "students," "children," "learning environments," "science education," "skills," "performance," and "achievement," which indicate the effectiveness of AI within educational technology. Contemporary EdTech research is characterized by terms "Learning analytics" (the process of students' learning behaviors) and "training systems" (methods and tools used to train students), playing a pivotal role in understanding and improving the learning process through data analysis and personalized training methods.

The term "technology acceptance model" (TAM) and its core attributes: "intention," "adoption," "self-efficacy," "user acceptance," and "perceptions," which appear in the graph, represent the Acceptance Model paradigm that indicates that the research is concerned with understanding and predicting how and why users (learners and educators) adopt technological tools.Human-Computer Interaction (HCI) is another learning concept that brings the user and computer together more naturally. Terms like "engagement," "feedback," and "user acceptance" focus on the interaction between the learner and the technology, which is combined under the HCI umbrella. (See Fig. 5). To sum up, the spatial arrangement reveals meaningful patterns in how educational technology concepts relate. Mapping technique effectively visualizes the complex interdependencies within educational technology research and AI.

Figure 5. Conceptual strucutre of network based on MCA (Multiple Correspondence Analysis)

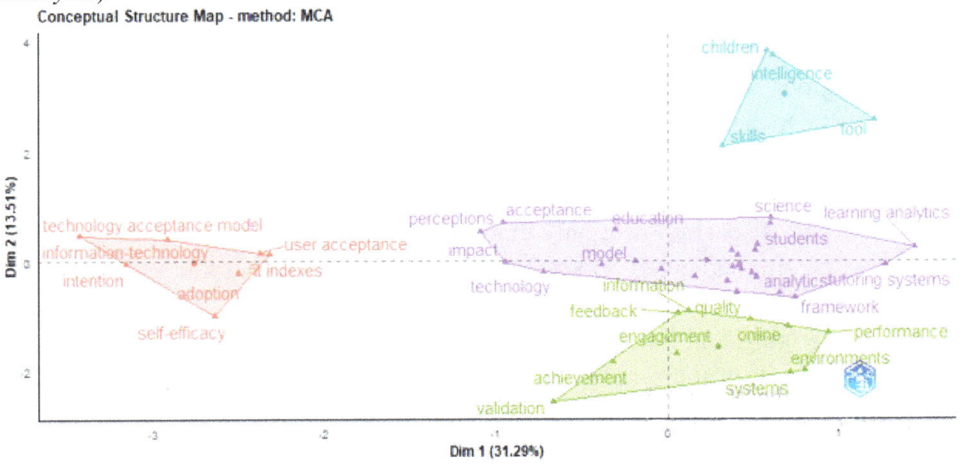

CRITICAL REFLECTIONS AND PEDAGOGICAL IMPLICATIONS

Although bibliometric analyses reveal a rapid expansion of research on artificial intelligence in education, high technology trends often obscure the realities that educators face in the field.Just relying on technological awareness does not achieve AI integration into teaching; it is not only about integrating AI into teaching but also requires a reconfiguration of pedagogical knowledge, classroom management, and ethical sensitivity. A qualitative study by Ren and Wu (2025) highlights that several teachers struggle to adapt AI tools to their subject matter and pedagogical goals, emphasizing the pertinence of frameworks such as TPACK (Technological Pedagogical Content Knowledge).

Concrete examples illustrate these challenges. For example, Knewton, as an adaptive learning platform, provides individualized learning pathways, but teachers often lack sufficient training to interpret data dashboards effectively, leading to underuse of the system's potential (Perrotta & Williamson, 2018).

Teachers having difficulties integrating Duolingo, one example of an I-powered feedback mechanism (language learning applications), enhance learner engagement and willingness to communicate in online settings. Duolingo integration as an AI tool into formal school curricula is not fully accomplished, and it is fragmented, because it often depends on teacher initiative rather than institutional strategies (Ouyang, Jiang, & Liu, 2024). These two cases highlight the pressing need for professional training programs that move beyond technical fluency toward critical evaluation, curricular integration, and reflective pedagogy.

In the context of Equity, Access, and Global Imbalances, the bibliometric patterns mapped in this chapter confirm that AI research in education is concentrated in a few regions, with the United States, China, and Europe emerging as leading contributors. On the other hand, "Global South" countries, having different cultural, linguistic, and infrastructural diversity, are significantly underrepresented, raising concerns about epistemic inequality and the danger of "one-size-fits-all" (Donthuet al., 2021). This disparity is not only in academia, since students and teachers cannot access pro-implemented AI systems designed without considering their local pedagogical needs.

Acknowledging and addressing these needs is of utmost importance. To accomplish the task, a more balanced and inclusive global research approach that AI innovations reflect the local educational and pedagogical needs, as advocated in reviews of AI adoption in higher education (Zawacki-Richter, Marín, Bond, & Gouverneur, 2019). Sustainability and ethics are two important priorities as AI integrates significantly into educational systems. Evidence in the literature shows an increasing emphasis on fairness, transparency, and data privacy. However, these discussions remain unevenly distributed across disciplines, often failing to translate into practical guidance for educators (Zawacki-Richter et al., 2019).

The complexity of AI abstract principles challenges students and teachers to implement it in everyday classroom activities. In their study, Baker and Hawn (2021) claimed that algorithmic bias may affect student agency, teacher autonomy, and institutional accountability questions (Baker & Hawn, 2021), a severe ethical issue. Although sustainability concerns about tangible objects such as resource usage, environmental costs, and long-term social implications. sustainability within AI in education entails technical innovations to enhance critical AI literacy among students and teachers alike.

These insights point to the need for a transformative agenda that moves beyond descriptive mapping of research output toward actionable strategies for policy, practice, and pedagogy. Selwyn (2022) argued that "transformative AI should be seen from pedagogical intentionality, and not from technological determinism to, where AI is framed as a tool rather than an end; second, from global concentration to distributed participation, ensuring the voices of underrepresented regions and contexts are included in shaping the AI-in-education landscape; and third, from abstract ethical discourse to concrete pedagogical practices that embed sustainability and responsibility in day-to-day teaching."

UNESCO (2021) sets AI and education policy guidelines that include supporting inclusion, teacher empowerment, cultural sensitivity, and a framework that bridges global collaborations, which is inscribed in its transformative agenda. Likewise, the European Union's AI Act explicitly incorporates education into its risk-based approach, highlighting the potential harms of opaque AI systems on vulnerable learners. By integrating bibliometric evidence with such critical reflections, scholars and practitioners can bridge the gap between research trends and educational realities, ensuring that AI adoption in education is innovative but also equitable, ethical, and sustainable.

AI IN INSTRUCTIONAL TECHNOLOGY FOR STUDENTS WITH DISABILITIES

Recent research suggests that artificial intelligence (AI) has become a valuable tool for supporting students with disabilities in instructional technology. Rice and Dunn (2023) conducted a systematic review of studies on the use of AI tools in students with special needs. They concluded that researchers of AI tools should not only be concerned with the use of technology in schools, but also that educators should advocate for the well-being of young adults. Their systematic review revealed that AI can provide personalized feedback, adapt content to meet student needs, and support inclusion in a digital learning environment. In addition, Marino et al. (2023) discussed how emerging AI technologies enable teachers to transform special education using data-driven insights and adaptive systems that adjust learning pathways in real-time. They emphasized that these technologies can help bridge gaps in accessibility for a wide range of students with disabilities, if applied correctly, thereby fostering inclusive learning. Moreover, they are against banning the use of AI technologies in class, as it can help students with diverse learning abilities.

Paglialunga and Melogno (2025) similarly noted that although AI-based interventions can be effective for students with learning disabilities, strong evidence still depends on consistent research methods and ethical safeguards. Saborío-Taylor and Rojas-Ramírez (2024) argued that technology should promote autonomy and inclusion rather than dependence. Ethical concerns, including data privacy, bias, and equitable access, are crucial issues that must be considered in the design and implementation of AI in academic settings. Rakap (2024) warns that educators must ensure AI tools align with the values of inclusive education, including respect for diversity in terms of cultural background. Together, these studies demonstrate that AI can significantly benefit students with disabilities. However, its successful integration requires not only thoughtful design and ethical awareness but also collaboration between technologists and educators, emphasizing the importance of teamwork in implementing AI in education

EQUAL LEARNING IN AN AI WORLD

Artificial intelligence (AI) is transforming the way students learn, the way teachers teach, and the way schools operate. From personalized tutoring systems to automated feedback tools, AI promises to make education more efficient and adaptive. However, we need to ask the following question: Does AI bridge or widen the existing digital divide? According to research conducted by the OECD (n.d.) from 2022 to 2025, AI can support inclusion and accessibility on the one hand; however, it may also exacerbate educational inequalities if students lack the necessary skills and access to well-sourced infrastructure (Marino et al., 2023). In well-resourced infrastructure, students and teachers benefit from AI-rich tools, while those with limited internet, devices, or training risk being left behind.

Nevertheless, a new form of inequality, referred to as the AI divide, is emerging alongside the traditional digital divide (UNESCO, n.d.). AI divide is not only about owning technology but also about knowing how to use it effectively and ethically. Therefore, AI systems should be deployed with consideration for fairness, transparency, and digital literacy, as they often deepen existing disadvantages among low-income, rural, or marginalized communities (Varsik & Vosberg, 2024). Therefore, AI advocates, including educators, policymakers, and researchers, emphasize the need for human-centered strategies. They should combine investments in technology with teacher training, equitable policy frameworks, and inclusive design, ensuring that AI in education truly empowers all learners, rather than an elite few.

ARTIFICIAL INTELLIGENCE IN EDUCATION: DURING AND AFTER THE PANDEMIC

The COVID-19 pandemic has rapidly accelerated the digital transformation of education worldwide, compelling educators and policymakers to adopt innovative technologies to maintain continuity, equity, and quality in learning. In this evolving landscape, artificial intelligence (AI), often integrated with the Internet of Things (IoT), has played an instrumental role in reshaping teaching and learning practices across various dimensions, from language acquisition and student well-being to decision-making and sustainability.

In South Korea, Um et al. (2024) examined the use of AI-Pengtalk, an AI-based conversational English program developed by the Educational Broadcasting System (EBS). Conducted with 108 fourth-grade classes in 54 elementary schools, the study found notable improvements in students' English proficiency, confidence, and motivation compared to control groups. More importantly, AI-Pengtalk helped narrow learning disparities linked to socioeconomic background, illustrating how AI-driven tools can foster more equitable educational opportunities in public schools.

Building on this technological vision, Kamruzzaman et al. (2022) explored how the integration of AI and IoT can support sustainable education systems, particularly during crises such as the COVID-19 pandemic. Their research emphasized the potential of AI- and IoT-assisted learning environments to deliver personalized, real-time, and immersive learning experiences. By leveraging smart devices, sensors, and AI-powered algorithms, education can adapt dynamically to each learner's pace and preferences while enabling remote participation. This approach offers a sustainable solution for smart cities, where technology ensures the continuity of education even in times of disruption.

Similarly, Mehrabi et al. (2024) investigated how AI can enhance decision-making in higher education, with a focus on engineering programs in the post-pandemic era. Using advanced machine learning models, the study analyzed student preferences for course modalities—online, hybrid, or face-to-face—and demonstrated that AI systems can help institutions make informed, data-driven decisions that align with both student and faculty needs. These findings highlight how intelligent analytics can optimize teaching strategies and improve flexibility in modern learning environments.

Meanwhile, Nguyen et al. (2024) conducted a bibliometric review exploring the role of AI-based support systems in promoting psychological well-being among university students. Their analysis revealed a growing scholarly focus on AI-mediated mental health tools that monitor emotional states, provide digital counseling, and strengthen social connectedness in virtual learning contexts. The study underscores that AI's impact extends beyond academics, supporting holistic student development and fostering emotional resilience in the post-COVID era.

Together, these four studies demonstrate the multifaceted capabilities of AI in education. From language learning and sustainability to institutional decision-making and student well-being, AI technologies are helping create adaptive, inclusive, and human-centered learning systems. As educational institutions worldwide continue to rebuild after the pandemic, the responsible and ethical integration of AI and IoT will remain vital for ensuring equitable, data-informed, and sustainable educational futures.

CRITICAL REFLECTIONS ON AI AND FUTURE DIRECTIONS

With its transformative potential, AI holds the promise of significant societal and ethical advancements. As AI technologies mature, they have the power to reshape social structures and their implications, offering a hopeful future. The evolution of AI technologies necessitates the active involvement of interdisciplinary approaches in shaping their future research directions. This involvement, which highlights responsible implementation, ethical frameworks, and community engagement, is crucial to harnessing AI for social good. AI is not just about quantifying data and its applications. It is about understanding and analyzing all its aspects from a social context perspective, which is crucial for enlightenment and awareness. A critical review examines the complex impact of AI on social structures, the ethical challenges it poses, and the necessity for multidisciplinary approaches to address the societal implications of AI (Zhou, 2024).

Critical theory delves into AI and explores its power network, economics, and social implications in the context of sociology. According to Latour(2005), as non-human representatives, AI acts as humans for decision-making processes. Although AI technologies are creating innovative opportunities for society! Nevertheless, we must ensure their benefits reach everyone, regardless of gender, race, or economic status, to thrive together truly. For example, AI can be categorized in the context of social classes in three terms: 'Digital divide', which refers to the unequal access to and use of digital technologies; 'Bias and algorithmic discrimination', where AI systems can perpetuate biases present in training data or encoding algorithms, resulting in discriminatory outcomes; and 'Threats to democracy and fairness', where AI can influence democratic processes and fairness by shaping information flows, political discourse, and decision-making (Zhou,2024). These are some of AI's societal challenges, and understanding them is crucial for responsible AI implementation. Regarding labour markets and wage inequality, Acemoglu et al. (2020) analyse the impact of AI and automation, offering a nuanced perspective on the economic Implications of AI-driven social change.

The ethical aspect of AI is another important issue that plays an important role in society regarding the ethical implications of AI. “Ethics in AI refers to moral considerations and principles guiding the design, development, and use of AI technologies (Wachter et al. 2021).” Fairness, transparency, accountability, and privacy are necessary to maintain ethical standards when implementing AI applications in society. Buolamwini et al. (2018) found that in commercial facial recognition, there is a need for various and representative datasets from all genders in AI development. Transparency in AI deals with more 'explainable AI,' a concept where complex AI models are designed to be more interpretable, thereby increasing trust and understanding. Conversely, accountability in the AI realm means that AI is responsible for its activities and should not harm anyone under any circumstances (Jobin et al., 2019). Moreover, privacy is a concern due to the nature of data-driven AI and its personal data usage (Wachter et al., 2017).

From a Critical theory perspective, AI is not only a neutral tool; it should be considered a socio-technical system embedded in the AI ecosystem development design that cares for institutions' values, assumptions, and priorities.

Critical theory examines how AI in instructional technology shapes and reproduces existing educational power structures and holds the potential to challenge and reshape them. Williamson & Piattoeva (2019) argued that the algorithms designed for educational needs should be trained to guide adaptive learning or assessment on datasets reflecting aspects of society holistically, not just a specific group of people based on their race, social class, and language, to cause biases unintentionally marginalizing students with underrepresented backgrounds.According to popular literature, critical theorists argue that AI imposes educational inequities without intentional interventions. However, we can counteract this potential with intentional, deliberate interventions, authorizing the privileged class to access high-resource contexts while addressing the less fortunate class. Therefore, reflective engagement with AI should be given importance to technological effectiveness and its deployment's political and ethical implications.

A second concern from a critical theory standpoint is the commodification of education through AI-driven platforms. Many commercial AI systems operate within liberal and capitalist frameworks, emphasizing efficiency, standardization, and measurable outcomes over holistic, transformative learning (Selwyn, 2019). AI design approaches should transform data generated from predictive analytics and profitable insights data into a shared public benefit for education. Critical theory perspective advoates that educators and policymakers to adhere to transparency, accountability, and participatory governance in AI-mediated learning environments. To keep the AI compliant with the abovementioned approaches, it is crucial to counter AI's potential adverse effects and design more inclusive and emancipatory educational practices.

CONCLUSION AND DISCUSSION

Using bibliometric analysis, this chapter examines how artificial intelligence has impacted educational technology by tracing its historical development within instructional technology from its inception to the present day. Drawing on data extracted from the Web of Science, the study mapped the evolution of research from early computer-assisted instruction to today's global surge in AI-related educational studies, suggesting a promising future for the field. Still, a few limitations should be acknowledged. Because the analysis relied primarily on one database, some relevant studies from Scopus, ERIC, or other open-access repositories may not have been included. Likewise, the retrospective design could not capture every possible keyword or topic variation. Despite these constraints, the study offers a valuable insight into how AI has evolved and established itself in education.

The findings indicate an exponential increase in publications since 2020, accompanied by growing diversification in publication outlets, author networks, and thematic directions. As previous research confirms (Keser Ateş et al., 2025; Donthu et al., 2021), AI in education is no longer a marginal topic but a central focus of global educational research, with China, the United States, and Europe contributing the largest share of scholarship. This expansion illustrates how the field has matured into a dynamic, internationally collaborative domain that mirrors broader technological, pedagogical, and societal transformations.

At the same time, the bibliometric evidence highlights new challenges and opportunities for the future. Emerging studies underscore the importance of critical reflection on equity and access when integrating AI into classrooms (Zawacki-Richter et al., 2019). Educators must be equipped with the necessary competencies to implement AI meaningfully (Ren & Wu, 2025). The shift toward generative AI necessitates careful consideration of its pedagogical potential and associated risks—particularly issues of bias, transparency, and student data privacy. Looking ahead, future research should build on bibliometric insights to bridge regional disparities, foster interdisciplinary collaboration, and establish frameworks for the responsible and ethical implementation of these insights.

In summary, artificial intelligence holds immense potential to transform instructional technology, particularly in designing adaptive, data-driven, and inclusive learning experiences for all learners, including those with disabilities. However, its success depends on ethical design, teacher readiness, and policy frameworks that ensure AI complements rather than replaces human interaction in education. Beyond mapping scholarly patterns, this analysis sheds light on how AI functions as both a technological catalyst and a pedagogical challenge. Responsible use demands transparency, ongoing evaluation, and a commitment to fairness, inclusivity, and accessibility.

Ultimately, bibliometric evidence reveals that artificial intelligence has become a pivotal and evolving force in shaping the field of instructional technology. The field now balances technical innovation with reflective inquiry into ethics and sustainability. As Selwyn (2022) reminds us, the real challenge ahead lies not only in perfecting AI as a tool but in ensuring it serves a pedagogically robust and ethically sound vision of education. Educational technology should invite both learners and educators to participate actively in this transformation. Practitioners must move beyond mapping the landscape to cultivating it—fostering global partnerships, strengthening AI literacy, and embedding equity and sustainability as the pillars of future innovation. The next chapter of AI in education should therefore be defined not by its computational power, but by its capacity to enhance human learning and promote educational justice.

REFERENCES

Acemoglu, D., & Restrepo, P. (2020). The wrong kind of AI? Artificial intelligence and the future of labour demand. *Cambridge Journal of Regions, Economy and Society*, *13*(1), 25–35.

Aksnes, D. W., Langfeldt, L., & Wouters, P. (2019). Citations, citation indicators, and research quality: An overview of basic concepts and theories. *SAGE Open*, *9*(1), 1–17. DOI: 10.1177/2158244019829575 PMID: 34290901

Anderson, J. R., Boyle, C. F., Corbett, A. T., & Lewis, M. W. (1990). Cognitive modeling and intelligent tutoring. *Artificial Intelligence*, *42*(1), 7–49. DOI: 10.1016/0004-3702(90)90093-F

Aria, M., & Cuccurullo, C. (2017). bibliometrix: An R-tool for comprehensive science mapping analysis. *Journal of Informetrics*, *11*(4), 959–975. DOI: 10.1016/j.joi.2017.08.007

Baker, R. S., & Hawn, A. (2021). Algorithmic bias in education. *International Journal of Artificial Intelligence in Education*. Advance online publication. DOI: 10.1007/s40593-021-00285-9

Bordons, M., Aparicio, J., González-Albo, B., & Díaz-Faes, A. A. (2015). The relationship between the research performance of scientists and their position in co-authorship networks in three fields. *Journal of Informetrics*, *9*(1), 135–144. DOI: 10.1016/j.joi.2014.12.001

Bradford, S. C. (1934). Sources of information on specific subjects. *Engineering (London)*, *137*(3550), 85–86.

Carbonell, J. R. (1970). AI in CAI: An artificial-intelligence approach to computer-assisted instruction. *IEEE Transactions on Man-Machine Systems*, *11*(4), 190–202. DOI: 10.1109/TMMS.1970.299942

Chen, C. (2004). Searching for intellectual turning points: Progressive knowledge domain visualization. *Proceedings of the National Academy of Sciences of the United States of America*, *101*(Suppl 1), 5303–5310. DOI: 10.1073/pnas.0307513100 PMID: 14724295

Chen, C. (2006). CiteSpace II: Detecting and visualizing emerging trends and transient patterns in scientific literature. *Journal of the American Society for Information Science and Technology*, *57*(3), 359–377. DOI: 10.1002/asi.20317

Chen, L., Chen, P., & Lin, Z. (2020). Artificial intelligence in education: A review. *IEEE Access : Practical Innovations, Open Solutions*, *8*, 75264–75278. DOI: 10.1109/ACCESS.2020.2988510

Derinalp, P. (2024). Past, present, and future of artificial intelligence in education: A bibliometric study. *Selçuk University Journal of Education Faculty*, *48*(1), 35–58.

Donthu, N., Kumar, S., Mukherjee, D., Pandey, N., & Lim, W. M. (2021). How to conduct a bibliometric analysis: An overview and guidelines. *Journal of Business Research*, *133*, 285–296. DOI: 10.1016/j.jbusres.2021.04.070

Doroudi, S. (2023). The intertwined histories of AI and education. *International Journal of Artificial Intelligence in Education*, *33*(3), 813–836. DOI: 10.1007/s40593-022-00313-2

Duolingo. (n.d.). Duolingo language learning platform. Retrieved September 7, 2025, from https://www.duolingo.com

Durak, G., Çankaya, S., Özdemir, D., & Can, S. (2024). Artificial intelligence in education: A bibliometric study on its role in transforming teaching and learning. *International Review of Research in Open and Distance Learning*, *25*(2), 120–139.

Ely, D. P. (1999). Toward a philosophy of instructional technology: Thirty years on. *British Journal of Educational Technology*, *30*(4), 305–310. DOI: 10.1111/1467-8535.00120

Garfield, E. (1955). Citation indexes for science: A new dimension in documentation through association of ideas. *Science*, *122*(3159), 108–111. DOI: 10.1126/science.122.3159.108 PMID: 14385826

Genç, H. N., & Kocak, N. (2024). Bibliometric analysis of studies on the artificial intelligence in science education with VOSviewer. *Journal of Education in Science, Environment and Health*, *10*(2), 132–152.

Jobin, A., Ienca, M., & Vayena, E. (2019). The global landscape of AI ethics guidelines. *Nature Machine Intelligence*, *1*(9), 389–399. DOI: 10.1038/s42256-019-0088-2

Kamruzzaman, M. M., Alanazi, S., Alruwaili, M., Alshammari, N., Elaiwat, S., Innab, N., Mohammad Elzaghmouri, B., & Ahmed Alanazi, B. (2022). AI- and IoT-Assisted Sustainable Education Systems during Pandemics, such as COVID-19, for Smart Cities. *Sustainability*, *15*(10), 8354. DOI: 10.3390/su15108354

Kasneci, E., Sessler, K., & König, C. (2023). ChatGPT for good? On opportunities and challenges of large language models for education. *Learning and Individual Differences*, *103*, 102274. DOI: 10.1016/j.lindif.2023.102274

Kelley, J., & Wenzel, A. (2025). Advancing artificial intelligence literacy in teacher education through professional partnership inquiry. *Education Sciences*, *15*(6), 659.

Koedinger, K. R., Anderson, J. R., Hadley, W. H., & Mark, M. A. (1997). Intelligent tutoring goes to school in the big city. *International Journal of Artificial Intelligence in Education*, *8*(1), 30–43.

Latour, B. (2005). From Realpolitik to Dingpolitik or How to Make Things Public. In Latour, B., & Weibel, P. (Eds.), *Making Things Public: Atmospheres of Democracy* (pp. 14–41). MIT Press.

Leibel, C., & Bornmann, L. (2024). Specification uncertainty: What the disruption index tells us about the (hidden) multiverse of bibliometric indicators. *Scientometrics*, *129*(12), 7971–7979. DOI: 10.1007/s11192-024-05201-1

Lotka, A. J. (1926). The frequency distribution of scientific productivity. *Journal of the Washington Academy of Sciences*, *16*(12), 317–323.

Marín, V. I., Bond, M., & Gouverneur, F. (2019). Systematic review of research on artificial intelligence applications in higher education – where are the educators? *International Journal of Educational Technology in Higher Education*, *16*(1), 1–27. DOI: 10.1186/s41239-019-0171-0

Marino, M. T., Vasquez, E., Dieker, L., Basham, J., & Blackorby, J. (2023). The Future of Artificial Intelligence in Special Education Technology. *Journal of Special Education Technology*. Advance online publication. 10.1177_01626434231165977

Mehrabi, A., Morphew, J. W., Araabi, B. N., Memarian, N., & Memarian, H. (2024). AI-Enhanced Decision-Making for Course Modality Preferences in Higher Engineering Education during the Post-COVID-19 Era. *Information (Basel)*, *15*(10), 590. DOI: 10.3390/info15100590

Nguyen, T. V., Mohd Daril, M. A., Ali, M., & Korejo, M. S. (2024). Enhancing psychological well-being in higher education post-COVID-19 pandemic: The role of AI-based support systems—Bibliometric reviews. [iJOE]. *International Journal of Online and Biomedical Engineering*, *20*(6), 139–152. DOI: 10.3991/ijoe.v20i06.48001

OECD. (n.d.). *OECD artificial intelligence papers. OECD*. https://www.oecd.org/en/publications/serials/oecd-artificial-intelligence-papers_74018992.html

Ouyang, Z., Jiang, Y., & Liu, H. (2024). The effects of Duolingo, an AI-integrated technology, on EFL learners' willingness to communicate and engagement in online classes. *International Review of Research in Open and Distance Learning*, *25*(3), 98–118. DOI: 10.19173/irrodl.v25i3.7677

Paglialunga, A., & Melogno, S. (2025). The Effectiveness of Artificial Intelligence-Based Interventions for Students with Learning Disabilities: A Systematic Review. *Brain Sciences*, *15*(8), 806. DOI: 10.3390/brainsci15080806 PMID: 40867139

Perrotta, C., & Williamson, B. (2018). The social life of learning analytics: Cluster analysis and the 'performance' of algorithmic education. *Learning, Media and Technology*, *43*(1), 3–16. DOI: 10.1080/17439884.2016.1182927

Price, D. J. de S. (1963). *Little science, big science*. Columbia University Press.

Pritchard, A. (1969). Statistical bibliography or bibliometrics*? The Journal of Documentation*, *25*(4), 348–349.

Rakap, S. (2024). Navigating the role of artificial intelligence in special education: Advantages, disadvantages, and ethical considerations. *Practice*, *6*(2–3), 99–104. DOI: 10.1080/25783858.2024.2411948

Ren, X., & Wu, M. L. (2025). Examining teaching competencies and challenges while integrating artificial intelligence in higher education. *TechTrends*, *69*(1), 519–538. DOI: 10.1007/s11528-025-01055-3

Rice, M. F., & Dunn, S. (2023). The Use of Artificial Intelligence with Students with Identified Disabilities: A Systematic Review with Critique. *Computers in the Schools*, *40*(4), 370–390. DOI: 10.1080/07380569.2023.2244935

Rudolph, J., Tan, S., & Tan, S. (2023). ChatGPT: Bullshit spewer or the end of traditional assessments in higher education? *Journal of Applied Learning & Teaching*, *6*(1), 1–22. DOI: 10.37074/jalt.2023.6.1.9

Saborío-Taylor, S., & Rojas-Ramírez, F. (2024). Universal design for learning and artificial intelligence in the digital era: Fostering inclusion and autonomous learning. *International Journal of Professional Development. Learners and Learning*, *6*(2), ep2408. Advance online publication. DOI: 10.30935/ijpdll/14694

Selwyn, N. (2019). *Should robots replace teachers? AI and the future of education*. Polity Press.

Selwyn, N. (2022). The future of AI and education: Some critical challenges. *Prometheus*, *37*(1), 22–36. DOI: 10.13169/prometheus.37.1.0022

Siemens, G., & Baker, R. S. (2012). Learning analytics and educational data mining: Towards communication and collaboration. *In Proceedings of the 2nd International Conference on Learning Analytics and Knowledge* (pp. 252–254). ACM. https://doi.org/DOI: 10.1145/2330601.2330661

Sleeman, D., & Brown, J. S. (Eds.). (1982). *Intelligent tutoring systems*. Academic Press.

Small, H. (1973). Co-citation in the scientific literature: A new measure of the relationship between two documents. *Journal of the American Society for Information Science*, *24*(4), 265–269. DOI: 10.1002/asi.4630240406

Suppes, P., & Morningstar, M. (1969). Computer-assisted instruction. *Science*, *166*(3903), 343–350. DOI: 10.1126/science.166.3903.343 PMID: 5812034

Um, H., Kim, H., & Choi, D. (2024). An AI-based English education platform during the COVID-19 pandemic. *Universal Access in the Information Society*, *23*(5), 1233–1248. DOI: 10.1007/s10209-023-01046-2

UNESCO. (2021). *AI and education: Guidance for policy-makers*. UNESCO Publishing.

UNESCO. (n.d.). Artificial intelligence in education. *UNESCO*. https://www.unesco.org/en/digital-education/artificial-intelligence

van Eck, N. J., & Waltman, L. (2010). Software survey: VOSviewer, a computer program for bibliometric mapping. *Scientometrics*, *84*(2), 523–538. DOI: 10.1007/s11192-009-0146-3 PMID: 20585380

Varsik, S., & Vosberg, L. (2024). *The potential impact of Artificial Intelligence on equity and inclusion in education, OECD Artificial Intelligence Papers, No. 23*. OECD Publishing., DOI: 10.1787/15df715b-

Wachter, S., Mittelstadt, B., & Floridi, L. (2017). Why a right to explanation of automated decision-making does not exist in the general data protection regulation. *International Data Privacy Law*, *7*(2), 76–99. DOI: 10.1093/idpl/ipx005

Williamson, B., & Piattoeva, N. (2019). Objectivity as standardization in data-scientific educational governance: Grasping the global through the local. *Research in Education*, *101*(1), 69–91. DOI: 10.1177/0034523718804718

Xu, H., Li, X., Tupayachi, J., Lian, J., & Omitaomu, O. A. (2024). Automating bibliometric analysis with sentence transformers and retrieval-augmented generation (rag): a pilot study in semantic and contextual search for customized literature characterization for high-impact urban research. *Proceedings of the 2nd ACM SIGSPATIAL International Workshop on Advances in Urban-*Ai, 43-49. https://doi.org/DOI: 10.1145/3681780.3697252

Zawacki-Richter, O., Marín, V. I., Bond, M., & Gouverneur, F. (2019). Systematic review of research on artificial intelligence applications in higher education—Where are the educators? *International Journal of Educational Technology in Higher Education*, *16*(1), 39. DOI: 10.1186/s41239-019-0171-0

Zhou, C. (2024). Artificial intelligence in sociology: A critical review and future directions. *Theory and Society*, *53*(2), 301–330. DOI: 10.1007/s11186-024-09542-z

Zipf, G. K. (1949). *Human behavior and the principle of least effort: An introduction to human ecology*. Addison-Wesley Press.

Zupic, I., & Čater, T. (2015). Bibliometric methods in management and organization. *Organizational Research Methods*, *18*(3), 429–472. DOI: 10.1177/1094428114562629

ADDITIONAL READING

Crompton, H., & Burke, D. (2024). Artificial intelligence in higher education: The state of the field. *International Journal of Educational Technology in Higher Education*, *21*(1), 22. DOI: 10.1186/s41239-024-00456-3

Kumar, S., Sharma, D., Rao, S., Lim, W. M., & Mangla, S. K. (2024). The evolution of supply chain resilience: A bibliometric analysis and future research directions. *Annals of Operations Research*. Advance online publication. DOI: 10.1007/s10479-024-05868-y

Perrotta, C., Selwyn, N., & Ewin, C. (2024). 'A necessary evil': The 'fixing' of educational data and the implication of AI for professional teaching identities. *Learning, Media and Technology*. Advance online publication. DOI: 10.1080/17439884.2024.2317831

Xie, K., Nelson, M. J., & Cheng, S.-L. (2024). Supporting self-regulated learning in online learning environments: A systematic review of AI applications and their ethical implications. *Computers & Education*, *216*, 105042. DOI: 10.1016/j.compedu.2024.105042

KEY TERMS AND DEFINITIONS

Artificial intelligence: Artificial intelligence is a technology that emulates the functions of the human brain.

Bibliometric Analysis: Bibliometric analysis studies any documentation in terms of numbers.

Bibliometrix: Bibliometric is a library pakege which runs under RStudio to carry bibliometric analyis from WoS, Scopus, Medline, to name three.

Critical Theory: Critical theory is a paradigm that deals with human well-being.

Edcautional Technology: Education technology illustrates the intersection of Education and Computers.

Compilation of References

Abbasi, B. N., Wu, Y., & Luo, Z. (2025). Exploring the impact of artificial intelligence on curriculum development in global higher education institutions. *Education and Information Technologies*, *30*(1), 547–581.

Acar, O. A. (2023, June 9). *AI prompt engineering isn't the future. Harvard Business Review*. https://hbr.org/2023/06/ai-prompt-engineering-isnt-the-future

Acemoglu, D., & Restrepo, P. (2020). The wrong kind of AI? Artificial intelligence and the future of labour demand. *Cambridge Journal of Regions, Economy and Society*, *13*(1), 25–35.

Adeleke, R., & Alabede, O. (2022). Geographical determinants and hotspots of out-of-school children in Nigeria. *Open Education Studies*, *4*(1), 345–355. DOI: 10.1515/EDU-2022-0176

Adiguzel, T., Kaya, M. H., & Cansu, F. K. (2023). Revolutionizing education with AI: Exploring the transformative potential of ChatGPT. *Contemporary Educational Technology*, *15*(3), ep429. DOI: 10.30935/cedtech/13152

Ahmed, D. F. (2024). Mapping Inequality: Spatial Dimensions of Social and Economic Disparities. *Liberal Journal of Language & Literature Review*, *2*(01), 1–12. https://llrjournal.com/index.php/11/article/view/34

Ahmed, E. (2024). Student performance prediction using machine learning algorithms. *Applied Computational Intelligence and Soft Computing*, *2024*(1), 4067721.

Aksnes, D. W., Langfeldt, L., & Wouters, P. (2019). Citations, citation indicators, and research quality: An overview of basic concepts and theories. *SAGE Open*, *9*(1), 1–17. DOI: 10.1177/2158244019829575 PMID: 34290901

Akudo, F. U., Igbokwe, I. C., & Oparaji, I. C. (2021). SCHOOL MAPPING AS THE DETERMINANT OF THE PROVISION OF EDUCATION RESOURCES IN PUBLIC SECONDARY SCHOOLS. *European Journal of Education Studies*, *8*(3). Advance online publication. DOI: 10.46827/EJES.V8I3.3644

Akyildiz, Y. (2025). The impact of virtual reality on vocabulary learning and cognitive efficiency. *Journal of Educational Technology and Online Learning*, *8*(2), 152–163.

Akyol, H. (2008). *Yeni programa uygun Türkçe öğretim yöntemleri*. Kök Yayıncılık.

Akyol, H. (2019). *Türkçe öğretimi: Okuma-yazma öğretimi*. Pegem Akademi Yayıncılık.

Alabdulhadi, A., & Faisal, M. (2021). Systematic literature review of STEM self-study related ITSs. *Education and Information Technologies*, *26*(2), 1549–1588. DOI: 10.1007/s10639-020-10315-z

Aleven, V., McLaughlin, E. A., Glenn, R. A., & Koedinger, K. R. (2017). Instruction based on adaptive learning technologies. In Mayer, R. E., & Alexander, P. A. (Eds.), *Handbook of research on learning and instruction* (2nd ed., pp. 522–560). Routledge., DOI: 10.4324/9781315736419-36

Alfayez, A. A., & Rasool, A. (2025). Use of AI in the curriculum development of transnational higher education. In *Bridging Global Divides for Transnational Higher Education in the AI Era* (pp. 401–422). IGI Global Scientific Publishing.

Al-Zawqari, A., Peumans, D., & Vandersteen, G. (2022). A flexible feature selection approach for predicting students' academic performance in online courses. *Computers and Education: Artificial Intelligence*, *3*, 100103.

Anderson, J. R., Boyle, C. F., Corbett, A. T., & Lewis, M. W. (1990). Cognitive modeling and intelligent tutoring. *Artificial Intelligence*, *42*(1), 7–49. DOI: 10.1016/0004-3702(90)90093-F

Anderson, L. W., & Krathwohl, D. D. (Eds.). (2001). *A taxonomy for learning, teaching, and assessing: A revision of Bloom's taxonomy of educational objectives*. Longman.

Anselin, L. (2024). An Introduction to Spatial Data Science with GeoDa: Volume 1 - Exploring Spatial Data. *An Introduction to Spatial Data Science with GeoDa: Volume 1 - Exploring Spatial Data*, 1–424. https://doi.org//DOI: 10.1201/9781003274919

Anselin, L., & Rey, S. J. (2022). Open Source Software for Spatial Data Science. *Geographical Analysis*, *54*(3), 429–438. DOI: 10.1111/GEAN.12339

Arévalo-Cordovilla, F. E., & Peña, M. (2024). Comparative analysis of machine learning models for predicting student success in online programming courses: A study based on LMS data and external factors. *Mathematics*, *12*(20), 3272.

Aria, M., & Cuccurullo, C. (2017). bibliometrix: An R-tool for comprehensive science mapping analysis. *Journal of Informetrics*, *11*(4), 959–975. DOI: 10.1016/j.joi.2017.08.007

Arizmendi, C. J., Bernacki, M. L., Raković, M., Plumley, R. D., Urban, C. J., Panter, A. T., & Gates, K. M. (2023). Predicting student outcomes using digital logs of learning behaviors: Review, current standards, and suggestions for future work. *Behavior Research Methods*, *55*(6), 3026–3054. PMID: 36018483

Aslan, I. A., & Sever, G. (2025). Fine arts high school students' experiences on the use of Tonic, an interactive instrument practice application. *Journal of Educational Technology and Online Learning*, *8*(3), 330–350.

Atalay, M., & Çelik, E. (2017). Büyük veri analizinde yapay zekâ ve makine öğrenmesi uygulamaları - Artificial intelligence and machine learning applications in big data analysis. *Mehmet Akif Ersoy Üniversitesi Sosyal Bilimler Enstitüsü Dergisi*, *9*(22), 155–172.

Bağlı, M. T. (2004). Oyun, Bilişsel gelişim ve toplumsal dünya: Piaget, Vygotsky ve sonrası. *Ankara Üniversitesi Eğitim Bilimleri Fakültesi Dergisi*, *37*(2), 137–169.

Bahroun, Z., Anane, C., Ahmed, V., & Zacca, A. (2023). Transforming education: A comprehensive review of generative artificial intelligence in educational settings through bibliometric and content analysis. *Sustainability*, *15*(17), 12983.

Baker, R. S., & Hawn, A. (2021). Algorithmic bias in education. *International Journal of Artificial Intelligence in Education*. Advance online publication. DOI: 10.1007/s40593-021-00285-9

Balaquiao, E. (2024). Optimizing students' performance through Artificial Intelligence (AI) technology: A gamified approach to smart learning environment. *Journal of Pedagogy and Education Science*, *3*(02), 104–114.

Bengio, Y. (2012). Practical recommendations for gradient-based training of deep architectures. In G. Montavon, G. B. Orr, & K.-R. Müller (Eds.), *Neural networks: Tricks of the trade: Second edition* (pp. 437–478). Springer.

Bereiter, C., & Scardamalia, M. (2013). *The psychology of written composition*. Routledge.

Bhose, M. (2024, August 23). *AI In STEM Education: Transforming Learning*. eLearning Industry. https://elearningindustry.com/ai-in-stem-education-transforming-learning

Biagini, G. (2025). Towards an AI-Literate Future: A systematic literature review exploring education, ethics, and applications. *International Journal of Artificial Intelligence in Education*, •••, 1–51.

Biesta, G. (2010). *Good education in an age of measurement: Ethics, politics, democracy*. Routledge., DOI: 10.4324/9781315634319

Bisdas, S., Topriceanu, C.-C., Zakrzewska, Z., Irimia, A.-V., Shakallis, L., Subhash, J., Casapu, M.-M., Leon-Rojas, J., Pinto Dos Santos, D., Andrews, D. M., Zeicu, C., Bouhuwaish, A. M., Lestari, A. N., Abu-Ismail, L., Sadiq, A. S., Khamees, A., Mohammed, K. M. G., Williams, E., Omran, A. I., & Ebrahim, E. H. (2021). Artificial Intelligence in Medicine: A Multinational Multi-Center Survey on the Medical and Dental Students' Perception. *Frontiers in Public Health*, *9*, 795284. DOI: 10.3389/fpubh.2021.795284 PMID: 35004598

Bjork, R. A. (1994). Memory and metamemory considerations in the training of human beings. In Metcalfe, J., & Shimamura, A. (Eds.), *Metacognition: Knowing about knowing* (pp. 185–205). MIT Press.

Bordons, M., Aparicio, J., González-Albo, B., & Díaz-Faes, A. A. (2015). The relationship between the research performance of scientists and their position in co-authorship networks in three fields. *Journal of Informetrics*, *9*(1), 135–144. DOI: 10.1016/j.joi.2014.12.001

Borenstein, J., & Howard, A. (2021). Emerging challenges in AI and the need for AI ethics education. *AI and Ethics*, *1*(1), 61–65. PMID: 38624388

Botzees. (2022, May 30). *Top 6 Trends in Stem Education in June 2022*. Botzees Toys. https://botzeestoys.com/blogs/news/top-trends-in-stem-education

Bozkurt, A., & Sharma, R. C. 2023. Generative AI and prompt engineering: the art of whispering to let the genie out of the algorithmic world. *Asian J. Distance Educ. 18* (2), 1–6. http://asianjde.com/ojs/index.php/AsianJDE/article/view/749

Bradford, S. C. (1934). Sources of information on specific subjects. *Engineering (London)*, *137*(3550), 85–86.

Braun, V., & Clarke, V. (2006). Using thematic analysis in psychology. *Qualitative Research in Psychology*, *3*(2), 77–101.

Breiman, L. (2001). Random forests. *Machine Learning*, *45*(1), 5–32.

Brookes, A., & Grundy, P. (1999). *Beginning to write: Writing activities for elementary and intermediate learners*. Cambridge University Press.

Bruner, J. S. (1960). *The Process of Education*. Harvard University Press.

Bruner, J. S. (1973). *Going Beyond the Information Given*. Norton.

Bruner, J. S. (1997). The culture of education. In *The culture of education*. Harvard University Press.

Bruner, J. S. (2009). *Actual minds, possible worlds*. Harvard University Press.

Buabbas, A. J., Miskin, B., Alnaqi, A. A., Ayed, A. K., Shehab, A. A., Syed-Abdul, S., & Uddin, M. (2023). Investigating Students' Perceptions towards Artificial Intelligence in Medical Education. *Health Care*, *11*(9), 1298. DOI: 10.3390/healthcare11091298 PMID: 37174840

Buluş, B., & Elmas, R. (2024). Yapay Zeka Uygulamalarının Kimya Eğitiminde Kullanımı Alternatif Araçlar. *Turkiye Kimya Dernegi Dergisi Kısım C. Kimya Egitimi*, *9*(1), 1–28. DOI: 10.37995/jotcsc.1366999

Burke, M., Driscoll, A., Lobell, D. B., & Ermon, S. (2021). Using satellite imagery to understand and promote sustainable development. *Science*, *371*(6535). Advance online publication. DOI: 10.1126/SCIENCE.ABE8628 PMID: 33737462

Burns, S., & Muscanell, N. (2024). EDUCAUSE QuickPoll results: A growing need for generative AI strategy. *EDUCAUSE Review*. https://er.educause.edu/articles/2024/4/educause-quickpoll-results-a-growing-need-for-generative-ai-strategy

Cain, W. (2024). Prompting change: Exploring prompt engineering in large language model AI and its potential to transform education. *TechTrends*, *68*(1), 47–57. DOI: 10.1007/s11528-023-00896-0

Cao, S., Chen, Y., & Zhang, L. (2025). An empirical study of an AI-driven platform in blended learning: Effects on Business English proficiency and engagement. *Language Testing in Asia*, *15*(1), 2–25.

Caquard, S., & Dimitrovas, S. (2017). Story Maps & Co. The state of the art of online narrative cartography. Http://Journals.Openedition.Org/Mappemonde, *121*. https://doi.org/DOI: 10.4000/MAPPEMONDE.3386

Carbonell, J. R. (1970). AI in CAI: An artificial-intelligence approach to computer-assisted instruction. *IEEE Transactions on Man-Machine Systems*, *11*(4), 190–202. DOI: 10.1109/TMMS.1970.299942

Carniel, A. C., & Schneider, M. (2021). A Survey of Fuzzy Approaches in Spatial Data Science. *IEEE International Conference on Fuzzy Systems, 2021-July*. https://doi.org/DOI: 10.1109/FUZZ45933.2021.9494437

Carvalho, A., Teixeira, S. J., Olim, L., Campanella, S. D., & Costa, T. (2021). Pedagogical innovation in higher education and active learning methodologies–a case study. *Education + Training*, *63*(2), 195–213.

Casal-Otero, L., Catala, A., Fernández-Morante, C., Taboada, M., Cebreiro, B., & Barro, S. (2023). AI literacy in K-12: A systematic literature review. *International Journal of STEM Education*, *10*(1), 29. DOI: 10.1186/s40594-023-00418-7

CAST. (2018). *Universal Design for Learning Guidelines version 2.2*. Retrieved from http://udlguidelines.cast.org

Çayak, S. (2024). Investigating the relationship between teachers' attitudes toward artificial intelligence and their artificial intelligence literacy. *Journal of Educational Technology and Online Learning, 7*(4-ICETOL 2024 Special Issue), 367–383. DOI: 10.31681/jetol.1490307

Çayak, S. (2024). Investigating the relationship between teachers' attitudes toward artificial intelligence and their artificial intelligence literacy. *Journal of Educational Technology & Online Learning*, *7*(4), 367–383.

Chan, C. K. Y., & Hu, W. (2023). Students' voices on generative AI: Perceptions, benefits, and challenges in higher education. *International Journal of Educational Technology in Higher Education*, *20*(1), 43. DOI: 10.1186/s41239-023-00411-8

Chen, C. (2004). Searching for intellectual turning points: Progressive knowledge domain visualization. *Proceedings of the National Academy of Sciences of the United States of America*, *101*(Suppl 1), 5303–5310. DOI: 10.1073/pnas.0307513100 PMID: 14724295

Chen, C. (2006). CiteSpace II: Detecting and visualizing emerging trends and transient patterns in scientific literature. *Journal of the American Society for Information Science and Technology*, *57*(3), 359–377. DOI: 10.1002/asi.20317

Chen, C., Guo, Z., & Judge, J. (2024). A QGIS Plugin for GIS-based Multicriteria Decision Analysis: An Application of Developing Alternative Future Land-Use Scenarios in Ghana. *Applied Spatial Analysis and Policy*, *17*(2), 779–797. DOI: 10.1007/S12061-024-09566-X

Chen, L., Chen, P., & Lin, Z. (2020). Artificial Intelligence in Education: A Review. *IEEE Access : Practical Innovations, Open Solutions*, *8*, 75264–75278. DOI: 10.1109/ACCESS.2020.2988510

Chiu, T. K. F. (2024). The impact of Generative AI (GenAI) on practices, policies and research direction in education: A case of ChatGPT and Midjourney. *Interactive Learning Environments*, *32*(10), 6187–6203. DOI: 10.1080/10494820.2023.2253861

Chiu, T. K. F., & Li, Y. (2023). How Can Emerging Technologies Impact STEM Education? *Journal for STEM Education Research*, *6*(3), 375–384. DOI: 10.1007/s41979-023-00113-w

Chiu, T. K. F., Xia, Q., Zhou, X., Chai, C. S., & Cheng, M. (2023). Systematic literature review on opportunities, challenges, and future research recommendations of artificial intelligence in education. *Computers and Education: Artificial Intelligence*, *4*, 1–15. DOI: 10.1016/j.caeai.2022.100118

Chiu, T. K., Meng, H., Chai, C. S., King, I., Wong, S., & Yam, Y. (2021). Creation and evaluation of a pretertiary artificial intelligence (AI) curriculum. *IEEE Transactions on Education*, *65*(1), 30–39.

Choi, W. C., Lam, C. T., Pang, P. C. I., & Mendes, A. J. (2025, June). A systematic literature review of explainable artificial intelligence (XAI) for interpreting student performance prediction in computer science and STEM education. In *Proceedings of the 30th ACM Conference on Innovation and Technology in Computer Science Education* V. 1 (pp. 221–227).

Chu, T. S., & Ashraf, M. (2025). Artificial Intelligence in Curriculum Design: A Data-Driven Approach to Higher Education Innovation. *Knowledge (Beverly Hills, Calif.)*, *5*(3), 14.

Ciampa, K., Wolfe, Z. M., & Bronstein, B. (2023). ChatGPT in education: Transforming digital literacy practices. *Journal of Adolescent & Adult Literacy*, *67*(3), 186–195. DOI: 10.1002/jaal.1310

Çoban, D., & Yıldız, D. G. (2025). An evaluation of the 10th grade robotic coding curriculum (2020) within a participant oriented curriculum evaluation approach. *Journal of Educational Technology and Online Learning*, *8*(2), 226–250.

Colangelo, M. T., Guizzardi, S., Meleti, M., Calciolari, E., & Galli, C. (2025). How to write effective prompts for screening biomedical literature using large language models. *BioMedInformatics*, *5*(1), 15. DOI: 10.3390/biomedinformatics5010015

Cole, M. (1996). *Cultural psychology: A once and future discipline*. Harvard University Press.

Cooper, G. (2023). Examining science education in ChatGPT: An exploratory study of generative artificial intelligence. *Journal of Science Education and Technology*, *32*(3), 444–452.

Couillard, B. K., Foote, C. L., Gandhi, K., Meara, E., & Skinner, J. (2021). Rising Geographic Disparities in US Mortality. *The Journal of Economic Perspectives*, *35*(4), 123–146. DOI: 10.1257/JEP.35.4.123 PMID: 35079197

Creswell, J. W., & Poth, C. N. (2018). *Qualitative inquiry and research design: Choosing among five approaches* (4th ed.). SAGE Publications.

D'mello, S., & Graesser, A. (2013). AutoTutor and affective AutoTutor: Learning by talking with cognitively and emotionally intelligent computers that talk back. [TiiS]. *ACM Transactions on Interactive Intelligent Systems*, *2*(4), 1–39.

Dai, Y., Liu, A., & Lim, C. P. (2023). Reconceptualizing ChatGPT and generative AI as a student-driven innovation in higher education. *Procedia CIRP*, *119*, 84–90.

Dang, H., Mecke, L., Lehmann, F., Goller, S., & Buschek, D. (2022). *How to prompt? Opportunities and challenges of zero-and few-shot learning for human–AI interaction in creative applications of generative models*. https://arxiv.org/abs/2209.01390

Davar, N. F., Dewan, M. A. A., & Zhang, X. (2025). AI Chatbots in Education: Challenges and Opportunities. *Information (Basel)*, *16*(3), 2–25. DOI: 10.3390/info16030235

Deng, X., & Yu, Z. (2023). A Meta-Analysis and Systematic Review of the Effect of Chatbot Technology Use in Sustainable Education. *Sustainability*, *15*(4), 2940. DOI: 10.3390/su15042940

Derinalp, P. (2024). Past, present, and future of artificial intelligence in education: A bibliometric study. *Selçuk University Journal of Education Faculty*, *48*(1), 35–58.

Dillman, D. A., Smyth, J. D., & Christian, L. M. (2014). *Internet, phone, mail, and mixed-mode surveys: The tailored design method* (4th ed.). John Wiley & Sons.

Ding, L., Li, T., Jiang, S., & Gapud, A. (2023). Students' perceptions of using ChatGPT in a physics class as a virtual tutor. *International Journal of Educational Technology in Higher Education*, *20*(1), 63. DOI: 10.1186/s41239-023-00434-1

Donthu, N., Kumar, S., Mukherjee, D., Pandey, N., & Lim, W. M. (2021). How to conduct a bibliometric analysis: An overview and guidelines. *Journal of Business Research*, *133*, 285–296. DOI: 10.1016/j.jbusres.2021.04.070

Doroudi, S. (2023). The intertwined histories of AI and education. *International Journal of Artificial Intelligence in Education*, *33*(3), 813–836. DOI: 10.1007/s40593-022-00313-2

Du, J., & Daniel, B. K. (2024). Transforming language education: A systematic review of AI-powered chatbots for English as a foreign language speaking practice. *Comput. Educ. Artif. Intell.*, *6*, 100230.

Duman, B. (2004). *Learning-teaching theories and process-based education.* Ani Publishing.

Dunn, W. E., & Lantolf, J. P. (1998). Vygotsky's zone of proximal development and Krashen's i+ 1: Incommensurable constructs; incommensurable theories. *Language Learning*, *48*(3), 411–442.

Duolingo. (n.d.). Duolingo language learning platform. Retrieved September 7, 2025, from https://www.duolingo.com

Durak, G., Çankaya, S., Özdemir, D., & Can, S. (2024). Artificial intelligence in education: A bibliometric study on its role in transforming teaching and learning. *International Review of Research in Open and Distance Learning*, *25*(2), 120–139.

EDUCAUSE. (2024). Higher education generative AI readiness assessment. *EDUCAUSE Library.* Retrieved from https://library.educause.edu/resources/2024/4/higher-education-generative-ai-readiness-assessment

Eke, O. E. (2024). Assessing the readiness and attitudes of Nigerian teacher educators towards adoption of artificial intelligence in educational settings. *Journal of Educational Technology & Online Learning*, *7*(4), 473–487.

Elmessiry, A., & Elmessiry, M. (2024). Navigating the evolution of Artificial Intelligence: Towards education-specific retrieval augmented generative AI (ES-RAG-AI). In *INTED2024 Proceedings* (pp. 7692–7697).

Ely, D. P. (1999). Toward a philosophy of instructional technology: Thirty years on. *British Journal of Educational Technology*, *30*(4), 305–310. DOI: 10.1111/1467-8535.00120

Erlingsson, C., & Brysiewicz, P. (2017). A hands-on guide to doing content analysis. *African Journal of Emergency Medicine : Revue Africaine de la Médecine d'Urgence*, *7*(3), 93–99. DOI: 10.1016/j.afjem.2017.08.001 PMID: 30456117

Ertmer, P. A., & Ottenbreit-Leftwich, A. T. (2010). Teacher technology change: How knowledge, confidence, beliefs, and culture intersect. *Journal of Research on Technology in Education*, *42*(3), 255–284.

Eskici, M., & Çayak, S. (2023). The Relationship between Teachers' Technology Proficiencies and their Levels of Integrating Technology into their Lessons. *Journal of Educational Technology and Online Learning*, *6*(4), 808–821.

Extance, A. (2018). How AI technology can tame the scientific literature. *Nature*, *561*(7722), 273–275. PMID: 30202054

Faheem, S. (2016). ESP Learners and the Language Based Activities. *Information Journal of English Language. Literature and Humanities*, *4*(1), 58–65.

Feng, Y., Wang, X., Wong, K. K., Wang, S., Lu, Y., Zhu, M., & Chen, W. (2023). Promptmagician: Interactive prompt engineering for text-to-image creation. *IEEE Transactions on Visualization and Computer Graphics*, *30*(1), 1–11. DOI: 10.1109/tvcg.2023.3327168 PMID: 37878445

Florian, L., & Black-Hawkins, K. (2011). Exploring inclusive pedagogy. *British Educational Research Journal*, *37*(5), 813–828.

Floridi, L. (2019). Establishing the rules for building trustworthy AI. *Nature Machine Intelligence*, *1*(6), 261–262. DOI: 10.1038/s42256-019-0055-y

Floridi, L., Cowls, J., & Beltrametti, M.. (2018). AI4People—An ethical framework for a good AI society. *Minds and Machines*, *28*(4), 689–707. PMID: 30930541

Flower, L., & Hayes, J. R. (1981). A cognitive process theory of writing. *College Composition and Communication*, *32*(4), 365–387.

Fowler, F. J. (2013). *Survey research methods* (5th ed.). SAGE Publications.

Gaftandzhieva, S., Talukder, A., Gohain, N., Hussain, S., Theodorou, P., Salal, Y., & Doneva, R. (2022). Exploring online activities to predict the final grade of student. *Mathematics*, *10*(20), 3758. DOI: 10.3390/math10203758

Garfield, E. (1955). Citation indexes for science: A new dimension in documentation through association of ideas. *Science*, *122*(3159), 108–111. DOI: 10.1126/science.122.3159.108 PMID: 14385826

Gary, K. (2019). Pragmatic Standards versus Saturated Phenomenon: Cultivating a Love of Learning. *Journal of Philosophy of Education*, *53*(3), 477–490. DOI: 10.1111/1467-9752.12377

Gašević, D., Dawson, S., & Siemens, G. (2016). Let's not forget: Learning analytics are about learning. *TechTrends*, *59*(1), 64–71.

Gedamu, W. T., Plank-Wiedenbeck, U., & Wodajo, B. T. (2024). A spatial autocorrelation analysis of road traffic crash by severity using Moran's I spatial statistics: A comparative study of Addis Ababa and Berlin cities. *Accident; Analysis and Prevention*, *200*, 107535. DOI: 10.1016/J.AAP.2024.107535 PMID: 38489942

Gee, J. P. (2003). *What video games have to teach us about learning and literacy*. Palgrave Macmillan.

Genç, H. N., & Kocak, N. (2024). Bibliometric analysis of studies on the artificial intelligence in science education with VOSviewer. *Journal of Education in Science, Environment and Health*, *10*(2), 132–152.

George, E. B., Senthilkumar, R., Al-junaibi, F., & Al-shuaibi, Z. (2025). Explainable AI methods for predicting student grades and improving academic success. *Journal of Information Systems Engineering & Management*, *10*(23s), 117–126.

Ghimire, S., Abdulla, S., Joseph, L. P., Prasad, S., Murphy, A., Devi, A., & Yaseen, Z. M. (2024). Explainable artificial intelligence–machine learning models to estimate overall scores in tertiary preparatory general science course. *Computers and Education: Artificial Intelligence*, *7*, 100331.

Goh, T. T. (2025). Learning management system log analytics: The role of persistence and consistency of engagement behaviour on academic success. *Journal of Computers in Education*, •••, 1–24.

Graham, S., & Harris, K. R. (2005). Improving the writing performance of young struggling writers: Theoretical and programmatic research from the Center on Accelerating Student Learning. *The Journal of Special Education*, *39*(1), 19–33.

Graham, S., & Perin, D. (2007). A meta-analysis of writing instruction for adolescent students. *Journal of Educational Psychology*, *99*(3), 445.

Graves, D. H. (1983). *Writing: Teachers and children at work*. Heinemann.

Guba, E. G., & Lincoln, Y. S. (1994). *Competing paradigms in qualitative research*. In N. K.

Gueldenzoph, L. E., & May, G. L. (2002). Collaborative Peer Evaluation: Best Practices for Group Member Assessments. *Business Communication Quarterly*, *65*(1), 9–20. DOI: 10.1177/108056990206500102

Guo, Y., Gunay, C., Tangirala, S., Kerven, D., Jin, W., Savage, J. C., & Lee, S. (2022). Identifying critical LMS features for predicting at-risk students. *arXiv preprint arXiv:2204.13700*.

Güven, G., & Sülün, Y. (2012). Bilgisayar destekli öğretimin 8. sınıf fen ve teknoloji dersindeki akademik başarıya ve öğrencilerin derse karşı tutumlarına etkisi. *Journal of Turkish Science Education*, *9*(1), 68–79.

Han, J., Kamber, J., & Pei, J. (2022). *Data mining: Concepts and techniques* (4th ed.). Morgan Kaufmann.

Harry, A. (2023). Role of AI in education. *Interdisciplinary Journal and Humanity, 2*(3), 260–268.

Helfenbein, R. J. (2021). Critical geographies of education: Space, place, and curriculum inquiry. *Critical Geographies of Education: Space, Place, and Curriculum Inquiry*, 1–110. https://doi.org//DOI: 10.4324/9781003178590

HEPI. (2025). Student generative AI survey 2025. *Higher Education Policy Institute*. Retrieved from https://www.hepi.ac.uk/2025/02/26/student-generative-ai-survey-2025/

Hokanson, B. (2022). New approaches on education technologies: A global perspective for digital transformation. *JETOL, 5*(4), 775–780.

Holmes, W.. (2022). *AI and education: Guidance for policymakers*. UNESCO.

Holmes, W., Bialik, M., & Fadel, C. (2019). *Artificial intelligence in education: Promises and implications for teaching and learning*. Center for Curriculum Redesign.

Holmes, W., Porayska-Pomsta, K., Holstein, K., Sutherland, E., Baker, T., Shum, S. B., & Koedinger, K. R. (2022). Ethics of AI in education: Towards a community-wide framework. *International Journal of Artificial Intelligence in Education, 32*(3), 504–526.

Holmes, W., & Tuomi, I. (2022). State of the art and practice in AI in education. *European Journal of Education, 57*(4), 542–570.

Holstein, K., & Doroudi, S. (2021). Equity and artificial intelligence in education: Will "AIED" amplify or alleviate inequities in education? *arXiv preprint arXiv:2104.12920.*

Holstein, K., McLaren, B. M., & Aleven, V. (2019). Co-Designing a Real-Time Classroom Orchestration Tool to Support Teacher–AI Complementarity. *Journal of Learning Analytics, 6*(2), 27–52. DOI: 10.18608/jla.2019.62.3

Hs Kumar, A. (2023). Analysis of ChatGPT Tool to Assess the Potential of its Utility for Academic Writing in Biomedical Domain. *Biology, Engineering. Medicine and Science Reports, 9*(1), 24–30. DOI: 10.5530/bems.9.1.5

Hurix Digital. (2025). AI-enabled assessment: Redefining evaluation in education. Retrieved from https://www.hurix.com/blogs/ai-enabled-assessment-redefining-evaluation-in-education/

Hwang, G.-J., Xie, H., Wah, B. W., & Gašević, D. (2020). Vision, challenges, roles and research issues of Artificial Intelligence in Education. *Computers and Education: Artificial Intelligence, 1*, 100001. DOI: 10.1016/j.caeai.2020.100001

Hyland, K. (2003). Genre-based pedagogies: A social response to process. *Journal of Second Language Writing*, *12*(1), 17–29.

İçen, M. (2022). The future of education utilizing artificial intelligence in Turkey. *Humanities & Social Sciences Communications*, *9*(1), 268. DOI: 10.1057/s41599-022-01284-4

Ifraheem, S., Rasheed, M., & Siddiqui, A. (2024). Transforming Education Through Artificial Intelligence: Personalization, Engagement and Predictive Analytics. *Journal of Asian Development Studies*, *13*(2), 250–266. DOI: 10.62345/jads.2024.13.2.22

Isiaku, L., Muhammad, A. S., Kefas, H. I., & Ukaegbu, F. C. (2024). Enhancing technological sustainability in academia: Leveraging ChatGPT for teaching, learning and evaluation. *Quality Education for All*, *1*(1), 385–416. DOI: 10.1108/QEA-07-2024-0055

Janowicz, K. (2023). Philosophical Foundations of GeoAI: Exploring Sustainability, Diversity, and Bias in GeoAI and Spatial Data Science. *Handbook of Geospatial Artificial Intelligence*, 26–42. https://doi.org/DOI: 10.1201/9781003308423-3

Jie, A. L. X., & Kamrozzaman, N. A. (2024). The Challenges of Higher Education Students Face in Using Artificial Intelligence (AI) against Their Learning Experiences. *Open Journal of Social Sciences*, *12*(10), 362–387. DOI: 10.4236/jss.2024.1210025

Jin, Y., Yan, L., Echeverria, V., Gašević, D., & Martinez-Maldonado, R. (2024). Generative AI in higher education: A global perspective of institutional adoption policies and guidelines. *arXiv preprint arXiv:2405.11800*. https://doi.org//arXiv.2405.11800DOI: 10.48550

Jobin, A., Ienca, M., & Vayena, E. (2019). The global landscape of AI ethics guidelines. *Nature Machine Intelligence*, *1*(9), 389–399. DOI: 10.1038/s42256-019-0088-2

Johnson, A. P. (2008). *Teaching reading and writing: A guidebook for tutoring and remediating students*. Rowman and Littlefield Education.

Jones, M. G., Rua, M. J., & Carter, G. (1998). Science teachers' conceptual growth within Vygotsky's zone of proximal development. *Journal of Research in Science Teaching: The Official Journal of the National Association for Research in Science Teaching*, *35*(9), 967–985.

Kacena, M. A., Plotkin, L. I., & Fehrenbacher, J. C. (2024). The use of artificial intelligence in writing scientific review articles. *Current Osteoporosis Reports*, •••, 1–7. PMID: 38227177

Kaival. (2025). Enhancing survey creation with generative AI: A guide to dynamic and customized questionnaires. *Medium.* Retrieved from https://medium.com/@Neopric/enhancing-survey-creation-with-generative-ai-a-guide-to-dynamic-and-customized-questionnaires-91dc8961d854

Kaldırım, A. (2014). The effect of 6+1 analytical writing and evaluation model on the sixth-grade students' writing expression skills (Unpublished master's thesis). Kütahya Dumlupınar University, Graduate School of Educational Sciences.

Kaldırım, A., & Tavşanlı, Ö. F. (2021). A thematic review of using digital teaching technologies in Turkish language teaching. *Journal of Educational Technology and Online Learning*, *4*(2), 70–95. DOI: 10.31681/jetol.898014

Kalkan, Ç. (2024, June 5). What is the Importance of STEM Education in Climate Change and Sustainability Education for Children? - Scientix blog Sustainable Development Goals. *Scientix Blog*. https://blog.scientix.eu/2024/06/what-is-the-importance-of-stem-education-in-climate-change-and-sustainable-development-goals-for-children/

Kamruzzaman, M. M., Alanazi, S., Alruwaili, M., Alshammari, N., Elaiwat, S., Innab, N., Mohammad Elzaghmouri, B., & Ahmed Alanazi, B. (2022). AI- and IoT-Assisted Sustainable Education Systems during Pandemics, such as COVID-19, for Smart Cities. *Sustainability*, *15*(10), 8354. DOI: 10.3390/su15108354

Kandlhofer, M., Steinbauer, G., Hirschmugl-Gaisch, S., & Huber, P. (2016). Artificial intelligence and computer science in education: From kindergarten to university. *2016 IEEE Frontiers in Education Conference (FIE)*, 1–9. DOI: 10.1109/FIE.2016.7757570

Karadağ, N. (2023). The impact of artificial intelligence on online assessment: A preliminary review. *Journal of Educational Technology & Online Learning*, *6*(4), 822–837.

Karadağ, N. (2023). The impact of artificial intelligence on online assessment: A preliminary review. *Journal of Educational Technology and Online Learning*, *6*(4), 822–837. DOI: 10.31681/jetol.1351548

Karataş, F., Eriçok, B., & Tanrikulu, L. (2025). Reshaping curriculum adaptation in the age of artificial intelligence: Mapping teachers' AI-driven curriculum adaptation patterns. *British Educational Research Journal*, *51*(1), 154–180.

Karelkhan, N., Kadirbek, A., & Schmidt, P. (2023). Setting Up and Implementing ArcGIS to Work with Maps and Geospatial Data with Python for Teaching Geoinformation Systems in Higher Education. *International Journal of Emerging Technologies in Learning*, *18*(14). Advance online publication. DOI: 10.3991/ijet.v18i14.39833

Kaşcı, T., & Selçuk, G. (2021). Examination of classroom teachers' technological pedagogical content knowledge and teacher self-efficacy beliefs. *Journal of Educational Technology and Online Learning*, *4*(4), 774–792. DOI: 10.31681/jetol.1018879

Kasneci, E., Sessler, K., & König, C. (2023). ChatGPT for good? On opportunities and challenges of large language models for education. *Learning and Individual Differences*, *103*, 102274. DOI: 10.1016/j.lindif.2023.102274

Katiyar, N., Awasthi, M. V. K., Pratap, R., Mishra, M. K., Shukla, M. N., Tiwari, M., & Singh, R. (2024). AI-driven personalized learning systems: Enhancing educational effectiveness. *Educational Administration: Theory and Practice*, *30*(5), 11514–11524.

Kauffman, H. (2015). A review of predictive factors of student success in and satisfaction with online learning. *Research in Learning Technology*, •••, 23.

Kayabas, İ. (2024). Innovative curriculum development and content creation with generative AI. In *Transforming Education With Generative AI: Prompt Engineering and Synthetic Content Creation* (pp. 462-473). IGI Global Scientific Publishing.

Kearney, M.-L. (2009). Higher education, research and innovation: Charting the course of the changing dynamics of the knowledge society. In Meek, V. L., Teichler, U., & Kearney, M.-L. (Eds.), *Higher education, research and innovation: Changing dynamics* (pp. 7–23). INCHER and UNESCO.

Kelley, J., & Wenzel, A. (2025). Advancing artificial intelligence literacy in teacher education through professional partnership inquiry. *Education Sciences*, *15*(6), 659.

Kellogg, R. T. (1994). *The psychology of writing*. Oxford University Press.

Keskin, S., & Yurdugül, H. (2022). E-learning experience: Modeling students' e-learning interactions using log data. *Journal of Educational Technology and Online Learning*, *5*(1), 1–13.

Khallaf, A. N., & Alqerafi, M. (2024). Using Ai to Help Reduce the Effect of Global Warming. *Power System Technology*, *48*(1), 1927–1947. DOI: 10.52783/pst.464

Khlaif, Z. N., Ayyoub, A., Hamamra, B., Bensalem, E., Mitwally, M. A., Ayyoub, A., Mogannam, B., Sanmugam, M., Joma, A. I., Itmazi, J., Shaqour, A. Z., & Tairab, H. (2024). University teachers' views on the adoption and integration of generative AI tools for student assessment in higher education. *Education Sciences*, *14*(10), 1090. DOI: 10.3390/educsci14101090

Khurana, V. (2024). Accelerating pace of scientific discovery and innovation through big data enabled artificial intelligence and deep learning. *Emerging Trends in Machine Intelligence and Big Data*, *16*(1), 38–53.

KIDSPARK. (2024, July 16). *AI & STEM Education: Leveraging Technology to Teach STEM*. https://kidsparkeducation.org/blog/ai-stem-education-leveraging-technology-to-teach-stem

Kılınç, S. (2024). Comprehensive AI assessment framework: Enhancing educational evaluation with ethical AI integration. *Journal of Educational Technology and Online Learning*, *7*(4), 521–540. DOI: 10.31681/jetol.1492695

Kitila, F. (2023). The Impact of Writing Through Integrated Skills Intervention on English Students' Writing Skills: Focus on Vocabulary and Grammar. *Journal of Language Teaching and Research*, *14*(2), 297–303.

Kıyıcı, O. D., & Dikkartın Övez, F. T. (2021). Examination of technology acceptance and TPACK competencies ofmathematics teachers who are involved in distance education practices during the pandemic process. *Journal of Educational Technology and Online Learning*, *4*(4), 805–821.

Kleesiek, J., Wu, Y., Stiglic, G., Egger, J., & Bian, J. (2023). An opinion on ChatGPT in health care—Written by humans only. *Journal of Nuclear Medicine*, *64*(5), 701–703. DOI: 10.2967/jnumed.123.265687 PMID: 37055219

Koedinger, K. R., Anderson, J. R., Hadley, W. H., & Mark, M. A. (1997). Intelligent tutoring goes to school in the big city. *International Journal of Artificial Intelligence in Education*, *8*(1), 30–43.

Koehler, M. J., Mishra, P., & Cain, W. (2013). What is technological pedagogical content knowledge (TPACK)? *Journal of Education*, *193*(3), 13–19.

Koh, W. Y. (2017). Effective applications of automated writing feedback in process-based writing instruction. *English Teaching*, *72*(3), 91–118.

Kolhe, N. P., Dhote, K. K., & Parihar, A. (2023). *Mapping the Access of Internet Facility to Schedule Tribe Population—An Approach Towards Digital Education*. 1–20. https://doi.org/DOI: 10.1007/978-981-19-8967-4_1

Kose, U., & Arslan, A. (2017). Optimization of self-learning in Computer Engineering courses: An intelligent software system supported by Artificial Neural Network and Vortex Optimization Algorithm. *Computer Applications in Engineering Education, 25*(1), 142–156. DOI: 10.1002/cae.21787

Kotei, E., & Thirunavukarasu, R. (2023). A systematic review of transformer-based pre-trained language models through self-supervised learning. *Information (Basel), 14*(3), 187. DOI: 10.3390/info14030187

Krasovskiy, D. (2020, October 30). *The Challenges and Benefits of Adopting AI in STEM Education.* https://upjourney.com/the-challenges-and-benefits-of-adopting-ai-in-stem-education

Krullaars, Z. H., Januardani, A., Zhou, L., & Jonkers, E. (2023). *Exploring Initial Interactions: High School Students and Generative AI Chatbots for Relationship Development.* DOI: 10.18420/MUC2023-MCI-SRC-415

Labadze, L., Grigolia, M., & Machaidze, L. (2023). Role of AI chatbots in education: Systematic literature review. *International Journal of Educational Technology in Higher Education, 20*(1), 56. DOI: 10.1186/s41239-023-00426-1

Lantolf, J. P., & Pavlenko, A. (1995). Sociocultural theory and second language acquisition. *Annual Review of Applied Linguistics, 15*, 108–124.

Latour, B. (2005). From Realpolitik to Dingpolitik or How to Make Things Public. In Latour, B., & Weibel, P. (Eds.), *Making Things Public: Atmospheres of Democracy* (pp. 14–41). MIT Press.

Lave, J., & Wenger, E. (1991). *Situated learning: Legitimate peripheral participation.* Cambridge University Press.

Law, N. (2014). Comparing pedagogical innovations. In *Comparative education research: Approaches and methods* (pp. 333–364). Springer International Publishing.

Leal, D. C., Capetillo, A., & Castorena, D. G. (2025, January 28). *Prompting literature review: The impact of Transformer models and ChatGPT on prompt engineering and AI research publications.* In *2025 Institute for the Future of Education Conference (IFE)* (pp. 1–7). IEEE. doi:DOI: 10.1109/IFE62519.2025.1234567

Lee, H., Chae, M. S., Park, J. Y., Lim, K. J., & Park, Y. S. (2022). Development and Application of a QGIS-Based Model to Estimate Monthly Streamflow. *ISPRS International Journal of Geo-Information, 11*(1). Advance online publication. DOI: 10.3390/ijgi11010040

Lee, S., Choe, H., Zou, D., & Jeon, J. (2025). Generative AI (GenAI) in the language classroom: A systematic review. *Interactive Learning Environments*, •••, 1–25. DOI: 10.1080/10494820.2025.2498537

Lee, U., Jung, H., Jeon, Y., Sohn, Y., Hwang, W., Moon, J., & Kim, H. (2024). Few-shot is enough: Exploring ChatGPT prompt engineering method for automatic question generation in English education. *Education and Information Technologies*, *29*, 11483–11515. DOI: 10.1007/s10639-023-12249-8

Leibel, C., & Bornmann, L. (2024). Specification uncertainty: What the disruption index tells us about the (hidden) multiverse of bibliometric indicators. *Scientometrics*, *129*(12), 7971–7979. DOI: 10.1007/s11192-024-05201-1

Levin, N. A. (2021). Process mining combined with expert feature engineering to predict efficient use of time on high-stakes assessments. *Journal of Educational Data Mining*, *13*(2), 1–15.

Li, M. Z. (2024, March 9). *Using prompt engineering to enhance STEM education*. In *2024 IEEE Integrated STEM Education Conference (ISEC)* (pp. 262–267). IEEE. https://doi.org/DOI: 10.1109/ISEC61299.2024.10664775

Li, B., Lily Tan, Y., Wang, C., & Lowell, V. (2025). Two years of innovation: A systematic review of empirical generative AI research in language learning and teaching. *Computers and Education: Artificial Intelligence*, *9*, 1–27.

Lincoln, Y. S., & Guba, E. G. (1985). *Naturalistic inquiry*. Sage Publications.

Lin, Y., Li, C., & Li, H. (2025). Comparing AI-generated and traditional textbook multiple-choice questions in nursing education: A prompt engineering-based Delphi study. *Medical Teacher*. Advance online publication. DOI: 10.1080/0142159X.2025.2533401 PMID: 40684326

Liu, M., Li, Y., Xu, W., & Liu, L. (2017). Automated Essay Feedback Generation and Its Impact on Revision. *IEEE Transactions on Learning Technologies*, *10*(4), 502–513. DOI: 10.1109/TLT.2016.2612659

Liu, P., Yuan, W., Fu, J., Jiang, Z., Hayashi, H., & Neubig, G. (2021). Pre-train, prompt, and predict: A systematic survey ofprompting methods in natural language processing. arXiv: 2107.13586.

Liu, T., Gao, Z., & Guan, H. (2021). Educational information system optimization for artificial intelligence teaching strategies. *Complexity*, •••, 1–13.

Li, Z., & Ning, H. (2023). Autonomous GIS: The next-generation AI-powered GIS. *International Journal of Digital Earth*, *16*(2), 4668–4686. DOI: 10.1080/17538947.2023.2278895

Long, T. T., Lam, N. T., & Cuong, T. Q. (2025, January). AI Integration into Curriculum Design and Development: Theoretical Framework and Application. In *International Conference on Mathematical Modeling and Computational Science* (pp. 352-361). Cham: Springer Nature Switzerland.

Lotka, A. J. (1926). The frequency distribution of scientific productivity. *Journal of the Washington Academy of Sciences*, *16*(12), 317–323.

Lubowitz, J. H. (2023). ChatGPT, An Artificial Intelligence Chatbot, Is Impacting Medical Literature. *Arthroscopy*, *39*(5), 1121–1122. DOI: 10.1016/j.arthro.2023.01.015 PMID: 36797148

Luckin, R., Cukurova, M., Kent, C., & Du Boulay, B. (2022). Empowering educators to be AI-ready. *Computers and Education: Artificial Intelligence*, *3*, 100076.

Luckin, R., Holmes, W., Griffiths, M., & Forcier, L. B. (2016). *Intelligence unleashed: An argument for AI in education*. Pearson Education.

Lundberg, S. M., & Lee, S. I. (2017). A unified approach to interpreting model predictions. *Advances in Neural Information Processing Systems*, **•••**, 30.

Lundstrom, P. (1996). Task-based language teaching in a learner-centered ESP setting: A case study. *Revista de Lenguas para Fines Específicos*, *3*, 199–213.

Lykourentzou, I., Giannoukos, I., Mpardis, G., Nikolopoulos, V., & Loumos, V. (2009). Early and dynamic student achievement prediction in e-learning courses using neural networks. *Journal of the American Society for Information Science and Technology*, *60*(2), 372–380.

Macfadyen, L. P., & Dawson, S. (2010). Mining LMS data to develop an "early warning system" for educators: A proof of concept. *Computers & Education*, *54*(2), 588–599.

Macías, M. (2023). English for specific purposes in Spain: Project based learning classroom proposal in vocational education. *International Journal of Professional Development. Learners and Learning*, *5*(1), 1–9.

Madanipour, A., Shucksmith, M., & Brooks, E. (2022). The concept of spatial justice and the European Union's territorial cohesion. *European Planning Studies*, *30*(5), 807–824. DOI: 10.1080/09654313.2021.1928040

Mao, J., Chen, B., & Liu, J. C. (2024). Generative artificial intelligence in education and its implications for assessment. *TechTrends*, *68*(1), 58–66.

Marginson, S. (2011). Higher education and public good. *Higher Education Quarterly*, *65*, 411–433.

Marino, M. T., Vasquez, E., Dieker, L., Basham, J., & Blackorby, J. (2023). The Future of Artificial Intelligence in Special Education Technology. *Journal of Special Education Technology*. Advance online publication. 10.1177_01626434231165977

Maron, M. E. (1961). Automatic indexing: An experimental inquiry. *Journal of the Association for Computing Machinery*, *8*(3), 404–417.

Marras, A., Fornara, F., & Pasqualotto, A. (2025). Harnessing AI for Inclusive Teaching: Professional Development Strategies for Early Educators. *AI in Early Education: Integrating Artificial Intelligence for Inclusive and Effective Learning*, 267-290.

Martin, R., Martinelli, F., & Clifton, J. (2022). Rethinking spatial policy in an era of multiple crises. *Cambridge Journal of Regions, Economy and Society*, *15*(1), 3–21. DOI: 10.1093/CJRES/RSAB037

Maspul, K. A. (2024). Exploring STEM Education for Real-World Climate Change Concerns to Empower Students as Change Agents. *Journal of Physics Education and Science*, *1*(2), 12. DOI: 10.47134/physics.v1i2.249

Mayer, R. E. (2005). *The Cambridge handbook of multimedia learning*. Cambridge University Press.

MEB. (2024). *Eğitimde kullanılabilecek yapay zekâ araçları rehberi*. Yenilik ve Eğitim Teknolojileri Genel Müdürlüğü.

Mehrabi, A., Morphew, J. W., Araabi, B. N., Memarian, N., & Memarian, H. (2024). AI-Enhanced Decision-Making for Course Modality Preferences in Higher Engineering Education during the Post-COVID-19 Era. *Information (Basel)*, *15*(10), 590. DOI: 10.3390/info15100590

Melo-López, V. A., Basantes-Andrade, A., Gudiño-Mejía, C. B., & Hernández-Martínez, E. (2025). The Impact of Artificial Intelligence on Inclusive Education: A Systematic Review. *Education Sciences*, *15*(5), 539.

Merriam, S. B., & Tisdell, E. J. (2016). *Qualitative research: A guide to design and implementation* (4th ed.). Jossey-Bass.

Miles, M. B., & Huberman, A. M. (1994). Qualitative Data Analysis: An Expanded Sourcebook. *Sage (Atlanta, Ga.)*.

Mishra, P., & Koehler, M. J. (2006). Technological pedagogical content knowledge: A framework for integrating technology in teacher knowledge. *Teachers College Record, 108*(6), 1017–1054.

Mollick, E. R., & Mollick, L. (2022). New modes of learning enabled by AI chatbots: Three methods and assignments. (SSRN *Scholarly Paper* 4300783). 10.2139/ssrn.4300783

Moraga, P. (2023). Spatial Statistics for Data Science: Theory and Practice with R. *Spatial Statistics for Data Science: Theory and Practice with R*, 1–279. https://doi.org//DOI: 10.1201/9781032641522

Mosly, I. (2024). Artificial intelligence's opportunities and challenges in engineering curricular design: A combined review and focus group study. *Societies (Basel, Switzerland), 14*(6), 89.

Murari, U. K., & Parmar, H. (2025). Ethical Integration of Artificial Intelligence in Inclusive Education: Addressing Challenges and Advancing Opportunities for Equitable Learning. In *Ethics and AI Integration Into Modern Classrooms* (pp. 439-470). IGI Global Scientific Publishing.

Murray, D. M. (1982). Teaching the other self: The writer's first reader. *College Composition and Communication, 33*(1), 140–147.

Musikhin, I. (2016). English for specific purposes: Teaching English for science and technology. *ISPRS Annals of the Photogrammetry, Remote Sensing and Spatial Information Sciences, III-6*, 29–35. DOI: 10.5194/isprs-annals-III-6-29-2016

Mystakidis, S., Christopoulos, A., & Pellas, N. (2022). A systematic mapping review of augmented reality applications to support STEM learning in higher education. *Education and Information Technologies, 27*(2), 1883–1927. DOI: 10.1007/s10639-021-10682-1

National Centre for AI. (2024). AI: Empowering inclusive education - Supporting special needs and tackling language barriers. Retrieved from https://nationalcentreforai.jiscinvolve.org/wp/2024/01/09/ai-empowering-inclusive-education/

Neuman, S. B., & Roskos, K. (2007). Literacy knowledge in practice: Contexts of participation for young writers and readers. *Early Childhood Research Quarterly, 22*(1), 27–43.

Ngo, T. N. (2025). Artificial intelligence for academic purposes (AIAP): Conceptualizing AI literacy and educational practices. *Educational Research Review, 28*, 102–118.

Nguyen, T. V., Mohd Daril, M. A., Ali, M., & Korejo, M. S. (2024). Enhancing psychological well-being in higher education post-COVID-19 pandemic: The role of AI-based support systems—Bibliometric reviews. [iJOE]. *International Journal of Online and Biomedical Engineering*, *20*(6), 139–152. DOI: 10.3991/ijoe.v20i06.48001

Nixon, N., Lin, Y., & Snow, L. (2024). Catalyzing Equity in STEM Teams: Harnessing Generative AI for Inclusion and Diversity. *Policy Insights from the Behavioral and Brain Sciences*, *11*(1), 85–92. DOI: 10.1177/23727322231220356 PMID: 38516055

Nnadi, L. C., Watanobe, Y., Rahman, M. M., & John-Otumu, A. M. (2024). Prediction of students' adaptability using explainable AI in educational machine learning models. *Applied Sciences (Basel, Switzerland)*, *14*(12), 5141.

Noble, S. U. (2018). *Algorithms of oppression: How search engines reinforce racism*. NYU Press.

Nowell, L. S., Norris, J. M., White, D. E., & Moules, N. J. (2017). Thematic analysis: Striving to meet the trustworthiness criteria. *International Journal of Qualitative Methods*, *16*, 1–13.

O'Connor, S., Peltonen, L. M., Topaz, M., Chen, L. Y. A., Michalowski, M., Ronquillo, C., & Denis-Lalonde, D. (2024). Prompt engineering when using generative AI in nursing education. *Nurse Education in Practice*, *74*, 103825. DOI: 10.1016/j.nepr.2023.103825 PMID: 37957062

O'Connor, S., Permana, A., Neville, S., & Denis-Lalonde, D. (2023). Artificial intelligence in nursing education 2: Opportunities and threats. *Nursing Times*, *119*(11). https://www.nursingtimes.net/roles/nurse-educators/artificial-intelligence-in-nursing-education-2-opportunities-and-threats-09-10-2023/

O'Neil, C. (2016). *Weapons of math destruction: How big data increases inequality and threatens democracy*. Crown.

OECD. (n.d.). *OECD artificial intelligence papers. OECD*. https://www.oecd.org/en/publications/serials/oecd-artificial-intelligence-papers_74018992.html

Okonkwo, C. W., & Ade-Ibijola, A. (2021). Chatbots applications in education: A systematic review. *Computers and Education: Artificial Intelligence*, *2*, 100033. DOI: 10.1016/j.caeai.2021.100033

OkusFocus. (2025). AI-Powered Reading Analysis. https://www.okusfokus.com/

Öncü, S. E., Gevher, M., & Erdoğdu, E. (2025). Exploring the potential use of generative AI for learner support in ODL at scale. *Journal of Educational Technology & Online Learning*, *8*(1), 80–99.

Öncü, S., Çolakoğlu, M., & Cigdem, H. (2025). Leveraging AI-Managed Learning Analytics and Micro-Credentials for Enhanced Student Engagement. In *Integrating Micro-Credentials With AI in Open Education* (pp. 133–152). IGI Global Scientific Publishing. DOI: 10.4018/979-8-3693-5488-9.ch007

Öncü, S., Çolakoğlu, M., & Colak, H. (2024). Engagement dynamics in information technology education: A comparative analysis of online vs. face-to-face instruction. *Journal of Educational Technology and Online Learning*, *7*(3), 321–333. DOI: 10.31681/jetol.1508735

Oppenlaender, J., Linder, R., & Silvennoinen, J. (2023). Prompting AI art: An investigation into the creative skill of promptengineering. arXiv. Doi:10.48550/arXiv.2303.13534

Ouatik, F., Ouatik, F., Fadli, H., Elgorari, A., Mohadab, M. E. L., & Raoufi, M. (2021). E-learning & decision-making system for automate students assessment using remote laboratory and machine learning. *Journal of E-Learning and Knowledge Society*, *17*(1), 90–100.

Ouyang, F., & Jiao, P. (2021). Artificial intelligence in education: The three paradigms. *Computers and Education: Artificial Intelligence*, *2*, 100020. DOI: 10.1016/j.caeai.2021.100020

Ouyang, F., Jiao, P., McLaren, B. M., & Alavi, A. H. (2022). *Artificial Intelligence in STEM Education: The Paradigmatic Shifts in Research, Education, and Technology*. CRC Press.

Ouyang, F., Zheng, L., & Jiao, P. (2022). Artificial intelligence in online higher education: A systematic review of empirical research from 2011 to 2020. *Education and Information Technologies*, *27*(6), 7893–7925. DOI: 10.1007/s10639-022-10925-9

Ouyang, Z., Jiang, Y., & Liu, H. (2024). The effects of Duolingo, an AI-integrated technology, on EFL learners' willingness to communicate and engagement in online classes. *International Review of Research in Open and Distance Learning*, *25*(3), 98–118. DOI: 10.19173/irrodl.v25i3.7677

Özen, E., & Kurtuluş, A. (2023). A study on mathematics teachers' technological pedagogical content knowledge (TPACK) and frequency of use of educational information network (EBA) assessment tools. *Journal of Educational Technology and Online Learning*, *6*(4), 1009–1026.

Paglialunga, A., & Melogno, S. (2025). The Effectiveness of Artificial Intelligence-Based Interventions for Students with Learning Disabilities: A Systematic Review. *Brain Sciences*, *15*(8), 806. DOI: 10.3390/brainsci15080806 PMID: 40867139

Pai, K.-C., Kuo, B.-C., Liao, C.-H., & Liu, Y.-M. (2021). An application of Chinese dialogue-based intelligent tutoring system in remedial instruction for mathematics learning. *Educational Psychology*, *41*(2), 137–152. DOI: 10.1080/01443410.2020.1731427

Pali ă, E. (2023). Teaching English in the artificial intelligence context. *Research and Science Today*, *2*(26), 56–62.

Panjwani-Charania, S., & Zhai, X. (2024). AI for Students with Learning Disabilities: A Systematic Review. *Uses of Artificial Intelligence in STEM Education*, 469.

Pan, Z., Biegley, L., Taylor, A., & Zheng, H. (2024). A systematic review of learning analytics: Incorporated instructional interventions on learning management systems. *Journal of Learning Analytics*, *11*(2), 52–72.

Papamitsiou, Z., & Economides, A. A. (2014). Learning analytics and educational data mining in practice: A systematic literature review of empirical evidence. *Journal of Educational Technology & Society*, *17*(4), 49–64.

Park, J., Teo, T. W., Teo, A., Chang, J., Huang, J. S., & Koo, S. (2023). Integrating artificial intelligence into science lessons: Teachers' experiences and views. *International Journal of STEM Education*, *10*(1), 61. DOI: 10.1186/s40594-023-00454-3

Pebesma, E., & Bivand, R. (2023). Spatial Data Science: With Applications in R. In *Spatial Data Science: With Applications in R.* https://doi.org/DOI: 10.1201/9780429459016

Pereira, G. W., Valente, D. S. M., de Queiroz, D. M., Coelho, A. L. de F., Costa, M. M., & Grift, T. (2022). Smart-Map: An Open-Source QGIS Plugin for Digital Mapping Using Machine Learning Techniques and Ordinary Kriging. *Agronomy 2022, Vol. 12, Page 1350, 12*(6), 1350. https://doi.org/DOI: 10.3390/AGRONOMY12061350

Peres, R., Schreier, M., Schweidel, D., & Sorescu, A. (2023). On ChatGPT and beyond: How generative artificial intelligence may affect research, teaching, and practice. *International Journal of Research in Marketing*, *40*(2), 269–275. DOI: 10.1016/j.ijresmar.2023.03.001

Perrotta, C., & Williamson, B. (2018). The social life of learning analytics: Cluster analysis and the 'performance' of algorithmic education. *Learning, Media and Technology*, *43*(1), 3–16. DOI: 10.1080/17439884.2016.1182927

Piaget, J. (1972). *The psychology of the child.* Basic Books.

Price, D. J. de S. (1963). *Little science, big science.* Columbia University Press.

Pritchard, A. (1969). Statistical bibliography or bibliometrics? *The Journal of Documentation*, *25*(4), 348–349.

Puranik, C. S., & Lonigan, C. J. (2014). Emergent writing in preschoolers: Preliminary evidence for a theoretical framework. *Reading Research Quarterly*, *49*(4), 453–467. PMID: 25316955

Quansah, R., & Essiam, C. (2021). The use of learning management system (LMS) moodle in the midst of covid-19 pandemic: Students' perspective. *Journal of Educational Technology and Online Learning*, *4*(3), 418–431.

QuestionPro. (2024). QuestionPro AI: Build surveys using artificial intelligence. Retrieved from https://www.questionpro.com/features/qxbot.html

Quinlan, J. R. (1993). *C4.5: Programs for machine learning*. Morgan Kaufmann.

Raji, I. D., Scheuerman, M. K., & Amironesei, R. (2021, March). You can't sit with us: Exclusionary pedagogy in ai ethics education. In *Proceedings of the 2021 ACM conference on fairness, accountability, and transparency* (pp. 515-525).

Rakap, S. (2024). Navigating the role of artificial intelligence in special education: Advantages, disadvantages, and ethical considerations. *Practice*, *6*(2–3), 99–104. DOI: 10.1080/25783858.2024.2411948

Rawat, A. K., Dahiya, M., & Khushpal. (2025). Comparative study of Sondh village through Geospatial data analytics using QGIS, Tableau and GeoPandas. *Progressive Computational Intelligence, Information Technology and Networking*, 474–480. https://doi.org//DOI: 10.1201/9781003650010-78

Razzaq, L., Patvarczki, J., Almeida, S. F., Vartak, M., Feng, M., Heffernan, N. T., & Koedinger, K. R. (2009). The ASSISTment Builder: Supporting the Life Cycle of Tutoring System Content Creation. *IEEE Transactions on Learning Technologies*, 2(2), 157–166. DOI: 10.1109/TLT.2009.23

Ren, X., & Wu, M. L. (2025). Examining teaching competencies and challenges while integrating artificial intelligence in higher education. *TechTrends*, *69*(1), 519–538. DOI: 10.1007/s11528-025-01055-3

Reynolds, L., & McDonell, K. (2021). Prompt programming for large language models: Beyond the few-shot paradigm. arXiv: 2102.07350. doi:10.48550/arXiv.2102.07350

Ribeiro, M. T., Singh, S., & Guestrin, C. (2016, August). "Why should I trust you?" Explaining the predictions of any classifier. In *Proceedings of the 22nd ACM SIGKDD International Conference on Knowledge Discovery and Data Mining* (pp. 1135–1144).

Rice, M. F., & Dunn, S. (2023). The Use of Artificial Intelligence with Students with Identified Disabilities: A Systematic Review with Critique. *Computers in the Schools*, *40*(4), 370–390. DOI: 10.1080/07380569.2023.2244935

Riegler, A., Wintersberger, P., Riener, A., & Holzmann, C. (2019). Augmented Reality Windshield Displays and Their Potential to Enhance User Experience in Automated Driving. *I-Com*, *18*(2), 127–149. DOI: 10.1515/icom-2018-0033

Riestra-González, M., del Puerto Paule-Ruíz, M., & Ortin, F. (2021). Massive LMS log data analysis for the early prediction of course-agnostic student performance. *Computers & Education*, *163*, 104108.

Rizvi, I., Bose, C., & Tripathi, N. (2025). Transforming Education: Adaptive Learning, AI, and Online Platforms for Personalization. In *Technology for Societal Transformation: Exploring the Intersection of Information Technology and Societal Development* (pp. 45–62). Springer Nature Singapore.

Rodríguez-Ortiz, M. Á., Santana-Mancilla, P. C., & Anido-Rifón, L. E. (2025). Machine learning and generative AI in learning analytics for higher education: A systematic review of models, trends, and challenges. *Applied Sciences (Basel, Switzerland)*, *15*(15), 8679.

Rogoff, B. (2003). *The cultural nature of human development*. Oxford University Press.

Romadhon, R. (2024). AI in language learning: English for specific purposes perceptions toward ChatGPT. *Lingua Journal*, *2024*(4), 120–135.

Romero, C., & Ventura, S. (2020). Educational data mining and learning analytics: An updated survey. *Wiley Interdisciplinary Reviews. Data Mining and Knowledge Discovery*, *10*(3), e1355.

Roscoe, R. D., Varner, L. K., Crossley, S. A., & McNamara, D. S. (2017). Unlocking the potential of automated writing evaluation: Feedback, coaching, and revision. *Educational Psychology Review*, *29*(1), 139–165.

Rosé, C. P., McLaughlin, E. A., Liu, R., & Koedinger, K. R. (2019). Explanatory learner models: Why machine learning (alone) is not the answer. *British Journal of Educational Technology*, *50*(6), 2943–2958. DOI: 10.1111/bjet.12858

Rose, D. H., & Meyer, A. (2002). *Teaching every student in the digital age: Universal Design for Learning*. Association for Supervision and Curriculum Development.

Rudolph, J., Tan, S., & Tan, S. (2023). ChatGPT: Bullshit spewer or the end of traditional assessments in higher education? *Journal of Applied Learning & Teaching*, *6*(1), 1–22. DOI: 10.37074/jalt.2023.6.1.9

Ruiz Viruel, S., Sánchez Rivas, E., & Ruiz Palmero, J. (2025). The Role of Artificial Intelligence in Project-Based Learning: Teacher Perceptions and Pedagogical Implications. *Education Sciences*, *15*(2), 1–18.

Saborío-Taylor, S., & Rojas-Ramírez, F. (2024). Universal design for learning and artificial intelligence in the digital era: Fostering inclusion and autonomous learning. *International Journal of Professional Development. Learners and Learning*, *6*(2), ep2408. Advance online publication. DOI: 10.30935/ijpdll/14694

Sarker, I. H. (2021). Data Science and Analytics: An Overview from Data-Driven Smart Computing, Decision-Making and Applications Perspective. *SN Computer Science*, *2*(5), 1–22. DOI: 10.1007/S42979-021-00765-8 PMID: 34278328

Schiff, D. (2022). Education for AI, not AI for education: The role of education and ethics in national AI policy strategies. *International Journal of Artificial Intelligence in Education*, *32*(3), 527–563.

Segal, M. (2019). A more human approach to artificial intelligence. *Nature*, *571*(7766), S18–S18. PMID: 31341307

Selwyn, N. (2019). *Should robots replace teachers? AI and the future of education*. Polity Press.

Selwyn, N. (2021). *Education and Technology: Key Issues and Debates*. Bloomsbury Publishing.

Selwyn, N. (2022). The future of AI and education: Some cautionary notes. *European Journal of Education*, *57*(4), 620–631.

Selwyn, N. (2022). The future of AI and education: Some critical challenges. *Prometheus*, *37*(1), 22–36. DOI: 10.13169/prometheus.37.1.0022

Senemoğlu, N. (2012). *Gelişim öğrenme ve öğretim: Kuramdan uygulamaya*. Pegem Akademi.

Sevim, N., Erol, O., & Başer Gülsoy, V. G. (2023). Examination of the correlation between e-learning readiness and achievement goal orientation of college students. *Journal of Educational Technology and Online Learning*, *6*(1), 184–201.

Shelton, B. E., Hung, J. L., & Lowenthal, P. R. (2017). Predicting student success by modeling student interaction in asynchronous online courses. *Distance Education*, *38*(1), 59–69.

Shi, Y. (2022). Advances in Big Data Analytics: Theory, Algorithms and Practices. *Advances in Big Data Analytics: Theory, Algorithms and Practices*, 1–728. https://doi.org//DOI: 10.1007/978-981-16-3607-3

Siemens, G., & Baker, R. S. (2012). Learning analytics and educational data mining: Towards communication and collaboration. *In Proceedings of the 2nd International Conference on Learning Analytics and Knowledge* (pp. 252–254). ACM. https://doi.org/DOI: 10.1145/2330601.2330661

Silva, G., Godwin, G., & Jayanagara, O. (2024). The Impact of AI on Personalized Learning and Educational Analytics. [ITEE]. *International Transactions on Education Technology*, *3*(1), 36–46. DOI: 10.33050/itee.v3i1.669

Silver, R. E., Kogut, G., & Huynh, T. C. D. (2019). Learning “new” instructional strategies: Pedagogical innovation, teacher professional development, understanding and concerns. *Journal of Teacher Education*, *70*(5), 552–566.

Singha, S., & Singha, R. (2024). Revolutionizing content creation and curriculum development through generative AI. In *Transforming Education With Generative AI: Prompt Engineering and Synthetic Content Creation* (pp. 261-280). IGI Global Scientific Publishing.

Sivarajkumar, S., Kelley, M., Samolyk-Mazzanti, A., Visweswaran, S., & Wang, Y. (2023). An empirical evaluation of prompting strategies for large language models in zero-shot clinical natural language processing. *arXiv*. https://arxiv.org/abs/2309.08008

Skinner, F. (1958). Teaching Machines: From the experimental study of learning come devices which arrange optimal conditions for self-instruction. *Science*, *128*(3330), 969–977. PMID: 13592277

Sleeman, D., & Brown, J. S. (Eds.). (1982). *Intelligent tutoring systems*. Academic Press.

Slee, R. (2013). How do we make inclusive education happen when exclusion is a political predisposition? *International Journal of Inclusive Education*, *17*(8), 895–907.

Small, H. (1973). Co-citation in the scientific literature: A new measure of the relationship between two documents. *Journal of the American Society for Information Science*, *24*(4), 265–269. DOI: 10.1002/asi.4630240406

Smith, A. B. (1993). Early childhood educare: Seeking a theoretical framework in Vygotsky's work. *International Journal of Early Years Education*, *1*(1), 47–62.

Smith, A., Leeman-Munk, S., Shelton, A., Mott, B., Wiebe, E., & Lester, J. (2019). A Multimodal Assessment Framework for Integrating Student Writing and Drawing in Elementary Science Learning. *IEEE Transactions on Learning Technologies*, *12*(1), 3–15. DOI: 10.1109/TLT.2018.2799871

Smith-Mutegi, D., Mamo, Y., Kim, J., Crompton, H., & McConnell, M. (2025). Perceptions of STEM education and artificial intelligence: A Twitter (X) sentiment analysis. *International Journal of STEM Education*, *12*(1), 9. DOI: 10.1186/s40594-025-00527-5

Somasundaram, M., Latha, P., & Pandian, S. S. (2020). Curriculum design using artificial intelligence (AI) back propagation method. *Procedia Computer Science*, *172*, 134–138.

Song, Y., Weisberg, L. R., Zhang, S., Tian, X., Boyer, K. E., & Israel, M. (2024). A framework for inclusive AI learning design for diverse learners. *Computers and Education: Artificial Intelligence*, *6*, 100212.

Srikanthan, G., & Dalrymple, J. (2002). Developing a holistic model for quality in higher education. *Quality in Higher Education*, *8*(3), 215–224.

Srinivasa, K. G., Kurni, M., & Saritha, K. (2022). Harnessing the Power of AI to Education. In *Learning, teaching, and assessment methods for contemporary learners: pedagogy for the digital generation* (pp. 311–342). Springer Nature Singapore.

Stake, R. E. (2024). *The Art of Case Study Research*. SAGE Publications Ltd. https://uk.sagepub.com/en-gb/eur/the-art-of-case-study-research/book4954

Stein-Smit, K. 2023. The Independent Self-Directed Language Learner and the Role of the Language Educator — Expanding Access and Opportunity. *Journal of Language Teaching and Research*, Vol. 14 (2), 269-277.

Stoller, F. (2006). Establishing a Theoretical Foundation for Project-Based Learning in Second and Foreign Language Contexts. In Beckett, G. H., & Miller, P. C. (Eds.), *Project-Based Second and Foreign Language Education: Past, Present, and Future* (pp. 19–40). Information Age.

Strobelt, H., Webson, A., Sanh, V., Hoover, B., Beyer, J., Pfister, H., & Rush, A. M. (2022). *Interactive and visual prompt engineering for ad-hoc task adaptation with large language models*. IEEE.

Strobl, C., Boulesteix, A. L., Zeileis, A., & Hothorn, T. (2007). Bias in random forest variable importance measures: Illustrations, sources and a solution. *BMC Bioinformatics*, *8*(1), 25. PMID: 17254353

Su, J., & Zhong, Y. (2022). Artificial Intelligence (AI) in early childhood education: Curriculum design and future directions. *Computers and Education: Artificial Intelligence*, *3*, 100072.

Sun, C., & Feng, G. (2009). Process approach to teaching writing applied in different teaching models. *English Language Teaching*, *2*(1), 150–155.

Suppes, P., & Morningstar, M. (1969). Computer-assisted instruction. *Science*, *166*(3903), 343–350. DOI: 10.1126/science.166.3903.343 PMID: 5812034

Swamy, V., Radmehr, B., Krco, N., Marras, M., & Käser, T. (2022). Evaluating the explainers: Black-box explainable machine learning for student success prediction in MOOCs. *arXiv preprint arXiv:2207.00551.*

Tang, J., Zhang, P., & Li, R. (2023). Artificial intelligence–based needs analysis for English for specific purposes. *Journal of Applied Linguistics*, *44*, 210–229.

Tanık Önal, N., & Önal, N. (2023). Online learning and teaching experiences of preservice science teachers during Covid-19 pandemic. *Journal of Educational Technology and Online Learning*, *6*(2), 295–314.

Tanweer, M., & Ismail, A. (2024). Generative AI in curriculum development: A framework for adaptive, customized, and personalized learning. In *Impacts of generative AI on creativity in higher education* (pp. 193–226). IGI Global.

Tappan, M. B. (1998). Moral education in the zone of proximal development. *Journal of Moral Education*, *27*(2), 141–160.

Tatar, C., Jiang, S., Rosé, C. P., & Chao, J. (2025). Exploring teachers' views and confidence in the integration of an artificial intelligence curriculum into their classrooms: A case study of curricular co-design program. *International Journal of Artificial Intelligence in Education*, *35*(2), 702–735.

Taylor, D. L., Yeung, M., & Bashet, A. Z. (2021). Personalized and Adaptive Learning. In Ryoo, J., & Winkelmann, K. (Eds.), *Innovative Learning Environments in STEM Higher Education* (pp. 17–34). Springer International Publishing. DOI: 10.1007/978-3-030-58948-6_2

Temel, T., & Yılmaz, C. (2025). Investigating the impact of digital storytelling on EFL learners' language motivation levels. *Journal of Educational Technology and Online Learning*, *8*(2), 164–189.

Titti, G., Sarretta, A., Lombardo, L., Crema, S., Pasuto, A., & Borgatti, L. (2022). Mapping Susceptibility With Open-Source Tools: A New Plugin for QGIS. *Frontiers of Earth Science, 10*, 842425. DOI: 10.3389/FEART.2022.842425

Tominc, P., & Rožman, M. (2023). Artificial Intelligence and Business Studies: Study Cycle Differences Regarding the Perceptions of the Key Future Competences. *Education Sciences, 13*(6), 580. DOI: 10.3390/educsci13060580

Tompkins, G. E. (2012). Teaching writing: Balancing process and product. Pearson Higher Ed.

Tompkins, G. E. (2004). *Teaching writing: Balancing product and process* (4th ed.). Merrill/Prentice Hall.

Tonbuloğlu, B. (2023). An evaluation of the use of artificial intelligence applications in online education. *Journal of Educational Technology & Online Learning, 6*(4), 866–884.

Tonbuloğlu, B. (2023). An Evaluation of the Use of Artificial Intelligence Applications in Online Education. *Journal of Educational Technology and Online Learning, 6*(4), 866–884.

Tonbuloğlu, B. (2023). An evaluation of the use of artificial intelligence applications in online education. *Journal of Educational Technology and Online Learning, 6*(4), 866–884. DOI: 10.31681/jetol.1335906

Torres, M. N. (1996). *Teacher-Researchers in the" Zone of Proximal Development.* Insights for Teacher Education.

Torrisi-Steele, G. (2026). AI and Curriculum: Designing for the Future. In *Foundations and Frameworks for AI in Education* (pp. 147-170). IGI Global Scientific Publishing.

Toyokawa, Y., Horikoshi, I., Majumdar, R., & Ogata, H. (2023). Challenges and opportunities of AI in inclusive education: A case study of data-enhanced active reading in Japan. *Smart Learning Environments, 10*(1), 67.

Türkben, T. (2021). Examination of classroom writing practices in the context of process-based approach to teaching writing. *Journal of Language and Linguistic Studies, 17*(SI-1), 619–644.

Ullah, R. S., Hashim, F., Bandeali, M. M., & Akbar, A. (2025). Artificial Intelligence in Curriculum Design a Roadmap for Adaptive and Personalized Learning in Higher Education. *The Critical Review of Social Sciences Studies, 3*(3), 304–322.

Um, H., Kim, H., & Choi, D. (2024). An AI-based English education platform during the COVID-19 pandemic. *Universal Access in the Information Society*, *23*(5), 1233–1248. DOI: 10.1007/s10209-023-01046-2

UNESCO. (2021). AI and education: Guidance for policy-makers. Paris: United Nations Educational, Scientific and Cultural Organization (UNESCO).

UNESCO. (2021). *AI and education: Guidance for policy-makers.* UNESCO Publishing.

UNESCO. (n.d.). Artificial intelligence in education. *UNESCO.* https://www.unesco.org/en/digital-education/artificial-intelligence

University of Pittsburgh Teaching Center. (2024). Using generative AI to create more accessible student learning experiences. Retrieved from https://teaching.pitt.edu/resources/using-generative-ai-to-create-more-accessible-student-learning-experiences/

Valeri, F., Nilsson, P., & Cederqvist, A.-M. (2025). Exploring students' experience of ChatGPT in STEM education. *Computers and Education: Artificial Intelligence*, *8*, 100360. DOI: 10.1016/j.caeai.2024.100360

van Eck, N. J., & Waltman, L. (2010). Software survey: VOSviewer, a computer program for bibliometric mapping. *Scientometrics*, *84*(2), 523–538. DOI: 10.1007/s11192-009-0146-3 PMID: 20585380

Varsik, S., & Vosberg, L. (2024). *The potential impact of Artificial Intelligence on equity and inclusion in education, OECD Artificial Intelligence Papers, No. 23.* OECD Publishing., DOI: 10.1787/15df715b-

Vaz, E. (2024). Innovations in Spatial Analysis: The Impact of GIS and Python in Knowledge Societies. *Regional Knowledge Economies*, 73–85. https://doi.org/DOI: 10.1007/978-3-031-76906-1_6

Venkatesan, R. G., & Mappillairaju, B. (2023). Detection of hotspots of school dropouts in India: A spatial clustering approach. *PLoS ONE, 18*(1 January). https://doi.org/DOI: 10.1371/journal.pone.0280034

Vettriselvan, R., & Ramya, R. (2025). Sustainable Curriculum Design and Development: A Comprehensive Approach. In *Smart Education and Sustainable Learning Environments in Smart Cities* (pp. 471-486). IGI Global Scientific Publishing.

Vojteková, J., Žoncová, M., Tirpáková, A., & Vojtek, M. (2022). Evaluation of story maps by future geography teachers. *Journal of Geography in Higher Education*, *46*(3), 360–382. DOI: 10.1080/03098265.2021.1902958

Vygotsky, L. S. (1978). *Mind in society: The development of higher psychological processes* (Cole, M., John-Steiner, V., Scribner, S., & Souberman, E., Eds.). Harvard University Press.

Wachter, S., Mittelstadt, B., & Floridi, L. (2017). Why a right to explanation of automated decision-making does not exist in the general data protection regulation. *International Data Privacy Law*, *7*(2), 76–99. DOI: 10.1093/idpl/ipx005

Waghid, Y. (2002). Knowledge production and higher education transformation in South Africa: Towards reflexivity in university teaching, research and community service. *Higher Education*, *43*(4), 457–488. DOI: 10.1023/A:1015211718131

Wahidur, R. S., Tashdeed, I., Kaur, M., & Lee, H.-N. (2024). Enhancing zero-shot crypto sentiment with fine-tuned language model and prompt engineering. *IEEE Access : Practical Innovations, Open Solutions*, *12*, 10146–10159. DOI: 10.1109/access.2024.3350638

Walder, A. M. (2014). The concept of pedagogical innovation in higher education. *Education Journal*, *3*(3), 195–202.

Walder, A. M. (2017). Pedagogical Innovation in Canadian higher education: Professors' perspectives on its effects on teaching and learning. *Studies in Educational Evaluation*, *54*, 71–82.

Walker, K. (2023). Analyzing US census data: Methods, maps, and models in R. *Analyzing US Census Data: Methods, Maps, and Models in R*, 1–368. https://doi.org//DOI: 10.1201/9780203711415

Wang, L., Bi, W., Zhao, S., Ma, Y., Lv, L., Meng, C., & Lv, H. (2024). Investigating the impact of prompt engineering on the performance of large language models for standardizing obstetric diagnosis text: Comparative study. *JMIR Formative Research*, *8*(1), e53216. DOI: 10.2196/53216 PMID: 38329787

Wang, Y. (2025). A scoping review of empirical studies on generative AI in language education (2022–2024). *Journal of Educational Technology & Society*, *28*(2), 1–22.

Wang, Y., & Johnson, T. E. (2021). Emotion regulation and learning engagement in intelligent tutoring systems. *Computers & Education*, *165*, 104148.

Warschauer, M., Tseng, W., Yim, S., Webster, T., Jacob, S., Du, Q., & Tate, T. (2023). The Affordances and Contradictions of AI-Generated Text for Second Language Writers. SSRN *Electronic Journal*. DOI: 10.2139/ssrn.4404380

Wertsch, J. V. (1991). *Voices of the mind: A sociocultural approach to mediated action*. Harvard University Press.

White, J., Fu, Q., Hays, S., Sandborn, M., Olea, C., Gilbert, H., Elnashar, A., Spencer-Smith, J., & Schmidt, D. C. (2023). Aprompt pattern catalog to enhance prompt engineering with ChatGPT. https://arxiv.org/abs/2302.11382

Widodo, H. P. (2008). Process-based academic essay writing instruction in an EFL context. *Bahasa dan Seni. Tahun, 36*(1), 101–111.

Williamson, B., & Eynon, R. (2020). Historical threads, missing links, and future directions in AI in education. *Learning, Media and Technology, 45*(3), 223–235.

Williamson, B., & Piattoeva, N. (2019). Objectivity as standardization in data-scientific educational governance: Grasping the global through the local. *Research in Education, 101*(1), 69–91. DOI: 10.1177/0034523718804718

Wilson, J. A., & Roscoe, R. D. (2020). Adaptive learning systems and writing instruction. In *Adaptive educational technologies for literacy instruction* (pp. 75–96). Routledge.

Winne, P. H., & Hadwin, A. F. (2008). The weave of motivation and self-regulated learning. In Schunk, D. H., & Zimmerman, B. (Eds.), *Motivation and self-regulated learning: Theory, research, and applications* (pp. 297–314).

Wollny, S., Schneider, J., Di Mitri, D., Weidlich, J., Rittberger, M., & Drachsler, H. (2021). Are We There Yet? - A Systematic Literature Review on Chatbots in Education. *Frontiers in Artificial Intelligence, 4*, 654924. DOI: 10.3389/frai.2021.654924 PMID: 34337392

Wong, C. (2022). Spatial thinking and policymaking in the UK: A spatial planning perspective. *Space and Polity, 26*(2), 135–142. DOI: 10.1080/13562576.2022.2090060

Wood, D., Bruner, J. S., & Ross, G. (1976). The role of tutoring in problem solving. *Journal of Child Psychology and Psychiatry, and Allied Disciplines, 17*(2), 89–100. PMID: 932126

Wood, D., & Moss, S. H. (2024). Evaluating the impact of students' generative AI use in educational contexts. *Journal of Research in Innovative Teaching & Learning, 17*(2), 152–167. DOI: 10.1108/JRIT-06-2024-0151

Xiaofan, W. (2025). Investigating the use of AI tools in English language learning: A phenomenological approach. *Contemporary Educational Technology, 16*(4), 301–320.

Xiao, R., Xu, P., Liang, X. L., Zou, Z., Zhong, J. G., Xiang, M. Q., & Hou, X. H. (2024). Effects of the special olympics unified sports soccer training program on executive function in adolescents with intellectual disabilities. *Journal of Exercise Science and Fitness, 22*(2), 103–110. PMID: 38268818

Xu, H., Li, X., Tupayachi, J., Lian, J., & Omitaomu, O. A. (2024). Automating bibliometric analysis with sentence transformers and retrieval-augmented generation (rag): a pilot study in semantic and contextual search for customized literature characterization for high-impact urban research. *Proceedings of the 2nd ACM SIGSPATIAL International Workshop on Advances in Urban-Ai*, 43-49. https://doi.org/DOI: 10.1145/3681780.3697252

Xu, W., & Ouyang, F. (2022a). A systematic review of AI role in the educational system based on a proposed conceptual framework. *Education and Information Technologies*, *27*(3), 4195–4223. DOI: 10.1007/s10639-021-10774-y

Xu, W., & Ouyang, F. (2022b). The application of AI technologies in STEM education: A systematic review from 2011 to 2021. *International Journal of STEM Education*, *9*(1), 59. DOI: 10.1186/s40594-022-00377-5

Yağci, A., & Çevik, M. (2019). Prediction of academic achievements of vocational and technical high school (VTS) students in science courses through artificial neural networks (comparison of Turkey and Malaysia). *Education and Information Technologies*, *24*(5), 2741–2761. DOI: 10.1007/s10639-019-09885-4

Yang, S. J. H., Ogata, H., Matsui, T., & Chen, N.-S. (2021). Human-centered artificial intelligence in education: Seeing the invisible through the visible. *Computers and Education: Artificial Intelligence*, *2*, 100008. DOI: 10.1016/j.caeai.2021.100008

Yannier, N., Hudson, S. E., & Koedinger, K. R. (2020). Active Learning is About More Than Hands-On: A Mixed-Reality AI System to Support STEM Education. *International Journal of Artificial Intelligence in Education*, *30*(1), 74–96. DOI: 10.1007/s40593-020-00194-3

Yin, R. K. (1994). Discovering the future of the case study method in evaluation research. *Evaluation Practice*, *15*(3), 283–290. DOI: 10.1016/0886-1633(94)90023-X

Yuan, J., Qiu, X., Wu, J., Guo, J., Li, W., & Wang, Y. G. (2024). Integrating behavior analysis with machine learning to predict online learning performance: A scientometric review and empirical study. *arXiv preprint arXiv:2406.11847.*

Yukselturk, E., & Bulut, S. (2007). Predictors for student success in an online course. *Journal of Educational Technology & Society*, *10*(2), 71–83.

Yurdakul, B. (2010). Yapılandırmacılık. In *Eğitimde Yeni Yönelimler, Editör: Özcan Demirel* (pp. 39–65). Pegem Akademi Yayıncılık.

Zawacki-Richter, O., Marín, V. I., Bond, M., & Gouverneur, F. (2019). Systematic review of research on artificial intelligence applications in higher education – Where are the educators? *International Journal of Educational Technology in Higher Education, 16*(1), 1–27.

Zawacki-Richter, O., Marín, V. I., Bond, M., & Gouverneur, F. (2019). Systematic review of research on artificial intelligence applications in higher education – where are the educators? *International Journal of Educational Technology in Higher Education, 16*(1), 39. DOI: 10.1186/s41239-019-0171-0

Zeng, D. (2005). The process-oriented approach to ESL/EFL writing instruction and research. *Teaching English in China, 28*(5), 67–72.

Zhai, X. (2022). ChatGPT User Experience: Implications for Education. SSRN *Electronic Journal*. DOI: 10.2139/ssrn.4312418

Zhai, X., Chu, X., Chai, C. S., Jong, M. S. Y., Istenic, A., Spector, M., & Li, Y. (2021). A Review of Artificial Intelligence (AI) in Education from 2010 to 2020. *Complexity, 2021*(1), 8812542.

Zhang, K., & Aslan, A. B. (2021). AI technologies for education: Recent research & future directions. *Computers and Education: Artificial Intelligence, 2*, 100025. DOI: 10.1016/j.caeai.2021.100025

Zhang, K., Zhou, F., Wu, L., Xie, N., & He, Z. (2024). Semantic understanding and prompt engineering for large-scale traffic data imputation. *Information Fusion, 102*, 102038. DOI: 10.1016/j.inffus.2023.102038

Zhao, Q., Yu, L., Du, Z., Peng, D., Hao, P., Zhang, Y., & Gong, P. (2022). An Overview of the Applications of Earth Observation Satellite Data: Impacts and Future Trends. In *Remote Sensing* (Vol. 14, Issue 8). https://doi.org/DOI: 10.3390/rs14081863

Zhao, H. G., Li, X. Z., & Kang, X. (2024). Development of an artificial intelligence curriculum design for children in Taiwan and its impact on learning outcomes. *Humanities & Social Sciences Communications, 11*(1), 1–17.

Zhou, C. (2024). Artificial intelligence in sociology: A critical review and future directions. *Theory and Society, 53*(2), 301–330. DOI: 10.1007/s11186-024-09542-z

Zimmerman, B. J. (2013). From cognitive modeling to self-regulation: A social cognitive career path. *Educational Psychologist, 48*(3), 135–147.

Zipf, G. K. (1949). *Human behavior and the principle of least effort: An introduction to human ecology*. Addison-Wesley Press.

Zupic, I., & Čater, T. (2015). Bibliometric methods in management and organization. *Organizational Research Methods*, *18*(3), 429–472. DOI: 10.1177/1094428114562629

About the Contributors

Gürhan Durak is currently a visiting scholar at The Open University (UK) and serves as the president of the International Conference on Educational Technology and Online Learning (ICETOL). His research interests include Generative Artificial Intelligence, Learning Analytics, Instructional Design, and Mixed Research Methodologies. Gürhan Durak serves as the Editor-in-Chief for several international journals, including the Journal of Innovations in Learning and Technology (JILT), Journal of Educational Technology and Online Learning (JETOL), Journal of Online Learning Studies (Jour-OLS), and Journal of Innovations in Learning and Technology (JILT). He holds a PhD in Distance Education from Anadolu University, one of the leading global institutions in distance education.

Serkan Çankaya is an Associate Professor at İzmir Demokrasi University, Faculty of Economics and Administrative Sciences, and the director of the university's Distance Education Center. He holds a PhD in Distance Education from Anadolu University, with research focusing on educational technology, special education technology, online course design, and interactive learning environments. He serves as Editor-in-Chief of the International Journal of Computers in Education (IJCE) and the Journal of Online Learning Studies (Jour-OLS), and as an editor for the Journal of Educational Technology and Online Learning (JETOL). Serkan has contributed significantly to research and practical projects aimed at improving educational experiences through technology.

***

Müge Adnan is currently a faculty member in the Department of Instructional Technology, Head of Informatics Department, and Director of Distance Education at Muğla Sıtkı Koçman University. She performed various key roles in national education and technology projects financed by the World Bank in Turkey including

National Education Development Project, Basic Education Project, and Social Risk Mitigation Project implemented by the Ministry of National Education and the Turkish Prime Ministry before academia. She graduated with a PhD in Computer Education and Instructional Technology from Middle East Technical University in 2005. Her research interests include open and distance learning, technology integration, faculty development, digital skills, learning analytics and digital divide. She has participated in several local, national and EU-funded projects as senior researcher or coordinator.

Munir Ahmad is a seasoned professional in the realm of Spatial Data Infrastructure (SDI), Geo-Information Productions, Information Systems, and Information Governance, boasting over 25 years of dedicated experience in the field. With a PhD in Computer Science, Dr. Ahmad's expertise spans Spatial Data Production, Management, Processing, Analysis, Visualization, and Quality Control. Throughout his career, Dr. Ahmad has been deeply involved in the development and deployment of SDI systems specially in the context of Pakistan, leveraging his proficiency in Spatial Database Design, Web, Mobile & Desktop GIS, and Geo Web Services Architecture. His contributions to Volunteered Geographic Information (VGI) and Open Source Geoportal & Metadata Portal have significantly enriched the geospatial community. As a trainer and researcher, Dr. Ahmad has authored over 50 publications, advancing the industry's knowledge base and fostering innovation in Geo-Tech, Data Governance, and Information Infrastructure, and Emerging Technologies. His commitment to Research and Development (R&D) is evident in his role as a dedicated educator and mentor in the field.

Çağatay Bal is currently a research assistant in the Department of Statistics, at Muğla Sıtkı Koçman University. He graduated with a PhD in Statistics from Muğla Sıtkı Koçman in 2025. He has held academic positions as a visiting scholar at Texas A&M University. His research interests include statistics, machine learning, artificial neural networks, deep learning and artificial intelligence. He has participated in several local and national funded projects as senior researcher. At Muğla Sıtkı Koçman University, he teaches data structures and algorithms.

Hamid Derviş is an Associate Professor in the Department of Information Management and Records at Kastamonu University. He is currently the department chair. He holds a Ph.D. in Information Management and Records from Hacettepe University, Ankara, Türkiye, where his research focused on the diffusion of nanotechnology in Turkey using social network analysis. Dr. Derviş has published numerous scientific articles in both national and international journals, including the Journal of Informetrics and Scientometrics. He has been selected as one of the world's top 2% of scientists in the research field of Information & Library Sciences, as determined by Stanford University and Elsevier, for 2024 and 2025, respectively.

Eralp Doğu is a Professor of Statistics at Muğla Sıtkı Koçman University, Turkey. He earned his B.Sc. in Statistics from Ege University (2002) and his M.Sc. and Ph.D. from Dokuz Eylül University (2006, 2011). He has held academic positions as a visiting scholar at Pennsylvania State University and as a postdoctoral researcher at Northeastern University Khoury College of Computer Science. His research focuses on biostatistics, artificial learning, statistical methods for biomolecular systems, and process monitoring. At Muğla Sıtkı Koçman University, he teaches data science, statistical software, and scientific research methods, while also serving as Coordinator of Digital Transformation and Data Management.

S. Ida Evangeline, presently working as an Assistant Professor in the Department of Electrical and Electronics Engineering at the Government College of Engineering, Tirunelveli, Tamilnadu, India. She obtained her Bachelor's in Electrical and Electronics Engineering from Manonmaniam Sundaranar University in 2003, and Master's in Power Systems Engineering from Anna University, Chennai, Tamilnadu, India in 2005. She completed her PhD degree in 2023 at Anna University, Chennai, Tamilnadu, India. She has published six research papers in international journals. Her current research interests include optimal power flow, renewable energy, soft computing, machine learning, and deep learning.

Rejon Kumar Ray is an accomplished business and data analyst, researcher, IT professional and a Google certified Analyst with over 13 years of experience across machine learning (ML), artificial intelligence (AI), and data science. He currently serves as an IT Business Analyst where he integrates advanced analytics, machine learning, and artificial intelligence into strategic decision-making and digital transformation initiatives. With a robust academic backgrounds, Mr. Ray holds an MBA from Gannon University, USA focus on Business Analytics, and an MBA in Strategic International Management from the University of Dhaka, Bangladesh. His academic background bridges quantitative analytics with managerial insight, enabling him to analyze complex data systems and develop scalable solutions for business growth. Throughout his professional journey, Mr. Ray has demonstrated his expertise in artificial intelligence (AI), ML framework, SQL, Python, SPSS, SAS, alongside his proficiency in analytical acumen extends to predictive modeling, natural language processing, and dynamic pricing systems. His work consistently focuses on transforming data into actionable intelligence to optimize operations, forecast market trends, and drive profitability. Mr. Ray's research contributions reflect his interdisciplinary interests in AI and ML-driven economic modeling, digital finance, healthcare system, and predictive modeling. His recent publications appear in peer-reviewed international journals, including Journal of Ecohumanism, Journal of Computer Science and Technology Studies, and Journal of Economics, Finance and Accounting Studies. His scholarly works explore cutting-edge topics such as the impact of digital finance on urban economic resilience, machine learning in breast cancer detection, and harnessing AI and ML applications to analyze the impact of digital financing, Financial fraud detection are remarkable. Mr. Ray's professional philosophy centers on data ethics, innovation, and evidence-based decision-making. He is blend of analytical precision and strategic foresight continues to shape his contributions to academia, business, and emerging technologies.

Rayhon Sapaeva is a scholar in the Department of Roman–Germanic Philology at Urgench State University, Urgench, Uzbekistan. Her academic interests include English and German linguistics, translation studies, and comparative literature. She is active in university teaching, curriculum development, and research projects that bridge language theory with classroom practice, and she presents her work at regional and international conferences.

Jean Mathieu Tsoumou holds a PhD in English studies and a Masters in English linguistics and communication from Complutense University of Madrid/Spain. He currently works for La Universidad Europea de Madrid, where he teaches ESP to undergraduate students. He is mainly interested in Pragmatics, Multilingualism, (Im) politeness, Discourse Analysis, Sociolinguistics and Politics. He has published in international journals, including the Journal of Pragmatics and Journal of Politeness: Language, Behaviour, Culture.

Seçil Tümen Akyıldız is an Associate Professor in the Department of English Language and Literature at Fırat University, Türkiye. She holds a PhD in Curriculum Development and Instruction. Her research interests include applied linguistics, foreign language teaching, educational technologies, artificial intelligence in education, prompt engineering, and teacher professional development. She is the Director of the Academic Writing Application and Research Center at Fırat University and has extensive experience in curriculum development, teacher education, and technology-enhanced language learning. Her recent work focuses on the pedagogical use of generative AI and the development of creative and reflective thinking skills in higher education.

Index

A

Academic Integrity 70, 76, 84, 85, 89, 99, 102, 114, 152, 177, 187
Accessibility 2, 3, 4, 7, 8, 9, 11, 12, 17, 19, 25, 26, 31, 32, 33, 34, 40, 48, 84, 85, 86, 87, 91, 92, 93, 94, 99, 100, 101, 105, 106, 107, 108, 109, 111, 113, 114, 138, 185, 196, 255, 256, 260
adaptive learning systems 119, 120, 121, 125, 126, 130, 131, 140, 146
AI 1, 2, 3, 4, 5, 6, 7, 8, 9, 10, 11, 12, 13, 14, 15, 16, 17, 18, 19, 21, 22, 23, 24, 25, 26, 42, 48, 49, 50, 52, 55, 56, 57, 58, 59, 60, 61, 64, 66, 67, 68, 69, 70, 71, 72, 73, 74, 75, 76, 78, 79, 80, 81, 83, 84, 85, 86, 87, 88, 89, 90, 92, 93, 94, 96, 98, 99, 100, 102, 103, 105, 106, 107, 108, 109, 110, 111, 112, 113, 114, 115, 116, 117, 118, 119, 120, 121, 122, 123, 124, 125, 126, 127, 128, 130, 131, 132, 133, 134, 135, 136, 137, 138, 139, 140, 141, 143, 144, 145, 146, 149, 150, 151, 152, 153, 154, 156, 157, 162, 166, 171, 172, 173, 174, 175, 176, 177, 178, 179, 180, 181, 183, 184, 185, 186, 187, 188, 189, 190, 191, 192, 193, 194, 195, 196, 197, 198, 199, 200, 201, 202, 203, 204, 205, 207, 209, 211, 212, 213, 214, 218, 220, 228, 230, 231, 232, 234, 237, 238, 239, 241, 242, 243, 244, 245, 246, 247, 248, 249, 250, 251, 252, 253, 254, 255, 256, 257, 258, 259, 260, 261, 262, 263, 264, 265, 266
AI in Education 7, 8, 9, 22, 24, 66, 79, 124, 144, 146, 173, 186, 187, 218, 230, 238, 239, 241, 245, 247, 248, 250, 254, 256, 257, 260
Artificial Intelligence 1, 5, 17, 21, 22, 23, 24, 25, 26, 42, 48, 50, 52, 56, 57, 78, 79, 80, 81, 83, 85, 110, 117, 119, 120, 121, 122, 123, 126, 127, 131, 134, 135, 136, 137, 138, 139, 140, 143, 146, 147, 149, 150, 154, 180, 181, 183, 184, 185, 187, 190, 192, 194, 198, 199, 200, 201, 202, 203, 204, 205, 208, 212, 232, 233, 237, 238, 241, 242, 243, 245, 246, 247, 250, 253, 255, 256, 259, 260, 261, 262, 263, 264, 265, 266
artificial intelligence in education 21, 22, 23, 24, 123, 138, 140, 143, 180, 187, 199, 200, 202, 204, 233, 242, 246, 247, 253, 256, 261, 262, 263, 265
Assessment 4, 18, 22, 24, 55, 56, 60, 68, 69, 72, 73, 79, 81, 83, 84, 85, 86, 87, 88, 89, 90, 91, 92, 93, 94, 96, 97, 98, 99, 100, 102, 103, 104, 105, 109, 110, 111, 112, 113, 114, 115, 116, 117, 132, 133, 134, 145, 151, 152, 153, 155, 157, 159, 160, 161, 177, 179, 185, 188, 189, 203, 211, 212, 214, 215, 216, 217, 218, 220, 221, 224, 225, 226, 228, 229, 230, 249, 259
Attitude 10, 121

B

Bibliometric Analysis 74, 237, 238, 239, 240, 242, 245, 250, 259, 262, 265, 266, 267
Bibliometrix 240, 245, 261, 267

C

ChatGPT 22, 57, 58, 74, 79, 80, 82, 84, 85, 97, 116, 150, 152, 153, 154, 161, 172, 173, 177, 178, 181, 186, 188, 189, 193, 194, 198, 199, 200, 201, 202, 204, 205, 238, 248, 262, 264
Climate Change 189, 190, 200, 201
communication 15, 61, 89, 103, 108, 109, 129, 141, 143, 144, 149, 150, 151, 153, 157, 158, 161, 162, 163, 164, 166, 168, 175, 177, 178, 192, 193, 194, 195, 200, 237, 239, 240, 264
Culturally Responsive Pedagogy 1, 9, 11

D

data governance 9, 27, 41, 43, 44, 50
Data Privacy 14, 42, 43, 87, 96, 98, 113, 123, 131, 137, 138, 187, 196, 254, 255, 260, 265
Differentiated Instruction 1, 6, 9, 11, 25
digital literacy 45, 131, 137, 193, 199, 256
Distance Education 36, 144, 207, 208, 211, 234

E

educational equity 26, 83, 85, 114, 119, 137, 138, 140
education policy 27, 28, 29, 30, 32, 34, 38, 41, 44, 48, 50, 116, 254
EDUCAUSE 95, 99, 112, 114, 116
EMIS 27, 31, 38, 40
equity in education 36
ESP 149, 150, 151, 152, 153, 154, 157, 162, 163, 165, 168, 169, 172, 175, 176, 177, 178, 179, 180

G

Generative Artificial Intelligence 1, 5, 21, 22, 26, 83, 85, 183, 185, 194, 202
geographic disparities 27, 28, 51
Globalization 150
GPT-4 87, 106

H

Higher Education 12, 21, 22, 24, 25, 52, 53, 55, 56, 57, 61, 65, 66, 68, 72, 73, 74, 75, 76, 79, 80, 81, 83, 84, 85, 86, 90, 113, 114, 116, 117, 147, 150, 178, 184, 189, 199, 200, 201, 203, 205, 234, 241, 243, 244, 254, 257, 263, 264, 266

I

Inclusive Curriculum Design 1, 3, 11, 17, 19, 26

L

Language learning 122, 123, 142, 149, 150, 162, 172, 175, 177, 178, 180, 181, 253, 257, 262
Learning Analytics 84, 111, 137, 141, 200, 202, 207, 208, 210, 231, 232, 234, 241, 242, 248, 249, 252, 264
LMS Interaction Data 209

M

Machine Learning 5, 26, 28, 33, 42, 48, 49, 50, 53, 58, 78, 81, 84, 91, 108, 203, 207, 208, 209, 210, 211, 213, 214, 216, 217, 220, 232, 233, 234, 235, 241, 242, 243, 249, 257

N

NLP 92, 249

O

Online Learning 21, 24, 56, 78, 79, 81, 117, 143, 144, 145, 146, 199, 202, 208, 209, 210, 217, 223, 229, 233, 234, 235, 252, 266
OpenAI 97

P

PBL 149, 150, 151, 152, 153, 154, 155, 161, 162, 163, 164, 165, 166, 167, 168, 169, 170, 171, 172, 175, 176, 177, 178, 179
Perception 18, 28, 55, 192, 194, 198
primary school students 119, 124, 130, 131, 139, 140
process-based writing 119, 121, 125, 128, 144
Prompt Engineering 22, 23, 55, 57, 58, 59, 60, 61, 62, 64, 66, 67, 68, 69, 70, 71, 72, 73, 74, 75, 76, 78, 79, 80, 81, 82

Q

Qualitative Research 65, 78, 79, 80

R

real-time dashboards 40, 49, 50

S

Spatial Data Science 27, 28, 29, 32, 33, 34, 36, 37, 38, 39, 40, 44, 45, 46, 51, 52, 53
STEM 23, 73, 80, 168, 183, 184, 185, 186, 187, 188, 189, 190, 191, 193, 194, 195, 196, 198, 199, 200, 201, 202, 203, 204, 231, 232
Student Engagement 12, 56, 67, 68, 69, 99, 113, 132, 133, 151, 186, 187, 196, 202, 207, 216
Survey Methodology 83, 84, 85, 86, 87, 97, 101, 113
Sustainability 21, 27, 52, 90, 105, 116, 137, 189, 190, 192, 193, 195, 199, 200, 254, 256, 257, 260, 262
sustainable education systems 257, 262

T

teacher scaffolding 119, 124, 125, 131, 137, 139, 140, 141
Technology 2, 4, 5, 7, 13, 15, 17, 18, 21, 22, 23, 24, 25, 36, 44, 50, 53, 75, 78, 79, 81, 83, 86, 88, 90, 92, 99, 103, 104, 105, 108, 112, 113, 114, 115, 117, 121, 122, 123, 124, 126, 127, 131, 132, 133, 136, 137, 138, 139, 140, 142, 143, 144, 145, 146, 147, 154, 164, 166, 172, 178, 181, 184, 186, 187, 190, 192, 193, 195, 196, 198, 199, 201, 202, 203, 205, 212, 213, 224, 232, 233, 234, 235, 237, 238, 239, 241, 243, 244, 245, 247, 248, 249, 250, 251, 252, 253, 255, 256, 257, 259, 260, 261, 262, 263, 264, 266, 267

U

UDL 1, 2, 7, 9, 10, 11, 16, 19, 26, 86, 87, 92
Universal Design for Learning 1, 9, 10, 11, 15, 26, 85, 86, 113, 116, 117, 264

W

writing instruction 119, 120, 121, 122, 124, 125, 128, 129, 131, 133, 134, 136, 141, 143, 144, 146, 147

www.ingramcontent.com/pod-product-compliance
Lightning Source LLC
LaVergne TN
LVHW080859300926
849162LV00003B/475
* 9 7 9 8 3 3 7 3 8 8 0 5 2 *